THE DISCOVERY OF MANKIND

THE
DISCOVERY OF
MANKIND

ATLANTIC ENCOUNTERS IN
THE AGE OF COLUMBUS

DAVID ABULAFIA

YALE UNIVERSITY PRESS
NEW HAVEN AND LONDON

Set in Caslon by J&L Composition, Filey, North Yorkshire
Printed in the United States of America

ISBN 978–0–300–12582–5 (alk. paper)

Book Club Edition

for Bianca and Rosa

Muchas dueñas fizieron auer, y tu pujaste sobre todas ellas.
Ladino Bible of Ferrara (1553): Proverbios de Selomoh 31:29

Adam's children in form, face and human
intelligence, and God's own handiwork.
Heinrich von Hesler (fourteenth century)

Have we not all one father?
Has not one God created us?
Malachi 2:10

They too are of the generation of Adam.
Gomes Eanes de Zurara (fifteenth century)

CONTENTS

ILLUSTRATIONS

11 A group of Gomerans wearing kilts, from the Rouen manuscript of *Le Canarien*, *c.* 1490, MS mm 129: f 47v (Collections Bibliothèque municipale de Rouen. Photograph Thierry Ascensio-Parvy).

12 Armed natives of the island of Enfer, 'Hell' (Tenerife), with a European ship approaching from the left, from the Rouen manuscript of *Le Canarien*, *c.* 1490, MS mm 129: f 48v (Collections Bibliothèque municipale de Rouen. Photograph Thierry Ascensio-Parvy).

13 An Arawak woman carrying a bow and arrow, from a late eighteenth-century account of Surinam by J.G. Stedman (Codrington Library, All Souls College, Oxford).

14 Wooden *duho* or ceremonial stool from Hispaniola, possibly made around 1400 (The Trustees of the British Museum).

15 Three-pointed stone *zemí* or idol from Hispaniola (Photo by Dirk Bakker. Photo courtesy of El Museo del Barrio, NY).

16 Three-pointed stone *zemí* or idol from Hispaniola (Photo courtesy of Museo Arqueológico Regional, Altos de Chavón, Dominican Republic).

17 Hawk's bell excavated at La Isabela, Hispaniola. From Kathleen Deagan and José María Cruxent, *Archaeology at La Isabela: America's First European Town*, 2002, p.201.

18 Early printed edition of a letter by Columbus describing his first voyage, 1493 (The New York Public Library, Astor, Lenox and Tilden Foundations).

19 Cover illustration of an Italian verse translation of a letter by Columbus describing his first journey (© The British Library).

20 German woodcut inspired by Vespucci's account of South America, *c.*1505 (The New York Public Library, Astor, Lenox and Tilden Foundations).

21 Vespucci's *Mundus Novus*, from a Leipzig edition of 1505 (Herzog August Bibliothek, Wolfenbüttel: QuH 26 (5)).

22 A family of Tupí Indians from Brazil, after John White, *c.* 1582–90 (© The Trustees of the British Museum).

23 A Tupí war dance, illustration in Theodore de Bry, *America*, part 3, Frankfurt, 1593, p.221. (Library of Congress).

24 Woodcut of Hans Staden's experiences among the Tupí Indians, 1557, from his *Warhaftig Historia* (Regionalmuseum Wolfhager Land. Photograph S.H. Siemers).

MAPS

PREFACE

By the end of the fifteenth century European horizons were vastly enlarged. What had been discovered was not just land but peoples; most of these were what used to be called 'primitive' peoples. Traditionally, though, the literature on the early discoveries has been dominated by geographical and navigational questions about knowledge of the Atlantic, types of ship, exact points of arrival. This book is about something else. For what Christian Europeans experienced was nothing less than their own discovery of mankind – of the variety and range of human activity and expression. This discovery continued to be debated for several centuries, and much has been written about these discussions from the mid-sixteenth century onwards, presenting the discovery of new peoples as a long process. The moment of discovery and its immediate aftermath have, strangely, received much less attention. In order to convey some sense of the shock of discovery, of the realisation that millions of people existed whose societies, beliefs and practices were vastly different from those of contemporary Europeans, I have based myself here as far as possible on eyewitness accounts of the very first encounters between Europeans and peoples previously unknown to them.

The history of these encounters began, in fact, a century and a half before Columbus first arrived in the Caribbean, in the eastern Atlantic, in the small but significant territory of the Canary Islands. Earlier still, in medieval Europe, images of monstrous peoples supposed to inhabit the edges of the world shaped attitudes and expectations among the European explorers. Some others were engaged in the discovery of far-off peoples in the fifteenth century: the Chinese voyages, led by the eunuch Zheng He, brought China detailed knowledge of the peoples and animals of the Indian Ocean; but they ended suddenly in 1433, for reasons that have been much debated. If anything, their effect was to close China off from the world after 1433, rather than to create links across unimagined distances. Still, the theme of the discovery of these lands and peoples now faces a challenge from those who say, with some justice, that the native peoples had mostly been there a long time, and were perfectly aware of themselves; so to talk of 'discovery' is to write a Eurocentric interpretation of history that insults their identity. But, frankly, coming into contact with these peoples, was such a major event in human history, resulting in the creation of great empires and the destruction of entire peoples, that the European dimension stands very much to the front. It was the beginning of a process that started with the establishment of a Spanish and a Portuguese empire, but continued in later centuries with the creation of English, French and Dutch dominions across the globe. The important point to remember is that this was a two-way encounter. The Europeans met them for the first time; but they also met the Europeans for the first time. The events described in this book did not merely lead to the discovery of what Europeans called a New World; they changed the entire world.

Many recent discussions of the early Atlantic encounters have taken place among literary scholars whose 'post-modernist' and 'post-colonialist' approaches to their material, and even highly politicised readings of the key texts, have not necessarily done much to illuminate the evidence. The Europeans, it is sometimes said, destroyed a paradise, in which mankind lived in harmony with nature. Cannibals become colonialist constructs. We are to blame. Others would argue that the inhabitants of the Caribbean were almost as good at destroying the surrounding habitat as the Europeans. I am convinced there were cannibals in the Caribbean and Brazil; and I am convinced that the disgust of European observers at the eating of human flesh was genuine. The fact that their cousins back home in Spain roasted (but did not eat) human flesh on the pyres of the Spanish Inquisition adds a certain irony, as the great Renaissance essayist Montaigne was aware. I also dislike the jargon in which many post-modernist discussions are garbed; one book about the first Portuguese description of Brazil solemnly informs the bemused reader that 'it considers the discourse as the place where Brazilian colonial subjectivity fights the stasis of Otherness by constantly creating and recreating itself through language'. Those puzzled by such language are heartily recommended to re-read Hans Christian Andersen's 'The Emperor's New Clothes'.

Among historians who have been happy to discuss the period before and after Columbus I should like to mention in particular Felipe Fernández-Armesto, now Príncipe de Asturias Professor of History at Tufts University, from whom I have learned an enormous amount in conversation and from his writings. Among those who have transformed our understanding of later developments, I should like to mention my former colleague Anthony Pagden, now at UCLA. I also have some quite ancient debts: to Peter Brooks of Robinson College, Cambridge, who spiritedly introduced me to the whole topic of European exploration when I was his pupil at St Paul's School; to the late Geoffrey Scammell of Pembroke College, Cambridge, who introduced me to a whole world of French scholarship on the early modern period. Caroline Dodds (Sidney Sussex College, Cambridge) and my Brazilian-born sister-in-law Inês Sapir-Cohn read earlier versions of this book and made very helpful comments. Bianca Abulafia compiled the index. I owe much in Cambridge to Peter Stacey (Sidney Sussex), William O'Reilly (Trinity Hall), John Marenbon (Trinity), David Phillipson (Caius), Chang Na (Caius); also to Eyda Merediz (University of Maryland), Francisco Béthencourt (King's College, London), Stefan Halikowski Smith (Swansea University), Amanda Power (University of Sheffield), Joan-Pau Rubiés (LSE), François Soyer (Lisbon), Debra Blumenthal (University of California, Santa Barbara), Ulpiano Bezerra Toledo de Meneses and Marlene Suano (University of São Paulo), Hiroshi Takayama (University of Tokyo), Katherine Spears (Bernard Quaritch Ltd); and very importantly to my agent, Bill Hamilton of A.M. Heath, and my editor, Heather McCallum, at Yale University Press, who has been an extremely attentive and helpful reader, as has Candida Brazil. I have benefited greatly from my use of the unrivalled collections at the Cambridge University Library, the Bodleian Library in Oxford (enhanced by the great hospitality of the Principal and Fellows of Brasenose College to Fellows of their sister college in Cambridge) and the British Library in London. The origins of this book go back to a study I wrote of the first encounters between Europeans and Canary islanders in the fourteenth century, and to a talk I have been giving to those willing to listen at seminars in Cambridge, at the Oxford University History Society, Dulwich College, Harrow School, Madrid (UNED) and the Mediterranean Studies Association in Coimbra and Genoa. This book also arose out of a Special Subject paper I have been offering in the History Faculty at Cambridge entitled 'Atlantic Encounters in the Age of Columbus', and I want very much to thank those who took part in it and made it such a rewarding experience for me and, I hope, for them. I was then able to claim release from the office of Chairman of the History Faculty and to write the book during a sabbatical year. As ever, and above all else, I have benefited from the support and interest of Anna Sapir Abulafia, with the added benefit that my wife knows an enormous amount about several of the theoretical issues mentioned in this book. She has also accompanied me to some of the places in the eastern Atlantic, Portugal and Spain that feature in this book. Above all, she has read this book in manuscript and criticised the text with enormous care and attention. This time, however, the book is for my daughters, Bianca and Rosa, who are also excellent companions whether at home or while travelling, and it is dedicated to them with much love.

David Abulafia
Gonville and Caius College, Cambridge
6 March 2007

DRAMATIS PERSONAE

Abreu Galindo, Juan de: Franciscan friar: at end of sixteenth century wrote influential account of conquest of Canary Islands; defended human status of islanders.

Alexander VI, Pope: capable and ambitious member of Borgia family from Valencia; reigned as pope 1492 to 1503; issued papal bulls dividing world between Spanish and Portuguese spheres of dominion.

Aquinas, St Thomas (d. 1274): prolific Dominican friar from Naples; student of Aristotle; reformulated in Christian setting ideas about natural law derived from Cicero and other classical writers; argued that pagan rulers may in certain circumstances have right to rule their subjects; greatly influenced las Casas (q.v.) and other Dominicans.

Arosca: Brazilian Indian chieftain; greeted Gonneville (q.v.) in 1504; sent son Essomericq to France with Gonneville.

Béthencourt, Jean de: lord of Grainville in Normandy; co-leader of French expedition to Canaries in 1402; invaded Lanzarote, Fuerteventura.

Bobadilla, Francisco de: Spanish investigator into Columbus' affairs in Hispaniola; had dubious reputation before reaching New World in 1500.

Boccaccio, Giovanni (1313–75): prolific Florentine author in Latin and Italian; enthusiastic student of classical antiquity and a founding father of Renaissance humanism; author of letter *De Canaria* on discovery of Canary Islands.

Buyl or Boyl, Bernat: Catalan friar entrusted with evangelisation of Hispaniola; returned quickly to Spain.

Cabot, John (d. 1498?): Venetian sea captain based in Genoa and Valencia; reached North America in English service, 1497.

Cabral, Pedro Álvarez: Portuguese explorer; led second Portuguese expedition to India; discovered Brazil en route to India, 1500.

Cadamosto: see da Mosto, Alvise da Cà.

Caminha, Pero or Pedro Vaz de: Portuguese knight on board fleet of Cabral bound for India (1500); wrote description of Brazilian Indians, sent to Portuguese king; died in India.

Caonabó or Caonabaò: powerful *cacique* or chieftain on Hispaniola; rival of Guacanagarí (q.v.); eventually captured by ruse; sent to Spain but ships sank and he drowned. Possibly born in Bahamas.

Cerda, Luis de la: footloose Castilian prince, mid-fourteenth century; offered kingdom in Canary Islands by Pope Clement VI (q.v.).

Chanca, Dr Diego Álvarez: Spanish physician; accompanied Columbus to Caribbean on second voyage (1493); wrote account of native peoples emphasising cannibalism.

Clement VI, Pope: able southern French lawyer; reigned as pope 1342–52; claimed papal dominion over pagan lands; attempted to create new realm in the Canaries.

Columbus, Christopher (1451–1506): Genoese sea captain who saw himself as God's agent; led four voyages across the Atlantic in search of route to Japan, China and India; appointed Admiral of the Ocean Sea and responsible for government of Hispaniola; wrote several surviving letters describing his voyages.

Columbus, Ferdinand (Hernán Colón): illegitimate son of Christopher Columbus; travelled on father's disastrous fourth voyage; defended father's reputation in biography; highly cultured collector of books and prints.

Cosa, Juan de la: Spanish explorer; accompanied Columbus and Vespucci; drew map showing newly discovered lands, 1500.

Da Gama, Vasco (c. 1460–1524): Portuguese explorer; led first Portuguese expedition to India round southern tip of Africa, 1497–8.

Da Mosto, Alvise da Cà: Venetian captain; entered service of Portuguese prince Henry the Navigator (q.v.); in 1450s travelled in West Africa; left detailed account of travels.

Dias, Bartholomew: Portuguese explorer; reached Cape of Good Hope, 1487; accompanied Cabral to Brazil and India, 1500.

Espinosa, Alonso de: Dominican friar; admirer of las Casas (q.v.); c. 1590 wrote account of conquest of Tenerife, built around story of miraculous image of Virgin of Candelaria.

Ferdinand II of Aragon, V of Castile (d. 1516): son of King John II of Aragon; married Isabella, claimant to Castile, in 1469; co-ruler of Castile and after her death (1504) regent of Castile; conquered Muslim Granada (1492) and expelled Spanish Jews same year.

Fernando Guanarteme: see Semidan.

Fonseca, Juan de: archdeacon of Seville, charged with organisation of Columbus' second voyage; rapidly fell out with Columbus.

Glas, Captain George: mid-eighteenth-century student of Canary history, translated work of Abreu Galindo (q.v.); murdered at sea by mutinous crew.

Gonneville, Binot Paulmier de: Norman sea captain; led expedition to India; reached Brazil instead, 1503–4; made friends with local chieftain Arosca (q.v.).

Guacanagarí: *cacique* or chieftain in northern Hispaniola; met Columbus during first voyage; leader of pro-Spanish faction among Taíno Indians.

Guarionex: *cacique* or chieftain in Hispaniola; opposed Columbus and Guacanagarí (q.v.).

Hemmerlein, Felix: early fifteenth-century canon of Zurich cathedral; mugged after he denounced immoral conduct of Swiss; wrote vivid description of early voyage to Canaries, later printed in 1497.

Henry the Navigator (1394–1460): intensely ambitious Portuguese prince, younger son of King João I and his English queen; won spurs at conquest of Ceuta in North Africa, 1415; became administrator of crusading Order of Christ; patron of settlers in Madeira, Azores; sent campaigns against Canaries; never travelled further than Ceuta and Tangier; detested Castilians.

Hojeda or Ojeda, Alonso de: accompanied second voyage of Columbus; sent by Columbus to *cacique* Caonabò (q.v.); later helped govern Hispaniola; also active in slave trade from Caribbean and South America.

Isabella of Castile (d. 1504): sister of King Henry IV of Castile; married Ferdinand, king of Sicily and heir to the kingdom of Aragon, 1469; usurped crown of Castile from rival Juana, queen of Portugal, winning war of succession (1474–9); shared government of Castile with husband; deeply devout; attempted to protect American Indian subjects from slavers.

João (John) II, king of Portugal: reigned 1481–95; patron of voyages down west coast of Africa; refused to back Columbus; first ruler to meet Columbus on Columbus' return from first voyage in 1493.

Juana 'the Mad', queen of Castile: daughter of Ferdinand and Isabella, succeeded to Castilian throne in 1506 with husband Philip of Flanders, who soon died; remained nominal queen of Castile till death in 1555 but mentally unbalanced.

Las Casas, Bartolomé de (1484–1566): impassioned Dominican friar; lived as young man in Hispaniola and Cuba; spoke and wrote in defence of rights of American Indians, arguing that they fought a just war against the rapacious Spanish conquerors; author of lengthy *History of the Indies*; admirer of Columbus, whose logbook he edited.

Lugo, Alonso de: Castilian soldier; conqueror of Tenerife in 1496.

Mandeville, John: late fourteenth-century travel writer, English; probably never travelled beyond Flanders but left popular description of wonders of the East.

Manuel I, king of Portugal: reigned 1495–1525; patron of voyages to India by Vasco da Gama and Cabral (q.v.); led forced conversion of Portuguese Jews.

Margarit, Pedro or Pere: Catalan soldier in Columbus' service; asked to tame interior of Hispaniola (1495).

Martyr, Peter Martyr d'Anghiera (1457–1526): Italian humanist who became Spanish royal secretary; author of *Ocean Decades* describing early discoveries; never visited New World but sometimes presented idyllic view of native population.

Ovando, Nicolas de: governor of Hispaniola; denied Columbus access to Hispaniola, 1503–4.

Palacios Rubios, Dr Juan López de: Castilian lawyer; helped compose 'The Requirement' (1511–13), declaration to be read to native peoples by Spanish conquerors; author of 'Book about the Ocean Islanders'.

Pané, Ramón: Hieronymite friar from Badalona in Catalonia; travelled on Columbus' second voyage (1493); sent into interior to evangelise American Indians; wrote account of native beliefs preserved by Ferdinand Columbus (q.v.) in biography of his father.

Peraza: Castilian family that acquired rights in several Canary islands from family of Jean de Béthencourt (q.v.); still present at time of Columbus, who met Doña Inés Peraza during his first voyage.

Petrarch, Francesco (1304–74): energetic student of classical antiquity; poet (in Latin and Italian); born near Florence; leading figure in emerging humanist movement in early Renaissance Italy.

Pinzón, Martín Alonso: captain of the caravel *Pinta*; accompanied Columbus' flagship on his first voyage, with brother Vicente Yáñez Pinzón; later quarrelled with Columbus.

Polo, Marco (1254–1324): Venetian traveller; visited China as young man; left record in dictated description of Asia, much read in later Middle Ages; had great influence on Columbus' assumptions about Asia.

Roldán, Francisco: Spanish soldier; Columbus' chief justice in Hispaniola (1496); leader of rebellion against Columbus.

Salle, Gadifer de la: nobleman from Poitou; co-leader of French expedition to Canaries in 1402; invaded Lanzarote, Fuerteventura; dispossessed by Béthencourt (q.v.).

Semidan: native chieftain on Grand Canary in 1470s/1480s; accepted Castilian authority, 1482; baptised as 'Fernando Guanarteme'.

Torriani, Leonardo: late sixteenth-century military architect and engineer; produced illustrated account of defences of Canaries for the king of Spain, including account of native peoples of each island.

Velázquez, Diego Velázquez de Cuellar: conqueror of Cuba (1511–12); employed Cortés of Mexico; hosted tobacco parties.

Vespucci, Amerigo (1454–1512): well-educated Florentine navigator; crossed Atlantic at least twice and recorded contacts with native peoples of South America in widely printed letters; insisted this was New World, not China or India; gave his name to 'America'.

Zurara, Gomes Eanes de: also known as Azurara; follower and encomiast of Henry the Navigator (q.v.); important chronicle describes Canary Islands, origins of black slave trade, etc.

GLOSSARY

Antilia: legendary land lying across the Atlantic.

Antilles: island chains in Caribbean; Greater Antilles include Cuba, Hispaniola, Puerto Rico, Jamaica; Lesser Antilles chain of islands runs down towards South America.

Antipodes: possible continent lying to the south of the equator.

Arawak: term used to describe peoples of northern South America from whom Taínos (q.v.) descended; also, language family including Taíno languages.

Behique: shaman and medicine man among Taíno Indians.

Berbers: native population of northern Africa, generally islamised in Middle Ages following Arab invasions.

Bohío: house of Taíno Indians.

Brazil: legendary island in Atlantic; name later applied to land discovered by Portuguese in South America, major source of brazilwood.

Cacique (*kasike*): word for king or chieftain on Hispaniola; term extended by Spaniards to all rulers in Spanish America.

Canarians: native population of Grand Canary.

Canary islanders: native population of all Canary Islands.

Caney: house in Taíno villages where many *zemís* (q.v.) kept and *cacique* (q.v.) may reside.

Caravel: small lateen-rigged ship used by Portuguese in exploration of African waters.

Caribs: island raiders coming up chain of Lesser Antilles into Taíno heartlands; accused of cannibalism.

Cathay: China.

Cipangu: Japan.

Conversos: converts from Judaism or Islam to Christianity and their descendants, often accused of keeping up ancestral religion; persecuted by the Inquisition.

Duho: ceremonial stool of Taíno Indians.

Encomienda: in Caribbean, grant to Spanish settlers of several dozen Indians obliged to deliver set quantity of gold or other items; developed into forced labour system across Spanish America.

Feitoría: trading station of Portuguese merchants in Africa, northern Europe, Mediterranean.

Greater Antilles: see Antilles.

Guanarteme: king or chieftain on Grand Canary.

Guanches: native population of Tenerife.

Guanín: natural alloy of gold and copper traded in Caribbean islands.

Indies, India: any of the lands bordering the Indian Ocean, from Ethiopia eastwards.

Lesser Antilles: see Antilles.

Lucayos: Bahamas.

Majoreros: native population of Fuerteventura.

Majos: native population of Lanzarote.

Maravedí: small, debased coin also used in accounting in Castile.

Mencey: king or chieftain on Tenerife.

Moors (*Moros*): term used in Spain and Portugal for Iberian Muslims, Moroccans and often natives of Sahara and parts of West Africa, especially when Muslim.

Moriscos: converted Muslims in Granada, Valencia and other parts of Spain, and their descendants, generally maintaining Islamic practices; expelled, 1609–14.

Nao: literally, ship, often square-rigged, as in case of Columbus' *Santa María*.

Portolan chart: charts showing meticulously detailed coastlines drawn on parchment, possibly as aids to navigation; often highly decorated.

'Requirement, The' (*El Requerimiento*): statement drawn up in Spain, to be read to native peoples at time of arrival of Spanish conquering armies/fleets, requiring submission to Spanish monarchy as condition of peace.

Taínos: literally, 'noble', 'good'; term in use to describe native population of Bahamas, Cuba, Hispaniola, Puerto Rico, Jamaica at time of Columbus' arrival.

Tupí, Tupinambá: native peoples of large swathes of eastern South America, including inhabitants of Brazil encountered by Portuguese.

Zemí, cemí: cult objects or idols of Taíno Indians, often in form of small animal, made of stone, wood, beads, bone, etc.

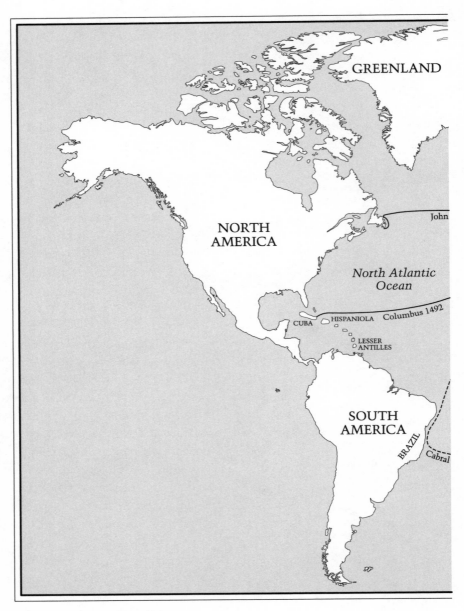

The Atlantic, 1492–1500

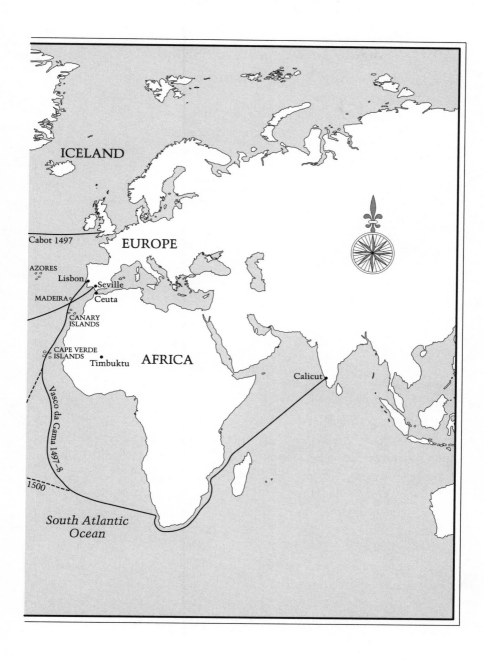

ICELAND

Cabot 1497

EUROPE

AZORES

Lisbon
Seville

MADEIRA

Ceuta

CANARY
ISLANDS

CAPE VERDE
ISLANDS

AFRICA

Timbuktu

Calicut

Vasco da Gama 1497–8

1500

South Atlantic
Ocean

PART I

MENTAL HORIZONS
The Peoples, Islands and Shores of the Imagination

CHAPTER 1

FINDING PEOPLE FROM OTHER WORLDS

Was Mankind Created More Than Once?

In the age of the Renaissance, roughly between the mid-fourteenth century and the early sixteenth century, western Europeans rediscovered aspects of the classical past that stimulated radical new ideas about man's place in the universe, as well as transforming arts and letters in Italy and north of the Alps. It was also a period when knowledge of the physical form of the world grew, not because the earliest explorers were Renaissance men engaged in a pure search for knowledge, but because they pursued more traditional goals: to find sources of gold and spices; to defeat the Muslim enemy. And this culminated in the opening of sea routes round Africa to the East Indies, by the Portuguese, and across the Atlantic to the West Indies, by the Spaniards. This extension of geographical knowledge has been described many times and very well. What has been treated as more of a side issue is the discovery not of lands but of people. For it was at this time that Europeans first encountered Atlantic peoples from whom they had previously been totally isolated, peoples who had never, to their puzzlement and alarm, heard the name of Christ (or Moses, or Muhammad), peoples who lived in what it later became fashionable to call 'Stone Age' cultures, lacking knowledge of hard metals, lacking cities, often lacking clothes, and sometimes, it was reported, taking a perverse pleasure in eating one another. Some of these peoples were found in the island chain of the Bahamas when Columbus arrived there in October 1492; and further investigation brought to light very many more in the bigger Caribbean islands to the south, especially Hispaniola (now divided between Haiti and the Dominican Republic). In fact, there had been even earlier contact with 'primitive' peoples in islands much closer to Europe, the Canaries, visited from the 1340s onwards, but only finally subdued by Spanish conquerors in 1496. Later, in 1520, the conquerors of the Americas would have their first sight of the great metropolis of Tenochtitlán, on the site of modern Mexico City, with its temple pyramids, its bloody sacrifices and its wealth in gold; and at this moment they knew that they had reached a different sort of world from that of the simpler peoples who lived around the shores of the Caribbean or down the coast of Brazil. They had at last found the great civilisation rich in gold for which they had been searching; but it was the wrong civilisation, in the wrong place.

Were these 'primitive' men and women really human or were they beasts in human form, conveniently created as subordinates who could be put to work for the conquerors? The definition of these folk as humans might depend on their appearance, and here experience did not quite match the stories of dog-headed people found in medieval literature. They looked fully human. But maybe it was their conduct that defined them as less than human: sexual licence, the nature of their religious beliefs and practices, a failure to appreciate the verities of the True Faith, not that it was offered to them with a great amount of effort. Why had the Word of Christ not reached them? Was it so that Spain under its 'Catholic Monarchs', Ferdinand and Isabella, would have the glorious mission of evangelising these peoples? That sounded like a cruel delay in securing the salvation of many millions of souls, so maybe they had indeed been visited by St Thomas, Christ's apostle in the Indies, but had been too obstinate or stupid to hold to his teaching; or maybe they were descendants of the Ten Lost Tribes of Israel, a lineage that might prove of little help at a time when the Jews were being persecuted in Spain.

The encounter with these peoples opened the eyes of Europeans to a vast range of practices and beliefs that no one had previously suspected to exist. It had enormous repercussions for those who were discovered – put to work in gold mines, or even enslaved, most died of overwork and from European diseases; few of their descendants are alive today. It is hard to argue that this was a deliberate act of 'genocide', for the massive mortality was unplanned, and indeed added to the difficulties of the conquerors, who needed labour in order to extract gold, and later sugar, from their new conquests. It has been well said that what lay behind this terrible loss of life was sheer stupidity on the part of the conquerors. The labour shortage that resulted from their disappearance from the West Indies had a further tragic consequence: the massive importation of black African labour from the Portuguese trading stations along the outer edges of West Africa, though this was only just beginning in the period with which this book deals.

This discovery of new peoples was a surprise for several reasons. Of course Europeans had heard tales of strange races at the edge of the world, but these were located in Asia or Africa, in areas contiguous with Europe, to which the Word of Christ had surely spread. Beginning with the Canary islanders, the puzzle of the Atlantic peoples grew in scale as the scale of the Americas themselves became obvious. Columbus, it is true, saw the peoples he encountered in the Caribbean as in some way subjects of the Chinese or Japanese emperor, and as inhabitants of islands off the coast of East Asia about which he had read in Marco Polo's book of travels. But they were still isolated, simple, living unadorned lives, more like the 'Stone Age' Canary islanders than like the silk-clad natives of the Far Eastern empires. Not for nothing did the earliest printed accounts of Columbus' first voyage to the Caribbean refer to his discoveries as the 'New Canaries'.

Perhaps the best way to envisage the experience of those who encountered the newly discovered peoples of the islands of the Atlantic is to imagine that somewhere in the mountains of Mongolia living specimens of pre-modern humans such as Neandertalers were found; or to imagine, equally, that scientists identified noises in outer space as signs of intelligent life beyond this planet. There have been repeated reports of bulky, hairy 'men', deep in the forests of south-east Asia or even high in the Himalayas and the Rocky Mountains; and, though many must refer to sightings of bears or apes, it is not clear why humans survive only in one species, while other creatures tend to survive in very many. If Neandertalers, or similar people, were found today, we would immediately begin weighing up the human rights of beings less advanced than *Homo sapiens*. Even though it is no longer suggested that Neandertalers were clumsy, stooping figures who grazed their knuckles on the ground as they tried to walk, it is clear that they looked different from *Homo sapiens*, with their large brow ridges, barrel chests and short but strong legs.[1] That is to address the question of appearance; but there is also the question of behaviour. Assuming that these people were lacking in many of the skills we associate with human society, possibly lacking speech, probably lacking art, we would debate how far they could take an equal place in civil society: for example, whether they should possess the right to vote. Today we would want to ensure these people were not held in captivity, whether as slaves or as objects of curiosity in a zoo, as circus exhibits or as slave labour. And yet theories still being propounded in the mid-twentieth century by Carleton Coon argued that the great 'races' of mankind were descended from different species of early human, including 'Peking Man', 'Java Man' and

'Rhodesia Man'.[2] In some hands, this led to dangerous assumptions about differences in mental capacity and physical skills. These arguments, now amply discredited, have interesting points of comparison with the arguments propounded by writers in sixteenth-century Spain who were hostile to the American Indians and who occasionally raised the question whether they were actually descended from Adam, or whether they were part of a separate creation of an inferior class of humanity. For how else could they have spread themselves in such great numbers across such vast spaces within the time since Noah's Flood and the seeding of the world's population by his sons Shem, in Asia, Ham, in Africa, and Japheth, in Europe? Fortunately for the defenders of their humanity, Augustine of Hippo had taken the view 1100 years earlier that even the 'monstrous races' were Adam's children, sharing a 'common human nature'.[3]

The barriers in the human mind between human identity and the animal world have not always been sharp.[4] The great apes have sometimes been dignified with human status by those who lived among them and could see that they do possess some skills also found among humans, such as the use of tools (though so do birds). Chimpanzees appear to teach their young (but even parrots – who will fly past later in this book – are numerate and capable of conducting conversations). In Europe, attempts to confer human status on orang-utans began in the eighteenth century; but the inhabitants of south-east Asia already knew them as 'men of the forest', the meaning of their name in Malay. What European interest in these great apes proves is that the great debate about who is human, and what it is to be human, which had become so important in the age of Columbus, remained very much alive thereafter. Medieval observers would have wanted to know if those they encountered could speak, if they were aware of God and whether they could apply reason, for example by adding up figures. These criteria were generally held to matter more than hairiness, skin colour, shape of skull or size.

The dilemma of the late medieval or early modern observer was not dissimilar to that of a modern discoverer of living Neandertalers. Canary islanders and, more particularly, the Taíno inhabitants of the Caribbean were treated as a source of cheap labour, and were forced to work in degrading conditions, with appalling loss of life, which gave rise to the bitter criticisms of Bartolomé de las Casas in the sixteenth century. Before her death in 1504, Queen Isabella of Castile emphatically demanded that they should not be enslaved, since they were her subjects, even if they were not Christian; they could be seen as weak humans, childlike (as las Casas himself observed), in need of protection and completion, that completion to be achieved by making them into Christian converts and thus into fully fledged human beings, able to take part in civilised life. Despite the horrific ill-treatment accorded to the American Indians, their suffering did generate a fierce and long-lasting debate at the Spanish court about their rights, in the presence of the Spanish rulers Charles V and Philip II.[5] The sorry truth is that by then it was too late to save the American Indians or the Canary islanders.[6] Nor did the disappearance of the native Guanches of Tenerife stimulate much debate before las Casas' admirer and imitator Alonso de Espinosa wrote vigorously in their defence a full hundred years after the conquest of the island by Spanish toughs. Once they were almost extinct, they became a subject of fascination for several writers, well into the seventeenth century.[7]

Was Intelligent Life Created More Than Once?

It has been seen that an analogy can be made between the discovery of 'primitive' peoples in the era of Columbus and the discovery of other types of human being. Another analogy would be the discovery of advanced life elsewhere in the Universe. Here we would probably be dealing with a more and not less advanced culture; yet the comparison is very instructive, especially from the theological perspective, which mattered enormously to those who first dealt with 'primitive' peoples in the fifteenth century. The cosmologist Paul Davies has written: 'It would surely be the greatest discovery of all time, eclipsing the findings of Newton, Darwin and Einstein combined. The knowledge that we are not alone would affect people's psyches, and totally transform our world view. The mere fact alone would be disruptive.'[8] In this case we would presumably have to adjust to types of civil association, religious belief and codes of morality constructed on very different foundations in a very different physical setting. The question 'are we alone?' is not simply one for physicists; it marks a point where science and religion converge, 'part of a longstanding religious quest as well as a scientific project', for all scientists, even those hostile to religion, 'accept an essentially theological world view' and look for pattern and meaning in the entire Universe.[9] As well as science and religion, history, human history, converges at this point: the opening of new worlds in the late fifteenth century provides an important precedent. A central problem for European Christians in the age of discovery was bound to be whether the Word of Christ had reached the peoples who seemed so

numerous, so remote and so ignorant of Christian beliefs. Could many
millions of humans over dozens of generations have been left stranded on the
shores of Original Sin without hope of rescue through baptism and grace?
But the Christian message was supposed to have reached all the peoples of
the Earth: St Mark had insisted that Christ had ordered his 'good news' to be
despatched to all living creatures throughout the world, and St Augustine had
asserted that 'the Word of God was spread through the entire Universe'. Mark
testified: 'And he said to them, "Go into all the world and proclaim the good
news to the whole creation. The one who believes and is baptised will be
saved; but the one who does not believe will be condemned."'[10]

Today, the Vatican has begun to express interest in the possibility of other
inhabited worlds far out in the Universe.[11] Have they been visited by Christ?
Do they have any understanding of the concept of the Trinity? And Jews
might ask whether they know the Torah, Muslims whether they know the
Koran, and so on. The Copernican and Galilean revolutions gradually undermined the view that the Earth was at the centre of the Universe; but there
remains an articulate school of thought, theological as well as biological, that
argues that the evolution of life based on DNA is so very complex, and indeed
improbable to the point of being very nearly impossible, that one could
perfectly well argue that it has only arisen in one out of roughly $10^{40,000}$
galaxies, if that.[12] Some modern theologians have argued that a Universe of
billions of galaxies must contain billions of places in which intelligent life
exists (or, better: has existed, sometimes many millions of years ago), and that
those places too are part of the divine plan. One argument is that, by making
contact with such worlds, the belated knowledge of Christ can be spread
not just to the Americas in the sixteenth century but to the galaxies beyond
in future centuries, while others have suggested that divine incarnation on a
planet inhabited by 'mudpods' would necessitate Christ in the form of a
mudpod.[13] (Just as medieval speculation about lands beyond the edges of
civilisation included fantastic creatures, imaginative modern scientists have
drawn images of monsters we could expect to meet in other worlds: a sky
whale with honeycomb wings and a six-legged 'mudpod' with eyes on stalks
that could have come straight out of medieval bestiaries.)[14]

The question of other worlds has already generated a great variety of
answers. Equally, there existed a vast variety of opinions about native peoples
in the decades after Columbus reached America. This is not a book about a
single 'intellectual tradition', though there were plenty of guidelines to be
found in the works of Aristotle, who identified barbarians as 'natural slaves'

suited to menial tasks, or of Thomas Aquinas in the thirteenth century, who identified those features of 'natural law' that could give legitimacy even to a pagan society. Their ideas lay at the centre of the debates that emerged in the sixteenth century about the rights of native peoples.[15] This book goes further back in time and looks at the experience and moment of contact, examining how those who were present described what they thought they saw, or at least how others back home heard their reports and tried to create order out of what at times seemed senseless information about peoples whose style of life it was hard to imagine. To do that, writers had to go back to ancient and medieval images of strange races, and so they sometimes grafted on to information about the New World assumptions drawn from older books, which were rich in fiction. All this information did not create a single, stable image of primitive mankind, and some of the most expressive writing was not widely circulated, such as the first Portuguese account of Brazil sent to the king in Lisbon in 1500. On the other hand, Amerigo Vespucci's tendentious account of areas close by was rushed into print, became a bestseller and influenced wider thinking about the inhabitants of the New World, not least because it portrayed some of them as guzzling cannibals, naked and beast-like.[16]

A historian writing today can go several stages beyond either Vespucci's fancies or the serious-minded debates at the Spanish court. There was a real, inhabited New World out in the Atlantic. It was not just a post-modernist 'construct', but a series of societies for whose existence we have hard physical proof, in their bones, and in the trinkets and idols excavated by archaeologists. All this evidence provides a fascinating picture of the native societies and how they were dramatically transformed by contact with European explorers and conquerors. There was no master idea of how to deal with newly discovered peoples, but many competing ideas; there was no agreement about the human status or rights of these peoples; and yet there was a consistent series of reactions to discoveries as far apart as Brazil and Tenerife – curiosity about the lives of the people combined with a mercenary wish to know how rich their lands were and, very often, aspirations to political authority over the people who had come to light. The central theme of this book is, then, how Europeans attempted to deal with peoples whose looks, behaviour and morality were strikingly different from what they were familiar with, peoples who appeared to represent a more primitive form of human life.

CHAPTER 2

WILD MEN AND WANDERERS

Columbus Sets his Course, August 1492

Christopher Columbus set off from the little port of Palos, opposite Huelva in the south of Spain, for Japan, China and the Indies on 3 August 1492. 'So it was,' he wrote, 'that, after having expelled all the Jews from your kingdoms and domains . . . your highnesses commanded that I should go to the said regions of India with a suitable fleet.'[1] This deliberately conjures up an image of a great armada. In fact, he set out with the small *Santa María*, and the smaller still *Niña* and *Pinta*. Castile, once the home to three religions existing side by side in the fragile but productive harmony known to historians as *convivencia* (that is, 'living together'), had proclaimed its Christian identity by receiving the surrender of the last Muslim kingdom on Iberian soil, Granada, on 2 January 1492, after 780 years of Muslim rule over part or even most of the Iberian peninsula – a surrender Columbus claimed to have witnessed. A few months later, in the Alhambra palaces overhanging Granada, Ferdinand and Isabella issued decrees commanding that all Jews in their kingdoms of Castile, Aragon, Sicily and Sardinia either depart or convert to Christianity. The pope, Alexander VI Borgia, himself a Spaniard, would before long reward Ferdinand and Isabella with the title *Reyes Católicos*, 'Catholic Monarchs', in recognition of their service to the Christian faith in conquering Granada, and of their plans to carry their conquests further into North Africa, as far, indeed, if God so willed, as the Holy Sepulchre in Jerusalem.[2] Columbus and his patrons Ferdinand and Isabella saw the conquest of Granada as part of the same great venture on which Columbus was about to embark:

Your highnesses, as Catholic Christians and princes who love the holy Christian faith, exalters of it and enemies of the sect of Muhammad and of all idolatries and heresies, thought to send me, Christopher Columbus, to those abovementioned regions of India to see the princes, peoples, and lands, and their disposition and all the rest, and determine what method should be undertaken for their conversion to our holy faith; and you ordered that I not go by land to the Orient, the customary route, but instead by a western route, where we do not know with certainty to this day that anyone has gone.[3]

Ferdinand would not simply carry the war against Islam across the Straits of Gibraltar to Morocco. It must become a global struggle. It must bring Christianity to the whole world. For at times a messianic fervour gripped Ferdinand. At other times, he seemed hard-headed, ruthless, pragmatic.

The year 1492 saw Spain 'purged' of its Jews, and all its Muslims mastered. Yet this was also the moment when Ferdinand and Isabella were gaining

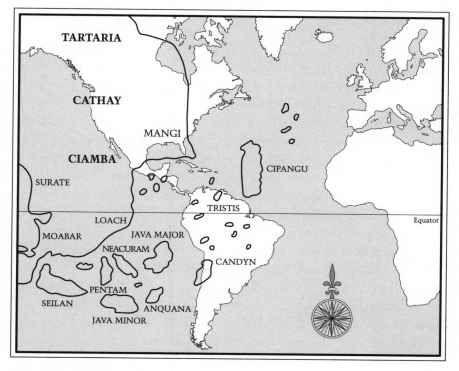

Martin Behaim's world globe of *c.*1492 imposed on a modern map of the Atlantic [after Fernández-Armesto, *Columbus*]

dominion over numbers of non-Christians far vaster than the Muslim population of Granada or the Jewish populations of their many kingdoms in Spain, Sicily and Sardinia. Together, these Jews and Muslims cannot have numbered more than half a million. Columbus would bring the Catholic Monarchs dominion over Hispaniola, home to maybe two million Taíno Indians, and a claim to dominion over a myriad of further islands and – if Columbus was right – a great Asiatic mainland as well. Elsewhere, too, the Catholic Monarchs were acquiring thousands of new 'heathen' subjects. The conquest of Grand Canary had at last been achieved and that of Tenerife, completed in 1496, was approaching its climax. Here, as in the Caribbean, were peoples who knew nothing of iron, possessed no books and knew nothing of Moses, Jesus or indeed Muhammad, until they met Europeans. 'Pagans' had been encountered before, by missionaries sent to Mongol lands who encountered shamanists and Buddhists, or by the Teutonic Knights who were engaged until the late fourteenth century in unsavoury wars with the pagan grand dukes of Lithuania; but these were peoples who had access to the Word of Christ, peoples among whom Christian missionaries circulated and among whom Christian peoples lived, even if many were heretics and schismatics – Nestorian and Orthodox Christians. In West Africa, it was true, there were areas penetrated by Islam and not by Christianity; and further south there were animists who either rejected Islam or were ignorant of it; but these lands too were part of a geographical continuum.

Columbus was a fervent reader of travel literature and a careful and skilled navigator. Thus he combined practical and theoretical knowledge. That, indeed, was the problem. In common with his contemporaries, he was inclined to give the written word, sanctified in some cases by centuries of acceptance (particularly within the Church), priority, and to assume that the answers to fundamental questions about the identity of the lands he aimed to discover, and did discover, was revealed in a series of books that began with Genesis and continued to the works of Marco Polo, Pierre d'Ailly (the fifteenth-century cardinal) and Aeneas Sylvius Piccolomini (the fifteenth-century Pope Pius II).[4] He had dipped into Aristotle's scientific works, too, but his reading was eclectic, a search for information to bolster his theories about the extent of the globe.[5] He had an obstinate, determined, inflexible character; he was self-important and brooked no contradiction. He was obsessed with the certainty that he would discover a route to Asia; and, once he had reached the New World, he hardly wavered in his insistence that what he had discovered was Asia and its outlying islands.[6] At one point he made his sailors swear that Cuba was part of the Asian mainland; the penalty for subsequently denying this was to be a fine of 10,000 *maravedís* and the excision of the culprit's tongue.[7] By its nature, this act revealed his own hidden doubts.

Columbus was learned, but he was also self-taught; the story that he studied at the University of Pavia can be discounted, as can tales of his noble pedigree.[8] It can easily be proved that he was the son of a Genoese weaver.[9] He was not a Jew. It is important to stress this because many claims have been made that he was Jewish, or Corsican, or Majorcan, or Portuguese.[10] His thinking did display a messianic fervour that is also visible in Jewish writings of the same time, an expectation of imminent deliverance. For the Jews the deliverer must surely be the Messiah, son of David. Christian writers, including converted Jews, picked up this theme; but for the Christians the deliverer would be Ferdinand, king of Castile and Aragon, who would recover Jerusalem, smash the power of Islam and the Turks, convert the remaining Jews and usher in the last days of mankind, culminating in the Second Coming of Christ. As his career progressed, Christopher Columbus, the 'bearer of Christ' (*Christophoros*), God's dove (*colomba*), increasingly saw himself too as someone sent by God to help deliver the world. The discovery and conversion of the people of the New World was part of God's plan for mankind.

He was an imposing, charismatic figure, tall and ruddy.[11] Even before his first voyage in 1492 Columbus was a well-travelled man. The traditional term 'first voyage' implies that he was less experienced than was the case; he knew the Atlantic islands well, especially the Madeira archipelago; he had sailed the Guinea coast and constantly compared what he saw in the New World with West Africa, to the detriment of Africa. He apparently visited Bristol and Ireland and sailed northwards to 'Thule', which could be a literary term for Iceland.[12] Indeed, he may have picked up from the men of Bristol or even from Icelanders tales of lands far to the west that had been visited by fishing fleets in search of cod, or by the Vikings half a millennium earlier when they had briefly settled in Newfoundland. Later in his life Columbus was struck by what seemed to be the prophetic words of the Roman sage Seneca (generally hailed as a secret Christian): 'A time will come in a number of years, when the Ocean will unfasten its bounds, and a huge land will stretch out, and Typhis the pilot will discover new worlds [*novos detegat orbes*], so the most remote land will no longer be Thule.'[13] He seems to have read papers in the possession of the Perestrello family of Porto Santo near Madeira that provided further evidence of land to the west. But Columbus became obsessed with his social advancement, and throughout his life he worked hard to improve the standing of his family, first marrying into the Perestrello family, of Italian origin but with links to the Portuguese nobility. He eventually assigned high office in the New World to his brothers Bartolomeo and Diego. He ensured that his legitimate son, also named Diego, made a truly excellent marriage, appropriate to someone who now had noble status, following the generous grants of rights and titles conferred by the king and queen on Christopher.[14] But just as 'Old Christians' murmured increasingly loudly at the success of converted Jews who had been admitted into the higher ranks at court, so they murmured too at the success of this Genoese parvenu, and of all the Genoese who so successfully managed the trade of Andalucía in these years.

Strange Peoples

The realisation that there existed new worlds inhabited by human beings, beyond the boundaries of Europe, western Asia and northern Africa, needs to be distinguished from the many myths and rumours of dog-headed people, even no-headed people, of giants and pygmies, which had deep roots in classical and other traditions. From 1492 – earlier, if one counts, as one should, the discovery of the Canary islanders as an important moment – European Christians actually saw in the flesh people from new worlds. Importantly, they were neither dog-headed nor headless. In 1493, Italian reports of the early arrival of Taíno Indians from the Caribbean remarked that some looked rather like Tartars, with round heads and 'oriental' eyes.[15] Rumours continued to circulate for many centuries of peoples with bizarre physiognomies; however, there was a rapid consensus that those new peoples who were actually encountered, rather than heard about, were human in shape of body. Did that mean they were human in type of soul? Monstrous races might not be descendants of Adam, might not therefore be part of the divine scheme for mankind. The Bible spoke mysteriously of giants who lived before the Flood, though these had presumably been swept away in the great deluge. The great hordes of Gog and Magog, mentioned in the Bible, were (Mandeville related) descendants of the Ten Lost Tribes of Israel who were hemmed in among impenetrable mountains in Further Asia, awaiting the coming of Antichrist, when they would be unleashed on mankind as a great scourge.[16] On the other hand, some had already taken the view that the unwashed Mongol hordes who swept westwards as far as Hungary in 1241 were part of the same army of Gog and Magog, a view that seemed to be confirmed by their strange appearance and wild habits. These included a failure ever to change their clothes, drinking fermented mare's milk and cooking slabs of meat by placing them between the saddle and the sweaty flanks of their small but sturdy horses as they rode at speed across the steppes.

The European response to the Mongols shows that there were two basic criteria for the assessment of human status. One was appearance, form, zoology: what might be called the evidence of physical or biological anthropology, and the other was the evidence of behaviour, conduct, technology: what might be called the evidence of social anthropology. Columbus, as will be seen, from the first moment of contact defended the argument that the people he encountered were physically human, and this was repeated independently by other observers, such as the first Portuguese to reach Brazil in 1500. This did not prevent Columbus and others from speculating about the existence of stranger races just over the horizon. Moreover, evidence of peoples who, by their everyday conduct, did not seem to be fully human was closer at hand. The Jews lived in the midst of European cities, whether or nor segregated in ghettoes; they wore similar clothes (indeed, it was the Christian authorities who tried to mark them out by requiring many to wear a special sign); and their diet, though more restricted by religious law, included nothing extraordinary like the reptile meat consumed in the Caribbean. There were, it is true, accusations that Jews ritually consumed the blood of Christian boys, and these revived in Spain, Italy and Germany at the end of the fifteenth century; these dark fantasies of Jews as bloodthirsty cannibals clearly raised questions about their human status. In the fourteenth century, Heinrich von Hesler was relentless in his insistence that the Jews were an accursed race whose only chance of humanisation lay in their conversion to Christianity.[17]

Jews lived in society, in families, communities, often within separated areas. They sometimes wandered from land to land, as in 1492 following their expulsion from Spain, but this wandering was always in search of places to live and settle. However, there were other types of people who did not conform to this basic norm, real nomads, for instance, whether Lapps in the north or Gypsies from the east. In the twelfth century, tent-dwelling Magyars were derided as ugly 'human monsters'.[18] The arrival of the nomadic Roma in fifteenth-century Europe caused much puzzlement. They claimed to be Christians, expelled from 'Little Egypt' somewhere in the east, and this gave rise to the name 'Gypsy', or 'Egyptian', though there is no doubt that they originated in India. As they reached Germany, Austria, Italy and France local lords sought to treat with them as they would with any other society, addressing their 'dukes' with due respect, and assuming that they possessed a similar social structure to that of aristocratic Christendom. As early as 1425 they had begun to trickle into Spain, apparently coming up from Africa as well as down from France; in the 1480s a second wave arrived, who claimed to be Greeks fleeing from the Turks. What protected them, however, was their self-declared Christian identity.[19] Even so, Ferdinand and Isabella ordered them to leave if they did not settle down and work for a master, accusing them of dishonesty and vagabondage.[20] Rootlessness suggested a lack of civilised ways.

A better example of wandering people is provided by someone who lived apart, among the beasts, even perhaps looking more beast-like than human: the wild man of the woods. He or she was a constant subject in late medieval art that drew on biblical references: the mad King Nebuchadnezzar condemned to live in the fields like an ox; Elijah or John the Baptist wearing a few skins and living in the desert; St John Chrysostom doing penance naked and alone.[21] A sixteenth-century painting by a follower of Pieter Brueghel the Elder portrays the common folk drama in which a wild man was captured and killed. This was a frequent theme of pageants at the end of the Middle Ages, as for example in a display in Brussels in 1496, in honour of the Spanish Princess Juana ('the Mad'), where fourteen actors dressed as wild men were part of the cast.[22] Cannibalistic female ogres or giants clad in skins had their place in the classic literary works of the Middle Ages by such authors as Chrétien de Troyes, writing in the twelfth century, and also in colourful folk tales from southern Germany. Characteristically, the wild man (or woman) was covered with hair, fur or scales, or at least wore skins, lived off berries and roots as a primeval hunter-gatherer, ate raw flesh (in some versions, human flesh) and had to use his own strength and wiles to survive, but without the advantages of late medieval technology. Often, he went around on all fours like any other animal. He might wield a heavy club, and avoided even his own kind, apart from the occasional fleeting encounter with a wild person of the opposite gender, which meant that the race was perpetuated. Lacking speech, expressing only 'senseless words, which nature did him teach' (to cite Edmund Spenser), he found it difficult to reason.[23] Could he then know God? It seemed not. Von Hesler, who was relatively sympathetic to wild men and saw them as indeed God's creatures, remarked that they are 'shaped like humans, but they are so crude and wild that they have never heard God's word'. Not all agreed with this judgment. Geiler von Kayserberg, a fifteenth-century theologian based in Strasbourg, took the view that there were several categories of 'wild men', including *diaboli*, satyrs or devils, surely created by Satan. Others clearly did belong to humanity: desert saints, Pygmies and the *Hispani*, which could mean lunatics or Gypsies, or which could just possibly be an unsubtle dig at all Spaniards.[24] South-eastern Europe was a special preserve of wild forest men, a tradition preserved in the name of one of its more mysterious regions, Transylvania.[25]

There was no single, overpowering image of the wild man or woman in late medieval and Renaissance Europe. This was a fantasy that could be expressed in dozens of distinct ways; one only has to look at Dürer's many etchings of wild people to see how classical themes could combine with German literary and folkloric traditions to produce a whole Noah's Ark of wondrous figures.[26] But the beast-like attributes of most wild men in late medieval literature and art were not generally seen as innate, the result of being created by God in a category that was neither fully human nor fully animal. Rather, the wild man was often understood to have fallen from his place in society, to be an exile, as a result of some misfortune that might even have begun in early childhood – after all, the founders of Rome, Romulus and Remus, had been raised in the forests by a wolf. It was therefore possible to recover one's human state and to return to civilisation, and the most direct route to recovery was through the Christian faith. In that sense, the negative image of the wild man always had a positive counter-image, a hope of redemption.

There was another image of wild people, the most fertile of all in its influence on those who discovered new peoples at the end of the Middle Ages. This was the image of primitive mankind living in a Golden or Silver Age, as portrayed, for example, in the 1520s and 1530s by Lucas Cranach in paintings now hanging in London, Dublin, Weimar and elsewhere.[27] While the Golden Age described by the classical poets (especially Hesiod and Ovid) had been an age of peace, it had also been one of technological simplicity; in the Silver Age mankind learned to build and to cultivate the soil; an understanding of the difference between good and evil developed, but, in its final phases, the harbingers of the Age of Bronze arrived, introducing strife. This was a primitive age of mankind characterised by a pristine purity that gradually declined, for 'civilisation' brings its temptations and corruptions. Thus the simple folk of the first ages of mankind were not grunting wild people covered in thick hair, unused to social intercourse; their nakedness was the nakedness of innocence rather than of sexual licence. This classical imagery remained at the forefront of early descriptions of the New World by writers at the royal court in Spain. It fused with imagery of the Garden of Eden, a favourite theme of the Bible-reading Columbus, even though it was hard for any theologian to accommodate the idea of part of mankind surviving in pristine purity from the days before the Fall of Man.[28] In the first place, there had only been one man and one woman in the Garden of Eden, and in the second even Columbus in his most ardent moments agreed that the Garden was inaccessible to humans. Still, the notion of mankind living in a prelapsarian state was a theme that kept recurring thanks to classical imagery.

Wild Men of the West

Another place to look for people who, by their conduct, did not lead fully human lives was the edges of Europe. Unconverted peoples in the far north, around the shores of the Baltic, were a source of morbid fascination. They were 'rude and animal-like', and were accused of savage idolatry and ferocious cruelty, which converged in the barbarous rite of human sacrifice. But the Irish too were seen as little better than pagans: 'Christians in name, pagans in fact', to cite St Bernard.[29] Gerald of Wales, a garrulous Norman, left a description of Ireland in the 1180s that at many points anticipates the descriptions of the New World over three centuries later. Whatever his reservations about the Irish themselves, Gerald praised the island for its freshness, its healthy (if rain-filled) air, its verdant fields, its lack of snakes; all this meant that few people fell sick there, and that Ireland preserved some of the pristine qualities of the world at the time of its creation, before corruption crept into almost everything.[30] But it was also a place of miracles and, it had to be said, of monsters. He told of werewolves who took animal form for seven years as a result of a local curse, but remained human underneath: 'the wolf then said some things about God that seemed reasonable'; 'the wolf gave a Catholic answer in all things.'[31] The credulous Gerald was fascinated by tales of men and women with animal features: there was a severely deformed man from Wicklow who was thought to be half-ox; while a woman in Connacht had intercourse with a magnificent white goat, which, he opined, was less abominable for the animal, for a rational human should not descend to the level of beasts.[32] And that, in essence, was his problem with the Irish as a whole. He could not see them as his equals. That they were physically human was by and large the case. It was their culture that was barbarous: 'but although they are fully endowed with natural gifts, their external characteristics of beard and dress, and internal cultivation of the mind, are so barbarous that they cannot be said to have any culture.'[33] He thought their simple cloaks and leggings were crude. They went into battle 'naked', that is, without armour and proper weapons, using spears, darts, axes and stones.

In the end, frankly, 'they are a wild and inhospitable people. They live on beasts only, and they live like beasts. They have not progressed at all from the primitive habits of pastoral living.'[34] Gerald's point was that mankind starts in the forests, moves to the fields and then to villages and towns. That, for him, was the sign of human progress. But the Irish were too lazy even to make much use of the fields. They could not be bothered to mine for the gold that could be found on the island, despite the value they placed on it. They avoided as far as possible the arts of linen-weaving and wool-weaving: 'they think that the greatest pleasure is not to work, and the greatest wealth is to enjoy liberty.' They were still in large measure people of the woods: 'all their habits are the habits of barbarians.'[35] They lived so far from the world of men that they had no know-ledge of (to use a modern term) civilisation. It was living together that gave people their culture. These were wild people on the wild edge of the world. Their one redeeming quality was their superlative music.[36] Their material culture was primitive; and on a moral plane they were deplorable too, 'a filthy people, wallowing in vice'. They had no proper marriages, and ignored the laws against incest.[37] They were faithless in two ways: treacherous in their dealings with one another, readily breaking solemn pacts; and barely Christian, for many remained unbaptised. Gerald had spoken with some mariners aboard a large ship who had been caught in a storm off Connacht and put in at an island off a shore they had never seen before. They told how they then caught sight of two men rowing a simple boat made of wickerwork and animal skins; these men were naked, though they had pieces of animal skin around their waist, and their blond hair was so long that it covered much of their body. Everything they were shown seemed new to them; they were offered bread and cheese but refused to eat them, saying they did not know what they were. What they normally ate was meat, fish and milk, and they were therefore very disappointed when the mariners refused to serve them meat, on the grounds that these were the days of Lent. Lent itself was meaningless to them, as was Christianity, or indeed the calendar of months, weeks and days. They normally went around naked, but would cover themselves with skins when it was vital to protect themselves from the weather. They were sent away with samples of bread and cheese to show to their own people.[38]

There is no evidence that Columbus had ever read, or even heard of, the book by Gerald of Wales, though he did visit Galway in western Ireland. It is clear, though, that Gerald's account of Ireland was read widely, as far south as Province. What his words reveal is an extraordinary consistency in the way medieval Europeans assessed peoples they regarded as less advanced than themselves. There was the question of their appearance, including their use of clothes; of their technology, in weapon-making, weaving and (raised by other writers) house-building; of their sexual habits and moral behaviour, including, very importantly, their knowledge of Christianity; and of their ability to associate with one another, to form a true 'society'. So those who told tales of an encounter with Irish 'barbarians' off Connacht acted in a strikingly similar way to those who encountered Canarians on Grand Canary in 1341, Taíno Indians in the Bahamas in 1492 or Tupí Indians in Brazil in 1500: they showed them their food, they observed their reaction to their ships and equipment.

Wild Men of the East

In fact, Columbus' informants were far more ancient than Gerald of Wales. A direct source of information to Columbus and his contemporaries was the Elder Pliny, who had died in the eruption of Vesuvius in AD 79; he told how Ethiopia was the home of many strange peoples, from the Pygmies of classical tradition to the naked Gymnetes and peoples without mouths. Elsewhere in Africa were the Blemmyae, with their eyes and mouth in the upper chest and no head, and man-eating Anthropophagi. India contained people with their feet turned backwards. Bearing in mind that the terms 'India' and 'Ethiopia' were interpreted very broadly to embrace all the southern and western shores of the Indian Ocean, there was a reasonable expectation that Columbus' ships would encounter such strange peoples. The stories grew in the retelling, as they passed through such writers as Augustine of Hippo in fifth-century Africa, Isidore of Seville in sixth- and seventh-century Spain, the author of the legend of St Brendan in the tenth century, medieval gossips such as Gervase of Tilbury in the twelfth century and Cardinal Pierre d'Ailly in the early fifteenth century – the latter's writings were closely studied by Columbus.[39] Marco Polo had plenty of space in his travel book for headless peoples or folk who shaded themselves from the sun by using their one immense foot as an umbrella. He liked to insist on the value of his eyewitness evidence: when he had not actually visited a place he described, he still tried to invest his account with similar authority. Thus he wrote of an island called Andaman in the Indian Ocean that it was full of wild people without a king, 'idolaters' who 'live like beasts', which was not surprising since they were dog-headed. If they ever encountered a normal human, they seized him and ate his flesh.

Columbus also knew the very popular travel book by John Mandeville, written in the late fourteenth century. In reality, Mandeville may never have travelled much further than Flanders, despite his claim to have circumnavigated the globe.[40] Mandeville was even more eloquent than Marco Polo about the Andaman islanders. One group would eat the bodies of their dead relatives – sons their fathers, fathers their sons – in an act of what would now be called endocannibalism: cannibalism within the tribe, a substitute for burial that, Mandeville says, was based on the principle that it was far more painful to be eaten by worms underground.[41] But on Nicobar the dog-headed people 'are fully reasonable and intelligent'. This is in contrast to Tracota, next door, where 'the people are like animals lacking reason' and hiss like adders rather than speaking; they live in caves because they are not intelligent enough to build houses.[42] Mandeville's account of monstrous peoples in the Indian Ocean therefore raises a question to which observers of newly discovered peoples would endlessly return: are these rational, intelligent people who are capable of living like the human beings known in Europe, capable, indeed, of understanding Christian truth, or are they more like animals, lacking, as some do, kings, houses, language, and following strange diets that might even include human flesh? In that case, several sixteenth-century Spanish writers would often argue, they were better placed to serve than to command.

Men without Reason

If there was one criterion that seemed most concisely to define the right to human status, it was religious identity. This is not to say that Muslims (for instance) were treated as less than human in their physical being; by the mid-thirteenth century some canon lawyers and theologians argued that their political institutions, so long as they followed 'natural law' and did not threaten Christianity, could be legitimate. But baptism was seen as the sacrament that in a very real sense completed the process of humanisation. All children were born with the taint of Original Sin, but it could be washed away so that life could begin afresh, or rather the true, spiritual life could begin in place of the merely carnal life into which each child was born. It turned the newly baptised

individual into a 'new person', a *novus homo*, able to subsist on the spiritual as
well as the physical plane, and able to reach out to the grace of Christ. In the
final analysis, for any fifteenth-century political thinker or theologian in
Catholic Europe, society consisted of Christendom; only a Christian could be
a citizen of the world. In Spain and Portugal, of course, the meeting of the
faiths, with the Jews squeezed comfortably or uncomfortably in the middle,
gave these issues added force.

Broadly speaking, the Jews became the target of theological campaigns,
which culminated in their segregation, expulsion, extermination and (especially in Spain) their conversion; the Muslims became the target of military
ones, which culminated in the loss of sovereignty over any part of al-Andalus,
Spain. The issue of Jewish unbelief became the subject of increasingly intense
discussion among the theologians of medieval Europe. From the twelfth
century onwards, Christian philosophers and theologians had argued that
anyone who applied reason, 'the quality which they believed separated man
from beast', could only conclude that Christianity was correct; 'in this way,' a
modern scholar has observed, 'Jews began to be discussed as if they were less
than human', lacking 'that quality which they believed separated man from
beast'. 'Just as Jews were perceived as standing outside the realm of human
reason, they were seen in this context as deliberately distancing themselves
from the rest of mankind': 'to be human was in effect to be a Christian.'[43] Jews
failed to apply reason, and this placed them dangerously close to the realm of
non-human animals. For Cicero had observed, in a work that was much read
in the Middle Ages, that mankind is unique among animals in possessing this
faculty of reason: 'he is the only one among so many kinds and varieties of
living beings who has a share in reason and thought, while all the rest are
deprived of it.' He concluded: 'the first common possession of God and man
is reason.'[44]

Applied to the Jews, this demotion from fully human status had tragic
consequences. (Conversion might elevate them to fully human status, for in
undergoing conversion, with the support of divine grace, they had grasped
hold of reason and had been wiped clean not merely of the taint of Original
Sin but of the further sin of Deicide.) This 'dehumanisation' of the Jews was
an idea that circulated among medieval intellectuals, but began to acquire a
practical application as missions in lands such as Catalonia failed to have the
desired effect. From the thirteenth century onwards the Dominican and
Franciscan friars launched vigorous and well-planned campaigns of conversion aimed at Jews and Muslims under Christian rule and, when opportunity

arose, at non-Christians in Muslim lands such as North Africa as well. Their strategy consisted of immersing themselves in the sacred texts of Judaism and Islam in the original Hebrew, Aramaic and Arabic, so that the friars could debate publicly with rabbis and imams; if they could convert the leaders, it was argued, then the masses would rapidly follow. Even the generally good-natured and tolerant Majorcan missionary Ramon Llull (d. 1316) simply assumed that when Jews, Muslims or pagans understood his elaborate argu-ments about how the Trinity was reflected in all Creation, they could not fail to turn Christian; he wrote well over three hundred books on the theme, but converted no one. At least he seemed to accept that Jews had some rational powers, and that Jews and Muslims worshipped the same God as Christians, a view many of his contemporaries appear not to have shared.[45] The friars began to range even further afield, sending missions to East Asia, to the courts of the Mongol khans, where the first public disputations with Buddhists took place in the late thirteenth century. This approach was one that Columbus would revive when he tried to find out about the religious beliefs of the Taíno Indians in the Caribbean. However convinced the friars might be of the truth of Christianity, their success in winning converts among both Jews and Muslims was modest. Violence, notably the Spanish pogroms of 1391, tended to win more converts, as did the expulsion of unconverted Jews in 1492; but then there was the fear that the converts were half-hearted at best. All this seemed to prove that the Jews in particular were obstinate and lacked reason. In mid-fifteenth-century Spain, the argument began to emerge that even after their conversion the blood of Jews and their descendants remained tainted, a line of reasoning that led to the exclusion of those of Jewish descent from high office in the Church and State by the middle of the next century. Thus even within Europe there was an established debate about whether all those who had human form possessed human mental capacities, and this debate would resonate throughout the period of the discovery of new peoples in the Atlantic.

CHAPTER 3

IMAGES OF ASIA

Rumours of Japan

Columbus expected to reach Japan and then China. His source of information about Japan, and everyone else's, was the dictated memoirs of the late thirteenth-century Venetian traveller to the Far East, Marco Polo. Polo had not merely visited the court of the Mongol emperor of China, Qubilai Khan, he also claimed to have been one of his civil servants. Polo's was not actually the first mention of Japanese gold to reach the ears of an audience in Europe. Around 1154, the geographer Idrisi, writing at the court of Roger II of Sicily, had mentioned that gold was so abundant in Japan that dogs wore collars of solid gold.[1] But Idrisi wrote in Arabic, and there is no evidence that his remarkable account of the world was ever read or used by Christian writers. On the other hand, there still exists a copy of Polo's *Travels* owned by Columbus, marked up with marginal notes by Columbus and his son and biographer Ferdinand, and preserved in Columbus' library in Seville. This copy was acquired, apparently from England, after 1493, so some sceptics have argued that he had not actually read the book before he went on his first and second voyages. However, he already owned a Latin paraphrase, the friar Pipino's *On Customs*, which he annotated with comments about Japan and elsewhere.[2] It was a very popular book – about fifty medieval manuscripts of Pipino's work still survive, before the first printed edition of 1482.[3] Columbus' logbook and letters from the first voyage make plain his knowledge of Polo's reports, so we have to conclude that if he had not read all of it, he had at least read parts or summaries of what Polo recorded. One obviously does not need to have owned a book in order to have read it.[4] Mandeville's account was also available; but this offered increasingly fantastic tales of rivers that flowed with precious stones on the edge of Paradise, and of the lands of the Christian king Prester John, whose Indian, Far Eastern or Ethiopian empire had been the subject of speculation since as early as the twelfth century.[5]

What was clear from Polo's writings was that one was very likely to reach Japan well before reaching China if one sailed west. On medieval world maps, the Atlantic Ocean was often portrayed as a quite narrow ring around the three continents of Europe, Asia and Africa; but in fact a rich literature spoke of inhabited and empty islands out to the west, in the Atlantic, and out to the east, in what would later be called the Pacific. Medieval writers about the Atlantic often assumed the existence of large, settled islands such as the Isle of the Seven Cities or *Antilia* lying west of Portugal, which had supposedly been colonised by shiploads of Christian exiles from eighth-century Spain, fleeing from the Muslim conquerors of their homeland under the guidance of seven bishops.[6] Thus it was not a great leap of the imagination to assume that these islands formed part of the chain of thousands of islands that were believed, with partial accuracy, to lie off the coast of Asia – the Spice Islands. Columbus was certainly not the first to search for such lands; for example, in 1487 the Fleming Ferdinand van Olmen set out with two ships from the Azores on such a mission, intending to report back to the king of Portugal; he seems to have misjudged the prevailing winds, sailed off into the mists and was never heard of again. Still, there was a growing consensus that Japan might be within reach. Martin Behaim was a German cartographer and traveller who had visited the outer edges of what was known of the Atlantic; in 1486 he was in the Azores, and very nearly joined the ill-fated expedition of Ferdinand van Olmen in search of land to the west. In 1492–3, before news of the New World voyages could be integrated into his understanding of the shape of the world, he made a great globe, now preserved in Nuremberg; here, Behaim portrayed Japan as a massive island, about three times the size of the Iberian peninsula, roughly as far from the Azores as the Azores are from Portugal, with the northern tip of Cipangu lying on the same latitude as the Straits of Gibraltar.[7] Polo began his account of Japan, or 'Cipangu', by locating it far further from the coast of Asia than is really the case: 'Cipangu is an Island towards the east in the high seas, 1500 miles distant from the Continent; and a very great Island it is.' Beyond Japan would lie Cathay, with its great port of Quinsay (Hangchow), where the Italian friar Andrew of Perugia had functioned as archbishop only a century and a half before, and beyond that was Malacca and the greatest spice market in the world; its harbour brimmed with merchants of diverse origins, and even the parrots were said to speak a great number of languages. And around all these places there was reliably said to exist a myriad of islands.

Columbus' ships passed though the Canary Islands in September 1492; thereafter, the winds, the crew's prayers and the skills of their admiral would carry them to what he was certain was the edge of Asia. He could expect first of all to reach Japan. Had any news filtered across to Spain from the great port of Fukoaka to the ports of China and down to Malacca, there to be carried along the spice routes through Calicut and Aden to Alexandria and Venice, Genoa or Barcelona, without being metamorphosed in a sequence of Chinese whispers, it would have told of the disintegration of central government, of a ruler, Yoshimasa, who made Isabella's unsuccessful predecessor and half-brother, Henry IV of Castile, look a political genius by comparison; though by now Yoshimasa had entered a Buddhist monastery, leaving others to attempt to sort out the chaos.[8] Just when the Spanish monarchs were bringing the rivalry of over-mighty subjects under control, the shoguns in Japan ceded local power to ruthless warlords. The news might also have carried reports of an empire that was, in the midst of this chaos, a vibrant centre of culture (much influenced by China) and a lively centre of trade in silk, paper and precious articles.[9] But no such news was available. Columbus travelled with the latest information he had: its author was the Venetian traveller Marco Polo. Polo had heard that Japan was fabulously rich in gold and pearls. He had lived two hundred years before. He had never been to Japan.

Polo's point was not so much that Japan was geographically far from China but that it was isolated from China:

> The people are white, civilised, and well-favoured. They are Idolaters [by which he may mean Buddhists], and are dependent on nobody. And I can tell you the quantity of gold they have is endless; for they find it in their own Islands, *and the King does not allow it to be exported. Moreover* few merchants visit the country because it is so far from the mainland, and thus it comes to pass that their gold is abundant beyond all measure. [*Passage in italics:* some manuscripts only.][10]

The claim that trade between the Asian mainland and Japan was limited has some basis in fact, as does the claim that Japan was rich in gold. Indeed, it was the mention of gold that set alight Columbus' enthusiasm for finding a direct route to Japan and China; no less enticingly, Polo went on to mention pearls and precious stones as well.[11] The emperor of Japan was said to have a palace roofed with gold, 'just as our churches are roofed with lead', with floors made of great golden slabs, 'so that altogether the richness of this palace is past all bounds and all belief'.[12] This wealth was to be used not simply to enrich Columbus and his family, but, above all, to meet the needs of the Castilian monarchs as they planned their great wars of conquest in the Mediterranean against Islam, which would culminate in the recovery of Jerusalem and the beginning of the era of human redemption.

There is quite a lively debate about the authenticity of Marco Polo's account of the Far East. Frances Wood's book *Did Marco Polo Go to China?* emphasised that, if he had travelled so far, he would have surely mentioned some of the real marvels of the East such as the Great Wall, which he did not describe (though it may well have been in a state of neglect in his time); his memoirs were dictated to a publicity-conscious, somewhat sensationalist writer named Rustichello who clearly added further spice, and they survive in several different versions.[13] Yet what matters from a fifteenth-century perspective is not the veracity of Polo's account but the ways in which it was understood, and believed, by men such as Columbus. Indeed, what seemed to give Polo's book greater authenticity was the readiness with which its author would dismiss as old wives' tales traditional myths about the East. A good example of this deflation of medieval myths is Polo's argument that the sala-mander was not a lizard that could live in the midst of fire; rather, it was a grey and fibrous mineral that did not burn; in other words, asbestos. This did not prevent him from supporting rumours of dog-headed Asiatic peoples and of cannibals in Furthest Asia. Two centuries later, Polo's words, combined with real evidence for cannibalism among the Caribs of the Lesser Antilles, only strengthened the conviction of the Spanish explorers that they had found a route to the Asian lands Polo had described. Polo probably did travel deep into Asia, followed by a handful of pioneering Venetian and Genoese merchants who lived and died in the great fourteenth-century port of Zaytun (Hangchow, Quanzhou). On the other hand, few would agree that he achieved the high office and influence he attributed to himself.

Letters to the Rulers of the Orient

Columbus too expected to reach the courts of the rulers of the East. In 1492 he bore letters across the Atlantic addressed to the Great Khan of the Mongols and other eastern potentates. (So exiguous was information about

China that western Europe was unaware that the Mongol dynasty, the Yüan, had been overthrown by the Ming emperors in 1368.) The letters contained a request that Columbus be granted a safe-conduct, as well as a recommendation of his good character to whomever he might encounter among the kings of the East. The text of this demand for a safe-conduct, preserved in the Archives of the Crown of Aragon in Barcelona, was published in 1985 but is little known. In this letter, Ferdinand and Isabella ask any ruler, prince, lord, captain, official, or indeed anybody else, to provide all necessary facilities for Christopher Columbus, who is travelling 'through the Ocean Sea to the parts of India' (a term that encompassed virtually all of Asia and East Africa).[14] A second letter was, somewhat hypocritically, addressed to 'the most serene prince [*blank space*], our most dear friend'; three copies were prepared, two with blanks in which the name of a ruler such as the emperor of Japan could be filled in, and one copy specifically addressed to the Great Khan, that is, the Chinese emperor.[15] The letter stated that the Catholic Monarchs had heard news of the unnamed prince's good disposition towards them, from their own subjects and from other accounts (presumably Polo), and they wanted to assure the prince that they were well and flourishing. It is all rather vague, and the reference to information from the Spanish monarchs' own subjects is odd, though some news of India had arrived from Portugal and ambassadors from Ethiopia had earlier reached Ferdinand's uncle King Alfonso of Aragon;[16] but the assumption was certainly that Columbus would meet characters straight out of Marco Polo's book of travels. His logbook suggests that the documents he carried also included an invitation to learn more about the Christian faith, following the pattern of letters sent eastwards in the thirteenth century with friars bound for the Mongol court. In the first lines of the logbook he insists that the king and queen asked him to see how the natives of the Orient could best be converted (or converted back) to Christianity, and that a principal motive in sending him across the Atlantic was to spread the Word of Christ, speaking of the Great Khan and asserting

> that many times he and his predecessors had sent to Rome to request teachers of our holy faith, who might instruct him in it, but that the Holy Father never had provided him with this, and so many peoples had been lost, falling into idolatries and adopting for themselves damnable sects.[17]

While he was in the Bahamas in October 1492 he resolved to press ahead beyond Cipangu to 'the mainland', to Quinsay, the Chinese port visited in the fourteenth century by Italians, 'and to give your Highnesses' letters to the Grand Khan and request an answer and return with it'.[18]

Nonetheless, there is a strong hint elsewhere in Columbus' logbook that the Spanish monarchs' letters were not particularly concerned with the preaching of Christianity – indeed, there were no priests or friars on board to preach it until the second voyage in 1493. The opening lines of the logbook (which in any case only survives in much altered versions) were probably added after Columbus' return, to flatter King Ferdinand and Queen Isabella. Nor were these latter's letters simply concerned with a strategic alliance with the Great Khan against Islam, a standard motif in European literature about the Mongols and their successors since the thirteenth century. For Columbus believed that he had reached the outer edges of a trade network serviced by the massive ships of the Great Khan, which came to obtain gold and pearls; Japan, he was sure (and this at least was correct, as it happens), was linked by regular sailings to China.[19] Noticing, however, that cotton was widely grown in the islands he had discovered, he observed:

> I believe it would sell very well over here, without bringing it to Spain, but rather to the large cities of the Grand Khan, which will be discovered, without a doubt, and to many others belonging to other lords who will be happy to serve your Highnesses in that business, and in those cities other things from Spain and from the lands of the East will be offered for sale, since the latter are to the west of us here.[20]

So here Columbus, reverting to the role of a Genoese sailor and merchant, was blithely suggesting that the Spaniards could intrude themselves very successfully as middlemen into the cotton trade between the islands he had discovered, trading not with Europe but with Asia.

In fact, Columbus and the Catholic Monarchs were aware of the need to keep their options open. On arriving in San Salvador, the first island he discovered, Columbus confidently laid claim to the territory in the name of Ferdinand and Isabella; this was easily done in the presence of uncomprehending but friendly natives who clearly lived simple lives on quite a small island. But he knew that, had he in fact arrived on the Asian mainland, in a great trading city such as Hangchow, any attempt to assert Castilian sovereignty would have done him and his monarchs no good. In those circumstances he would immediately have unwrapped the letters of recommendation and sought out the highest official he could find (this was what Vasco da

Gama did when he arrived in Calicut on his own epic voyage round Africa to the Indies in 1498). It is clear what he would then be requesting. The other option throughout the planning of his voyage had to be the creation of a trading station, what the Portuguese called a *feitoría* ('factory') or the Genoese, of whom Columbus was one, knew as a *fondaco*: a reserved area containing the facilities foreign merchants would need, such as an inn, a storehouse, a chapel, a bakery and a bathhouse. Columbus had seen how this type of institution, developed in the Mediterranean, served very well in the Atlantic trading posts of the Portuguese in West Africa; the Portuguese had displayed little interest in claiming direct rule over vibrant African kingdoms and had simply reserved to the king of Portugal the grand title 'Lord of Guinea'.[21] The creation of trading factories would be a much more grand but empty outcome than the privileges Columbus received from the king and queen suggested: they had showered on him extensive commercial and financial rights, including a tenth of all gold, pearls and other precious cargoes, the title of Admiral of the Ocean Sea, the post of 'viceroy and governor general in all those islands and any mainland and islands that he may discover', none of which would be very useful if he strayed into the heart of a great empire with its own fleets, armies, tax system and provincial governors.[22] All these open-ended promises and gifts to Columbus thus reflected deep uncertainty about what he would discover, combined with undoubted optimism that there was something accessible out there in the Atlantic.

Not merely was that something not Japan or China, it was a chain of islands inhabited by people closer in appearance and style of life to the 'Stone Age' peoples of the Canaries than to the silk-clad subjects of the Far Eastern emperors. It was a society simpler in its technology than the complex city-based societies they already knew in black Africa from the Portuguese explorers and traders. Columbus was convinced that the people he found were Asiatic, but the immediate comparison that came to mind was indeed with the Canary islanders: 'none of them are dark, but rather the colour of Canary islanders, nor should one expect anything else, since this island is in the same latitude as the island of El Hierro in the Canary Islands.'[23] He could only think in the categories that were already familiar to him. He responded to the shock of the new by asserting all the time that it was not new.

PART II

EASTERN HORIZONS
*The Peoples, Islands and Shores of the
Eastern Atlantic*

CHAPTER 4

INNOCENCE AND WILDNESS IN THE CANARY ISLANDS, 1341–1400

Seven Miniature Continents

Dominating the archipelago, the great volcano of Mount Teide on Tenerife, 3718 metres above sea level, was visible from afar. The Canary Islands were close enough to one another for the inhabitants of each to be aware that the world was a little larger than the island they knew. But in many respects the islands are miniature continents. Although they stand off the African coast, they are not part of the African continental shelf but are, like Madeira and the Azores further west, volcanic peaks that have risen out of the Atlantic Ocean. Unlike Madeira and the Azores, however, each island of any size had a human population well before the arrival of the Iberian conquerors. The Canaries are distinct from one another in climate, with internal variations on the larger islands. They are also distinct in topography and soil; some, such as the eastern islands, are sandy and dry; the western islands, benefiting more from Atlantic winds, have a moister subtropical climate and in consequence richer foliage, a characteristic they share with Madeira to the north-west. The islands were never physically connected to Africa, but emerged volcanically out of the Atlantic, and the only large mammals known to the early inhabitants – dogs, sheep, goats, pigs – arrived from Africa, as did the human population.[1]

The Canary Islands were an ideal setting for all types of fantasy. They provided an almost infinitely adaptable stage-set. There is a view that Mount Teide inspired Dante in the early fourteenth century, when he described the mountain of Purgatory on the edge of the world.[2] A version of the *Chronicle of King John II of Castile* of 1417, by the Jewish convert Alvar García de Santa María, told how the islands had been colonised by seafaring

Spanish Muslims who had brought the Canaries under the authority of the great general al-Mansur. This piece of bogus history could be used to justify Castilian claims to the islands, since conquering them could then be seen as part of the process of reconquering Muslim Spain. Perhaps this was the origin of a later and extraordinarily colourful account of the 'Muslim' Canary islanders. The late fifteenth-century Valencian writer Joannot Martorell recorded in the enormously popular prose romance *Tirant lo Blanc* how Abraham, 'the king of Canary, a hardy youth whose virile and restless soul was stirred by dreams of conquest', launched a great fleet, invaded England via Southampton, attacked London and Canterbury, and even captured Kenilworth Castle.[3] Martorell was making free use of an English romance, *Guy of Warwick*, in which the enemy was, more appropriately, the Danes; but here the Canary islanders became Muslims and great mariners. They were, of course, neither.

Indeed, the Muslims of Africa were as puzzled by the Canary islanders as were the Christians. Although Muslim authors such as the great twelfth-century geographer Idrisi, living in Sicily, knew the islands existed, the Canaries had always proved strangely unconquerable.[4] They attracted very similar legends among Muslim geographers to those that gathered around them in Christian Europe – for Muslims too they were the 'Happy Islands', or *Kalidat*.[5] Idrisi told of ferocious beasts on an island called Lamghoch, where there was a great tomb and a temple; he claimed that amber and other stones were gathered on the islands and sold to the Lamtuna Berbers on the mainland; indeed, the islanders practised magic with the help of their remarkable stones. This all seems pure fantasy, based on rumours collected over the centuries.[6] Even the most energetic Muslim armies seem to have found the inhabitants of the islands too fierce for comfort: they were left alone by the Almoravid Berbers in their triumphant re-islamisation of the facing shores of north-west Africa during the eleventh century; and the Canary islanders beat back raids by another Berber sect, the even fiercer Almohad rulers of twelfth-century Morocco. Considering the fact that the islanders were armed with weapons made of hardened wood, bone and chipped stone, this was a remarkable achievement.

Vague knowledge about these islands, derived from classical and early medieval writers such as Pliny the Elder in the first century and Isidore of Seville in the sixth and seventh, was passed on to medieval Christendom when the first scientific mapmakers in western Europe began to produce the careful, intricately detailed and extraordinarily accurate maps known as

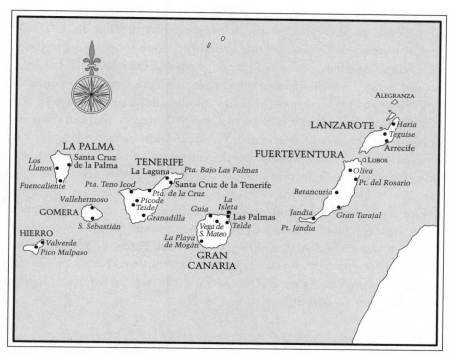

The Canary Islands

portolan charts, which survive from about 1300 onwards. The best mapmakers, in Venice, Genoa and, above all, Majorca, may have seen Arab maps; many were Majorcan Jews who came from a multilingual community with contacts to both Africa and Spain. What they produced reflected experience as well as traditions passed down from one cartographic atelier to another. There was a strong awareness that diagrammatic world maps revolving around Jerusalem were of no use to serious navigators. From 1277 an active trade linking the Mediterranean to the Atlantic developed. Not surprisingly, the Italian and Catalan merchants who dominated this trade wanted to sell their goods in Flanders and England, and from the latter they could acquire excellent wool for looms back home.[7] However, the prevailing winds tended to blow ships southwards as they left the Straits of Gibraltar. Thus ships from Majorca, Genoa and elsewhere came to know the ports of Atlantic Morocco such as Safi, and edged their way

closer to the Canaries themselves.[8] The idea that this might be the start
of the route to the spices of the Indies began to develop. In 1291 the
Vivaldi brothers of Genoa announced that they were setting out for 'India'
via a route that would take them past Majorca and Gibraltar and down the
African coast. They disappeared somewhere off Africa, which presumably
they hoped to circumnavigate, although another, less plausible view is that
they planned to head westwards across the Atlantic, in the same way as
Columbus.[9] The son of one of the Vivaldi brothers went looking for his
father and uncle in the mid-fourteenth century; and well into the fifteenth
century sailors travelling down the coast of West Africa kept their eyes
open for evidence that the Vivaldi brothers had reached so far, even
looking for supposed descendants of these intrepid pioneers. To all intents
and purposes, however, the Canaries marked the southern limit of
European penetration of the Atlantic until Gil Eanes of Lagos in the
Algarve, after earlier attempts, rounded the low but treacherous sandbanks
of Cape Bojador in 1434, and opened a route for Portuguese shipping
down the coast of Africa.[10]

II: The View from Florence, 1341

Christopher Columbus tried to make sense of the people he met in
Guanahaní on 12 October 1492 by comparing them with the people he had
left behind in the Canaries, whose waters he had left by 9 September. For
it was in the Canaries that Europeans first encountered 'uncontaminated
Gentiles', to use the phrase of a historian of the islanders, Alonso de
Espinosa, writing about a hundred years later: that is, pagan peoples living
on seven islands isolated from the African continent, and even isolated from
one another. The existence of such peoples raised the difficult question of
why God had allowed them to fester in ignorance of His Word during the
thirteen centuries that had elapsed between the Crucifixion and the first
known landing by European sailors, in 1341. The same question would be
posed again and again in the Americas after 1492. This remarkable
encounter in the Canaries, the first known encounter of medieval Europeans
with a Neolithic society, was recorded by the great fourteenth-century
Florentine writer Giovanni Boccaccio in his essay *De Canaria*, and what
follows is a reconstruction of events as he described them.[11] This he did at
second-hand, relying on a letter or letters he had received from Florentine
friends in Seville, who had heard or read the story as it was recounted by a

Genoese sea captain, Niccolò da Recco; Boccaccio himself never went on this journey.

In July 1341, two sizeable ships accompanied by a smaller vessel set out for the Canaries from Lisbon, carrying, as was common at the time, a mixed crew composed of Portuguese, Castilians, Catalans and Italians.[12] The explorers took horses and heavy armaments on the assumption that they would be waging war against well-defended towns and fortresses.[13] Thus they knew of the islands' existence from previous reports, now lost (another Genoese in Portuguese service, Lançalotto Malocello, had been in those waters around 1336),[14] but they evidently had no knowledge of the sort of societies to be found there, which lacked horses, castles and fire-power: hence their astonishment when they encountered their first native islanders. On the first island they could see rocks and forests inhabited by naked men and women and by animals; the people they saw were 'rough in manners', *asperis cultu et ritu*.[15] They obtained some modest goods – goatskins, sealskins, fats – but they were not tempted to create a base there and so sailed on.

The little fleet reached a second, rather larger island, *Canaria*, the island now known as Grand Canary. Standing close offshore, their ships attracted the wonder of the natives. The explorers saw a great gathering of men and women, who had come to watch them; most were naked, though some, 'who seemed superior to the others', were clad in fine, soft goat's leather dyed red and yellow, with delicate stitching made of animal gut.[16] It is apparent from later remarks in the same report that such clothing as the Canary islanders wore generally indicated status.[17] The explorers also discovered (presumably later) that the natives were familiar with marriage, a point that in their eyes would have confirmed that they were not bestial savages; married women wore a kilt much in the same way as men, but unmarried girls went completely naked, going about their business without any sense of shame. On this island the inhabitants showed reverence to a leader: 'these people seemed to have a prince', a sign that they were less 'rude' than those on the first island.[18] The islanders wanted to make contact with the sailors, who were discouraged by their failure to make themselves understood. What the visi-tors heard of their language was mellifluous; they were said to speak fast and in an animated way, like the Italians. Not to be put off, some of the islanders swam out to the ships. Later the explorers realised that this island was more intensively cultivated in the north than in the south, and had many houses; it possessed fig trees, palm trees and vegetable gardens. They later decided that it was also the most densely populated island in the archipelago.[19] Everything mentioned here fits well with what is known from other evidence, such as archaeology, of the greater sophistication of Grand Canary compared to the other six islands.

The first contact had been encouraging, so twenty-five armed sailors went ashore, encountering about thirty entirely naked natives, who in fact were terrified and ran away. To the alarm and fury of the natives, the sailors then broke into some houses, which were skilfully constructed of square stones with wooden roofs, as well as being very clean inside. The sailors found excellent dried figs and grain of various types, including a species of wheat longer and broader than any found in Europe. The explorers discovered that the inhabitants did not make bread but ate their grain in the form of seed ('like birds') or flour, which must be the ancestor of the *gofio* flour still eaten in the Canaries. They drank water, not wine. One of the buildings the explorers entered proved to be a temple made of dressed stone blocks, which contained no paintings or decorations. Inside there was little more than a statue of a naked man carrying a ball, his private parts modestly covered by a fig leaf. This they took away with them back to Lisbon, though it disappeared long ago.[20]

The ships sailed round Grand Canary, and the sailors observed the bleaker landscape of the south of the island; they also explored as many of the adjacent islands as they could, noticing the handsome trees character-istic of El Hierro and the fine wood and flowing watercourses character-istic of La Gomera. The report implies that the explorers landed on or coasted past all but one of the inhabited islands and made contact with the natives, attempting to speak with them and to gauge their numbers. They were impressed by high peaks on Tenerife and La Palma, but they were scared away by a strange mast adorned with something like a sail which they saw on one of the islands, believing it to be enchanted – presumably it was some sort of cult object. The expedition established that six out of thirteen islands were inhabited (seven out of twelve would have been more accurate); however, the density of population varied from place to place.[21] The languages of the islands differed, and the natives had no knowledge of navigation, so that the only way they could travel from island to island was by swimming. The visitors were able to take a much closer look at the islanders when they carried back with them from Grand Canary four young men, barefooted, beardless, uncircumcised, long-haired, wearing kilts made of goatskin or palm fronds that only revealed their genitals when the wind blew strongly. They seem to have been quite ready to go to Europe. They were as tall as Europeans and strong. Probably they were very intelligent, but it was hard to say because they spoke no known language, so communication had to be by sign language. They were friendly and trusting towards one another and had the habit of sharing their food equally; but there was one, who wore a loincloth made of palm leaves, who was more honoured than the others; these others wore loincloths of goatskin, coloured yellow and red.[22] They sang and danced well and were sweet-tempered, in fact they were rather superior to a good many Spaniards, a somewhat xenophobic remark that Boccaccio probably copied from his Italian informants.

Once on board, their hosts showed them familiar foods and objects from Europe, to see how they would respond. The explorers discovered that the native Canarians were quite interested in bread, which was a novelty to them, but they refused wine and continued to drink water. They were very familiar with cheese and the meat of sheep and goats.[23] But they had no knowledge of camels, which only reached the islands in the sixteenth century and later; cattle and donkeys were also unknown to them. And of course when they were shown gold and silver coins, gold necklaces, vases and swords, or invited to take a whiff of perfume, these were all complete novelties.[24] This act of showing them gold and silver objects prefigures very closely attempts by Columbus and others to discover sources of gold by dangling such trinkets in front of native Americans. One commentator on Boccaccio's report has seen this as an attempt at a systematic scientific experiment 'designed to test their knowledge and understanding', and perhaps therefore to test their capacity for human reasoning – they were also asked to recite numbers from one to sixteen in Canarian, as numeracy was regarded as one sign of the capacity for rational thinking in medieval Europe.[25] Baser motives seem more credible, however, for there were persistent rumours of a River of Gold debouching on the West African coast no great distance from the Canaries. It seems more likely that they were shown gold in the hope that they would direct the sailors to new sources of the yellow metal. Here there was complete disappointment. 'These do not appear to be rich islands,' Boccaccio reports, and the costs of the expedition were scarcely met from its exiguous profits; only simple products such as goatskins, tallow and dyestuffs were acquired during the voyage.[26]

A Pastoral Idyll

The story of this expedition was, then, written down by one of the great pioneers of the literary revival in early Renaissance Italy, Giovanni Boccaccio (1313–75); what he recorded was the reaction of the explorers to the people they encountered rather than dry navigational data. Boccaccio entered the brief text of his *De Canaria* into a commonplace book now preserved in Florence, and the impression remains that this was just a rough draft of an exercise that he proposed at some stage to expand. Indeed, it was evidently based on a letter he had received from Italian correspondents in the Iberian peninsula. Boccaccio polished his correspondents' account in various ways, turning it into Latin and giving it a classical, pastoral flavour.[27] The resulting essay expressed his fascination with a society quite unlike anything with which he was familiar from everyday experience, yet one which reminded him of the idyllic pastoral societies portrayed in classical texts. Boccaccio knew his Virgil and other Roman writers; he was hungrily hunting for more data. In his hands the letter from Spain was transformed from a description of strange wonders at the edge of the world into an ethnography of primitive peoples who were otherwise only familiar from his reading of classical texts.[28] Of course, Boccaccio was tempted to pull his description towards his ideal of a simple pastoral society, honest in toil, in contact with nature and free of cares. He wanted to prove that these people were free of materialistic corruption, and he probably wanted to imply that they lived in a simple and pure 'state of nature'. Their nakedness was the nakedness of lustlessness, not lustfulness; the genitals of the idol in their temple were decently covered by a fig leaf, a conceit that must surely be Boccaccio's, since his description of the statue bears no relation to surviving Canarian cult objects. His imagination had generated nothing less than a classical statue of a young man.

Like his contemporaries in late medieval Europe, Boccaccio tended to trust texts, especially ancient texts, more than modern observation. He faced the problem of reconciling the Florentine report with received knowledge. He knew that the Elder Pliny's *Natural History* reported the discovery of the Canaries, or 'Fortunate Isles', by the Moroccan king Juba in the reign of Emperor Augustus. Pliny mentioned six islands, just as the Boccaccio essay talked of six inhabited islands; Pliny and the *De Canaria* shared references to such features as the palm trees on *Canaria* or Grand Canary and the clouds on Mount Teide, overhanging Tenerife. Like

Boccaccio, Pliny based his account on a letter he had read, this time by King Juba. In Pliny's account, the only inhabitants appeared to be goats, lizards and *canes* or dogs (hence the name *Canaria*), but ruined buildings, even a temple, proved the islands had been inhabited in earlier times; after all, the dogs and goats must have been brought by somebody.[29] There can be no doubt about the ancient discovery of the 'Fortunate Isles'. The islands were occasionally mentioned as the limit of the known world; and several Italian works of the fourteenth and fifteenth centuries returned to the image of the Fortunate Isles as a place halfway to the blessed abode of the departed in Elysium.[30] They were freely confused with legendary mid-Atlantic lands such as the Isle of St Brendan, named after the intrepid Irish navigator, or the Isle of the Seven Cities.[31]

Boccaccio's report was not published, in the sense applicable to the word before printing: it was not copied and diffused, with or without its author's permission, though it is thought that a couple of Florentine writers a century later may have been influenced by seeing his text.[32] What matters is that it reveals a common outlook quite independently developed by later observers of primitive societies: some writers, such as the Italian humanist Peter Martyr d'Anghiera, described the inhabitants of the Caribbean islands, which they saw initially as 'New Canaries', as people living in a state of innocence, even bliss, similar to the pastoral societies they imagined from their reading of classical authors such as Theocritus and Virgil. From Boccaccio onwards, Italian humanists were fascinated by the evidence that there really did exist a society that lived life as a pastoral idyll. Still, Boccaccio was a literary craftsman, not a historian or ethnographer.[33] *De Canaria* marks a stage in the evolution of his enthusiasm for the classical past, and bears comparison with the idealisation of the gods and spirits of ancient Greece and Rome in his charming work *The Nymphs of Fiesole*: as one modern writer has commented, 'he was seeking exotic settings in which to locate his imaginative fictions'. To the word 'exotic' one could add the word 'erotic', because, as will become clear, the nakedness, real or imagined, of native peoples was something that also drew in curious readers.

Wild Solitude

Boccaccio was not the only literary giant to respond to news of the discovery of these extraordinary people. There is a telling reference to the Canaries in the widely diffused essay 'On the Solitary Life' written in 1346 by Boccaccio's great friend Francesco Petrarca, or Petrarch (1304–74), an even more influential figure in the revival of Latin letters at the time.[34] Boccaccio's description of the Canarians stands in stark contrast with that provided, much more briefly, by Petrarch. Petrarch praised at length the virtues of a solitary life over the active life in the community; this solitary life was something he tried to practise in Provence and the Paduan hills at various times in his own life. However, Petrarch had some difficulty fitting the inhabitants of the islands into a description of the advantages of the solitary life, for the solitude of the Canary islanders was of a different order from that of a hermit; he identified their solitude as that of solitary places rather than solitary lives.[35] He wrote:

> Its people enjoy solitude beyond nearly all men, but are without refinement in their habits and so little unlike brute beasts that their action is more the outcome of natural instinct than of rational choice, and you might say they did not so much lead the solitary life as roam about in solitudes either with wild beasts or with their flocks.[36]

Petrarch's comments were remembered by later visitors to the Canaries, even if Boccaccio's were not. The late sixteenth-century military architect Torriani thought Petrarch had described perfectly the rather morose solitary disposition of the natives of La Gomera:

> They were great lovers of solitude as Petrarch tells in his book on the solitary life and in consequence they were melancholy, for they sang sad songs of eight, nine or ten syllables, and with such sorrow that they wept, as one still sees among those who are descended from the last inhabitants.[37]

Petrarch knew of the investiture of Luis de la Cerda as ruler of the 'Fortunate Isles' by Pope Clement VI in 1344; ironically he compared the heavy rainfall on the day of the investiture, and the name 'Fortunate Isles', with the harsher realities of Canarian society. He defended the solitary life as a rational choice, but the Canarians had followed it by natural instinct, and they could barely be distinguished from their herds of animals.[38] He said he knew of past Genoese exploration of the islands; but, even if Petrarch knew Boccaccio's essay (or the report on which it was based), it is plain that Boccaccio's view of the Canarians was of a quite different order. Their naked simplicity was to him a sign of purity, not bestiality.[39]

Here, then, were two contrasting fourteenth-century images of Canary Island society that anticipated similar divisions of opinion concerning the American Indians after 1492. In one the inhabitants were a subject of wonder, expressed in admiration for their social skills such as sharing of food and deference to their leader; even their nakedness could be seen as a sign of innocence. They were intelligent and physically powerful. Their buildings were well constructed out of dressed stone. They had fine gardens and culti-vated grain of remarkable properties. Their ignorance of gold, though surely a great disappointment to the Portuguese visitors, was also a sign of their lack of materialism. In this, there were the makings of a rustic idyll, whose origins lay in the tradition that beyond the Pillars of Hercules there lay a collection of 'Happy Isles'. Against this, Boccaccio's friend Petrarch found a more gloomy message. These were wild men of the forest leading a bestial existence. The grounds for identifying them as near-animals were not that they were heathens, but that they lacked all signs of sociability, an odd complaint in a work devoted to the virtues of the solitary life. But theirs was not the type of solitude that Petrarch was seeking. What is important is the way Boccaccio revealed one possible reaction to their discovery, and Petrarch quite another.

It is revealing to compare the description of the first contact between the islanders and the Europeans in *De Canaria* with Columbus' logbook. Though a hundred and fifty years separated the two encounters, Columbus' arrival in the Bahamas generated remarkably similar behaviour by both the Europeans and the native Americans. As in the Canaries, the natives would innocently swim out to the explorers' boats, unafraid of any danger; as in the Canaries, the explorers then interviewed them about their obses-sion, gold. As in the Canaries, Columbus was struck by the nakedness of the inhabitants, which he apparently read as a sign of innocence, seeing the Taínos as a blank tablet or *tabula rasa*, intelligent and in many ways beau-tiful human beings who could surely be brought easily to Christianity – not monstrous races, not wild men of the woods. Columbus, at least at this point in his career, belonged in the tradition represented by the Boccaccio essay and not in that of Petrarch's remarks, though there is no sign that he knew either work. Even more remarkably, the same generally positive ideas appeared in the earliest accounts of the naked, innocent inhabitants of the Brazilian seaboard, first visited by Portuguese ships bound for India in 1500. But the negative view of Petrarch was also mirrored in other descriptions of the American Indians: Amerigo Vespucci emphasised their 'bestial' ways: nakedness became a sign of immodesty; they were consumed by sexual hunger and by hunger for human flesh. The complex interplay between these two views of primitive peoples is one of the major themes of this book.

The Revelation to the Pagans, 1400

There was a third view of the islanders, which was a variation on the positive view formed by Boccaccio, though it developed independently among authors who can have had no awareness of the commonplace book in Florence in which the lone copy of Boccaccio's essay survived. In this view they were idealised to the point where their paganism became a preparation for their conversion to Christianity, a sort of pre-Christianity. This view was most clearly articulated in the late sixteenth century by the Dominican friar Alonso de Espinosa, who told a most extraordinary tale. He claimed that, in around 1400, when Tenerife was entirely inhabited by the unconverted people known as the Guanches, two shepherds were looking after their flocks on the north-eastern shore of the island. They noticed that some of the sheep had wandered towards a gully near the beach, but that something had alarmed them. The shepherds assumed there must be rustlers in the area who were trying to steal their animals, so one of them went to take a closer look and saw a human figure standing on a rock in the gully. Looking more closely, he saw that it was actually a woman carrying a child, and she was dressed in colourful robes that were of a quite unfamiliar sort. It was the custom that Guanche men did not speak to lone women (they could be condemned to death for doing so). But the shepherd thought that he might signal to the woman to go away, so as to let him and his sheep pass through the gully. The woman did not react. Although he was not allowed to speak to a lone woman, he was apparently allowed to throw a stone at her; at any rate, he tried to do this, but his arm stiffened and he could not release the stone. He and his friend did then try to speak to her, to no avail. The second shepherd began to suspect that she was not animate, so he took a sharp stone used for cutting (the local equivalent of a knapped flint, called a *tabona*) and tried to saw into one of the woman's fingers, but, amazingly, the stone passed through as if it were not there and cut his own fingers instead. By the end of this encounter, then, one shepherd had a miraculously stiff arm and the other a bleeding hand.[40]

The shepherds then went to see the local ruler or *mencey*, the Lord of Guimar, to inform him about this wonder. The latter, for his part, consulted his counsellors, and they all marched down to the beach to see the woman, who was still where the shepherds had left her: 'what caused most astonishment was that they saw no movement, and heard no voice nor reply, although they spoke to it, and saw the splendour of its countenance and its dress, and the majesty it represented.'[41] The *mencey* decided that the image must be taken to his house; no one dared touch the woman, but the two shepherds who had found her were ordered to pick her up, and when they did so their injuries healed at once. Realising that there was something supernatural about the figure, the *mencey* took charge and carried the image home, as if she were an honoured guest.

Espinosa recounted these events about two hundred years later, around 1590. What had arrived from the sea was 'one of the greatest relics in the world, and the one that has worked most miracles'. According to Espinosa, the Virgin Mary herself had taken the islanders under her protection: it was a very special miracle, for divine blessings were not usually conferred on pagan peoples in this way, and so the miracle had to be seen as a reward for the simple, natural purity of life as it was lived in the Canary Islands before the Christian conquest. Indeed, he insisted, Tenerife was specially blessed. The Word of Christ had come late, but it had come not through an apostle, in the way that St James evangelised Spain or St Thomas evangelised India; rather, it was the Virgin herself who evangelised Tenerife: 'although she did not divulge the evangel by words, by her presence she disposed souls to receive it with much facility, and to keep it with fidelity.'[42] The powerful Lord of Guimar in northern Tenerife had understood the significance of the relic and spread word of its arrival, which caused great wonder among the Guanche chieftains. Indeed, a raiding party consisting of Spanish and French interlopers on the islands of Lanzarote and Fuerteventura tried to steal the statue after they had heard about it on a trading or slaving trip to Tenerife, but the Virgin herself did not wish to be carried away; plague broke out on Fuerteventura, and the image was promptly sent back.[43] This account mirrors, as Espinosa was well aware, that in the Bible concerning the seizure by the Philistines of the Ark of the Covenant from the defeated Israelites, followed by an outbreak of plague among the Philistines.[44]

For Espinosa, then, this was a powerful object capable of working remarkable miracles. He described the image with loving care, just as he saw it on a visit to Candelaria, on 25 October 1590, insisting that it was very beautiful.[45] It appears to have been more than half-lifesize, with a long face and curious eyes that seemed to watch the onlooker from whatever angle one approached the statue; its majesty and gravity made one's hair stand on end. Although the face was brownish in colour, with rosy cheeks, the hues tended to change from one moment to another. This miraculous face was surrounded by long plaits of golden hair. The woman held a naked child, while in his left hand the child carried a stump of green candle (hence the name 'Virgin of Candelaria'). The woman was dressed in a gold costume, adorned with red 'Latin' characters; Espinosa could not read the inscriptions at all well, and his transcriptions are nonsensical – they were clearly written in an unfamiliar script and language which he found impossible to read, most likely ornate Gothic capital letters of the sort that were by then long out of use: LPVRINENINPEPNEIFANT, one inscription seemed to say, NARMPRLMOTARE another, and so on. For it was most probably a large piece of flotsam (most likely the figurehead) from a ship that had been swept south and had foundered in the Atlantic, possibly a fourteenth-century Flemish or German sculpture. Espinosa denied this, in the face of rational explanations by sceptics:

> In the year 1400, which is the year when the holy image appeared, although the navigation of this sea was known, and there was information respecting these islands, yet the sea was not then navigated freely, nor did it lead anywhere until Cape Verde was discovered, and the route to the Indies. Therefore to say that some ship of Christians brought it, and when they brought it that they left it to be dashed about among rocks and stones, is not credible. For the image is the most beautiful and the best finished piece of work that can be seen. To say that the sea brought it, some ship which had it on board having been lost (as we have seen other things brought in that way), and cast it up where it was found, is nonsense.[46]

Rather, he averred, this was an image brought by angels, and indeed made by angels. Today there is nothing of the statue left to examine; in 1826 a flash flood carried it off into the sea and it has never been recovered, though the cult continues. Espinosa attributed sixty-five miracles to the image, mostly consisting of recovery from illness, but he also recorded cases of ships being saved by its miraculous powers.[47]

Here, then, were 'uncontaminated Gentiles', as he called the Guanches, people who were totally isolated from the Iberian battleground of Christianity, Judaism and Islam, but who were nonetheless worthy of divine protection mediated by the Virgin Mary.[48] 'They were Gentiles without any law, nor ceremonies, nor gods like other nations' (by 'law' he meant a religious code like the Torah or the Koran); but, like all rational creatures, they were searching for a perfect knowledge of God, and 'the seed of the faith fell into their hearts on hearing the Word'.[49] The Virgin loved the people of the islands, and their salvation was planned decades before the Christian armies under the violent conquistador Alonso de Lugo overwhelmed the last Guanche resistance in 1496.[50] It was a similar story, in many ways, to that of the peoples of the Americas in the sixteenth century, who also had their share of miraculous images and had similarly been oppressed by conquerors who purported to act in Christ's name. Before he wrote his book on the Virgin of Candelaria and the history of the Guanches, around 1590, Alonso de Espinosa had served in a Dominican mission in Guatemala; he was deeply influenced by the radical thinking of his Dominican predecessor las Casas, who had denounced the Spaniards for their catastrophic mistreatment of the American Indians.[51] In central America Espinosa had already heard of the reputation of the Virgin of Candelaria, no doubt because ships bound for the New World often touched in at the Canaries for supplies.[52] Espinosa was also influenced by the thinking of the great Dominican St Thomas Aquinas; bearing Aquinas' views in mind, he was anxious to prove that the Guanches practised a form of 'natural religion' that combined an awareness of God's existence and of the need to worship Him through ceremonies with an extraordinary and unique blessing: the protection, even while they were unconverted, of the Virgin Mary.[53] It was easier to make this case for Tenerife than it was for Grand Canary, which had been visited by missionaries regularly since the mid-fourteenth century, with only limited success. Espinosa's sense that the islanders lived in a state of semi-grace, not so much as non-Christians but rather as pre-Christians, was strongly affirmed in his story of the miraculous arrival on the eastern shore of Tenerife of the statue of the Virgin Mary. Paradoxically, the last island to be conquered by the Spaniards was, Espinosa insisted, the most favoured by the Virgin.

Espinosa therefore offered an important variant on the pastoral idyll of Boccaccio. Boccaccio had actually rejoiced in the paganism of these islanders, which he saw as a survival from the remote past; Espinosa identified within their paganism the foundations of a new, Christian identity. Who the inhabitants were, and how they resisted conquest and indeed conversion for so long, now needs to be examined.

CHAPTER 5

THE CANARY ISLANDERS, 1341–1496

Uncontaminated Gentiles

From the early or mid-fourteenth century an 'uncontaminated' group of peoples lay open to inspection by European missionaries, mercenaries and merchants, as Genoese, Majorcans and Portuguese, among others, made their way into Atlantic waters in the hundred and fifty years before Columbus' first voyage to the Caribbean.[1] There are two ways of describing the natives of the Canary Islands: there is the old evidence from the accounts left by the Spaniards and other conquerors, and there is the new evidence from archaeology, anthropology and linguistics. Often, though not always, the two converge. Sometimes one set of evidence fills gaps left by the other; archaeology can also correct false assumptions in the narratives. The early narratives of and about the European discovery and conquest are rich in fascinating information regarding the social life, political organisation and religion of the islanders, particularly the inhabitants of the two largest islands, Tenerife and Grand Canary. Of course, there is much in these accounts that is suspect: the chivalric qualities attributed to the islanders may be a sign of genuine European respect, or they may be an attempt to prove that the Europeans were facing a tough enemy, and that the Europeans therefore deserved respect for their tenacity. Still, there are few informative accounts of the politics, customs and beliefs of a prehistoric society, so these, for all their bias, cannot be disregarded.

Those who sought to describe native society in the century and a half after the conquest knew how much had vanished since the last strongholds in Tenerife fell in 1496. The Canary islanders were all but extinct: their numbers had fallen, as a result of the arrival of European diseases; some had been taken away by slavers or simply expelled to Spain; others lost their identity by marrying Iberian settlers, a familiar story to anyone who knew what had also been happening in the Americas. However, around 1600, observers such as the friar Espinosa seem to have had access to older written accounts, now lost; Espinosa even discovered some old Guanches on Tenerife whom he could interview, though he found them 'timid and fearful'.[2] Oral traditions are easily dismissed; but oral histories recorded in black Africa have proved impressively solid when set alongside European records.[3] Among early observers of the Canaries, awareness that the native peoples had been swept away was sharpened by knowledge of the massive depopulation in the Americas following Spanish colonisation of the Caribbean, Mexico and Peru; this prompted Espinosa's defence of yet another native people that had suffered at Spanish imperial hands, the Guanches. Building on the story of the Virgin of Candelaria, he provided a detailed account of the history of the final conquest of Tenerife by Alonso de Lugo in the 1490s, and of Guanche society; but his book also forms part of a romanticising tradition that laid emphasis on the heroism and indeed chivalry of the Guanche warriors, producing an image of a society recast in a western European mould. Clearly, care must be taken in interpreting his account of the religion of the islanders, but it nonetheless provides a fascinating insight into European views that were highly critical of the behaviour of the Spanish conquerors.[4]

Espinosa established something of a tradition. Juan de Abreu Galindo, a Franciscan friar, wrote a *History of the Conquest of the Seven Isles of the Canaries* around 1600, and had obviously read Espinosa's work and some of the (now lost) works from which Espinosa himself drew. He laid more emphasis on Grand Canary, and described the customs of the Canarians and the early history of their contacts with Europe, including an extraordinary series of visits by ships and friars from Majorca in the fourteenth century. He also described the conquest of Grand Canary by Spanish conquistadores in the 1480s. He was anxious to place the history of the Canaries in a classical and biblical setting, addressing, for instance, the argument that the islanders were a remnant of the Ten Lost Tribes of Israel, and looking for Jewish origins in their rites; he thought the American Indians were better candidates for what, in the age of the Inquisition, was a very dubious honour.[5] He even denied the presence of 'idols' among the Canary islanders, apparently so that they would not run the risk of being investigated as idolaters by the Inquisition. He argued that some Majorcan missionaries who arrived in the fourteenth century were at first much loved by the Canarians (thus suggesting that the islanders had an easy disposition towards Christianity) and that the missionaries taught them useful skills in the fine arts and even in government: 'the means to govern with great skill and propriety'.[6] In fact, the main evidence for the borrowing of Western technology consists in the trade in fish hooks and old tools for figs and the dyestuff known as dragon's blood.[7]

Alongside this evidence, there are the results of archaeological and anthropological research in the Canaries, which offer some idea of the islanders' material culture and help explain where they originally came from, as does the study of surviving fragments of their languages. Here too the information that is presented cannot be accepted without question; archaeology is certainly not politically neutral. Racial theorists landed on the Canaries in the twentieth century, looking among the bones of the ancient islanders for their own type of human perfection: tall, agile, blond Aryans. Others have suggested that the Canary islanders were unsuspected monumental architects, who had carried with them to the islands the ancient Egyptian art of pyramid-building. Setting aside bizarre theories of this sort, plenty of data can be found: the bodies of mummified islanders; their tools; their stone goddesses; their leatherwork, woodwork and wickerwork, all wonderfully preserved in a dry climate. All this can then be compared with what is found in European accounts, which, for example, describe mummification in detail.[8] Remarkably, a 'Stone Age' society can be observed in the round, in a way that is not possible for the builders of Stonehenge or the founders of Jericho.

Island Berbers

How far back the settlement of the Canary Islands can be traced is a difficult question. It has been seen that the Elder Pliny wrote of a visit by the fleet of King Juba of Mauretania to uninhabited but abandoned islands in around AD 1; later traditions spoke of political exiles sent there as punishment, perhaps with their tongues cut out. Nowadays, no one really doubts that the islands were inhabited by Berber-speakers.[9] In fact, early European observers worked this out for themselves. In the late sixteenth century, an Italian engineer, Leonardo Torriani, affirmed that they were 'Azanaghi', that is Sanhaja Berbers, of the same stock as the Tuareg and many of the brown slaves who had been carried to Portuguese slave markets from western Africa since the mid-fifteenth century. Abreu Galindo's sympathetic account of the islands was translated into English in the middle of the eighteenth century by a learned English sea captain, George Glas. Captain Glas was a man of deep intellectual curiosity and some courage who wandered the seas, carrying with him his wife and daughter. Taking ship for England from Orotava in Tenerife, he was stabbed to death by a mutinous crew, and his wife and daughter were thrown overboard (the mutineers were caught and hanged at Dublin).[10] This is how he paraphrased and expanded Abreu Galindo's words:

> He adds, that in the skirts of Mount Atlas, in Africa, there is a tribe of Africans called Canarios, who perhaps first discovered and peopled this island, and called it after their own name. . . . From this similitude of names one would naturally be led to believe that the natives of the island Canaria and those of the neighbouring continent of Africa, were one and the same people.[11]

In fact, the same point was made in 1494 by the Sicilian humanist Scyllacius.[12] This evidence from place-names is still cited, even if the true origin of the term 'Canary' is in doubt. The island of La Gomera may be connected in some way to the Ghomera tribe in the mountains of north-western Sahara. The Canaries were and still are filled with places whose names are clearly Berber, beginning with the characteristic feminine syllable *Ta-*: Tacaronte, Taoro, Tamarazeyte among locations known to the conquerors, Tazacorte, Tamaduste, Taganana among present-day ones.

To this can be added the evidence from the fragments of Canary Island speech that have been recorded since the sixteenth century. As Boccaccio had already warned, the language of each island was distinct, providing evidence of extreme isolation (they diverged over time), or possibly of varied origins within the vast Berber world of north-west Africa, for there is no single 'Berber language' but many interrelated languages and dialects. Thus Canarians travelling in the boats of early explorers could not readily be understood on the other islands (nor was there any sense of inter-island loyalty; the Gomerans became enthusiastic mercenaries serving the Spanish conquerors of Tenerife). The Gomerans have become famous for their 'whistling language'; this was supposed to have originated among a group of exiles who were sent to the island after their tongues had been cut out, and it was reported as early as the fifteenth century as a type of speech that was generated solely with the lips. It survives today as a means to communicate across distances, rather like the Alpine yodel, and it is highly unlikely that it was ever a form of everyday speech. The isolation of the islanders was all the greater because they had lost the art of navigation, even though they had evidently arrived on the islands by ship. There is very little evidence of Arabic influence in surviving examples of the islanders' speech, further suggesting isolation at a time when Arabic was competing with Berber in North Africa; that is, from the seventh century onwards, following the rise of Islam. In other words, the islands were genuinely isolated from the Islamic world. But there is evidence that some of the islanders had writing; the script found on several (but not all) islands is quite similar to the very beautiful Tifinagh writing of Berber North Africa and, with the help of Carbon-14 dating, it has been shown that one example scratched into a wooden funeral bier dates from around AD 1000. Espinosa referred cryptically to ancient inscriptions. Captain Glas was fascinated to find that some Berber words appeared in Canary Island dialects of Spanish: the word for barley, *tumzzen*, found among some of the Atlas Berbers, has a parallel in *tamozen*, a word used with the same meaning on Fuerteventura.[13] However, several words may have arrived in the fifteenth and sixteenth centuries, when the Europeans began to import labour from the facing coast of Africa.

The Berber identity of the islanders did not please everybody who studied them. In Spain, from the mid-nineteenth century onwards, there were attempts to prove that some of the islanders were 'European', even Iberian, in origin; the islanders could thus be seen as ethnically Spanish, whatever their style of life, for even if they were not Christians they were also not Jews or Muslims, but rather, as Espinosa would have insisted, pre-Christians. For Franco's generation, this bizarre image of the islanders suggested that the conquest of the Canaries in the age of the Catholic Monarchs was as much part of a process of 'national reunification' as the victory over Granada, the expulsion of the Jews, the acquisition of Navarre or the marriage of Ferdinand and Isabella. Thus the conquest of the islands did not consist of the subjection of an alien race, and Spanish 'racial purity' remained unsullied.[14] Since, by the mid-sixteenth century, there were few pure-blooded islanders left, the issue was resolved long before Franco. In addition, over-enthusiastic experts in 'racial science' from Germany and elsewhere became fascinated by the Canary islanders in the 1930s; they wondered if they were perfect specimens of Cro-Magnon man, and even perhaps the forerunners of the 'Aryan' racial type. Much measuring of skulls (most of which remain on gruesome display in the Las Palmas Museum) established that they were of Berber ethnic origin, though there was some variation in skulls and skeletons between different islands, further confirming that they had become isolated from one another several centuries before the arrival of the Europeans.

The tendency in some of the modern literature to call all the Canary islanders 'Guanches' (pronounced in modern Canary Spanish *Wanches*) is unhelpful, implying a cultural uniformity that clearly did not exist.[15] This term properly applies only to the population of one of the two biggest islands, Tenerife, while 'Canarians' is best used only for the natives of Grand Canary. As has been seen, in the late Middle Ages the islands in the archipelago were known collectively as the *Insulae Fortunatae*, the 'Fortunate' or 'Happy Islands', following classical tradition, and the name *Canaria* was generally reserved for Grand Canary.[16] Culturally there were clear distinctions between the Guanches of Tenerife,[17] the Canarians of Grand Canary,[18] the Auaritas of La Palma,[19] the Majos of Lanzarote,[20] the Gomeros of La Gomera,[21] the Bimbachos of El Hierro[22] and the Majoreros of Fuerteventura,[23] the natives of the seven inhabited Canary Islands. Thus the collective term 'Canary islanders', rather than Guanches or Canarians, serves best to describe all the different native groups, who still had more similarities than differences in their style of life.[24] The name of the Majoreros has been preserved in the name of Fuerteventura's cheese, then as now excellent.

The Naked and the Clothed

Fifteenth- and sixteenth-century observers tried to make sense of the islanders. A chronicler close to Ferdinand and Isabella, Andrés Bernáldez, expressed his disapproval of the way they went around naked, and was puzzled by their religious life – they were 'idolaters without law', but also intelligent and faithful.[25] The Italian military architect Leonardo Torriani, sent by Philip II of Spain to write a report on the defences of the Canaries, became fascinated by what he could discover of the life and customs of the pre-conquest inhabitants, and left a finely illuminated manuscript, now the pride of Coimbra University Library, based on what he saw and heard between 1586 and 1593, that is, the time when Espinosa was also writing.[26] Alongside the drawings of fortifications that he had been commanded to produce, there are pictures of a man and a woman from Grand Canary, the man wearing a cape and shirt, the woman a long shift; Torriani greatly admired the deftness of the natives in fabricating a substitute for cloth made of palm leaves.[27] By contrast a pair of Gomerans are shown wearing much less – a short kilt for the man, a short skirt and open cape for the woman, partially exposing her breasts.[28] This was certainly closer to the image that fascinated European observers from the start, of naked or nearly naked natives, innocent, perhaps, and unaware of their sexual power when they encountered visitors from Spain.

Writing in Portugal, Zurara, the biographer of Henry the Navigator, described differences between the islands in diet, living quarters and religious practices.[29] He remarked that most Canarians 'went entirely naked', though some wore palm kilts, while 'the people of La Gomera were less civilised, and they had no clothing and no houses'.[30] His Venetian contemporary Alvise da Cà da Mosto reported that the Guanches of Tenerife went around naked, apart from some who wore goatskins; they protected themselves from the cold (even though the climate was generally mild) by rubbing animal grease into their skins, and they used the juices of various herbs to paint themselves in green, red and yellow patterns (similar customs were later observed among naked peoples in southern South America). Da Mosto thought these designs quite beautiful, and he noted how varied they were, expressing individuality in much the same way as properly civilised people do by the way they dress.[31] On Grand Canary, clay stamps were made, for 'printing' designs on the skin and other surfaces. (Elaborate decoration with henna of exposed parts of the female body such as the hands is a feature of Berber societies to this day.) Clearly, on the warmer sides of the islands and in summer nakedness was widespread; even in winter the temperature remains mild, so clothing seems often to have been used to signify high status. However, despite their facility with palm leaves, the islanders had no knowledge of textile-weaving, and apart from the leaves they relied on animal skins for clothing, sewing pieces together with animal gut, just as Boccaccio described.[32] This is confirmed by the evidence of the mummified bodies of the islanders: the Canary Museum in Las Palmas displays well-preserved examples of jackets, boots and utensils made of goat and sheep leather, sewn together in just this way.

Diet was one of the features that varied between islands, with some inhabitants relying more on fish and others showing a greater ability to cultivate the soil. The Canary islanders fit the standard image of Neolithic populations in showing knowledge of animal husbandry, throughout the archipelago, and of agriculture, on Grand Canary and several smaller islands. Some islands, such as Fuerteventura, were ill-suited to agriculture. The eastern islands lacked watercourses, and rainwater was carefully preserved in small reservoirs; the societies of Lanzarote and Fuerteventura were closer to the Sahara Desert in more than one way. Analysis of the internal organs of Guanche mummies in Tenerife reveals that barley was the staple cereal there, not baked into bread but consumed in a toasted form similar to the *gofio* that still forms a significant part of the islanders' diet. Grand Canary, ever the most complex in its technology, was the one island on which attempts were made to cultivate the soil using irrigation.[33] Animal products such as sheep's milk and animal fat were an essential part of the diet in most places. The fat or milk would be mixed with *gofio* to make it more digestible: a sort of Canary Island muesli.[34]

A fifteenth-century description, by Felix Hemmerlein of Zurich, portrayed islanders who ate raw flesh and knew nothing of the art of cooking; they were amazed and delighted when they first smelled and ate roasted and fried meat.[35] In another account, the inhabitants of the eastern islands were ignorant of fire, letting their meat cook solely by the heat of sun's rays. In yet another, the inhabitants of Fuerteventura ate their meat unsalted, after hanging it up to dry, and as a result were afraid to take refuge in their strongholds, since they could not store food for very long before it spoiled. The later narrative accounts say that meat was eaten half-roasted or rare; this was done, they assert, to make it more tasty, for it was important to demonstrate that the natives were not like beasts, 'eating, like dogs, raw flesh in great quantities'. In fact, 'the natives ate flesh very moderately, and never raw'. At the time Abreu Galindo wrote these words, everyone in western Europe was aware of tales of beasts in human form who ate uncooked meat like wild animals, and indeed Aristotle's works insisted on the importance of fire and cooking in human culture. The local diet seems to have been healthy; French and Spanish writers reported that some islanders were extremely tall and, even though this could easily be an example of European fantasies about giant races on the edge of the world, skeletal remains prove the existence of very tall islanders. There were also reports that people lived long, another common theme in descriptions of primitive peoples (such as the Tupí of Brazil in 1500) which may also have some foundation in fact. Isolation from the rest of the world meant isolation from Western diseases as well.

In most of the islands caves provided homes for the living and sepulchres for the dead. But there were also stone houses with wooden fittings in the eastern islands and on Grand Canary. Centres of population did emerge, for instance at Telde in north-eastern Grand Canary. On Lanzarote, the ruler appears to have had a small 'capital', and on Fuerteventura there were villages composed of groups of huts. Although Petrarch accused the islanders of being scattered and living isolated from one another, this was not the case. There were plenty of villages, no doubt with some of their dwellings cut into the rock face. The survival of village place-names such as Arguineguin in southern Grand Canary close to areas that have yielded quantities of native pottery is evidence that the islanders did live together in communities. The Canarians had better building skills and made less use of cave dwellings than the inhabitants of other islands. However, Torriani drew a picture of the royal palace or mausoleum in northern Grand Canary that looks like the decorated façade of a series of cave openings; and painted patterns have been found on the walls of some caves on Grand Canary: triangular designs, spirals, grids, in earth colours.[36] Abreu Galindo suggested that the art of building was one of the skills that the Canarians acquired from a small number of Majorcan missionaries active on Grand Canary in the late fourteenth century.

Not everyone is satisfied that the islanders' buildings were so modest. Claims have been made that the Guanches of Tenerife built great monumental platforms, described by the twentieth-century explorer Thor Heyerdahl as 'pyramids'; big stone platforms of this type do exist in the north of Tenerife, but excavation of the ground around them has not produced evidence that Guanches lived and worked close by.[37] Many consider these platforms to be piles of stone heaped up after the conquest by Spanish farmers and tidied up rather too enthusiastically by Heyerdahl's team of investigators. However, the Canary islanders did have cult centres, and Torriani drew a picture of a spiral-shaped temple or *fquenes* (in their language) on Fuerteventura. In the middle he placed a classical-looking statue of a young man; it has been seen that Boccaccio mentioned a mysterious temple containing just such a statue, while Torriani attributed similar buildings to the Majos of Lanzarote.[38] Abreu Galindo mentioned pyramid-type structures on Grand Canary, used for royal burials; but these were clearly tiny, more like broad-based obelisks than great platforms. It is not impossible that there were big platforms for major political and religious ceremonies, though the architect Torriani supplies a vivid drawing of a Canarian cult centre that consists simply of a mountain peak to which the semi-naked faithful are seen wending their way.[39] The massive rock Idafe on La Palma was a great centre of worship, and it was believed that one day it would collapse, leading to a great disaster; this anticipates modern fears that half of La Palma will slip into the sea, setting off a massive ocean-wide tsunami that will supposedly flood Manhattan. Since Torriani did not actually draw or describe Heyerdahl's 'pyramids', and since this was exactly the sort of structure that would have attracted his attention in a part of Tenerife he certainly visited, the chances that they go back to a period before Torriani's time, around 1590, seem very slim.

Comparing the islands, there is a general sense that Grand Canary had a higher level of culture, as can be seen for example in its pottery, which was more highly decorated than that of (say) La Gomera, though overall the islands' styles are quite similar to those of the African Berbers. The written sources suggest that women were especially active in the craft of pottery-making.[40] The ancient techniques have been perpetuated since the conquest, and Canary Island potters, whether partly of native descent or just descended from Spanish imitators of local potters, can still produce ceramics in traditional styles.[41] The small stone carvings and clay sculptures that survive seem to have had religious significance: mother goddess figures with outsize genitalia appear (it was these that European writers would imaginatively transform into classical statuettes). Wickerwork too was found on many archaeological sites in the islands. But the islanders knew nothing of metalworking. Their weapons were of fire-hardened wood, sharpened bones, including fish bones, and splintered stones; some survive, such as the *banot*, fighting staffs – the word itself was common to the dialect of several islands. Torriani drew a picture of a duel between half-naked Canary islanders in which they stand on a platform (much smaller than the top of one of Heyerdahl's 'pyramids') and attack one another with staves.[42]

There were some other skills that had been very well honed. One was the art of mummification, which was achieved without the elaborate evisceration of organs practised by the ancient Egyptians, and with a much more limited use of spices and unguents. It was, in fact, the art of desiccation. After death, the bodies of the most important members of Tenerife society were dried in the sun, clothed in skins and shoes, wrapped with selected herbs in reed mats or skins, and then taken to a burial cave where they were placed on a trestle.[43] Many of these mummies survive and can be admired (if that is the right word) in museums in the Canaries and elsewhere. For Espinosa, the existence of elaborate burial rituals was further proof that these were societies that operated according to a system of 'natural law', for reverence for the dead was seen by Aristotle and his followers as a sign of proper human behaviour.

Pagan Rites

The narrative accounts of the life of the Canary islanders before and during the European conquest do not merely confirm much of the archaeological record, but add a great amount of new information. The authors of these works – the two priestly authors of *Le Canarien*, the friars Espinosa and Abreu Galindo, the engineer Torriani – undoubtedly idealised the native population. Espinosa relied as far as he could on evidence from the Guanches themselves; but not many survived down to his time and, as he observed, 'if they know they do not wish to tell', for fear of causing harm to their community – the Inquisition might have taken an unhealthy interest in their knowledge of ancient rituals, for instance.[44] While it would be a mistake to assume that everything Espinosa and Abreu Galindo claim is trustworthy, they did have access to information about the political and religious life of these islanders in a way that simply does not exist for the inhabitants of Neolithic Europe. Model-building based on modern social science has been deployed in order to try to deduce the political structures of the people who built Stonehenge. Exercises of this type suffer from the simple fact that they are heavily influenced by the preoccupations of the social sciences today: highly politicised ideas of class, caste and gender that may be easier to apply to the twenty-first century AD than the twenty-first century BC. The narratives of the fifteenth to seventeenth centuries present similar difficulties, in the sense that their authors had religious or other preoccupations that coloured their writing, but they do contain what purport to be hard facts about political history before the conquest and about the customs of the native population. Even bearing in mind the problem of bias, it is possible to observe an ancient, largely non-literate (that is, prehistoric) society in remarkable detail. Or, to be precise, one can see how Western observers judged such a society, quite unlike any other society western Europeans had previously encountered. The two areas that attracted most attention were the religious beliefs of the natives and their political system, though there was some fascination also with their martial skills.

In describing the religious beliefs of the islanders, Abreu Galindo, Espinosa and most other early writers attributed to them (with some justice, but also as a result of a wish to reveal similarities to European religion) a belief in a single supreme God, even if they also worshipped lesser gods and spirits.[45] These commentators understood the urgency of the argument that the natives of the Canaries had some understanding of God, and that they practised rituals through which they worshipped Him, without indulging in the excesses of Aztec or Inca heathenism. In his highly influential 'On Laws', Cicero had argued that 'there is no race so highly civilised or so savage as not to know that it must believe in a God, even if it does not know in what sort of God it ought to believe'.[46] Knowledge of God, even if 'weak and confused', would be proof

that they followed 'natural religion', and lived just but as yet unenlightened
lives, not merely in the spirit of Cicero but in accordance with the principles
of natural law set out by Thomas Aquinas in the thirteenth century. For
Aquinas, who was, like Espinosa, a Dominican friar, even a non-Christian
society could exercise natural justice, based on fundamental principles that
any rational human could comprehend.[47] Belief in one God, sexual restraint
and the exercise of justice were markers indicating that this was a society
governed in accord with natural law. This then raised the question whether it
could be aggressively conquered, especially if its rulers had done nothing to
offend Christians. For example: if, as in Grand Canary, they allowed
Christian missionaries to settle and preach, then they should rightly be
immune from attack. Thus both Espinosa and Abreu Galindo were guiding
their readers, very adeptly, towards an acceptance of the fully human status of
the Canary islanders.

According to these authors, similar ideas of a Supreme Being existed on
both Grand Canary and Tenerife. On the latter island, Abreu tells us, their
God was known as *Achguayerxeran Achoron Achaman*, 'he who sustains the sky
and the earth'; on Grand Canary he was known as *Alcorán*.[48] Abreu and
Espinosa heavily emphasised the monotheistic element in native religion, and
it is possible that there was an idea of a Supreme God on some or all of the
islands, but the natives of Grand Canary appear also to have worshipped the
stars and planets. Abreu Galindo's defensive remark that 'the natives of this
island did not worship idols, nor had any images of the Deity' forms part of
his attempt to present the Canarians as pure monotheists rather than
heathens, and can easily be discounted using the excavation finds; in any case,
Torriani, without the friars' agenda, had already portrayed the natives of one
island after another as *idolatri*. Fifteenth-century Portuguese views of the
islanders' religion were recorded by Henry the Navigator's biographer: Zurara
reported that the Canarians did have a belief in God and that there were even
some who called themselves Christians (he was thinking of those converted
by the Majorcan missions); on Tenerife too 'they believed in the existence of
a God';[49] but the Gomerans believed in God without submitting to any code
of religious law, and the Auaritas of La Palma 'had no knowledge of God, nor
any faith at all', and 'like the other cattle they are very bestial', comments that
appeared to justify the slave raids that were launched against this island.[50]
When in need of rain, the islanders appealed to the gods by bringing their
herds to the high places where they worshipped; the bleating of the animals

was supposed to attract the gods' attention and, it was hoped, encourage them to release the rainfall that was needed.

Several practices described by Abreu Galindo and Espinosa attracted their attention because of their similarity to Christian customs and rituals; in particular, there were women known as 'Magadas' who performed a similar role to nuns. They wore long white robes and lived together in a single 'house'; their convents were sacred territory, houses of refuge to which criminals would flee and where they would have immunity.[51] Milk was important in the religious rites of the islanders in the same way as holy water among Christians: the milk of specially segregated goats (from whom the young were not taken) was sprinkled on their temples. In times of crisis, milk and butter were poured on the sacred rocks in the districts of Gáldar and Telde.[52] It is fairly certain that these stories of the votive pouring of milk are based on reality, for milk and milk products were an important part of the Canary Islands' economy; but there is still a need for caution. This type of ritual was also associated, in the minds of Renaissance writers, with an idealised paganism, a cult of nature in which gods, nymphs and humans lived side by side in harmony – a literary conceit found in the works of Boccaccio in the fourteenth century and of the Neapolitan Jacopo Sannazaro at the end of the fifteenth. In one of Sannazaro's descriptions of a prayer to a classical goddess he describes a shepherd 'pouring out a vessel of warm milk and kneeling with arms extended to the east'.[53] Gentle pastoral imagery helped protect the islanders by portraying them as innocent shepherds, and it also preserved the idea that these islands were the 'Happy' or 'Fortunate' Isles of classical literature. But the pouring of liquids also conjured up Christian imagery. In a book published in 1676 the Spanish writer Juan Nuñez de la Peña described how water was used in a ritual similar to baptism; in his account, the Guanches of Tenerife said they knew about this ritual, which was 'an ancient custom, from the time of their ancestors', and, departing from the idea that the natives had never heard the name of Christ before the arrival of the European conquerors, he surmised that they had in fact learned of baptism from St Bartholomew, St Brendan or another early witness to the Christian faith.[54] Espinosa had also heard of these missions (and indeed of similar rituals), but he attached no importance to the visits, since for him the principal evangelist in Tenerife was none other than the Virgin Mary.

Divided Realms

Espinosa, Abreu Galindo and Torriani also offered insights into the political life of the islands. Espinosa described the hierarchical power structure of Tenerife under its petty kings or *menceys*. There existed nine tribes on Tenerife.[55] The Guanches believed there had been a single ruler in the past, whose nine sons had carved up the island in his old age. This began the fragmentation of the island, though, interestingly, inheritance passed from elder brother to younger, and only to sons once the older generation had died out. Espinosa described elaborate coronation ceremonies at which the new *mencey* brandished a bone of one of his ancestors and made an oath, followed by a feast for the nobles (there were also occasional female rulers).[56] The political history of Grand Canary was similar. Instead of *menceys* the island was ruled by chieftains called *guanartemes*. The wise nun Antidamana married the chieftain Gomidafa at the end of the fourteenth century, and they managed to unify the island rather in the manner of Ferdinand and Isabella (a model Abreu Galindo may have had in mind when he told this story).[57] Their quarrelsome grandsons divided the island into two statelets, one based at the traditional power centre of Telde in the north-east, and the other at Gáldar in the north-west. These divisions naturally hampered the Canarians when they were attacked by the Spanish conquistadores, who had established mastery over Grand Canary by 1483.

Local legends told how, at the time when the gods created mankind, the noble caste came into being first, along with their flocks; subsequently, a second creation brought into being a subservient order of lesser men. In any case, Espinosa and Abreu Galindo were determined to show that this was a structured society in which there existed a true nobility; perhaps this is not surprising in authors of the sixteenth and seventeenth centuries, who were immersed willy-nilly in the culture of the proud Spanish hidalgo. Abreu Galindo was fascinated by the initiation ritual that young nobles had to undergo; he presented it as a verbal examination, testing the ethical qualities of the young man – 'whether he was in any way discourteous, ill-tongued, or guilty of any indecent behaviour, especially to women' (talking to lone women whom one met by chance could earn a death penalty, as the finders of the image of the Virgin of Candelaria had been aware). These were aristocrats, with chivalric values. At the same time the young noble had to show that he had not sullied his hands with unsuitable trades. Just as a Spanish nobleman would wish to distance himself from overt involvement in trade, Canarian nobles had to avoid the taboo of keeping, milking or, worst of all, slaughtering sheep or goats. Once ennobled, the young Canarian would abide by a code that insisted that he give honour to women and children, even enemy ones, and that he never damage the temples of his enemy.[58] Abreu Galindo took great delight in describing their duels, which he presented as gallant tournaments. Of course, by implying that the islanders were more chivalrous than the Spaniards, Abreu Galindo may have wished to teach a lesson to his European contemporaries.

At the other end of the social scale were butchers. The refusal to allow noblemen any contact with the slaughtering of sheep reflected social divisions on the islands. Butchers were the lowest caste in Canarian society: 'none of the Canarians exercised the trade of a butcher except the dregs of the people', to cite Glas' paraphrase of Abreu Galindo; as Untouchables, they were not allowed physical contact with normal people, but were supplied with all their needs by other means.[59] In the fifteenth century, both Zurara and da Mosto insisted that Christian captives were used as butchers on Grand Canary, to prevent the pollution of native Canarians (it is perhaps comforting to know that slave raiders sometimes ended up as slaves in the hands of the people they tried to despoil). This fear of pollution bears comparison with the taboos found in Berber and Middle Eastern societies, which might relegate certain groups such as Jews and Gypsies to metalworking.

Abreu Galindo was also anxious to show that the islanders' family life was acceptable to European observers. Once again, this concern had its roots in the long history of discussions about non-Christian societies: any evidence that they practised polygamy, polyandry, sodomy or (even worse) incest was seen as proof that primitive societies needed to be governed by Christian masters. The Canary islanders, however, were presented as paragons of good conduct, living in accordance with the principles of natural law. Thus they were strictly monogamous. Their marriage habits aroused interest; brides were fattened on milk and *gofio* before their wedding, to make them fertile.[60] On the other hand, there were negative images that, in their most extreme form, presented the inhabitants of some islands as near-beasts. Torriani thought that men on El Hierro (which he considered the most barbarous island) could have any and as many women as they wished as wives except their own mothers. There was even a report in the fifteenth-century chronicle known as *Le Canarien* that on Lanzarote most women had three husbands, rotating them month by month, though Torriani said it was the opposite: that men could have as many wives as they wished, but could not marry their sisters.[61] Da Mosto claimed to have heard from Portuguese slave raiders that on Tenerife the petty kings had the right to deflower virgins, a claim that does not seem to be corroborated elsewhere and that may just be a fantasy.[62] On La Gomera there may have been a custom by which men offered their wives for the night to visiting travellers, as an act of generosity; da Mosto's contemporary Zurara insisted that 'their women were regarded almost as common property, for it was a breach of hospitality for a man not to offer his wife to a visitor by way of welcome'; Zurara also said that the islanders ate like beasts and lived in holes in the ground, preferring to consume rats, lice and fleas rather than wholesome meat.[63] The Swiss canon lawyer Hemmerlein based himself on reports of a Portuguese expedition in the late fourteenth century when he described men and women having sexual intercourse in public, and women making themselves freely available to any man;[64] all the other evidence suggests that this was lurid fantasy, but the theme of primitive folk charged with irrepressible sexual energy remained powerful in descriptions of the first Americans as well.

Nonetheless, most Renaissance writers did not assume that these societies were primitive, in the sense of lacking complexity in their political, religious and social life. What was primitive was their technology, but even that gained grudging admiration when would-be conquerors found their resistance unbreakable. For one of the most remarkable facts about the history of European relations with the Canaries is quite simply how long it took to conquer the islands. Norman adventurers arrived in the eastern Canaries at the start of the fifteenth century; the conquest of the archipelago was not complete until four years after the fall of Granada and the discovery of the Caribbean islands by Columbus.

CHAPTER 6

RIGHTS OF DOMINION, 1341–1496

Contrasting Priorities, 1341–51

The Portuguese-Italian expedition of 1341 provided a basis for later claims by Portugal that it had been a pioneer in the waters of the Canary Islands, and so had a right to exercise sovereignty there. No thought was given to the wishes of the natives. But the expedition was followed by several decades in which Portugal was distracted from Atlantic adventures: the little kingdom suffered from plague, political disorder and social conflict, leading to the accession of a new dynasty under João or John I of Avis in 1383–5; and then, in alliance with England, Portugal was sucked into a bitter conflict with Castile, setting off a jealous rivalry that would last a century. During this time others, including the Castilians, became more interested in Canary waters. Boccaccio had reported that the expedition of 1341 brought little or no profit, and the business communities of Lisbon and Seville would have been aware of this disappointing fact. The fantasy that the islands contained imposing castles and cities was gradually replaced by knowledge that the inhabitants were neither rich nor (by European standards) sophisticated.

The first to attempt to raise their flag in the Canaries after Portugal were the Majorcans.[1] The Catalan kingdom of Majorca, established in 1276, consisted of the Balearic Islands, Roussillon and Montpellier; its economic strength, built on trade through Majorca, Perpignan and Montpellier, was not matched by political power. Its last ruler, the eccentric King James III, had grandiose ideas but was under constant pressure from his cousin and overlord, the king of Aragon, who eventually, exasperated by James' overtures to France and a supposed plot to kidnap him, seized most of his territories in 1343–4.[2] But the year before, James of Majorca decided to license a series of expeditions to the Canary Islands in the hope of making them into his personal domain, where he could operate without the interference of Aragon or indeed France; he seems to have given no thought to Portuguese claims. At least four ships were sent out in 1342; they were to head for 'the region of the newly discovered islands commonly known as the Fortunate Isles', a rather paradoxical phrase that betrays the fact that contemporary knowledge of the islands was a combination of traditional fantasy and exact information, as might be expected in Majorca, which was home to the best cartographers of the time: these islands had an old name, but were newly explored. The ships' captains were very precisely instructed that, should they capture any island, town or castle, they 'must recognise as prince and lord the said lord our king', for the king of Majorca would exercise all rights of jurisdiction. There was still, then, an assumption that the islands contained fortified strongholds, and it is likely that the Majorcan ships went out well armed, in the same way that the Portuguese explorers the year before had arrived equipped with horses and armaments. What happened to the four Canarians brought back by the Portuguese in 1341 remains a mystery. Conceivably they were treated honourably as Canarian nobles; but other Canarians taken back on later expeditions were enslaved. The Majorcans evidently also brought back some Canarians from their sally southwards in 1342: three years later, a document from Majorca reports that 'a certain captive from Canaria' was working in a vineyard near the island capital, and the casual way he was described hints at the presence of plenty more Canarians.[3]

Popes, kings and princes had their curiosity aroused. Claims to the Canaries would accumulate in the next few decades, without any thought for the wishes of the natives. After the kingdom of Majorca was absorbed into the Crown of Aragon in 1343–4, the Aragonese king, Peter the Ceremonious, assumed the rights claimed by his deposed cousin James III and sent his own ships to the Canaries.[4] There was a growing interest in the purple dye known as orchil which could be found in the islands, in sealskins and, ominously, in slaves. So many Majos had been taken off Lanzarote as slaves that the population had fallen to a mere three hundred by the start of the fifteenth century. The early voyages went further south as well. In August 1346 Jaume Ferrer set out from Majorca, now part of the Aragonese Crown, for the Canaries and the *riu d'oro*, the 'River of Gold'. Ferrer vanished, but throughout the fifteenth century his ship and its crew were routinely painted on the outer edges of world maps, such as that owned by the dukes of Ferrara in the mid-fifteenth century: a crowded little ship under sail, with an accompanying inscription to remind map-users that there were still secrets to be uncovered in West Africa. The River of Gold, speculatively marked on Majorcan maps, was thought to lead into the African interior towards Timbuktu, for it was assumed that the Niger River debouched into the Atlantic somewhere a little beyond the Canaries, and not, as it actually does, deep in the bend of Africa.[5] Gold, then, was one objective; news of its existence there reached Majorca from Jewish and Muslim merchants who maintained links with business partners in Saharan trading posts, from where gold dust was brought on the backs of camels to the ports of the Mediterranean.[6] To bypass the routes across the desert and to take business away from Muslim middlemen was one of the great dreams that motivated the search for gold in the late Middle Ages. The idea began to develop that the Canaries might be used as an offshore station from which to tap into the commerce in gold and, later, in slaves from West Africa. But Ferrer was sailing in the service of God as well. There were friars on board, ready to bring the Word of God to unenlightened peoples.

Once the pope became interested, saving souls became at least as important as finding gold. In 1351, the king of Aragon and the pope sent a Genoese and a Catalan captain, both resident in Majorca, to the Canaries as part of an ambitious plan to bring the natives into the Christian fold. Pope Clement VI wrote that the news of the discovery of the islands had caused great wonder at the papal court; the islands were fertile, full of good things and well populated, but had still not been brought to the true faith. Up to thirty missionaries accompanied the ships; and the pope indicated that they also planned to carry with them twelve Canary islanders who had been brought back to Europe by an earlier expedition and had been instructed in the Catalan language and the Christian faith. These islanders were said to be full of zeal to return to the islands, in order to work for the conversion of their fellow islanders. But in his licence for this voyage the king of Aragon wrote of the Canary islanders as *rurales* – simple country-dwellers – and *brutales*, a term that implied an animal-like savagery; they also, he said, 'lived according to no law but acted in a bestial way in all things'. Pope Clement VI created a missionary bishopric, staffed by Carmelite and Franciscan friars, on Grand Canary. The friars built a small church in Telde, the seat of one of the *guanartemes* on Grand Canary. But Christianity did not strike deep roots there. The church at Telde was a tiny Christian enclave. Fearful of slavers, the natives remained suspicious of the European visitors they encountered.

The Grumbling Canon of Zurich, 1370/1450

Felix Hemmerlein (or Hemmerlin) was a reforming canon of Zurich, and a canon lawyer of repute, who died around 1460. He led an eventful life: he vocally attacked the immoral life of the choristers in Zurich, whereupon they physically attacked him and tried to beat him to a pulp. He inserted into one of his learned tomes, much more concerned with the failings of the Swiss than with unknown peoples, a brief account of a voyage to the Canaries that he thought had occurred in about 1370.[7] The tract, which was completed in 1450, took the form of a dialogue between a nobleman and a rustic, and the description of the Canaries was put in the mouth of the nobleman, with a few curious questions attributed to the countryman. Since Hemmerlein was born in 1389, it had all happened some years before his own time.[8] Hemmerlein was active in Church circles, taking part, for example, in the great Basel Council where debates on the ownership of the islands were held; so his outlook may have influenced wider attitudes to the problem of whether the Canary islanders should enjoy a fully human status. For, despite his many very negative statements about the Canary islanders, he was not trying to argue that these wild men were merely beasts in human shape. He wanted to defend the native islanders against the accusation that they were incapable of rising above an animal existence. The way they could achieve that was by becoming Christians and by learning the 'mechanical arts' from Christian instructors. In much the same way, King Alfonso the Magnanimous (d. 1458) had fond schemes to send friars, artisans and even a princess to the court of Ethiopia, an ancient Christian kingdom that he felt was in need of a little European polish.[9] Hemmerlein, though, was telling a tale with a moral. Under the surface of the story lies a little sermon about the chance every human being has to abandon brutish behaviour and become a decent, devout, industrious citizen of (say) Zurich.

Hemmerlein told how a galley sailing in Atlantic waters had been chased by pirates southwards off its intended course; the galley flew the flag of the king of Aragon. The ship then ran before stormy winds further and further south for ten days and nights, until its crew glimpsed some islands in the offing, probably Fuerteventura and Lanzarote.[10] But as the Aragonese came near, they saw people of both sexes covered with simple animal skins, howling like dogs, with the appearance, frankly, of monkeys. For both sides this was (as Hemmerlein presents events) an encounter with a type of people previously unknown to them. The natives had never seen Europeans before, he asserted, 'nor did they have or know the use of ships', a constant refrain in descriptions of the Canary islanders.[11] The only point of comparison for Hemmerlein was the strange and primitive peoples of parts of India who dressed in simple skins, as described in the works of Isidore of Seville. The islanders were used to eating raw flesh, but once they began to realise that the visitors intended no harm, they made contact, even eating food together, which the sailors roasted and fried in the pots they had brought along. The islanders greatly appreciated the taste and smell of well-cooked meat. This receptivity to Western manners and skills was evidently important to Hemmerlein, for it demonstrated that the islanders were capable of being raised to a higher level of humanity. Then a few of the natives came along with the Aragonese sailors, apparently willingly, to visit three more islands, where they were once again well received, but found that the languages they spoke were 'special and distinct', another example of the fascination European writers showed for the variety of languages spoken in the Canaries.

The galley headed westwards through the archipelago. But the fifth island on which the sailors landed was an even greater surprise than the four they had seen already. There the natives were very hostile; they did not merely look like animals, but behaved like them too. Sexual intercourse took place in public and in any case all the women were shared sexually by the men. They gave birth in positions characteristic of animals rather than humans. In fact, they even ate 'like other wild animals'.[12] On leaving the archipelago, the explorers took away a few men and women, apparently from the first island they had visited. However, these natives soon indicated by sign language that they wanted to go back home, so 'by great benevolence' the sailors returned them, and sailed back in a month to Aragonese territory. Advice about what to do next was then taken from the University of Paris; it was agreed that the islanders urgently needed missionary friars and people who could teach them agriculture and the mechanical arts; and in fact the missions were, Hemmerlein insists, a success, for the natives of the 'good' islands learned about the Catholic faith and even learned the art of writing, while (unfortunately) the inhabitants of the fifth island were 'left in their bestial wildness'.[13]

According to Hemmerlein, the king of Aragon asserted his rights of dominion, and the islanders (or at least the good ones) accepted this, for they had never had any other lord; this was a revealing remark, because Hemmerlein would have been fully aware of the claims of the different Iberian kingdoms to dominion over the islands, and was well informed about Spanish matters. But Hemmerlein did not just tell the story. He also passed judgment, arguing that the islanders generally lived in a 'state of innocence' – 'indeed, they lived according to the law of nature' – by which he evidently did not mean a well-balanced pagan society operating in a reasonably sophisticated way according to the principles of natural law. His view was that natural man was as much (or more) animal as he was man.[14] One feature of their innocence was that the island men held things in common, even (surprisingly) women, but they soon learned to conduct themselves better once the missionaries arrived, and now understood the importance of marriage. The missionaries had apparently effected what he called a 'reformation' in the life of the islanders, turning them into proper humans as well as Christians. Thus from their primitive state, close to that of animals, the islanders had been humanised and had acquired the skills of civilised folk.

Hemmerlein was still left with the problem of who these people actually were. Where, the countryman of his dialogue asked the nobleman, did these people come from? The answer was that they had arrived on the islands 'in the cataclysm of the Great Flood'; had they been survivors of the antediluvian world population, they would of course have spoken the language of God and of early mankind, Hebrew.[15] But then the countryman had to ask a further question. The islanders appeared not to have received the Word of Christ when it was diffused across the world and, even if four islands had now become aware of the Christian faith, there remained the problem of the obdurate fifth island.[16] Of course, this was all rather far from the truth; missionary efforts had yielded little success, and Tenerife and Grand Canary, the largest islands, remained unconquered and seemed unconquerable. What Hemmerlein contributed was a note of optimism, even if it was combined with the strongly negative imagery of islanders who looked and behaved like monkeys. Or, to place him more exactly in the history of European attitudes to native peoples, his account of the Canary islanders combines the negative and the positive, side by side and in the same sentence, in a way that would be characteristic of later writers on the peoples of the Americas. It is hardly surprising that, faced with the sheer novelty of the types of people they encountered, in appearance, technology and beliefs, the earliest observers should often have conveyed messages that were in some respects quite contradictory.

Missions to the Edges of the World, 1344–1400

The planned conversion of the Canary islanders formed part of a wider strategy for dealing with the peoples who lived beyond the bounds of

Christendom, even if the Canary peoples were unique, having been totally isolated for many hundreds of years. The roots of the policy adopted by the Aragonese rulers and the popes can be found in the initiatives of missionaries of the thirteenth century, drawn mainly from the ranks of the Dominican and Franciscan friars, whose campaigns among the Jews and Muslims have already been described.[17] In his *Book of the Gentile and the Three Wise Men*, Ramon Llull of Majorca conjured up the image of an atheistic pagan 'philosopher' ignorant of Judaism, Christianity or Islam, wandering the world in search of truth; he received instruction in all three religions, and came to believe in God, though the reader is never told which religion the pagan chose.[18] Although Llull's evangelical academy at Miramar in the Majorcan mountains did not last, he sowed the seeds of a missionary movement among the Franciscans, with whom he had cordial ties; the Catalan and Majorcan missionaries who were being commended to the pope by the king of Aragon seventy years after his death were his spiritual descendants. There was only one method that could succeed: to insert Christian missionaries into native societies and, using gentle example and persistent preaching, to draw the unenlightened to the faith. The Canaries seemed the ideal terrain for this venture, and the Majorcans, long after their last autonomous king had died, remained enthusiasts for the cause. The king of Aragon, too, remained protective: in 1366 he gave his approval to an expedition from Majorca whose aim may well have been to clear the islands of intruders, such as slavers, who in his view had no right to be there.[19] Yet there were other factors that determined the outlook of popes, kings and missionaries to the Canary islanders.

For there was another great missionary enterprise that was pressing ahead at this time, politically more important and vastly larger in scale: the conversion of the Lithuanian pagans, who persisted in their unbelief, sandwiched between Catholic Poland and Orthodox Russia (making it important that, if they did convert, it was not to the wrong sort of Christianity). The Lithuanian grand dukes were rulers of a vast empire that, at its peak, stretched almost from the Baltic to the Black Sea. The Lithuanians had hundreds of thousands of Catholic, Orthodox, Jewish, Karaite and Muslim subjects. The Word of Christ had reached them, but, like the Jews, they refused to listen; nor were their grand dukes 'primitive' in their style of life. They knew iron perfectly well; they had secretaries who wrote letters for them (generally in Slavonic scripts and languages); they made trade treaties and even traded in cabbages with the West.[20] Nevertheless, Pope Clement VI saw the

Lithuanian and the Canarian enterprises as part of a common assault on
paganism. Letters from this pope and his predecessors were specially collected
together in a bound volume, 'Vatican Register 62', as it is now known; here
the compiler brought together 'the business of the Tartars, the lands overseas,
infidels and heretics'.[21] Indeed, just as the war against the Lithuanians, led by
the Teutonic Knights, was preached as a crusade, conferring spiritual privileges on participants such as the remission of past sins, the expeditions to the
Canaries could attract similar papal privileges, as happened in 1351. All this
provided important precedents for the way the popes and Spanish rulers
would react to Columbus' discoveries at the end of the next century.

In 1344 Pope Clement granted Luis de la Cerda the island; it was to be a
'perpetual fief', in recognition of papal authority over unconquered islands.[22]
Luis declared to the pope that his motive in claiming rule over the Canaries
was 'to eliminate their wicked pagan error so that the glory of the divine name
may be praised there and the glory of the Catholic faith might flourish', and
the pope remarked that Luis de la Cerda came from an illustrious family, well
known for its role in spreading the faith.[23] Luis never arrived in his remote
kingdom, however, and in fact died only four years later, leaving a vacuum that
the pope wisely filled not with princes with vain claims, but with the
Majorcan friars under their missionary bishop. Still, whether Luis made his
kingdom real or a bishop exerted authority instead, it was the pope who
gained most prestige from the lordship of the Canaries. Seen from Avignon
(or, in the fifteenth century, from Rome), the outlying, unconquered islands
of the world were at the pope's disposal, entrusted to him by Christ, with the
agreement of the Roman emperor, for their evangelisation and good government. Papal claims to islands in the Atlantic would be carried many stages
further in the 1490s under Alexander VI, who assumed the right to divide the
entire unconquered area of the Outer Ocean between Castile and Portugal.
Clement was an able canon lawyer, and he was well aware of the arguments
concerning the rights of Christians to exercise authority over non-Christian
peoples. Some of these had been set out in tracts by his great predecessor
Innocent IV in the mid-thirteenth century and by Thomas Aquinas a little
later – the argument that pagan rulers had a right to undisturbed dominion
so long as they ruled in accordance with 'natural law' was particularly important. Actually, Pope Clement dissented from this view, and was not alone in
doing so. He followed the alternative line of the great thirteenth-century
canon lawyer Hostiensis, who insisted that, with the coming of Christ, all
pagan rulers lost their right to govern themselves, which devolved instead on

the Christian faithful: 'the implication is that just as there was no salvation outside the Church so too there was no legitimate political authority outside the Church.'[24] Innocent IV had made it clear that pagan rulers could not be deprived of dominion simply because they were pagans; on the other hand, these rulers must not stand in the way of missions, as the Lithuanian dukes had often done.

On this point, the Canarians too had a mixed record. The Majorcan missions ended in disaster; the bishopric came to an abrupt end in the last months of the fourteenth century. Abreu Galindo provided a remarkable account of Canarian reactions to the Majorcan presence. It is not often that the voices of the natives themselves can be heard, even if here they are mediated through the distorting mirrors of oral tradition, on which Abreu relied, and of Abreu's own wish to show how the Canarians were indeed good folk who had been maltreated by the Europeans. The Canarians did remember the Majorcans in both positive and negative ways, but it is also clear that their memories telescoped events that took place across the entire second half of the fourteenth century into a much narrower band of time. In Glas' rendition:

We have no other account than from the relation of the natives, and what may be collected from their old songs, in which some account of those Majorcans is given. By comparing their different traditions of this affair and arranging them in order of time, it appears to have been as follows.[25]

After the death of Luis de la Cerda, soon after his investiture, some Majorcans set out again for the islands. They anchored in the north-east of Grand Canary, where they found natives who, 'being unaccustomed to the visits of strangers, lived in an unguarded manner, not thinking they had any thing to fear from the sea'. The Majorcans, he said, assumed the island was uninhabited (a strange assumption to make by this stage) and those who had disembarked were amazed when the natives emerged, apparently from nowhere, and 'attacked the Europeans with sticks and stones, and wounded several of them'. The Majorcans who had landed were taken prisoner, while those who had remained on board sailed off in fright without waiting. However, 'in the number of those who were taken prisoners were two priests, who were greatly respected by the natives. These fathers built two hermitages, of stone without cement.'[26]

Abreu Galindo stressed the benefits the Majorcans brought to Grand Canary; he insisted that the missionaries were at first much loved by the

Canarians and that they taught the islanders useful skills in architecture, the fine arts and even in the art of government: 'the means to govern with great skill and propriety'.[27] *Le Canarien* reports that in 1403 the French knight Gadifer de la Salle arrived on the shore near Telde and made a surprising discovery: the last will of one of the thirteen friars who had worked at the mission station there. This friar had written that he and his brethren had worked incessantly among the Canarians, teaching them the Christian faith, but he was convinced they were untrustworthy and treacherous. The chronicle speaks of thirteen, and not two, friars, and several more arrived in 1386 after being recommended to the pope by the king of Aragon, who retained a proprietorial interest in the far-off islands. The problem was not the friars but the laity, many of whom were more interested in the bodies than the souls of the islanders. Slave raiders arrived from Spain in increasing numbers, including not just Catalans but pirates from Cantabria and Andalucía in 1393. *Le Canarien* is adamant that Lanzarote had been largely depopulated by slave raiders before 1402, and the other islands were also treated as good hunting grounds. The crude activities of these raiders over many years incensed Canarian opinion, contributing to a fateful decision to exterminate the Europeans.

Abreu Galindo relates that, when a famine struck Grand Canary, the 'Council' of the Canarians met and decided that food was in such short supply that they could no longer support the Majorcan captives. Instead, they would kill all of them; indeed, they also decided to put to death all newborn girls except the first-born, 'to lessen the number of inhabitants in the island'.[28] They had no means to trade with the outside world in order to acquire food, nor any way to emigrate without knowledge of ships. Abreu Galindo admitted that the massacre of the Majorcan captives was a 'cruel and barbarous resolution' (in Glas' rendition), but they were impelled to do it by 'the scandalous behaviour of the strangers themselves'. Glas noted that Abreu Galindo had not revealed what their crimes were, 'but seems to insinuate that they had made some attempts of an heinous and unnatural kind upon some of the natives, which rendered them most detestable in their sight, as they were utter strangers to such abomination'. This sounds like a barely concealed accusation of sodomy. The Canarians massacred all but two friars, with whom they dealt in what was apparently a more honourable way, similar to the custom whereby disgraced noble islanders would throw themselves off high peaks and be dashed to pieces on the rocky floor of a ravine. The friars were taken up a mountain and thrown into a deep tunnel, whose exit was unknown until the clothes of the friars were found on the beach; the tunnel was evidently a volcanic shaft leading down to the seashore. In any case, the friars vanished, presumed dead.

The famine was eased by other forces, however. Plague hit the island and 'carried off two thirds of its inhabitants'; no doubt the bubonic plague which had been a scourge of Europe had at last been brought to the islands by visiting slavers. Without this massive population loss, Captain Glas observed, the island would have been unconquerable; he thought that fourteen thousand properly armed Canarians would have been able to defend the island against the Spaniards, with the help of its craggy and rugged landscape, 'where a hundred men may very easily battle the efforts of a thousand'.[29] He noted that in this respect Grand Canary, Tenerife and the smaller islands were different from the open landscapes of Lanzarote and Fuerteventura, the lower-lying, sandy islands closest to Africa, which were by their nature more exposed. And it was there, on the eastern edges, that the permanent conquest of the islands began.

CHAPTER 7

QUARRELSOME CONQUERORS, 1402–44

Chivalry and Greed, 1402–4

In 1402 an expedition set out from France for the Canaries, led by Jean de Béthencourt, lord of Grainville, a native of Normandy, and Gadifer de la Salle, a Poitevin nobleman. They had fought side by side in Tunisia in 1390, when a crusading army launched an attack on the city of Mahdia, a long-standing object of European ambitions because of its ancient links to the gold trade across the Sahara. The gold of Africa was certainly one of the great lures that now drew Béthencourt and de la Salle to the Canaries: there was talk of discovering the route to the River of Gold beyond Cape Bojador. However, even if their later conduct seems very materialistic, they were also guided by the traditional chivalric concern of many early explorers: the wish to acquire fame through good deeds, preferably in the service of Christ.[1] Although they were not Muslim territories, the Canaries could be seen as a back door leading into the Islamic world. Moreover, the expedition possessed exact information about the Canaries. Through family connections, Béthencourt knew about the Andalucían–Cantabrian expedition of 1393 (one of its dubious achievements had been the capture of a king and queen on the island of Lanzarote); and a French relative who had been involved in that raid also provided backing for Béthencourt.[2] The raiders of 1393 had returned home convinced that the conquest of the eastern islands was going to be straightforward, and the new invaders sought to create a domain for themselves, using their links both to the French and the Castilian crowns in the hope of securing lordship over the islands. The French king apparently approved of their venture, but he was looking in other directions, trying to capitalise on the fall from power of Richard II in England in 1399, and stirring up anti-English mischief in Scotland.

From the moment they set out from La Rochelle in May 1402 the two leaders discovered that they could no longer abide one another. It has been suggested that they had very different objectives: de la Salle was more the romantic crusader, while Béthencourt may have been seeking profits with which he could cover his mounting debts back home; perhaps even the crusade indulgences he acquired from the pope were simply a means to make more money, because these spiritual privileges could be sold for a good price to those willing to back the expedition.[3] However, Béthencourt must not be judged too harshly; the elegant manuscript of the *Le Canarien* chronicle from the library of the dukes of Burgundy, now preserved in the British Library in London, contains a sustained invective against him and makes no mention of the faults and mistakes of de la Salle. Another, rather fuller version of the same chronicle, preserved in a manuscript in Rouen, gives the opposite view and leans towards Béthencourt. Like the leaders of the expedition, the chronicle's two priestly authors, Le Verrier and Bontier, at first collaborated but then disagreed strongly about who was the real hero of the Canarian adventure. The journey south had many mishaps. They sailed in a 'très bon navire', beautifully drawn in the London manuscript. But problems began early with contrary winds in the Bay of Biscay, where they encountered a Scottish earl and some other dubious characters who were enjoying a career as pirates. The pirates allowed Béthencourt to take away a new anchor they had stolen, but this only landed the explorers in serious trouble later, as they rounded the Iberian peninsula. The Castilians arrested de la Salle for piracy, and he had to argue his way out of an Andalucían prison.

Arriving at last in Lanzarote, they built good relations with the natives, and managed to establish a fort at a place they called Rubicón on the tip of the island, conducting raids into the neighbouring island of Fuerteventura from there, with the tacit consent of the local ruler in Lanzarote. The latter was described by the chronicle as 'the Saracen king', *roy sarrasin*, a term that was not so much intended to disparage their new friend as to raise him in the estimation of readers. Béthencourt and de la Salle could thus be portrayed as paragons of chivalry, fighting a familiar type of war with other, unfriendly 'Saracens' on the romantically entitled island of Lanzarote, that is, 'Sir Lancelot', where their port of disembarkation received the suitably Arthurian name of La Porte Joyeuse (Sir Lancelot having lived at La Joyeuse Garde). Yet this was not quite the land of Arthur or Lancelot, and there was little to gain except empty titles over rather barren lands. The Majoreros of Fuerteventura quickly learned to distrust the French, who seemed no better than the Spanish slave raiders of past years – the expedition of 1393 had done immeasurable damage to relations between the Canary islanders and the Europeans. Béthencourt went back to Castile looking for reinforcements and, without consulting his colleague, made himself a vassal of the king of Castile, Henry III, who granted him title to all seven Canary Islands. Since past Castilian expeditions to the Canaries had been private ventures anyhow, the Castilian court must have seen no harm in offering its patronage while others did the work on its behalf; if the venture succeeded, all well and good, but if it failed Castile had at least asserted a claim that could be activated in future.

At some point the raiders acquired more ships. De la Salle set out on a voyage of reconnaissance, visiting Grand Canary where, as has been seen, he found the will of one of the thirteen friars from Telde. He traded advantageously with the Canarians, exchanging the dyestuff known as dragon's blood and vast quantities of figs for truck as simple as fish hooks, needles and old iron pots. Then he passed by an island called 'Enfer': the authors of *Le Canarien* played with the native word 'Tenerife' to make it sound like the French word for 'Hell', for volcanoes like Mount Teide were known to be the gateways to the Underworld. Then, at night, the crew arrived off La Gomera. They seized some Gomerans who were cooking and took them back to their ship; after this relations with the natives sharply deteriorated and they had to leave in a hurry without being able to take on water.[4] *Le Canarien* praised the natural resources of the islands (these would include slaves as well as dyestuffs and other goods); it presented them as worthwhile conquests, flowing with water and endowed with fine woods that could be profitably traded as lumber. The natives were seen as curious and, at times, noble people: the Auaritas of La Palma ate only flesh; the Gomerans 'speak from their lips', possibly a reference to the famous 'whistling language' whose existence was attributed by the chroniclers to the fact that the first settlers were exiles whose tongues had been cut out;[5] the handsome, noble Canarians decorated their bodies with printed and painted designs but mostly went naked, though women wore skirts made of skin to cover their genitals;[6] the Majoreros of Fuerteventura lived off excellent goat's cheeses, animal fat and dried meat, which they hung unsalted in their houses (rather smelly houses, in consequence), and were tall and strong, living together in tight communities, and 'very strong in their faith', worshipping in temples where sacrifices were offered; Lanzarote's settlements were more spread out, and the natives ate salt and barley, but the men went naked apart from a cloak and the women wore long leather shifts. These Majos were good fighters, too, and were skilled archers. In fact, the islanders were so skilled at throwing stones that 'it seems as if it were a bolt from a crossbow when they hurl it'; besides, they were very agile and could run like hares. They were well practised in warfare among themselves, and Fuerteventura, or 'Erbanie' as the chroniclers called it, was divided in half by a strong stone wall and contained 'the strongest *chasteaux* built in their way', presumably not so much 'castles' as fortified stockades.

While Béthencourt was away, then, de la Salle showed some initiative. He was embarrassed by his deputy who, during his absence, seized the Majo king while entertaining him to dinner; this caused unrest among the Majos, and even the French settlers were restive. When Béthencourt returned in 1404, de la Salle was not pleased to find that he had been left out of his colleague's arrangements with Castile. It seemed to de la Salle, in his exasperation, that there was only one option, though a risky one: he would go in person to Castile to plead his own cause. He failed outright, and disappeared from the islands, dying in obscurity in 1422. Left in charge without a rival, Béthencourt forged ahead, establishing a fragile dominion over Lanzarote and Fuerteventura, though mostly around the outer edges. In the interior, he had to depend on the highly variable goodwill of local rulers. Land was distributed to his followers, including family members such as his nephew Maciot. Béthencourt's achievement in capturing and settling El Hierro, the westernmost isle, with 160 Normans sent by Maciot, should not be belittled. Wisely he tried to create a ring around the two largest and most intractable islands, Tenerife and Grand Canary. Although a few women had accompanied the original voyage, there were now attempts to encourage more women to come from Europe; not surprisingly this proved difficult, and on El Hierro the Normans resorted, all too predictably, to violence, trying to seize twenty-three native women. Generally, however, the invaders learned to respect the native population as a doughty enemy. That did not mean they respected the right of the natives to live free of interference, however, for they were convinced of the justice of their Christian cause, quite apart from materialistic considerations.

Béthencourt and de la Salle had remembered their obligations to the Church, sending a message to Pope Benedict XIII in Avignon as soon as they had gained a foothold on 'the island called Lancelot', and securing a privilege in January 1403 that granted them the status of crusaders, in recognition of the work they would do in spreading the faith to unbelievers. This pope's enthusiasm was all the greater because he was in vigorous competition with his rival, the Roman pope, and the Great Schism was still ten years from resolution (not that this pope accepted its resolution; he went to live in state in a seaside castle at Peñíscola in the kingdom of Valencia, later made even more famous as the stage-set for the film of *El Cid*). Each pope tried to outdo his rival in extending benediction to great enterprises. The conquest of the outlying islands of the Ocean Sea might not appear to be a great enterprise, but Benedict, as spiritual lord of the world, made it plain in a bull issued in summer 1404 how important these islands were in the wider scheme of things: he had, he said, a paternal concern for all nations and all 'climates' of the world, and so, hearing that the Christian faith was spreading successfully in Lanzarote, he wished to erect there a bishopric of the Canary Islands that would be based in the stronghold of Rubicón. What must at this point have been little more than a French encampment of wood and earth was formally and pompously elevated to the rank of a cathedral city. So, within a few years of the extinction of the missionaries of Telde, the Canaries once again had a bishop. Curiously, reflecting perhaps the disorganisation of the Catholic Church at the time of the Great Schism, no one seems to have given any thought to the fact that the bishop of Telde, a Majorcan friar, was still alive and well and living in Aragon. Apparently he had never set out after his nomination in 1392, which saved him from the horrible fate of his fellow Franciscans on Grand Canary.

The clerical authors of *Le Canarien* had no doubt that the aim of the invasion of the islands was their conversion. In a passage boldly written in red ink the manuscript morosely says: 'These are the things to which we intend to introduce the Canarians living in the southern parts who are unbelievers [*mescreans*] and do not recognise their Creator and live in part like beasts and their souls are on the way to perdition.'[7] And the chronicle proclaims at the start that de la Salle and Béthencourt had travelled south 'for the honour of God and for the sustenance and enlargement of our holy faith', to islands 'inhabited by unbelievers of various religions [*loys*] and various languages . . . with the intention of converting them and bringing them to our faith'.[8] Béthencourt converted the king of southern Fuerteventura and his followers to Christianity; the king took the name Louis, and then another king arrived with forty-seven followers, this king taking the name Alfonse. Béthencourt carried three native men and one woman to France so they could acquaint themselves with French ways. But conversion entailed conquest too: the aim of the invaders was 'to conquer the land and place the people under the Christian faith'.[9] Béthencourt, his chroniclers insisted, was intent on opening up the route to the River of

Gold, and understood the strategic importance of his work in the Canaries for Christian interests in West Africa.

More is known about the endless struggle for control of the islands after 1402 than about the fate of the natives. For this, it is best to turn to the account of the islands by the architect Torriani two hundred years later. By his time the islands had to all intents been repopulated by Berber slaves taken from the opposite shore of Africa, and his information about the Majos and Majoreros was presented with some reservations: 'and this is as much as we have known about the ways of these barbarians,' he says of the people of Lanzarote. It was impossible to work out whom the idol in their circular temple represented, but he was intrigued to find that the custom of making shoes out of goatskins, which he attributed to the 'Maohs', had continued to his own day, except that nowadays they were made of camelskin. So too the Majoreros of Fuerteventura were a people of the past; they had lived simply and had not even known fire, for they cooked their meat by leaving it in the hot sun. They had a unique system of justice whereby it was not the perpetrator of a capital crime who was executed but a beloved member of his family, to make the criminal suffer all the more. And there were giant men on the island, for Torriani had seen the sepulchre of a man twenty-two feet tall; tallness had already been a theme in fifteenth-century accounts, emphasising the wondrous appearance of at least some islanders. *Le Canarien* had also mentioned people of 'great stature, strong and tough'.[10] Despite the conversions attributed to Béthencourt, by 1443 there were only about eighty Christians in Fuerteventura, according to Zurara, who had a keen interest in the island on behalf of the Portuguese. By this time, the surviving Majoreros seem to have taken to their stockades on the higher ground, leaving the edges to the Europeans.

The islands were poor and dry. The main struggle was to make ends meet; the gold of Africa seemed far away. French enthusiasm evaporated: Béthencourt passed his rights to his nephew, and Maciot also accepted the authority of the Peraza family in Spain, though he was willing to sell his notional rights in the islands again and again to any interested bidders. Still, this link to the Perazas helped prepare the ground for the defence of Castilian rights over the islands later in the fifteenth century. As time went by, Castilian settlers replaced the French, and Castilian became the language of government. The main legacy of Béthencourt was his name, which has spread widely in the Spanish-speaking world and beyond; all these Betancurs, Béthencourts and Betencourts may be descendants either of Jean de Béthencourt or of

Majoreros whom he and his followers converted to Christianity.[11] By 1440, Fernán Peraza had consolidated his control over the three islands originally taken by the French. He was then able to add La Gomera to his collection, though apparently on better terms for the natives, who found themselves treated as protected allies in recognition of their willingness to come to terms. La Palma, however, resisted forcefully, and Fernán's son died fighting there. Thus the programme of conquest remained in place, but progress was painfully slow. As Béthencourt and de la Salle had found, the costs were high and the returns on the investment very poor.

Prince Henry's Ambitions, 1424–36

Growing knowledge of the islands made them sound less like a demi-paradise. The elegiac descriptions of the individual islands in *Le Canarien*, emphasising the superb quality of the water, the fine trees and the agricultural potential of the islands, did not match the experience of the Europeans, who came to value only three products in trade: the dye orchil, seals slaughtered for their skins and the live bodies of enslaved islanders. But intractable, even unconquerable, as the islands seemed to be, they still attracted new claimants, of whom the most persistent was Prince Henry of Portugal (1394–1460), known as 'the Navigator', who became obsessed by the Canaries.[12] His energies were channelled through the crusading Order of Christ, which he governed, and which had succeeded to the Templar properties in Portugal. Throughout his life he juggled four objectives: an abiding desire to acquire lands for himself, for the Order of Christ and for Portugal in Morocco, despite counter-claims from Castile; a wish to explore and open up new uninhabited islands in the Atlantic (Madeira and the Azores); a determination to open up the coast of West Africa to trade and crusade; and, last but not least, a desire to establish dominion over the Canaries. To achieve all these objectives he spent beyond his means, irritated the Castilians (whom he regarded anyhow as sworn enemies), and trampled on the rights of those who stood in his way in Portugal.[13] Sir Peter Russell insisted that for Henry the Canaries were 'a prize worth winning for its own sake'.[14] They were seen as part of a wider assault on Islam, though everyone knew they were not Islamic; but this was the same Henry who told the pope that in acquiring empty Madeira he had scored a great victory against the Muslims – just as the early expeditions to the Canaries had been gazetted as part of a great campaign against 'Saracens'.[15] The obsession was not simply Henry's. The Portuguese had laid claim to the Canaries as a result of the expedition described by Boccaccio, in 1341, and maybe even earlier ones as well. They always resented Castilian or other claims; and it was this sense that they were being excluded from the prizes that lay open in the eastern Atlantic (including access to African gold) that propelled the Portuguese, and Henry most of all, to send ships down the coast of Africa. Without Luis de la Cerda and Jean de Béthencourt as stimuli, then, the Portuguese royal family might have concentrated its efforts on local targets such as Morocco, Granada and, indeed, enemy Castile.

The emergence of Portugal as a naval power at the end of the Middle Ages was in some senses predictable, in others surprising. The Portuguese kingdom lacked the rich *vegas* and *huertas*, valleys and gardens, that brought wealth to Andalucía and Valencia. There were one or two rare products that it did offer, notably ambergris, a secretion from the intestines of sperm whales, used then as now in perfume; this was washed up on the shores of Portugal. But as traffic between the Mediterranean and Flanders grew during the fourteenth century, Lisbon became a useful stopover for Genoese and other ships engaged in the trade in wool, alum (a fixative used in the cloth industry) and finished cloths. The Portuguese established a base at Middleburg in 1390, the first important *feitoría*, 'factory' or trading station, that they created overseas. Genoese merchants installed themselves in Lisbon, and a Genoese admiral helped create a Portuguese fleet in the early fourteenth century, both for trade and for crusade against the Muslims.[16] Links with the Mediterranean developed too, as sugar was brought from North Africa, while ties to Granada were sometimes close, because Spain's last Muslim kingdom shared Portugal's fear of Castilian ambitions.[17] Moreover, Portugal had a well-established fishing industry, which benefited from the intense demand for fish in Lent and on Fridays throughout the year, so that there was a constant traffic in fish small and large from the Atlantic to the Mediterranean.[18] Portugal developed its own commercial links as far afield as England, links that were reinforced by the Hundred Years' War, when a dynastic marriage between the royal houses of Portugal and England brought the English mother of Henry the Navigator to Lisbon. It is hardly surprising that, as they gained more confidence at sea, the Portuguese should have turned south towards Atlantic Africa and the Canaries as well as north towards Flanders and England.[19]

The first islands to attract Henry's interest, in the 1420s, were those of the Madeira archipelago; in the 1430s and 1440s he also developed a strong interest in the Azores, even further to the west. Even in his own time Madeira became a great centre of sugar production and was settled by large numbers of Italians as well as Portuguese, while the Azores, or 'Flemish islands', attracted many Flemings and were famous for dairy goods and wheat. Columbus' first father-in-law ruled Porto Santo, the sister island of Madeira, and the young Columbus conducted trade in sugar through Madeira.[20] But before these settlers arrived all these islands were uninhabited, and it was the Europeans who transformed them by planting wheat and sugar and breeding cattle. These Atlantic islands thus constituted a clean New World, the first New World, newer in fact than the New World that was soon to be discovered. Later, around 1460, a third set of uninhabited islands was discovered much further to the south, the Cape Verde Islands, and Portugal claimed these as well, and the royal privilege establishing Portuguese settlement in the Cape Verde Islands, dated 12 June 1466, grandly talked of the rivers, woods, fisheries, coral, dyes and mines on islands that could offer few of these resources; more importantly, the islanders could trade freely on the Guinea coast, and slave trading and raiding was to become their speciality.[21] The Cape Verdes became a vital supply station for fleets bound for America in the sixteenth century, just as the Azores became an important meeting point for fleets coming across from America and up from the Indian Ocean, on their way back to Iberia. But the Cape Verde Islands, as well as São Tomé on the equator (settled with Jewish children forcibly converted to Christianity), also became important slave stations, where black Africans were held until the slave ships were ready to cross the Atlantic and sell their human cargoes in the islands of the Caribbean. Sugar and slaves signalled the future of the Atlantic; but in Henry's day, when there was no knowledge of what lay across the ocean, it was understandable that attention focused on the islands closest to Africa, those that seemed to lie on the route to the River of Gold.

In 1424 Henry equipped an expedition to the Canaries. It seems to have been massive, if the sixteenth-century historian Barros (who was usually well informed) was right: Fernando de Castro was sent with thousands of soldiers, including cavalry, to attack Grand Canary. He repeated the mistake of assuming he would be fighting against a conventional enemy equipped with castles and modern weapons. But the expedition was a total failure. The clearest evidence of this can be found in the almost complete silence of his admiring biographer Zurara, who passed on from the subject as quickly as he could to other business: 'he also fitted out a very great armada against the Canary Islands, to show the natives there the way of the holy faith.'[22] In 1434 Prince Henry attacked the Canaries again, this time probably aiming at Tenerife; yet again the Portuguese were beaten off. The same year, encouraged by Portuguese captains who were returning from an expedition to the coast of West Africa, some Gomerans took passage in their caravels and gladly participated in raids on La Palma. Zurara stated that the aim of the expedition was to capture slaves on La Palma;[23] it was not a war of conquest, and the fleet only consisted of seven ships, one of which had been bound for the Guinea coast but joined the other six when its captain learned that there were rich pickings to be found in the Canaries. The caravels reached La Palma at dawn and the raiders decided that the easiest target was groups of young men and women who were tending sheep and goats amid the rocks. Taken by surprise, the shepherds and goatherds were forced to flee into a deep ravine that was so precipitous and dangerous, even for those who were accustomed to such terrain, that some of them fell from the rocks and died. They showered the invaders with stones and javelins, but in the end the Portuguese captured seventeen islanders, and were particularly pleased to carry off a vast woman who, they assumed, was a local queen.[24] However, it was all but impossible to carry off anything else such as the animals the islanders had been tending. This raid was probably the first close contact between La Gomera and La Palma for many centuries. But there was no sense that Canary islanders should make common cause against the Europeans. On the other hand, some Gomerans were apparently fascinated by European culture, and they found that an alliance with a Christian power brought some immunity from slave raiders. The Gomerans would remain the most enthusiastic collaborators with the Iberian conquerors throughout the fifteenth century. However, the captain of the seventh caravel, which had been bound for Guinea, considered that he was short of booty; he decided to seize twenty-one Gomerans, whom he despatched to Portugal, and whom an angry Prince Henry promptly sent back to La Gomera with gifts.

Henry wondered what combination of diplomacy and warfare would bring him the best results. The Castile-hating prince even wrote to King John II of Castile offering to rule the Canaries, presumably on behalf of Castile; this request must have raised a hollow laugh, especially since Henry's interest in Morocco was seen as undermining Castile's claims in that territory. A more obvious way forward was to win papal approval for the Portuguese claim to the islands. This was not straightforward. There was growing concern that Christian expeditions were doing more harm than good. Pope Eugenius IV received complaints from the bishop of Rubicón, who begged him to take action to defend the natives; some were already turning to Christianity, but they were being molested by Portuguese raiders. He told how one of Prince

Henry's expeditions had attacked a still-unconquered island, presumably Tenerife or Grand Canary, but had been beaten back. The raiders were determined not to lose the chance of profit, so they next attacked one of the islands where some of the natives had already converted (probably Lanzarote); they found settlements where Christian converts lived. Some they killed or wounded, and some they carried off as slaves; they also took their food and goods. In excuse, the Portuguese later informed the pope that the raiders had been starving because a supply ship failed to reach them. So they went in search of food, grabbing what they could. Henry, for his part, was very proud of this outcome: he boasted that he had won four hundred converts following his own expedition in 1434; it has been suggested that for 'converts' one should read 'slaves', Canary islanders transported back to a Christian life in Portugal, precursors of the black African slaves who, a decade later, would become a staple element in Portuguese trade in the eastern Atlantic. These contradictory reports led the pope to call a halt to expeditions against those Canary islands that had not so far been wholly or partially brought under Christian rule. It was not simply a political question; there was a moral issue that remained unresolved: did pagans possess the right to govern themselves without interference?

Nearly Wild Men, 1436–60

The Portuguese took advantage of the complaint against Henry's men to launch a vigorous diplomatic offensive at the papal court. Portugal would act as the agent of the Church, because only by the sword could these islands be tamed. But this meant that Portugal alone must be granted rights there; competition with other European powers would distract the Portuguese from their holy task. In 1436 King Duarte of Portugal, Henry's brother, wrote to Pope Eugenius IV, insisting that conversion was the driving force behind the Portuguese claim to the Canaries. He said that the natives were so wild that they prevented missionaries from living in their midst, and the pope was well aware that respected Christian authorities had long insisted on the absolute right of peaceful missionaries to work in pagan lands. Duarte said with some justice that there was no material gain to be had in ruling these poor and desolate islands.[25] For Duarte, the islanders were 'nearly wild men'; they lacked a common religion, 'nor are they bound by the chains of law; they are lacking normal social intercourse, living in the country like animals'.[26] They could not write, they did not use metals or money, and they did not even know how to cross the sea. In other words, their technological simplicity was used to justify their subjection. Duarte insisted that Prince Henry was not simply a grand slave raider: the prince had been doing his best to introduce proper laws and government to these folk. In other words, the claim that they lived according to natural law, and might therefore be permitted to go about their business unimpeded, was decisively rejected. Conquest was in their own best interests. Leaving them alone was condemning them to perdition. The pope was disconcerted. The issue depended on a broader question, that of the right to dominion of pagan rulers. He therefore put the matter out for consultation. Two canon lawyers, Antonio Minucci da Pratovecchio and Antonio Roselli, were recruited to examine the question.[27] They adhered in the main to the arguments of Pope Innocent IV two hundred years earlier, suggesting that pagan rulers could not be dispossessed simply because they were pagan, even if they were subject to papal overlordship, at least de jure, and even if there were circumstances in which the pope could intervene in the interests of all mankind, not simply of Christians.[28]

In the 1430s the papacy was under threat from the radical churchmen of the Council of Basel, who wished to limit papal authority. Papal universalism was on the defensive under Pope Eugenius, and it is no surprise that he took the opportunity to express his universal authority specifically by acting as arbiter of the fate of the Canary Islands. This aspect of the verdicts of Minucci and Roselli must have appealed to him. His arbitration also gave him a chance to look for friends in royal courts in Iberia. The problem was how to please Portugal without offending Castile. In September 1436 Eugenius decided that no harm would come of granting the islands to Duarte of Portugal; Duarte could press ahead with the evangelisation of all the Canary islanders. Eugenius did not distinguish between islands already partly settled and islands that were completely unconquered; indeed, he devoted a significant part of his papal bull authorising Portuguese conquests in the Canaries to the assertion not of Portuguese but of papal claims to dominion, over the world and its inhabitants. Thus the Canaries offered a platform for the declaration of a wider political manifesto.

Against Duarte there stood the indomitable Alonso de Cartagena, who was an expert at gaining the pope's ear. Alonso was the son of an equally remarkable rabbi from Burgos who had converted to Christianity and had become bishop of Cartagena and then of Burgos itself. He vigorously argued the Castilian case against Portugal. One issue now was which kingdom could claim the islands by virtue of proximity.[29] Alonso launched a vigorous campaign at the Basel Council, forcing Eugenius to retract his grant to Portugal after a mere two months. Eugenius, it is true, did not actually withdraw Portuguese rights but applied a version of the biblical law of the Medes and the Persians which, once issued, could not be revoked. He stated that he had now learned that Castile too had rights in this theatre, so Portugal could only enjoy the rights granted in September so long as they did not clash with those of others. In effect, this meant not at all. Clearly, supporting little Portugal against vociferous Castile created far too much trouble.

After this debacle, Henry for a time soft-pedalled on the question of the Canaries. He returned to his other enterprises, even though the Moroccan campaign was intensely irritating to Castile. He interfered in La Gomera, setting a pro-Portuguese faction of two chieftains named Bruco and Piste against a pro-Castilian faction consisting of the other two chieftains. Piste was delighted with his new allies from Portugal and resolved to visit Prince Henry, who received him with great pleasure and allowed him to stay with him for the rest of his life; Zurara met him at Henry's court.[30] Another way to gain power in the Canaries might be to dangle money in front of European landlords. In March 1448 the Portuguese offered Maciot de Béthencourt a large pension in return for Lanzarote; he accepted and retired to a quieter life in Madeira. Since Maciot had earlier also accepted the Perazas of Castile as his overlords, this new gesture was certain to inflame relations with Castile. Extraordinarily confident of its claims, the royal court in Lisbon sent Fernán Peraza a message telling him that he had to present himself at the Portuguese court to prove his claims in the Canaries.

There was an important sense in which all this did not matter to the kings of Castile and Portugal, whatever its effects on the native population of the Canaries. Henry was well known for his overweening ambitions. The Portuguese court did not allow him everything, insisting, for instance, that the Azores be shared with other royal princes. By the mid-1450s there were much bigger issues that would perhaps determine the future of the Iberian peninsula. King Henry IV of Castile was interested in marrying Juana, the sister of King Afonso V of Portugal. This would defuse the great rivalry between the two kingdoms, which Henry the Navigator had mischievously fostered for many years. What happened on the edge of the world was in this sense of limited importance and interest. But in another sense it had an enormous fascination to contemporaries. The debate about the ownership of the Canaries reawakened the interest of lawyers and theologians in the rights of pagan peoples. The Canaries posed new problems. They were remote; their inhabitants could not be classed as rebels, nor were they traditional enemies engaged in a Muslim counter-crusade, like the Nasrid sultans of Granada; they were brutish folk in need of Christian enlightenment. It seemed, then, that the negative message preached by Petrarch rather than the positive message associated with Boccaccio had won the debate over the nature of the islanders; and the outcome of that debate would determine their status and rights, and those of any other peoples who might be discovered out in the Atlantic.

CHAPTER 8

GOLD AND SLAVES, 1444–96

Black and Brown Slaves, 1444

The decision by Portugal to adopt the African rather than the transatlantic route in the hope of opening up trade with the Indies reflected years of experience in Africa, and knowledge of African peoples, for such a route would involve a close knowledge of eastern Atlantic waters. Portuguese caravels had been sailing along the coast of West Africa since 1434, in the service of Prince Henry and later in that of the Crown; they steadily increased their range until, by 1472, they had reached the south-eastern corner of West Africa, near the islands of São Tomé and Príncipe. But this was not a continuous process; Henry was easily diverted, and a disastrous campaign against Tangier took priority around 1437, while its messy aftermath, with his brother captured and imprisoned in Morocco, kept Henry quiet for a few more years. By 1440 the African traffic was running again. In the early days, slave raiding into the Canaries and into Africa were combined; Henry's ships were active around La Gomera in 1440 and 1442. As they mapped the coasts of Africa, the Portuguese left markers showing where their ships had been, crosses of wood (later, of stone) that still survive in some locations as far south as the Cape of Good Hope.[1] This was a way of staking a claim, literally; but the aim was not to establish mastery over the black peoples of Africa, merely over the waters linking them to Iberia, in the face of rival interests – interloping Castilians, Genoese, Aragonese, Flemings. In 1441 the Portuguese created their first offshore base on the western flank of Africa, at Arguim; it had a wooden tower and a chapel, where Mass was recited, to demonstrate that Prince Henry's endeavours had brought Christianity to the edges of black Africa.

Trade, then, rather than conquest, was what defined European relations with the Africans at this period. But trade was conducted in human beings as well as in inanimate goods. Domestic slavery was in fact a well-established feature of Mediterranean life in the late Middle Ages; in addition, young female slaves risked being treated as concubines. The sources of slaves varied from decade to decade: the northern coasts of the Black Sea, for instance, provided Genoa with thousands of Circassians whom they sold in Egypt (where some joined the elite Mamluk guard and even became sultan); Libya was an important source in the fourteenth century; the entire population of Muslim Minorca was sold into slavery by the island's Christian conquerors in 1287. Palermo, Majorca, Barcelona and Valencia were among the places to which those looking for a household slave would gravitate; Lisbon was soon to be added to the list. For the years after 1444 saw the Portuguese trade in black slaves become big business; they marked the beginning of the great slave trade that would last until the nineteenth century and that would constitute one of the most heartrending and shameful episodes in world history.[2] Still, it was only gradually that plantation slavery emerged. Most slaves in Africa were not sold to foreigners but instead lived in family-based communities, working the soil more as serfs offering labour and foodstuffs to their lords, rather than as slaves fully possessed by their masters. Others, including war captives, were sometimes sold on to the Portuguese.

On the other hand, slaves could be obtained by less formal means. Raiding rather than trading laid the foundation of the Atlantic slave trade: raids were launched into the Canaries and into Sanhaja territory on the western edge of Africa. In 1444, 240 Sanhaja Berbers were captured and sent back to Portugal on six caravels. They arrived in Lagos, capital of the western Algarve, where Henry himself was awaiting them – he had property in the area and often resided at Sagres nearby, while the town had already received slaves from the Canaries in the past. The Berbers seem to have been mixed together with a number of black slaves, whom the chronicler Zurara likened to creatures from Hell, 'spirits from the lowest hemisphere', describing them as 'deformed'. But even this hostile response was mitigated by Zurara's horror at the sight of families being split apart and the great distress this caused.[3] Still, Zurara piously thought that there was 'some consolation amid their current distress' in the opportunity to be saved as Christians, for 'many died in this faith', 'remembering that they too are of the generation of Adam'.[4] Such comments conveyed a mixed message about the human status of these folk. Aquinas had insisted that, while

slavery was permissible, the separate sale of parents and children, husbands
and wives, was not. Henry seems to have viewed this breach of Aquinas'
principles (if he was even aware of them) with equanimity: theory and practice stood a long way apart in the treatment of native peoples. He took his
cut, about fifty in all, some for himself, a few for the Order of Christ; a
couple of slaves were presented to the Church in Lagos.

   The opportunity now seemed to exist for Portugal to act as middleman in
the European slave trade. This aspiration was made real the next year, when
much larger numbers of slaves, this time mainly black, were taken directly to
Lisbon, exciting great wonder among the citizens, who came aboard the
caravels to see these strange people; so many flooded aboard that there was a
worry the ships would capsize. The slaves were then marched to Henry's
palace, thereby displaying to any sceptics what profits Henry's slow-maturing
schemes could produce. Before long Seville and Valencia were turning to
Portuguese suppliers in order to keep their slave markets stocked.[5] It is
thought that Henry and his agents were responsible for the import of up to
twenty thousand slaves from black Africa, the Berber lands facing the
Canaries and the Canaries themselves.

Africa in Western Eyes

The relationship with the African peoples was dominated by commerce, even
if the claim that the African expeditions were part of a great Christian crusade
was frequently reiterated. The Portuguese were keen to discover what
resources Africa could offer; as they moved south, they saw a world of towns,
mosques, river boats, metal foundries, horse traders and armed cavalry that
was much more easily recognisable than the simpler and very isolated worlds
of the seven Canary Island peoples. Perhaps nothing had quite as much reso-
nance in European ears as the news that the African states were ruled by
expansionist kings who possessed large mounted armies. In the Senegalese
interior opposite the Portuguese trading station at Arguim there lay a
successful empire, the Wolof state, which was ruled by elected kings or *burbas*
who could summon to arms 10,000 cavalry and 100,000 infantry, according
to Duarte Pacheco Pereira, writing in 1506; this was thus a polity worthy of
respect in European eyes. Also within West Africa, the powerful Songhay
state, which acquired control of Timbuktu in 1469, achieved its victories
partly on horseback, taking over the remnants of the far-famed empire of
Mali, whose easy access to vast gold supplies had impressed western

Europeans since the fourteenth century. These cavalry-based empires were thus the sort of entities Europeans might recognise as familiar, not totally dissimilar to their own ideas of political hierarchy and social organisation.

Christianity might not have arrived in West Africa, but Islam was present, though observers such as Alvise da Mosto insisted that it had laid only a light veneer over the lands to the south of the Sahara. This was actually a misconception, for there were vibrant Islamic revivals in West Africa in exactly this period: Ali, conqueror of Timbuktu, ruled over both Muslims and pagans, and in fact many of the slaves or serfs he settled on the land were pagan Mande from the south.[6] Further south still, in the area of Benin, with its massive and sophisticated capital city, were kingdoms into which Islam had not penetrated and where animist cults proliferated;[7] the Portuguese were fascinated by the evidence for wealthy cities and great kings in the interior, and the royal chronicler Pina reports how impressive the ambassador of Benin was: 'a man of good speech and natural wisdom'.[8] It was in this area that the Portuguese established the trading station of Elmina in 1482, a collection point for gold and slaves.

Vivid descriptions of the daily life of African peoples were included in da Mosto's record of his travels in the service of Henry the Navigator during the 1450s. He readily fitted much of what he saw into European categories.[9] Arab and Berber priests had impressed on the rulers the importance of living according to a set of 'laws'; da Mosto had said earlier of the nomads of the Sahara: 'those who inhabit this desert have no religion, nor any natural king.'[10] What shone through da Mosto's account was his conviction that here and elsewhere the people could be won to Christianity with only a moderate amount of work. Da Mosto, as a member of a Venetian business family, was not surprisingly fascinated by the resources of the lands he visited in West Africa. And yet his overall picture was of poor kingdoms, producing only modest goods, ignorant of money. He visited a market in a field and watched as Africans bartered cotton, oil, millet, wooden bowls, mats made of palm leaves and other simple goods. The most marvellous object in the market was himself: the Africans rubbed his skin with their spittle to see if his white colour would come off; they were astonished by his short grey woollen cloak, for wool was apparently a novelty, and by his black damask doublet (no doubt he was slowly roasting in these clothes).[11] Other Western goods fascinated them: candles were unknown in this land; they thought that a sailor's pipes were a strange singing animal; they even decided that the portholes on the Portuguese ships were eyes; they were amazed by crossbows and still more by guns, especially when da Mosto fired a cannon – the noise scared them, and when they heard that a cannon could mow down more than a hundred men, they averred that it was the Devil's invention.

It was true that in some places royal courts were much simpler in style than their European equivalents. King Budomel peregrinated from village to village, sowing his seed at a prodigious rate, with about nine wives in each village, while the wives were attended by five or six younger girls whom he also treated as his concubines. Budomel asked da Mosto if he knew some way of increasing his sexual potency so that he could have relations with many women in succession, and even offered a great reward; he thought that Christians were experts in many things, but here da Mosto seems to have failed him.[12] If da Mosto is to be believed, Budomel observed that God must be on the side of the Christians, because his people were so poor and the Christian kingdoms were so rich. But he could not risk conversion because he believed he would lose power if he did so.[13]

Some commentators made very negative remarks. Antonio Malfante was an intrepid Genoese who made his way across the Sahara to Timbuktu in 1444. He claimed to have encountered one tribe who 'act carnally like beasts', for in his view there were no laws of incest and fathers had intercourse with their daughters, as did brothers with their sisters.[14] The black peoples 'are unlettered, and without books', but 'they are great magicians, evoking by incense diabolical spirits'. Da Mosto called Africans 'lascivious'. Overall, the image of the Africans was thus a mixed one, combining the recognisable with the exotic, legends of great wealth (the king of Mali who tethered his horse to a massive lump of gold) with accounts of poor, dust-blown villages.[15] Africa did not conjure up a pastoral idyll, as the Canaries did in the minds of some writers; nor were the inhabitants lacking in sociability, in the way Petrarch described the Canary islanders. These were lands on the edge of the known world, connected to that world – a very different experience for European visitors from the remote islands of the eastern and later the western Atlantic.

As the slave trade developed, black Africans suddenly became a familiar sight on the streets of Lisbon and other European cities. There were certainly ambiguities in the way white Europeans reacted to blackness: on the one hand black was a negative colour, but on the other Caspar, one of the three Magi, was portrayed as a black king in Flemish, Spanish and Italian paintings of the Adoration produced at this time. Although some of the black people seen in Iberia were free, most of these were freedmen or freedwomen who had arrived as slaves; unfreedom seemed to characterise black people in the eyes of those Europeans who encountered them, whether as slave traders, slave owners or passers-by.[16] From this developed a sense that their inferiority was inherent. And yet in the mid-fifteenth century the Portuguese king had been content to treat with the African kingdoms as partners in trade and politics; the African king Bemoy was received at court. In other words, there were many variables in the relationship between Europeans and black Africans, but the starting point was the assumption that they were unquestionably the descendants of Noah's son Ham, and so formed part of the family of mankind. Ham, it is true, had a bad reputation in the Bible, and the argument was heard in Spain that his descendants were tainted, even, perhaps, condemned to servitude because Ham had mocked his drunken and naked father.[17] But they were still family, even if they were black sheep. Elsewhere in the world, more 'primitive' native peoples posed a more persistent problem.

Castile Claims its Share, 1479–96

From 1474 to 1479 a war of succession raged in Castile: King Afonso of Portugal launched invasions in support of his wife, Juana, legitimate heiress of King Henry 'the Impotent' of Castile, though eventually the usurper Isabella (Henry's sister) and her husband, Ferdinand of Aragon, gained the upper hand. In the struggle for Castile, the Atlantic islands were merely a side issue, though rival fleets ranged as far south as the Cape Verde Islands. Still, claims over the islands needed to be settled, and when, in September 1479, Portugal and Castile made peace at Alcáçovas, the two kingdoms agreed to divide the Atlantic islands between them, with Portugal securing all the previously uninhabited islands, and Castile only the Canaries. In essence the treaty recognised the *de facto* conquests as *de jure* ones, including in addition islands in the Canaries that were still to be conquered (Grand Canary and Tenerife), and islands that might yet be found by the Portuguese. Castile did not rush to make its claims effective in the unconquered parts of the Canaries. Once they were at peace with Portugal, the Castilian monarchs were fully committed to an expensive war against Granada, an opportunity to enhance their prestige at home and abroad.[18] Neither Columbus' plans, in reality not very expensive, nor dreams of island conquest in the far-off Canaries, could distract them for long until the Alhambra was in their hands. Therefore any campaigns in Grand Canary

or Tenerife would ideally have to be organised and equipped by conquistadores able to raise funds on their own, in what were effectively private
acts of conquest.

Behind these events a transformation was taking place within the economic
life of Spain. From the thirteenth century onwards, the maritime trade of the
Spanish kingdoms had been dominated by the Catalans, from their bases in
Barcelona, Majorca and Valencia. Despite crises, this trading network
survived largely intact into the reign of Ferdinand of Aragon, who well understood its importance to his finances.[19] The rise of the ports of Atlantic Spain
was a slower process, more or less simultaneous with the emergence of
Portugal as a trading power. The northern Spanish ports benefited from the
raw materials of the Spanish hinterland – from plentiful supplies of Spanish
iron and wool. With the conquest of Córdoba and Seville in the thirteenth
century, the Castilians also had access to the rich agricultural produce grown
in the fertile soils watered by the Guadalquivir. Finally, as in Portugal,
Genoese admirals helped the Castilians set up an efficient royal fleet. If
for no other reason, naval rivalry with Portugal would propel the Castilians
southwards to the Canary Islands.

Attempts to establish mastery over Grand Canary had already been gathering pace under Henry the Impotent. The soldier Diego Garcia de Herrera
married into the Peraza family and by 1468 had established a fort on the edge
of Grand Canary. He had a surprisingly lucky turn of fate when a Portuguese
raiding party arrived the same year, hoping to make gains in the Canaries; in
the event, he persuaded them to enter his own service, and he even married
his daughter to their leader. Loyalties were easily transferable in this island
world. The Canarians began to organise themselves better as the threat grew.
They forced back the European invaders, having cleverly copied Spanish
weapons; but the swords and shields they used were made of hardened wood.
Abreu Galindo describes how one *guanarteme* holed up European forces but
then chivalrously allowed them to leave, guaranteeing their safety by
pretending to be their hostage so that his own followers would not attack the
conquistadores. Once everyone was out of the stronghold, he threw a great
party for both sides. This story, whatever its basis in fact, forms part of the
tradition among the better-disposed European writers of seeing the Canary
islanders as paragons of chivalry, perfectly capable of operating according to
the ethical code of Spanish knighthood. The story also suggests that some
Canarian leaders were willing to co-operate with the invaders. In 1476 a deal
was struck with the Spaniards: the Canarians guilelessly allowed an 'oratory'

to be built, which looked strangely like a fortress; and they also agreed to trade relations.

It was at this point that Ferdinand and Isabella became worried by developments. They knew that the islands could become the theatre of a secondary conflict with the Portuguese, with whom they had still to make peace. They therefore paid five million *maravedís* to Diego Garcia de Herrera so that he would go away (less than it sounds: the *maravedí* was a heavily devalued coin). Next, thirty cavalry and nine hundred infantry arrived from Spain on 22 June 1477, under the command of an Aragonese soldier named Juan Rejón; among the troops was Alonso de Lugo, the future conqueror of Tenerife. They landed with the intention of reoccupying Herrera's fortress, now destroyed, and making it their centre of operations; but as they marched there, 'they were accosted by a woman in the Canarian dress, who asked them, in the Castilian language, whither they were going?' She told them that their route was long, the road was bad and broken by precipices; 'but that at a small distance from the place where they then were, was a commodious plain, with a rivulet of good water, plenty of fire-wood, with palms and fig-trees, from whence they might have access to all the principal places of the island'. When they reached the place she had pointed out to them, the woman had vanished, and Juan Rejón was convinced that this was no Canarian woman at all (after all she had spoken to them in their own language) but St Anne, to whom he was very devoted.[20] In any case, the palmy place where they settled became the city of Las Palmas, commanding a narrow peninsula at the top of Grand Canary and giving access to native centres nearby, most importantly Telde. At first, Las Palmas was simply a fortified wooden encampment; the natives of the interior continued to resist and even to defeat Spanish armies. St Anne's advice had not been so good after all; the Spaniards were confined to the northern tip of the island and even a victory over the *guanartemes* Semidan and Doramas did not enable them to break out permanently. Rejón clearly had to be replaced: he was politely told to go and conquer Tenerife and La Palma instead. In 1480 Ferdinand and Isabella appointed a new commander, Pedro de Vera, who had all the qualities needed for this enterprise: he was brave but thuggish, and he also proved successful, killing Doramas in battle (as he died, the *guanarteme* was baptised with water collected in a Spanish helmet).[21] The latter's successor appeared amenable to Spanish demands and was also baptised, going to live among the Christians for a while. But this was a ruse, for he wanted to learn the military secrets of his enemies, and when he was back among his people he turned against the Spaniards, who in any case were quarrelling among themselves; Rejón was still on the island, making difficulties for his successor. Native Gomeran mercenaries were brought to Grand Canary, since Pedro de Vera believed they were actually more reliable than European troops. The Gomerans had less sophisticated weapons, but they were tall and strong, and much better suited to fighting in the jagged landscape of the interior of Grand Canary.

The real Spanish breakthrough occurred finally in 1482, when a force under Alonso de Lugo took the Canarian stronghold of Gáldar and even captured the formidable *guanarteme* Semidan while he was asleep. Semidan was sent to Toledo where he decided that the time had come to acknowledge Spanish superiority; baptised under the name 'Fernando Guanarteme', with the king as his godfather, he was rewarded by Ferdinand and Isabella with a grant of land in the Canarian interior. This gesture was typical of the policy of generations of Spanish kings before them: conquered Muslim rulers had sometimes been allowed to retain local authority over their own people, within a restricted area. Of course, they hoped that Don Fernando Guanarteme would now convince the other *guanarteme* that he too should submit; but the political history of the island had to a large extent consisted of rivalries between *guanartemes*, and the Spaniards were rebuffed by showers of toughened javelins and darts. Still de Vera persisted, and when he captured a place called Ansite with the help of Fernando Guanarteme and Canarian troops loyal to Don Fernando, in April 1483, the conquest was to all intents at an end. The high priest of Gáldar accepted baptism, the inhabitants of Ansite, six hundred men and fifteen hundred women, accepted Spanish rule, and their leader saved his honour by leaping to his death off a high rock. There was some trouble in the mountains in 1485, but now that Fernando Guanarteme was on the European side, he could be sent to deal with the troublemakers.

No doubt the conquest could have been achieved much faster if the invaders had had proper support from Castile. But resistance had proved to be serious and sustained. Native weapons could prevail against modern Spanish armaments. The agility of the lightly armed and lightly clad Canarians, and their knowledge of the craggy landscape, gave them immense advantages. They seemed in the main to be unimpressed by what Spanish civilisation had to offer. The key to conquest was, predictably, the division of the enemy: the defection of Semidan was the guarantee that before long Grand Canary would fall under Spanish rule. But unconquered Tenerife was still larger and still more precipitous, and there were even more petty kings with whom the Spaniards would have to deal. Some had quite large armies at their disposal: Tmodat of Taoro is said to have been able to summon seven thousand men. Espinosa thought the island was home to 200,000 sheep and goats, and the size of its population and resources made it both an attractive target and a difficult land to conquer.[22] Herrera's attempt to proclaim Castilian sovereignty in 1464 was accompanied by the creation of a base at Añaza, which was a natural source of tension; five Guanches were executed for attacking a Castilian soldier, and the local *mencey*, with a thousand of his men, chased the invaders away. Tenerife was free of invasion for some years, though not of slave raiders if the appearance of Guanche slaves in Spain and Madeira is any guide to what was happening.[23]

Ferdinand and Isabella were still preoccupied with the costly war for Granada, and then with arrangements for the resettlement and good government of the former Muslim kingdom. This meant that in Tenerife, as had been the case on the other islands, there existed a promising opportunity for someone who was willing to raise the cash to pay for a war of conquest without the help of the Crown. The Crown would continue to claim dominion and its share of the spoils, the latter to be delivered once conquest was effected. Since Juan Rejón, the failed conqueror of Grand Canary, had not taken up the further offer of a licence to conquer Tenerife and was now dead, Ferdinand and Isabella granted that right to Rejón's old foe Alonso de Lugo instead. Espinosa relates that de Lugo agreed to pay for the conquest himself.[24] He took over a thousand men from Grand Canary to Tenerife, landing at Santa Cruz in May 1493, and making contact with the lord of Guimar, the owner of the Candelaria image and shrine.[25] While this *mencey* seemed well enough disposed to de Lugo and might prove a powerful ally, a visit de Lugo received from Bencomo, *mencey* of Taoro, was much less satisfactory. Bencomo was scornful of the demand that he turn Christian and seemed uninterested in what Christianity had to offer; he saw no reason to accept de Lugo and the king and queen of Castile as his masters. It was an attitude that reflected the deep suspicion that had built up in the Guanche communities after decades of European raids. Bencomo was confident: the Guanches knew that they were capable of beating Spanish armies in the field, and indeed Bencomo and his allies routed de Lugo's men, many of whom fled from the island. The *mencey* of Taoro appears in Espinosa's account of these events as a chivalrous prince who guaranteed the safe passage of the defeated Spaniards, while the Spaniards are portrayed as truly treacherous: de Lugo apparently enslaved and despatched to Spain three hundred Guanches from

Guimar who had arrived to fight on his side, and it was only on the emphatic orders of Ferdinand and Isabella that they were eventually freed.[26]

Guanche attacks on Christian strongholds grew more persistent. De Lugo realised he could no longer maintain control even of the small areas he thought he had subdued, and he withdrew with his tail between his legs in summer 1495. Nonetheless, he did not abandon his plans. The king and queen were still unwilling to become directly involved, but there were other sources of aid: first, Italian businessmen interested in the opportunities for profit that a conquered Tenerife might offer (profit from trade, from acquiring and selling Guanche slaves, from setting up sugar factories, from acquiring estates) and, second, Spanish noblemen with a tradition of pursuing their own foreign policy with the blessing of the Crown – most significantly, the duke of Medina Sidonia.[27] These investors provided de Lugo with six ships, over a thousand men, seventy horses and supplies. But they are said to have faced up to ten times as many armed Guanches in northern Tenerife. In fierce fighting 1,700 Guanches were killed, but only forty-five Castilian troops. This victory re-established the credentials of de Lugo, and the *mencey* of Guimar hastened to protest his obedience, sending troops of his own in support of the invaders, though they were of rather less use after the victory than they might have been before it.

In late 1495 the struggle for control of Tenerife was finely balanced. The Spaniards began to run out of vital supplies; the duke of Medina Sidonia forwarded chickpeas and flour from Spain. What also arrived from Spain was disease, and it was the lack of Guanche resistance to this, as in other New Worlds, that probably did most to break down their military resistance. In addition, small hunting parties, armed with crossbows and primitive muskets, searched out Guanche contingents and began to wreak havoc.[28] By summer 1496 several *menceys* had begun to negotiate a surrender, and the last four *menceys* to resist submitted on 29 September 1496. As in Grand Canary, this did not mean all resistance was at an end, but what remained could be contained within the highlands, and to all intents and purposes the territorial conquest of the Canaries was now complete. If one takes the Norman-Poitevin expedition of 1402 as the starting point, it had lasted nearly a century.

Although the territorial conquest was complete, the battle continued for the conquest of the islanders' souls: the Franciscan Alonso de Bolaños was engaged, on and off, in missionary activity in the 1460s and 1470s, with the help of a papal licence; it seems that one of his tasks was to introduce the 'mechanical arts' that the natives lacked. Felipe Fernández-Armesto has observed that he and his fellow missionaries represented a relatively positive approach to native society, seeking its spiritual and material improvement but emphasising that it possessed natural virtue. Against this, other observers were horrified by what they heard of the natives, perpetuating the negative outlook of Petrarch: a year after the final fall of Tenerife Hieronymus Münzer wrote about the bestial appearance of the islanders, while the royal chronicler Bernáldez was one of those who saw them as naked barbarians, idol-worshippers and enemies of the Christian religion; he also thought that the nakedness of the Canarians was proof of their 'bestial' ways.[29]

The Canary islanders had to adjust to the experience of rule by Spaniards, who divided much of the land up among themselves.[30] Madeira provided a model for the colonisation of subtropical islands, even if it lacked a native population; a sugar mill was built by de Lugo on Grand Canary in 1484, in other words the very moment the island was pacified. The Genoese appear to have been most active in providing essential capital for setting up sugar plantations and factories (they were already a powerful force in Seville, to which they exported Canary islanders as slaves), but this activity made them the focus of intense xenophobia in the islands, as also in Spain.[31]

Disease had set off a calamitous decline in the native population, especially on the easternmost islands; the answer was to import brown and black slaves from the facing shores of Africa, many of whom were Muslims.[32] Ferdinand and Isabella were worried that in consequence the Muslim population might grow dangerously large, so they discouraged the arrival of free Muslims and encouraged instead the importation of black slaves, who were often put to work in the sugar factories.[33] The native islanders who had been made captive in the wars of conquest, or for other reasons, tended to work as domestic slaves, and were often deported from their native island to another one, or to Spain itself – Seville soon developed a small Canary islanders' quarter. This treatment recalls what was beginning to happen in the 'New Canaries' which Columbus had discovered far to the west, nearly four years before the surrender of Tenerife.

PART III

WESTERN HORIZONS
The Peoples, Islands and Shores of the Western Atlantic

CHAPTER 9

FROM THE OLD CANARIES TO THE NEW CANARIES, 1492

The Island of the Holy Saviour, 12 October 1492

On 3 August 1492 Christopher Columbus at last set out with his single *nao* and two smaller caravels from Palos, carrying his letters to the Eastern potentates, with the blessing and financial support of the king and queen, various Italian backers and the rather less enthusiastic citizens of Palos, who were obliged to settle a fine they owed the Crown by fitting out two of his ships. Taking advantage of the rights assigned to Castile, he made course 'for the Canary Islands, which are in the Ocean Sea',[1] from where he proposed to sail due west into the sunset; passing Tenerife, where he saw Mount Teide belching fire, Columbus put in at La Gomera. His tiny fleet attracted interest there. Columbus, or (to give him his grand title) Don Cristóbal Colón, Admiral of the Ocean Sea, was graciously received by Doña Inés Peraza, who introduced him to a group of Spaniards who lived on El Hierro, the westernmost island in the archipelago. They told Columbus exactly what he wanted and expected to hear. They insisted that 'every year they saw land to the west of the Canaries in the direction of the setting sun'.[2] Thus the visit to La Gomera provided Columbus not merely with the meat, water and wood that he needed for his great voyage; in the Canaries he also acquired what seemed to him certain knowledge that land lay over the horizon. And so, on 6 September, he set out again, full of expectation; but his own energy was not matched by that of the wind and he was becalmed between La Gomera and Tenerife, which was especially embarrassing because he had news from a caravel that had just arrived from El Hierro that the Portuguese were intruding into Spanish waters and were keen to arrest him.

Columbus avoided the Portuguese men of war. It was only on Saturday 8 September that 'the northeast wind began to blow'[3] and he was at last able to make headway; even then he deliberately told his crew that each day they were travelling less far than was actually the case so that they would not be alarmed at the thought of travelling so far out of sight of land into uncharted waters. There is no need here to chronicle all the events of the voyage. Columbus was an observant navigator, anxious to see in the sky and water proof that his journey was taking him towards either islands or the great Asiatic mainland; he had a practised seaman's knowledge of water birds, so that every patch of seaweed and every flight of birds was studied intently. It was birds, las Casas said, that had led the Portuguese to the islands they had discovered in the Atlantic.[4] In addition, 'they saw a whale, which is a sign that they were near land, because whales always swim close to it'.[5]

The idea that Columbus continually faced rebellion on board is an exaggeration. There were moments when he exasperated his crew, who included some rough and unsavoury types, and there was apparently talk of throwing him overboard and of then reporting to the Spanish court that he had overbalanced while disporting himself with his fancy navigational instruments. The crew were certainly worried at the prospect of sailing in search of unknown lands; what worried them even more was the lack of contrary winds to take them back to Spain, a plausible reason why others had gone west and never been seen again. In early October, observing the birds and seaweed, Columbus was satisfied they were close to the islands that lay off the coast of Asia; they had merely to chance upon one. But Columbus preferred to press on, for turning south to find the islands would distract him from what was still his main objective, the Asiatic mainland or Japan. His direction of sail would carry him a little above the point where Japan was most likely to lie, in his opinion; on 6 October Pinzón urged him to head south-west to Cipangu, for that was the essential first stage in any attempt to open up Asian waters, and eventually he turned the ships in that direction.

By 9 October the crew were beginning to grumble loudly. But a couple of days later the signs of land were clear for all to see: staffs floating in the sea that seemed to have been fashioned by human beings; land grasses and a branch with some sort of fruit still attached, as well as the ubiquitous seaweed. Finally, after night had fallen, Columbus thought he could discern a light in the far distance, rather 'like a wax candle that was being raised and lifted'.[6] He promised a prize – a silk doublet and a 10,000 *maravedí* pension – to the sailor who first sighted land. Columbus appears in the logbook as the person who valiantly insisted that the light was real, and that they were close to land, in the face of the scepticism of his sailors. This enabled him to claim for himself the prize for seeing land, while the first actually to do so was a sailor from the Sevillian suburb of Triana named Rodrigo. As the explorers closed in, two hours after midnight, they realised that they were two leagues off the coast of an island, which they could make out amid the faint shadows of the night. The ships took in sail and hove to until dawn. It was early on the morning of 12 October 1492. Columbus' logbook gives no clue to the emotions of the admiral and his crew, but all the other evidence about Columbus' assumptions and behaviour makes it plain that he and his men combined warm satisfaction at finding land with trepidation at the thought of what might be found on the land – monstrous men or animals – and a belief that they had reached the myriad of offshore islands close to Asia. In fact, they had reached the Bahamas, or the Lucayos, to use the native name.

The first European encounter with the inhabitants of the Caribbean started in a small way and was strikingly similar to the first such encounters in the Canaries. Setting aside the visits of the Norsemen to 'Vinland' in the early eleventh century, where they met the native 'Skraelings', this is the first known contact in human history between Europeans and Americans.[7] It was a contact that had quite enormous consequences, as the short-lived and largely forgotten Viking settlements in Newfoundland did not.[8] And even if, as the conspiracy theorists insist, the Portuguese, the Bristolians or others knew about America already, there is no evidence of contact between these supposed pioneers and the native population, no evidence of an attempt to claim dominion over the 'Indies', no evidence of native Americans and their artefacts being brought to Europe before Columbus' first voyage of 1492–3.

At dawn the low-lying, lush island came clearly into view. The sailors saw pink, sandy beaches, green trees and water, as well as fruit trees; the sight of fresh water was a delight after the long sea journey. It is not desperately important to know which island this was, though the native name was Guanahaní; the general opinion is that it was the island long known as Watling Island, now renamed San Salvador.[9] Later the explorers observed that it had a large lake in the middle, and was flat and well-wooded; assuming it has been correctly identified with the modern San Salvador, it would be truer to say that the island had a whole network of lakes and cays, which now carry such names as 'Granny Lake', 'Duck Pond' and 'Gold Dust Pond', amounting to about one-third of the land area of the island, which is about ten miles by five in size. 'Soon they saw naked people',[10] and it was the encounter with the latter that determined what happened next. The three captains – Admiral Christopher and the Pinzón brothers – went ashore with

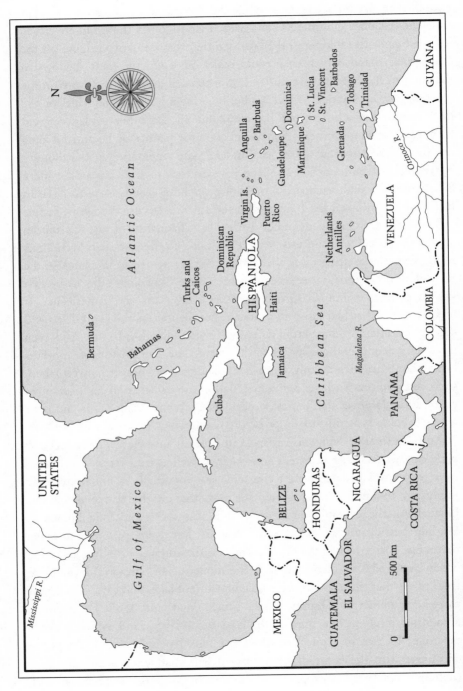

The modern Caribbean

royal banners, already intent on claiming the island for Castile and for Christ. This was odd, for they had no idea what sort of place they had reached or who else (such as the Great Khan of China) might regard it as his territory. Or rather, as their behaviour made plain, they saw Guanahaní as in very many respects another Canary island, similar in size and inhabited by similar folk. Accompanied by the Crown representative, Rodrigo Sánchez de Segovia, and by the notary who had travelled with the fleet and who duly recorded all these events in notarised documents, Columbus declared 'that he was taking, and had in fact taken, possession of that island, for his lords the king and queen'. A name had to be found, and the island was christened 'Holy Saviour', San Salvador. Meanwhile, natives of the island began to gather round Columbus and the Spaniards, wondering at the arrival of ships quite unlike the long dug-out boats with which they were familiar, and marvelling at this bizarre ceremony. At this stage they were inclined to think that the ships were giant birds and that the Europeans were gods who had flown to their island from the place of sunrise.

In any case, the inhabitants were 'people', not dog-headed monstrous races. Columbus wrote in his letter to his financial backer and patron, the *converso* courtier Luís de Santángel: 'On these islands until now I have not found any monstrous men, as many expected; rather, they are all people of very beautiful appearance.'[11] One could be sure that they were fully human in form because, male and female, they went around entirely naked, though at this stage he had seen only young men, and one small girl. The men were 'very well made', their bodies were 'very beautiful' and their features were very agreeable too. They had thick, short hair, in a basin cut, though at the back they wore a long pony-tail, which they refused to shear; they had unusually broad foreheads, as well as straight legs and trim stomachs. Rather than wearing clothes, they painted their faces or even their entire bodies (as he must have been aware, this was also the practice in the Canaries): white, red and black were all favoured. But even if they painted themselves black, their natural colour was much lighter: 'they are the colour of the Canary islanders, neither black nor white';[12] 'none of them are dark, but rather the colour of Canary islanders, nor should one expect anything else, since this island is in the same latitude as the island of El Hierro in the Canary Islands'[13] – a clear expression of the common belief that skin colour was simply determined by latitude, and that the closer one came to the equator and to the Sun, the more one would be burned brown and then black.

Simple and Beautiful People, October 1492

The reactions of Columbus have been preserved in his logbook or diary. This, addressed to the king and queen, was rather more than a daily journal of winds, currents and distances travelled. It was also an opportunity to advertise his talents, to express his opinions about what he found and why the Castilian monarchs should continue to support his enterprise; it was therefore filled with lyrical passages about the landscapes he saw and the gentle, docile people he met. It was revised as he travelled, for some passages were clearly rewritten in the light of slightly later knowledge, and comments about the lands he had discovered would be repeated from page to page, as if he were not quite sure where to drop them into the text. Very often an event ascribed to a particular day is then described in similar terms the next day or the day after. The conclusion must be that the logbook he finally presented to the king and queen was worked together from a series of more or less parallel drafts, notes and scribbles, copied, recopied and then merged not very neatly. This is only the beginning of the problem. Columbus' original logbook has vanished, but a partial transcription by his admirer Bartolomé de las Casas survives from the 1520s. Las Casas conveniently distinguished between the passages he was quoting verbatim (often expressed in the first person) and those that were merely a digest of the logbook (expressed in the third person). He also incorporated parts of Columbus' logbook in one of his histories of the Indies, but here he intruded more personal comment.

Columbus' son Ferdinand, in an attempt to defend Christopher's increasingly battered reputation, wrote a life of his father that also made extensive use of the logbook. In addition, several of Christopher Columbus' letters have survived, such as the letter to his Aragonese backer Luís de Santángel, as well as a copy of a letter to Ferdinand and Isabella in similar terms, which only came to light in the 1980s and makes many of the same points (if, as some have asserted, it is not genuine, it does not change the picture in any significant measure). So, once one has established which passages Columbus wrote, his voice can be heard, though with some outside interference. Purists might then argue that this is, after all, only Columbus' account, and that an independent writer needs to be found who can 'verify' his statements. That is not easy to do. Peter Martyr, the Italian humanist who flourished at the Spanish court, wrote elegantly about Columbus' voyages, but never visited the Americas and based himself on Columbus' descriptions of the New World. Everyone read Columbus; there was nothing else to read, at least in order to find out what had happened during the first of his four voyages. Therefore it is best to make a virtue of this dependence on the admiral's own views. If one is trying to establish how Europeans saw the native peoples of the Atlantic, and how successfully they separated myths about exotic peoples from the sober reality of what they encountered, then Columbus' writings are a superb source of information. In fact, they are much more useful for this purpose than they are for gauging exactly where he landed or what routes he took between the islands.

Columbus' first reactions to native peoples in the Americas provided a matrix into which all subsequent encounters were then fitted. As his continual reluctance to accept that he was anywhere other than the edges of Asia suggested, once Columbus made up his mind he could not easily be shifted. So it was with his view of the American Indians. Thus Columbus wrote of the natives of Guanahaní: 'they were a people who would be delivered and converted to our faith better by love than by force.'[14] These, las Casas insisted, were the 'exact words' of Columbus in his logbook, and they were bound to appeal to las Casas himself, for they expressed what he admired in Columbus, even if he regretfully accused Columbus, elsewhere in his vast works, of failing to work hard enough for the salvation of the souls of the Indians. Columbus asserted that they were simple in their way of life, accepting as gifts, in token of friendship, 'red caps and glass beads that they put around their necks and many other things of little value with which they were very pleased'.[15] The friendship between Columbus and the natives was sealed when they came swimming out to the ships (rather as the Canary islanders had swum out to the Portuguese ships a century and a half earlier), bringing gifts of their own: 'parrots, spun cotton in little balls, javelins, and many other things'.[16] They were willing to accept the simplest trifles: bits of broken pottery or glass; one could exchange sixteen balls of spun cotton for three small Portuguese coins. On one of the islands the ships visited during this voyage, a sailor secured a handsome gift of gold in return for a shoelace. Excavations on San Salvador have produced a few beads that appear to have been traded by the Spaniards; one would like to think that they date from Columbus' visit and that they prove the identity of Guanahaní as the modern San Salvador, though unfortunately that would be reading too much into the almost microscopic evidence. Having run out of things to offer, the natives of Guanahaní began to swim to the ships, take what they could and jump into the water to carry their loot away. But this was not evidence that they were thieves or animal-like: 'these people are very gentle'; 'they think they should take nothing unless they give something in return, but they are embarrassed that they can offer nothing.'[17] 'It seemed to me that they were a poor people in every way.'[18] This was not just a comment on their way of life, but also a warning that large amounts of gold would not be found on their island. They wore gold ornaments in their noses, but cotton was the main local product.

Columbus' logbook entries for 12 and 13 October portrayed a people ignorant of iron and heavy weapons, though they used javelins with tips made of sharp fish teeth. They had big boats, made of hollowed-out tree trunks, 'marvellously crafted', some of which could carry several dozen people.[19] In search of a word with which to describe these canoes, he repeatedly called them *almadías*, the same word that the Portuguese used for the native boats they saw in West Africa, where he had travelled as a young man. Scars on their bodies indicated that they were used to war, even with their simple weapons, and they complained (apparently in sign language) that they were the victims of raids by people from other islands who tried to capture them. Columbus, let loose on a flight of fancy, then concluded that what they were really saying was that people came to enslave them from the 'mainland', that is, from Cathay or perhaps Cipangu, which he was convinced must be nearby and which he would now find and identify. When he said in his logbook that 'they ought to make good and clever servants' he was, no doubt, thinking of the value these poor people might present to slave traders, but the primary meaning of his comment was (surely) that the raiders whom they feared, the men who came to take them captive, valued them as servants because they were physically fine men and gave the impression of real intelligence.[20] 'Our Lord being pleased, I will take six of them from here to Your Highnesses at the time of my departure, so that they may learn to speak' – by which he meant speak Spanish.[21] Those who came with him at this point were willing enough, though one decided to escape on the next island. This strategy of taking back natives had been practised many times in the Canaries and in Africa. It was not followed simply in order to aid communication. The native Indians were a source of wonder in themselves; they had potential as slaves; they were, above all, in need of religious enlightenment, for, as Columbus said of the islanders in general, 'I believe that they easily would become Christians, for it seemed that they had no religion [*me pareçió que ninguna secta tenían*].'[22] This was not a denial that they had any religious beliefs; it was more an answer to the question of whether they were members of a great organised religion or 'sect' with temples, priests, cult sacrifices and holy books – they were certainly not Muslims, which was a relief. In his logbook Columbus wrote of how they prostrated themselves, offering thanks to God (so it seemed) for having sent the great ships to them: 'an old man came aboard the launch, and others called loudly to everyone, men and women, "Come, see the people who have come from the sky; bring them something to eat and drink." '[23] Later, in his *Letter to the Monarchs*, he would say: 'nowhere in these islands have I seen signs of sects or idolatry'.[24] They knew 'that all power is in the sky', so they were clearly practitioners of a sort of natural religion, based on a knowledge of God, simple, pure, uncorrupted, though ignorant of Christian truth. His underlying suggestion was that, living in a natural state, they needed Christian dominion to be exercised over them. This was a view Columbus retained. Four years after his discovery, he still claimed, 'I have not succeeded in discerning among them either idolatry or other sects,' even though he then went on to describe their little idols or *zemís*. 'Idolatry' thus meant something highly organised, rich in ceremony, hieratic, an alternative Church.

The island of Guanahaní was large, low and green, lacking all animals apart from parrots. 'There are gardens of trees, the most beautiful that I have seen, very green, with leaves like the trees of Castile in the months of April and May, and lots of water.'[25] Columbus noted that the islands near Guanahaní were low-lying and fertile, that they were all inhabited, and that the people of the different islands, though 'very simple' and handsome, fought each other.[26] The inhabitants of Guanahaní seemed to be saying in sign language that there were over a hundred different islands, which they then proceeded to name (or so he believed – what they were actually saying is anyone's guess); and this confirmed Columbus in his belief that he had reached the thousands of islands that, according to Marco Polo, stood off Cipangu and Cathay. However, Columbus was more interested in gold than in parrot feathers, and the natives made plain the existence of another land to the south where the king dined off gold plate. There could be little doubt about the identity of such a place: 'so as not to waste time, I want to go and see if I can come upon the island of Cipangu.'[27]

It was so obvious to him that bigger and better lands lay to the south that he decided against building a stockade on Guanahaní or carrying off the entire population into slavery. He was convinced that a mere fifty men could control this docile island population. These thoughts might seem discordant after the eloquence with which he described the gentleness and pristine simplicity of the islanders. Las Casas himself saw in this ambiguous outlook, so often positive but also infused with sheer greed, the beginning of the calamity that would destroy the population of the Indies. For las Casas, Columbus was both God's agent and a thoughtless destroyer, to be succeeded by others who were agents of the Devil. Yet this combination of the positive and the negative in the same passage describing native peoples was absolutely characteristic of the first responses to them. This was not because of a learned misreading of the writings of Aristotle or Isidore of Seville; it was the result of the sheer puzzlement that the discovery of such peoples created in the minds of Europeans. They were peaceful in manner and lacked heavy weapons, but they fought wars among themselves. They were docile and intelligent, so they would make good slaves. But they also knew that there is a God, therefore they would make good Christians. On balance, though, Columbus' description of his first encounter on Guanahaní was an idyll. Readers in Europe, such as Peter Martyr, could recognise from it that the natives of the Bahamas lived in a sort of Golden Age. This was the world of the pastoral poets; but while Virgil, Boccaccio and Sannazaro had written of an invented world full of fauns, satyrs and classical gods, here was something real, of which tangible proof existed in the bodies of the living Indians brought back to Spain, in the parrots and trinkets Columbus could display, and, above all, in the little pieces of gold that suggested how much new wealth was waiting to be found on the islands he had uncovered.

Culturally and physically, the inhabitants of the fifteenth-century Caribbean and the Bahamas lived a long way from the rich, city-based civilisations of Mexico and Peru. It is important to remember that the Europeans' first contact with American Indians was with peoples whom they believed to be Asiatic, offshore islanders linked somehow to the empires of China or Japan, but lacking the magnificent cities and silk-clad courtiers they knew they would find in the Far East. In other words, they were puzzled to discover men and women whose style of life was closer to that of the Canary islanders. And yet their appealing simplicity was compromised by rumours of man-eaters and monstrous peoples to the south. There were always two images of native peoples that co-existed and interacted, one positive and one negative.

Archaeology has revealed a great amount about the life of the early inhabitants of the Caribbean region. As in the Canaries, it often offers striking confirmation of claims made by European writers. It is now time to examine the peoples of the Caribbean area at the time of Columbus' arrival, ranging beyond his initial area of contact, the Bahamas, north of the Caribbean Sea, to include the inhabitants of virtually all the islands of the Caribbean, islands that came to be known as the Greater and Lesser Antilles.

CHAPTER 10

TAÍNOS AND CARIBS

Early Peoples of the Caribbean

Guanahaní and the Bahamas were inhabited by an offshoot of the people generally known today as the 'Taínos', a word that meant, in their language, 'noble'.[1] Archaeologists have revealed a considerable amount about the Taínos, not just in the Bahamas but in their major settlements on Hispaniola (modern Haiti and the Dominican Republic), Cuba, Puerto Rico and Jamaica. In fact, the Bahamas were the farthest-flung Taíno settlements.[2] The Taínos had over many centuries migrated northwards from the coasts of South America, along the chain of the Lesser Antilles, finally arriving in the bigger islands at the end of the first millennium AD.[3] They formed a branch of the Arawak-speaking peoples whose language and customs still survive in parts of Venezuela, and they were (literally) pursued up the island chain by a second group of Arawak peoples, the Caribs, of whom more shortly.[4] There seem to have been at least four ethnic groups living in the islands in 1492. The people Columbus met were not the earliest inhabitants of the islands, if fragments of evidence from the early narratives and a modern Cuban reading of the archaeological finds are to be trusted, and it seems that these earliest inhabitants had not entirely disappeared by 1492.[5] In 1514 Diego Velázquez de Cuellar, the conqueror of Cuba, described the life of a people known as the Ciboneys, who may be the same as the Guanahatabeys or Guanahacibibes mentioned later by las Casas in a different location (just to add to the confusion, another writer, Oviedo, located the Ciboneys in south-western Haiti and not on Cuba at all). Anything that was known about the Ciboneys was vague and based on rumour. 'The life of these people,' Velázquez wrote, 'is of the manner of savages, for they have neither houses nor village quarters, nor fields, nor do they eat anything else than the flesh they take in the mountains and turtles and fish.'[6] The myths of the Taínos spoke of strange fishermen who lived a primitive existence on the seashore, but there were also European legends about fisherfolk who shaded their heads with a large foot which were well known to the Spaniards of the time, so it is quite possible that Velázquez simply conflated a number of similar pieces of pseudo-evidence to produce an image of people who lived more like animals than humans. Maybe indeed they were a 'creation of the Spanish or Taíno imagination', and as such by no means the first example of an imaginary different-people-over-there.[7]

Some historians have therefore been reluctant to believe that the Ciboneys (or Guanahatabeys or Guanahacibibes) were real people, or at any rate that they were still a distinct group in 1492. Others, notably archaeologists in Castro's Cuba, have invested a good amount in the presumption that they did exist. In the first place, they were most likely concentrated in western Cuba, in the area of Havana, which means that local archaeologists have been keen to identify their remains among the excavated sites on their own doorstep.[8] In the second place, they have a crucial role to play in a Marxist history of early Cuba. They would surely represent the original, communistic population living in a state of primitive equality before the coming of materialism. If this interpretation echoes the talk of a Golden Age found in the works of Columbus' contemporaries when they first contemplated the native Americans, this only proves that Marxism too has drawn on classical and biblical ideas of the pristine innocence of mankind. What archaeologists have shown is that the life of the inhabitants of western Cuba, presumed predecessors of the Taínos in the entire region, was simple: there was no use of pottery; there were simple stone tools, which included intriguing stone spheres, polished smooth, whose exact function remains a mystery; there are some pictographs from cave sites.[9] There is no evidence of the Ciboney language beyond a few place-names that may include very ancient roots, though the origins of the language seem to lie in South America, suggesting that they had worked their way up the island chain from the south.[10] On balance, it does seem that there was an earlier population which by 1492 had become confined to the outer edges of the Greater Antilles, that is, the tip of Cuba; their presence did, however, block easy access to Florida and Meso-America by the Taínos, sealing off the Taíno world from the complex civilisations of central America. Another small group, the Macorís in Hispaniola, used a language closer to that of Honduras, indicating links in the distant past with central America; but by 1492 their culture, if not their speech, was very similar to that of the dominant group, the Taínos.

The Taíno Indians

The Taínos seem to have assumed that the entire world consisted of their island chain; no myths of migration from a great southern landmass are known among the Taíno myths that survive. When Columbus first heard the Taínos speak of lands rich in gold over the horizon, it was he who attached unwarranted meaning to their words and gestures; and many Taínos whom he met on his voyages indicated these lands simply to encourage him and his men to leave, as they increasingly found the visitors troublesome. Yet it is very likely that the Taínos originally came from South America, more precisely from the Orinoco valley.[11] This can be established on archaeological evidence, documenting very exactly the spread of their pottery; on linguistic grounds, linking Taíno speech to the great Arawak family of languages;[12] and on biological grounds, using the evidence of skeletal remains to link their physical type to that of the Arawaks of South America.[13] Over the massive time span from 2000 BC to AD 600, a 'First Repeopling' has been postulated, as they gradually moved into the Guianas and then across the water to Trinidad and into Grenada (a distance of about eighty miles) and beyond into the great chain of the Lesser Antilles, though most likely this occurred slowly and in many phases. The spread of their distinctive 'Saladoid' pottery, named after a small South American site, Saladero, reveals the slow diffusion of their ancestors.[14] The Taínos did not strike permanent roots on each island. It is easy to imagine that as one location filled up with people, there was an incentive for some of the inhabitants to move away – competition for scarce resources, political struggles, family rivalries. It was a jerky expansion. They used a 'slash-and-burn' method of cultivation, clearing woodland, sowing it, exploiting it till its potential was exhausted, and then moving on. Their boats, made out of often massive tree trunks, enthralled European observers; they were masters of the seas between the islands, and lone mariners would think nothing of a quick trading trip to a neighbouring island, as Columbus was astonished to discover. Even so, it would be wrong to suppose that every generation experienced migration. The jump from the Lesser Antilles into the first of the larger islands, Boríquen or Puerto Rico, seems to have been accomplished during the centuries after AD 500; from there they arrived relatively quickly in Hispaniola, the future seat of Spanish government in the region, and passed through to Jamaica and to eastern and central Cuba, the largest island in the group.[15]

The discovery at Yuma in the modern Dominican Republic (Hispaniola) of what may be griddles for cooking cassava bread has been read as a sign that the Taínos were now leading a more settled existence. Important too is the way that local cultures developed: Taíno culture was not imported ready-made, but each island, or (within the bigger islands) each region, developed distinctive features, which were determined, obviously enough, by access to particular resources – fish, meat, different food crops. The Lucayan Taínos, in the Bahamas, had less complex political structures than those of Hispaniola, and this area was generally less 'developed' than the Greater Antilles.[16] This has led archaeologists to talk of the Taínos of Hispaniola, Puerto Rico and eastern Cuba as 'Classic Taínos', who reached a higher level of cultural sophistication and technological accomplishment than those of the outlying, smaller islands; or in some classifications to describe the Taínos of Cuba and Jamaica as 'Sub-Taíno', though it is abundantly clear from Columbus' descriptions that the Taínos of eastern Cuba lived a very similar existence to those of Hispaniola.[17] But there was much variation within the Classic Taínos as well. At Unión in the Dominican Republic a community developed whose life revolved around fishing, and of course trade networks developed out of these specialities, for the Taínos were practised navigators who have given the modern world the word 'canoe' (in their language, *canoa*). They brought with them from South America seeds and animals, introducing bitter manioc, dogs and the large rodent known as the agouti, which was a significant part of their diet. The successful implantation of increasingly diversified Taíno cultures in the Lesser and Greater Antilles is known to archaeologists as the 'Ostionoid expansion', dating roughly to the period 600 to 1200. The great champion of Taíno archaeology, Irving Rouse, was optimistically convinced that, but for the arrival of the Spaniards, Taíno civilisation would eventually have made contact with the civilisations of central America, from which it would have learned many arts and skills; before long it would have reached a level comparable to the Meso-American and Peruvian civilisations.[18] Possibly so; but in 1492 even the Classic Taínos were not city-builders and they lacked the political unity and elaborate mechanisms of government imposed by the Aztec and Inca emperors.

In Harmony with Nature?

The daily life of the Taíno Indians was dominated by the production of manioc or cassava (known to the Taínos as *yuca*).[19] This root crop had been brought from South America, where modern Arawaks still cultivate it in ways very similar to those employed by the Taínos. Cassava flour provided the base for tortillas, which were the staple element in the Taíno diet; it is also the source of tapioca. This starchy flour kept well and was highly nutritious. (With some exaggeration, the Indians complained that the Spaniards would eat in a day what one Indian consumed in a fortnight.) The Taínos did not eat large amounts of maize, unlike the inhabitants of the mainland bordering on the Gulf of Mexico and the Caribbean. Maize featured in their diet rather as it has featured in the modern European diet: it was generally eaten young as corn-on-the-cob, rather than made into corn bread or tortilla.[20] Whereas among the peoples of Mexico there were corn gods, these were not a feature of Taíno religious life; indeed, the chief god was most closely linked with cassava.

The dominance of cassava was instantly visible to anyone arriving in their villages: the Taínos heaped up small mounds, about a metre high and three metres across, which stood in neat rows, and planted them with cassava roots, in this way ensuring that the plants were properly drained and that weeding could be achieved easily.[21] The Arawak peoples had learned that the best yields came from a bitter type of manioc that contained a poisonous juice. Somehow in the past they had realised that this juice could be removed by squeezing the roots when they were harvested and flaked, and elaborate tubes made of palm fibres were constructed, which were twisted or pulled until the poisonous juice ran out. It was collected in bowls; once it had been boiled the juice lost its toxicity, and indeed was used in cooking. Modern investigations among the Arawaks of Surinam have shown how the work was done – children help to extract the poison, and the next stages are assigned to women, who flake the roots and grind them down into a flour which can be spread on griddles and baked into pancakes.[22] But the Taíno diet was not monotonous. They also ate large amounts of fish, shellfish and the flesh of sea mammals such as the manatee, as well as iguana meat (which initially disgusted the Spaniards) and the large rodents called agouti, and they caught parrots for food as well as to pluck their magnificent feathers.[23] Their preference was for boiled food, which simmered away in large pots; they added vegetables, peanuts and cassava juice, and they were strong believers in the use of chilli pepper, which naturally interested European visitors, who had a strong professional interest in spices. Similar 'pepper-pot stews' are still eaten by the Arawaks in Guyana.

For some modern commentators, this dependence on what could be harvested from the soil and the sea reveals how the Taínos lived in harmony with nature. In a twentieth-century recasting of Peter Martyr's encomium, the great historical geographer Carl Sauer wrote:

> The tropical idyll of the accounts of Columbus and Peter Martyr was largely true. The people suffered no want. They took care of their plantings, were dexterous at fishing and bold canoeists and swimmers. They designed attractive houses and kept them clean. They found aesthetic expression in woodworking. They had leisure to enjoy diversion in ballgames, dances, and music. They lived in peace and amity.[24]

Balance with nature would depend on human numbers. Estimates of the number of Taínos living on the islands vary enormously: two million on Hispaniola in 1492 may be about right, but it is just intelligent guesswork, based on Columbus' attempts to count tribute-paying Indians, who seem to have exceeded one million. In fact, estimates have reached as high as eight million and as low as 100,000.[25] Thus the question of whether they were over-using existing resources is hard to answer. For the first European visitors, such as Columbus, this harmony with nature was visible in the lack of dependence on the seasons, meaning that they could sow and harvest when they chose; it was visible in the lushness of the well-watered Caribbean forests; it was expressed too (as Peter Martyr insisted) in the lack of possessiveness of the Taínos, with their supposedly communistic approach to the ownership and management of their fields. Recent writers have taken this further, insisting that this semi-paradise was then shattered by the Spanish conquerors.[26] Yet it is important to be wary of an argument that is partly based on the initial wonderment of the Europeans at what they had found. Those who saw the Taínos in a positive light – by no means all early visitors and commentators – assigned to them an idealised place in their chart of humanity, as survivors from a pristine age of mankind before the Fall, or at least before the Flood.

Other aspects of material life are better known from the European narratives than from archaeology. They walked around naked, though some Taínos wore cotton loincloths and some women wore skirts whose length might indicate their social status. Cotton was important in their life, and it was one of the first products that Columbus encountered; their knowledge of cotton textiles marked them out from the Canary islanders, and must have brought to mind similarities with the black African peoples.[27] Later, the Taínos of Hispaniola would plead that they could offer the king and queen of Castile large amounts of cotton without difficulty; it was finding gold that was much more arduous. Rather than cotton, they used palm leaves to construct their *hamaca,* the hammocks in which they slept – another Taíno word that has passed into the European vocabulary. These hammocks were strung up in their big, round huts or *bohíos* (the word meant 'home').[28] These were made of wood and thatch, with conical roofs, and contained the living quarters of large numbers of families, who lived side by side. The Taínos used to hang their possessions from the rafters, in baskets and gourds, and the Spaniards were disturbed to find that sometimes these gourds contained human bones. These were understood in some places (the Carib islands) to be evidence of cannibalism, but in Taíno territory they were apparently the gathered bones of ancestors, who thus 'lived' amid their descendants. The huts were grouped together around a plaza, at one end of which there generally stood a round, square or rectangular house, the *caney,* where the images or *zemís* of their gods would be found and the chief might take up residence.[29] So there were villages of several hundred people, set among fields of cassava; but there were no towns or strongholds. As Peter Martyr noted, they did not mark off their territory or the possessions of an individual with fences. They led a communal existence.

The Taínos were very skilled craftsmen in wood, and some of their work has survived, notably the low stools called *duhos,* on which they placed their *zemí* idols. Some of these *duhos* contain intricately carved faces of mythical beasts, very occasionally gilded;[30] the *zemís* themselves were lovingly made from wood, stone, beads and other substances.[31] Beautiful objects made of bone and shell have survived, including a miniature dog's skull found on Antigua, delicately carved from a shell.[32] Necklaces made of beads, coloured stones and bone were much prized, and Columbus' gifts of beads and other small ornaments were therefore greatly appreciated. Gold featured on their necklaces, hammered into small flat plates of varying shapes; gold was used in nose ornaments, hanging down from the nostrils. Face masks of gold foil were also made. This gold excited the Europeans, and yet gold was virtually the only metal the Taínos knew, nor was it processed in forges. It was found in the riverbeds in the form of nuggets and grains and then simply pounded into shape. In addition, some alloyed metals, such as a gold, copper and silver mixture, were probably brought up the island chain, all the way from what is now Colombia.[33] In other words, the Taínos, like the Canary islanders, were technologically a 'Stone Age' population. In some respects they were more advanced than the Canary islanders, since they knew how to make cotton cloth and had developed cassava cultivation to a high pitch, but they did not have any experience of animal husbandry. Their weapons were quite similar to those of the Canaries (javelins tipped with sharp fish teeth), and the Caribs were especially good archers, sometimes using serrated fish teeth on their arrows to deadly effect. Some Taíno warriors favoured heavy wooden clubs.[34] At a more modest level, the Taínos were good potters; women were particularly active in the production of pottery, which was traded along the land and sea routes within the Taíno world.[35]

The Taínos had no pack animals; the only way to move around the islands was on foot, though their chieftains were sometimes carried around in a litter. If anything, this encouraged the use of boats around and between islands, and a lively trade developed in foodstuffs, cotton thread and carved *zemis*: Columbus was amazed to find that glass beads and coins traded by his men on 13 October were already being taken south in a native boat encountered off Long Island (Fernandina) on 15 October, along with some dried leaves and food. Not just European goods but also reports of the coming of the gods in their flying boats were diffused at top speed throughout the island chain.[36] The inter-island trade could only be conducted using the dug-out canoes, propelled by paddle power, that had attracted Columbus' attention from the moment he made contact with the Lucayan Taínos.[37] The largest of these canoes, made from a massive felled tree trunk, could seat as many as a hundred Taínos, and the chieftain's boat might be specially painted and carry on board a canopied area. The process of making these boats was long and complex, involving considerable effort on the part of the village. The tree trunk had to be split open and hollowed out by burning away the wood and chopping away at the residue. The outside of the boat was trimmed and 'marvellously carved in the native style', to cite Columbus' first reaction. Wood – wooden boats, wooden house frames, wooden weapons, wooden digging sticks, wooden thrones – was a vital but easily accessible raw material in Taíno life, and it is impressive how many wooden objects have survived from the Taíno lands.[38]

Another item in great demand was feathers, for headdresses and other ornamental use, although the Taínos were less lavish in their use of them than the Brazilian Indians, who might coat themselves entirely in a felt made of the finest feathers. For the naked body was not an unadorned body. These men and women were not the classical nudes who were being re-created by the sculptors of Florence in the age of Columbus, or who had been erotically evoked in the pastoral poetry of Boccaccio and his successors, even though sixteenth-century printmakers would often enjoy portraying them in just this manner. As in the Canary Islands, the use of body paint (as well as feathers, in the Americas) added further individuality, sometimes as a marker of status, sometimes as war paint, sometimes as heat insulation.

Chieftains and Families

One indication that the Taínos deserved to be accorded human status was the fact that they had political power structures: chiefs, nobles and commoners.[39] Much less is known about these features of Taíno society in the Bahamas, because Columbus did not linger there;[40] but he and his companions reported at length about the rulers they encountered in Hispaniola. The political life of the Classic Taínos was not dissimilar to that of the Canary islanders: there were many local rulers, known as the *kasikes*, or in Spanish spelling *caciques*, generally men but occasionally women; they controlled the larger villages and their dependencies, while a few major *caciques* exercised wider regional power in the bigger islands such as Hispaniola.[41] The *cacique* was not an autocrat; he was first among equals, receiving visitors to the village, seated on his elaborate *duho* stool, and enjoying a ceremonial role as organiser of festivities. The *cacique* would typically lead the singing at great public dances. The Spanish conquerors came to know a number of *caciques*, who deftly played them off against their rivals; warfare between caciquedoms was rife. There seems to have been a rough territorial division of the greater islands, but strict boundaries between caciquedoms did not exist. Alongside the *caciques* shamans exercised great influence in Taíno society, as religious leaders and medicine men – more of this shortly. Nor were the *caciques* able to go to war or conduct policy without the advice of the council of the *nitaínos* or nobles, the upper caste, to be distinguished from the general mass of people, or *naboría*.[42] Noble status seems to have depended on success in war, on one's reputation as a hardy fighter, and not simply on descent.

Grand ceremonies were held to mark events such as the *cacique*'s wedding, or to express thanks for deliverance from a hurricane (another Taíno word that has passed into the European vocabulary). Among the ceremonies over which the *cacique* presided was the ball game, or *batey*, played in the central plaza of the village with bouncy rubber balls which had to be propelled back and forth between the hips of the rival teams of twenty to thirty men or women, without being touched by the hands or the feet.[43] This involved great skill. (The Taínos did not follow the central American practice of sometimes condemning the losing team to death.) The ball games had a religious and social function. A ball-court has been excavated in the Caribbean, at what may have been one of the headquarters of Guarionex, a *cacique* well known to Columbus; but the Taínos also played in cleared open spaces, as happened in the Bahamas, where the style of life was somewhat simpler.[44]

The study of kinship patterns became a major topic in anthropology during the twentieth century, in the wake of famous studies of the Pacific islands by Malinowski, Mead and others. But observers in the years around 1500 were already struck by the sharp differences between European kinship patterns and the way family relationships operated in the Taíno world. European observers were also curious, persistently so at times, about the sexual life of the Taínos and their incest regulations. This was of some importance for the future of the Taínos. Evidence that they lived lives of unbridled lust, having intercourse with anyone, whether relative or neighbour, would suggest that they did not live according to natural law; it might therefore compromise their claim to humanity, or at least their right to govern themselves. One characteristic of classic Taíno society was what is called 'avunculocal residence': in other words, a newly married husband (followed by his bride) would go to live in the same house as his mother's brother. The rule was not 'honour thy father and mother' but 'honour thy mother's brother'.[45] The advantage of this system was that a Taíno male with several wives could take all of them into his uncle's house: this clearly would not have worked so effectively if he had moved into the household of the mother of one of his wives. In fact, descent passed through the female line, and it was through that line that goods were inherited (though the chieftainship seems to have passed mainly through the male line). Yet this did not reflect a polyandrous society in which women took many men as sexual partners and were uncertain of the paternity of their children. If anything, polygamy (or polygyny) was a Taíno institution, but mainly among the *caciques*, who could afford to maintain more than one wife. Matriarchy and patriarchy existed side by side in Taíno society. Women played a crucial role in the economy of the Taíno village, and the respect the sexes felt for one another is reflected in some of the Taíno myths. The latter, preserved by one of Columbus' followers, provide an extraordinary insight into the mental world of the Taínos. But before they can be explored the third major group of people in the pre-Columbian Caribbean must be examined: the Island Caribs, who gave their name to the sea they navigated, but also to the practice of eating human flesh.

The Caribs

Columbus and his contemporaries recorded very clearly the sharp fear of the Taínos in the face of raids from a pirate people who were passing up the line of islands from the south-east, reaching at least as far as Puerto Rico and Hispaniola. Their appearance was frightening. According to Dr Diego Álvarez Chanca, who travelled west on Columbus' second voyage, in 1493:

> The Caribs wear two bandages, made of cotton, on each leg, one near the knee and the other near the ankles. The result is to make the calves large and the places mentioned very small and to me it appears that they regard this as an attraction. So, by this difference, we knew the one race from the other. The customs of this race of Caribs are bestial.[46]

These garters can be seen on a three-foot statue of a man from the Caribbean, preserved in the British Museum and thought to date from around 1400, although Ferdinand Columbus believed that this was also a Taíno practice. According to Chanca, the Caribs were highly accomplished archers and ruthless warriors. The raiders carried off Taíno women; Dr Chanca maintained that the Caribs had children by these women, but if the children were boys they were castrated, employed as servants and raised to manhood in order to be slaughtered and eaten at their feasts. Indeed, what really struck horror into the Taínos was the fear that men would be carried off as prize trophies, to be killed and eaten by the cannibalistic Caribs: 'they say that the flesh of a man is so good that there is nothing like it in the world,' Chanca observed.[47] For it is from the term Cariba or Caniba that the word 'cannibal' as well as the name 'Caribbean' was derived. Dr Chanca said that he visited a village in Guadeloupe and found the neck of a man cooking in a pot. It is certainly possible that he added this detail to spice up his travel narrative, or that he was wrong about the type of meat he saw cooking, but the only land animals of any size on Guadeloupe were human beings, so he cannot have confused these bones with those of cattle or sheep. Columbus told the king and queen:

They eat human flesh, are great archers, have many canoes, almost as big as galleys, with which they navigate around all the islands of the Indies and they are so feared that they have no equal; they are as naked as the others, except that they wear their hair long, as women do.[48]

Columbus opined that the Taínos feared them because the Taínos were, frankly, cowards. Of course, this theory enabled Columbus to present himself as the protector of the Taínos against this horrible enemy.

The Spaniards found it convenient to classify the peoples of the Caribbean as 'good' or 'bad' in their customs, docility and appearance, and it is easy to see why post-modernist writers have often denied the existence of the cannibals, arguing that they were simply used as an excuse for the imposition of empire by the overweening Spaniards.[49] Against them, the argument goes, it would be permissible to wage a holy war, with the licence of the Church and of the king and queen; whereas against the more co-operative Taínos of Hispaniola, subjects of the Crown, no crusade could be launched. In 1503 Queen Isabella, who was always anxious to protect her Indian subjects, forbade their enslavement in the Caribbean, with the exception of the cannibals and those who violently resisted conversion.[50] This was not surprisingly taken by some as a licence to go raiding into any areas that had not fallen under direct Spanish rule, carrying off Taínos and Caribs as slaves. To argue that the American cannibals were a fiction, or indeed that all cannibalism is just an exercise in Western humiliation of subject peoples, is to ignore the detailed and persistent evidence from European visitors to South America, where very similar practices were documented by independent observers throughout the sixteenth century, and into modern times.[51] One modern commentator proclaims that even to give the equivocal verdict that Carib cannibalism is not proven is 'still to acquiesce to the implicit violence of colonialist discourse', before then taking the reader on a mystery tour of Dr Freud's ontologies and phylogenies.[52] But to say that cannibalism existed in the Americas is not to say that all native Americans were cannibals; that was clearly not the case, nor was it said by observers to be the case. The question here concerns the natives of the Caribbean (attention will focus on Brazil in later chapters), and it concerns the people known to the Spaniards as *Caribes*, and to the Taínos as *Cariba* or a variant of that; their names for themselves may have been *Kallinago* and *Kalliponam*.[53]

It was easy to label any 'bad' natives as Caribs, and the word became a shorthand term for troublesome raiders, above all for anyone suspected of making a feast of human flesh. It is not entirely clear whether they were a separate *gente*, 'people', as Chanca assumed; archaeologists differ on the question whether there was a distinctive Carib culture.[54] According to one view, Caribs and Taínos were branches of the same Arawak people who were colonising the Antilles in great waves throughout the millennium before Columbus' arrival. But the Taínos talked of the Caribs as people who did differ from themselves, in habits if not in all aspects of their culture; they were recognisable as a distinct group in the seventeenth century, and the starting point has to be the simple fact that the Taínos had a name for them. Indeed, a very small number can still be found on the islands. In reality, the term 'Carib' had and has many uses, from an ethnic description of mobile cannibal raiders to a description of settled Arawak-speaking peoples who lived in the Lesser Antilles and on the adjacent coast of South America.[55]

By 1492, the Caribs had become part of the Arawak world of the Caribbean, whether or not they were welcome there. A separate race of Island Caribs existed in the imagination of the explorers, and they were greatly feared by the Taíno Indians as well. They were led by male warriors who could trace their descent back to the coasts of Guyana. Lacking well-organised chiefdoms, they are thought to have reached a lower and looser level of social organisation than the Taínos, though they were skilled in cotton-weaving and in wickerwork.[56] They are hard to detect in the archaeological record. There may be a connection between the arrival of the Island Caribs and the production of the so-called 'Suazoid' pottery of the Lesser Antilles, including Barbados, from about 1100; but even this idea has generated invective among archaeologists and linguists, especially over the insoluble question of whether Carib potters were male or female and, if the latter, whether they might in fact have been captive Taíno women. Still, there is no evidence of the sudden, dramatic breaks that might be expected to follow the substitution of an old population by a new one. Most probably, they were replacing the Taíno population in areas such as the Windward Islands, not by exterminating all the Taínos but by killing their males, taking their females and then mixing with them, while they were also pushing northwards along the island chain and attacking the Greater Antilles as well. Overall, they are easier to identify by their behaviour than by their artefacts, language or skeletal remains: a Carib is as a Carib does.

Detailed accounts of the Caribs came quite late, notably that of Père Breton who lived among the Caribs of Dominica in the years around 1647. A word of warning is needed, because these Caribs may have been late arrivals from South America rather than descendants of the Caribs who were said to have terrorised the Taínos.[57] These accounts describe myths that have only a general similarity to those of the Taínos: the fish in the sea originated in shavings of manioc roots, rather than being metamorphosed from the bones of a slaughtered youth, as among the Taínos. European visitors were perplexed by their very different attitude to the boundaries between the world of the living and the world of the dead: 'they hold that someone they know is always alive,' said an English traveller of the Caribs in 1700.[58] These accounts also told how the men took any number of wives in rapid sequence, for, 'as there is no polity or law among the savages, they also have no fixed rule for their marriages'. They had no explicit rules about incest; it was merely Nature that held them back from sexual relations between parents and children, or between brothers and sisters.[59] Observers related how they liked to drink themselves into a stupor before launching their raids, swallowing vast amounts of beer whose secret ingredient was women's spittle (presumably containing some yeast-bearing agent – the Caribs also spent hours chewing narcotic leaves, as the explorers observed).[60] They enjoyed licking each other's body lice, a habit that was easier for European observers to bear than their constantly reported addiction to feasts of human flesh.

The Caribs no doubt changed in significant ways following the Spanish conquest of large areas of the Caribbean. From the late sixteenth century, there are accounts of their violent pirate raids which suggest that they became more, not less, ruthless as they came under pressure from the Europeans. It was reported that, armed with poisoned arrows, they attacked Spanish ships and settlements around Puerto Rico with impunity, killing Europeans and their black African slaves, and eating some of their victims.[61] Spanish slavers carried them off, seeing the Caribs, who knew all about slave raiding, as fair game. They had never been subdued, and from the start of the sixteenth century they were regarded as the object of a just war; even the question of whether they had souls was in doubt, because it was supposed that rational beings could not possibly conduct themselves so savagely; the word 'savage' appeared in early English accounts of the Caribs.[62] It was a word with a good heritage, derived from *selvage*, *silvestris*, 'of the forests', the image of the wild man that had remained potent since medieval times. Père Breton reported rumours of an indigenous population whom the Caribs had displaced in the Lesser Antilles, 'who are white like the French and have long white beards'; their whiteness seemed to be the result of living in the cold uplands to which they had fled after the Caribs enslaved them. Soon after Breton had arrived in Dominica, in 1642, several of these ancient inhabitants had been carried off by the Caribs: 'they killed and ate the man and made slaves of the woman and girl', but these 'Mountain-men' wreaked their revenge, burning a Carib hut and seizing Carib property.[63] Ill-feeling towards their escaped slaves meant that the Caribs generally ate any of these mysterious Mountain-men, or *Allouages*, on whom they laid their hands. On the other hand, the Caribs of the Lesser Antilles had been massacred by the Spaniards and had suffered terribly from smallpox, so that on Guadeloupe the Caribs were the descendants of a single woman and her children who survived mass extermination by the Spaniards by fleeing into the mountains. Menfolk were few and were the constant target of Spanish and other European raiders, who killed or enslaved those they could find. There was a constant game of tit-for-tat.

The Caribs had some sense of their origins on the mainland:

They all say that their first father Kallinago, having left the mainland accompanied by his family, set up home on Dominica. Here he had a long line of descendants and here lived the nephews of his nephews who through an extreme cruelty killed him with poison. But he was changed into a fish of monstrous size that they call *Akaiouman* and he is still full of life in their river. This fable makes known at least that they are descended from peoples of the mainland.[64]

Breton described the Caribs as red-skinned, their skin made even redder by the dyes they rubbed into it every day. He said they were a melancholy people, rather silent, but 'not overly stupid for savages'; physically agile, robust and healthy, they were 'without doubt capable of greater things'.[65] They were not cruel to one another, only to their enemies, but they became dangerous when they had been drinking, and then they would fight one another. They were lazy, assuming that the cassava crop would keep them in food; sometimes this lack of industry simply left them hungry. Chanca, describing the Caribs he encountered a century and a half earlier, emphasised that they wore their hair very long, while the Taínos cut their hair in various styles and decorated their faces with designs.[66] The Caribs, on the other hand, rubbed face paint around their eyes, to look more fearsome.[67]

One plausible view is that the Island Caribs resembled Viking warriors who did great damage, but largely adopted the customs and culture of the people whose lands they raided and settled. Culturally, they tended to assimilate; politically, they remained a threat because of their use of extreme violence and the fear that was generated by reports of their cannibalism. If, as the evidence suggests, the Caribs took local women and used them as servants, it is hardly surprising that a mixing of Taíno and Carib culture took place.[68] They all spoke dialects of Arawak anyhow, for the language of the Caribs had similar roots to the Taíno dialects; it may have been a sort of pidgin Taíno. Père Breton, whose works included a Carib dictionary, reported that Carib men spoke a different dialect from the women, and there were other dialects for grand orations and so on. It seems there was a specialised vocabulary, confined to males, which possibly derived from the Kalina, Galiba or Cariba languages of the South American shores. The existence side by side of different ways of speech is not unusual – many languages, including Japanese, have several registers, formal and informal, and understanding one register does not mean one is competent in another.

Some archaeologists, ignoring what they see as an artificial distinction between Taínos and Caribs, have treated raiding parties that seized women and male slaves as a fact of life right across the Caribbean islands. Is it really certain that the Taínos did not eat human flesh at least occasionally? Can the gourds full of human bones that hung from the rafters of their houses be explained entirely innocently? Dr Chanca remarked that the Indians of Puerto Rico often suffered Carib raids but, lacking boats of their own – which is implausible – responded by trying to capture the invaders, 'and if by chance they are able to take those who come to raid them, they also eat them as do the Caribs'.[69] 'Carib' thus described a style of life at least as much as a people; and some customs attributed to the Caribs may also have been typical of certain Taíno communities.

CHAPTER 11

TURTLES, SHAMANS AND SNORTING TUBES

A Humble Friar

The first European book written on the soil of the Americas is thought to have been the modestly presented tract on the religious beliefs and practices of the Taíno Indians, composed by Fray Ramón Pané, a Catalan friar, on the island of Hispaniola:

> I, Fray Ramón, a humble friar of the Order of St Jerome, am writing what I have been able to discover and understand of the beliefs and idolatries of the Indians, and of how they worship their gods, by order of the illustrious Lord Admiral and Viceroy and Governor of the Islands and Mainland of the Indies.[1]

Pané travelled out to Hispaniola on Columbus' second voyage, leaving Spain on 25 September 1493 with twelve to fifteen hundred other souls. What he had to say about native religion was far more detailed than any other account of the religious beliefs of newly conquered peoples written before the conquest of Mexico. Moreover, his words were studied, in first draft and then in later versions, by Christopher Columbus, and they determined his views on native beliefs; they were also read closely by Peter Martyr, the humanist intellectual whose writings were widely diffused across Spain and Italy; and they were also studied critically by the great defender of Indian rights Bartolomé de las Casas in the sixteenth century. This may suggest that all that is known of Taíno religion is built on a narrow base, the opinions of one man, full of detail but often vague, muddled and disordered, and then constantly recycled; on the other hand, the evidence of archaeology corroborates important points in Pané's account, such as the presence of small idols or *zemís*, and the use of hallucinatory drugs by Taíno shamans. The richness of his account has encouraged attempts to analyse the myths in sophisticated but controversial ways; in the wake of the famous studies of Brazilian myths by the French structural anthropologist Claude Lévi-Strauss, Jungian psychoanalysis has been applied to the myths recorded by Pané. Lévi-Strauss' method involved a sometimes heavy-handed attempt to make sense of myths by filling gaps with material from myths generated in other communities (on the grounds that all myths share certain 'archetypes' which are deeply embedded in the human consciousness). This allows a marvellous flexibility, so that analysis of this kind is littered with phrases such as 'I suggest the following interpretation', 'I suspect that', 'as I see it, then', and impressively punctuated with visits to the myths and legends of the Hebrews and the Greeks.[2]

In fact, the first problem is that of knowing what Pané actually wrote. His book does not survive as a separate work, but as a book within a book, inserted in the biography of Christopher Columbus written by Columbus' illegitimate son Ferdinand. Ferdinand Columbus shared with his father an impressive range of accomplishments: he was a great collector of books and prints, and assembled what is believed to have been the largest private library of his day in Seville (he owned 15,370 books and 3200 prints by the time he died in 1539). Only part of this vast collection still survives.[3] He developed his own 'project for a universal library', and, most importantly, he preserved some of his father's books, with their very revealing marginal notes. He was keen to defend Columbus' memory against the assaults of those who saw him as a ruthlessly ambitious social climber who had risen far above his natural station, and whose claims to authority and revenues in the Caribbean were repeatedly challenged in slowly maturing court cases. But in the process of defending Christopher Columbus' reputation, Ferdinand Columbus carefully assembled material from his father's logbook and other works, including Pané's tract, which he copied wholesale into his life of his father. However, Ferdinand's biography has not survived in its original Spanish version. It was translated into Italian by a Spaniard named Ulloa in Venice in 1571; Ulloa did not know what to make of Pané's strange material, and he garbled many passages, mangling personal names. To a large degree Pané's book can be reconstructed, however, by comparing Ulloa's version with the evidence of Christopher Columbus or Peter Martyr or las Casas when they cited Pané, but there are still many mysteries – even the spelling of Pané's name was long contested. Thus the rediscovery of the mental world of the Taínos has involved hacking through a forest of misunderstandings scattered in the text by Ulloa, only to reach another forest, Pané's own puzzled attempts to record Taíno myths. To say that Pané tried to make sense of them would be an exaggeration. Often he abandoned any attempt to order his material. He could not cope with the disordered time-frame, or lack of a time-frame, and he was convinced that the Taínos were a stupid and superstitious people.

Pané was not a great intellectual, unlike Ferdinand Columbus. He rued the day when the king and queen of Castile and Aragon had visited Barcelona and the little town nearby, Badalona, where he led a quiet life as a Hieronymite brother in the convent of San Jerónimo de la Murtra.[4] He may well have been present when Ferdinand and Isabella received Columbus there. The king and queen understood that, following the discoveries in the west, a massive programme of evangelisation was required; it was what Christ expected of them, and what Pope Alexander VI, with some insistence, saw as the justification for Spanish or Portuguese claims to dominion in newly discovered lands. Ferdinand and Isabella had in fact sent no priests or friars on the first voyage, which seems strange: there had been missionaries on board earlier voyages of exploration, such as those of the Vivaldi brothers and of Jaume Ferrer down the coast of Africa, though the Portuguese visited at least one African king who wished to be baptised, and had to apologise that they had no priest on board to perform the sacrament. Maybe the lack of priests confirms suspicions that the search for gold took priority over the search for souls in need of salvation. Or maybe no priests could be persuaded to go on the first voyage of Columbus. Or maybe the king and queen were worried that priests or friars would see themselves as representatives of the pope rather than of themselves. On the second voyage Father Bernat Buyl set up a base at La Isabela, Columbus' centre of government in Hispaniola, in January 1494, and about a dozen priests and friars worked with him.[5] Pané was sent into the interior; he had clearly drawn the short straw, though for a time he seems to have had the help of a French Franciscan friar who spoke the language rather better – las Casas had actually met both men.[6]

Pané's task, when he arrived, was to study in detail the language and beliefs of the natives of Hispaniola to provide the basis for a missionary programme there. This has been described as a great innovation, but in fact Pané was being inserted into a venerable tradition with particularly deep roots among Catalan friars.[7] As has been seen, for two and a half centuries the friars had immersed themselves in the languages and texts of Judaism and Islam as a prelude to preaching campaigns. Brave or foolhardy missionaries went to North Africa, seeking out emirs and imams, or proclaiming their faith and denouncing Muhammad in the public square. This became a Catalan speciality, a way the Catalans, who no longer possessed a frontier with Islam after the mid-thirteenth century, could continue to fight for the faith, with words rather than with arms. It is no surprise, then, that a similar venture in the lands of the newly discovered peoples should have been attempted. What was different – and what greatly frustrated Pané – was the lack of holy books among the Taínos. Dealing with an oral culture was different from studying the Talmud or the Koran. Las Casas thought, in any case, that Pané's intellectual abilities were slight and that the task was beyond his capabilities: he was 'a simple man of good intention', but not really a master of the local language.[8] But this was only to underline a generic problem: the standard of the clergy who travelled out to the New World in the first twenty years after Columbus' arrival was mediocre, and few priests or friars chose to stay long in such a difficult environment – Father Buyl gave up and returned to Spain as soon as he could. It was not simply the physical conditions that defeated them; the failure to convert more than a tiny number of Taínos prompted those who did stay behind to retreat into their thatched convents away from the native population, offering their services in the first place to the Spanish settlers (who often had other priorities than God).

Pané went to the New World as (figuratively speaking) a blind man. He had no prior knowledge of Taíno beliefs and practices. Columbus had been vague about their religious identity, even if his assertion that they had 'no religion' was not, as has been seen, quite as dismissive as has generally been assumed – he meant that they had no elaborate cult with temples and sacrifices. The result was that Pané had to develop his own strategy. Recently uncovered evidence, the testimony of Pané himself before a board of enquiry into Columbus' government of Hispaniola in 1499, shows Pané in a different light. Pané's deposition recorded that Columbus did not encourage the conversion of Indians, and indeed actively discouraged it. When Pané tried to interest him in several exciting opportunities Columbus made difficulties and 'he did not dare to turn them into Christians for fear of the admiral'.[9] On the other hand, Pané may have felt under pressure to criticise his former master to the board of enquiry. What the board was told cannot be taken entirely at face value: it was looking for evidence of Columbus' tyranny following a series of complaints. Its methods, though infinitely milder, had much in common with those of the Inquisition: it collected depositions to prove a particular case, and there was not much room for an active defence –

Columbus himself had gone back to Spain in humiliating circumstances in order to convince the king and queen of his good intentions. While they were both in Hispaniola, Columbus certainly did not neglect Pané, to whom he turned as a source of information;[10] the admiral knew that he would be flattering the sensibilities of Queen Isabella if he initiated the evangelisation of the Indians.

In late March 1495, Pané joined a Spanish commander at the fort of Magdalena, which the Europeans were defending against one of the most powerful and troublesome *caciques* on Hispaniola, Caonabó, and he managed to pick up the local tongue, Macorí (though 'he knew that language only imperfectly', las Casas said). However, the other Taínos did not understand Macorí, so this was a bad start.[11] Macorí seems to have been an archaic language spoken in northern Hispaniola by some descendants of pre-Taíno settlers, whose general style of life was otherwise very similar to that of the Taíno majority.[12] The Taíno term 'Macorí' meant 'the bad people', as opposed to themselves, 'the good people'. Las Casas pointed out that most Spaniards simply had no interest in the fate of the souls of the Taínos, for their real interest was in the work of their bodies:

> And this business of no one's knowing the languages of this island was not because they were very difficult to learn, but rather because in those days no man either of the Church or the laity took any care, great or small, to impart doctrine or knowledge of God to these people; instead, they all merely made use of them, wherefore they learned no more words in the languages than 'give the bread here', 'go to the mines', 'take out gold' and such words as were necessary for the service of the Spaniards and the execution of their desires.[13]

Columbus urged Pané to go to the lands of another *cacique* named Guarionex, who was said to be interested in conversion; Pané should learn the language spoken there, which was a form of Arawak and therefore much more widely understood. So he spent another two years with Guarionex, whose enthusiasm for turning Christian gradually waned as Taíno resentment at their treatment grew; and then Pané moved on to yet another *cacique*, Mabiatué.

Pané's attempts to imbue the Taínos of Guarionex's lands with a sense of Christian belief and conduct ended on a sour note. Six of Guarionex's people were found to have buried Christian images underground as if they were Taíno idols and to have urinated on them; as punishment they were burned at the stake by Columbus' brother and representative, Bartholomew, who had failed to understand that this was actually a way of showing respect to idols among the Taínos.[14] Such reactions did nothing to increase Taíno appreciation of the benefits of Spanish rule. On the other hand, on 21 September 1496, nearly four years after Columbus had arrived in the region, Pané baptised his first convert, who took the name Juan Mateo and was followed by his brother and six others; before long the two brothers were killed by rebellious Indians, to Pané's distress.[15] By the time of the baptisms, Christopher Columbus was on his way back to Spain; but he had already been briefed by Pané, for he incorporated part of the first draft of Pané's book into a letter he wrote that year.[16] After three years with Mabiatué Pané at last finished his book, in 1498; Peter Martyr had a copy in Spain a few years later (1500–4), and some years after that Bartolomé de las Casas saw a manuscript of the book in Spain.[17] It was largely through Martyr's retelling that knowledge of Taíno beliefs spread across Europe. It had taken Pané many years to produce a work that, in its authoritative modern edition, adds up to only forty-six pages (thirty-five in the English translation), including many modern editorial notes. His book did, then, arouse strong interest; and yet it was chaotic – Pané himself confessed that he felt he had placed things back-to-front, that he did not understand what he was told, that he often had nothing on which to write and so could not make proper notes. He could only describe the Taínos of Hispaniola, 'because I know nothing whatsoever of the other islands, for I have never seen them',[18] though las Casas later insisted that the beliefs of the Taínos in the other islands were very much the same, and archaeological evidence from Jamaica and Puerto Rico confirms this.[19]

Las Casas was irritated by Pané's persistent negativity, his insistence that the Taínos were ignorant fools, his poor Spanish. On the other hand, with his passion for the conversion of the Indians, las Casas was prepared to admit that Pané 'seems to have had some zeal and goodwill'.[20] To las Casas, Pané's attempts to convert the natives were, frankly, laughable:

> As a simple man, however, he did not know how to do it; rather, his efforts amounted to nothing more than to say the *Ave Maria* and *Pater Noster* to the Indians, and some words about there being a God in heaven who was the creator of things, according to what he was able to teach them with abundant flaws and in a muddled way.[21]

Pané had little faith in the Taínos: 'their ancestors have made them believe all this, for they do not know how to read, nor can they count except up to ten', a judgment that underestimated their ability to count effectively in multiples of ten.[22] He laid the blame for their ignorance on the *behiques* or shamans, charlatans who 'practise many deceptions'.

A World outside Time

Ramón Pané provided a window into the mental world of the Taíno Indians. This is a record of a vanished people; it is extremely precious. That said, it is also a record of European failure to understand what was being said; part of its interest lies in the bewilderment Pané felt when he heard old men and women retail Taíno stories of the creation of man and the sea, or when he witnessed their shamans having what were supposed to be two-way conversations with the recently deceased. In other words, it is a record of both the Taíno and the European mentality. Pané attempted to describe Taíno myths by fitting them within the obvious structure that any European would expect to find. How did they understand the creation of the world and of mankind? That seemed to him the obvious starting point: 'they know likewise from whence they came, and where the Sun and Moon had their beginning, and how the sea was made, and where the dead go.'[23] Whether the Taínos would have placed the same emphasis on Creation stories is another question. Their conception of the material world and its relationship to the world of the dead and of spirits was so different from that of medieval Christians, Jews or Muslims that Pané was well and truly puzzled. Still, he wanted at the outset to write about their knowledge of God. It was true, he said, that they worshipped little idols called *zemís*; but they also had some knowledge of a Creator God: 'they believe that he is in heaven and is immortal, and that no one can see him, and that he has a mother. But he has no beginning, and they call him *Yúcahu Bagua Maórocotí*', apparently meaning 'Giver of Cassava, Master of the Sea, Conceived without Male Intervention'.[24] This God had a virgin mother, then, whose name very approximately meant 'Mother of the Waters, Lady of the Moon, the Tides and Maternity, Universal Mother': *Atabey Yermao Guacar Apito Zuimaco*. No Christian could fail to see the implications of this, even if Pané made no attempt to explore further: a God with a mother was instantly recognisable. (It is instructive to compare Espinosa's comments on Guanche religion in Tenerife a century later, and on a Mother-of-God figure there, bearing in mind that he had read some of the works of las Casas, who had read Pané.) Pané wished to show that the Taínos were aware of the existence of a single Creator God, in other words that 'natural religion' lay at the root of their beliefs; but, typically, he soon switched his mood to one of scorn for the superstitions that he found himself recording.

Writing about a quarter of a century later, las Casas had his own agenda, and read Pané in a partisan way, looking for evidence in the Taínos' defence; he was anxious to prove that they possessed a knowledge of God, that they were not 'idolaters'. He said that they had a 'meagre, weak and confused knowledge of God, although more pure or less dirty in the horrors of idolatry than many others';[25] he argued that the greater a nation's understanding of God, the more elaborately would it worship Him, with temples, priests, sacrifices and rituals. The Taínos thus had both the advantage and the disadvantage of simplicity. Las Casas was able to compare Taíno ways with the elaborate and bloodthirsty rituals of the Aztec priests, which certainly had no parallel in Taíno practices – though las Casas was even prepared, when pressed, to defend Aztec human sacrifices as an expression of excessive religious zeal. Endowed with a 'universal and confused knowledge of a First Cause, which is God, and that he dwelt in the heavens', the Taínos, in las Casas' view, observed natural religion in its most basic form and could be easily converted to the Christian faith, or rather could have been, since by the time las Casas wrote it was difficult to find any surviving Taínos.[26] Everyone – Columbus, Pané, later las Casas – was prepared to accord to the Taínos a pure belief in a single God, however elementary, that underlay their cult of the *zemís*. And this was crucial in determining whether they should be granted fully human status, as rational beings who governed themselves according to the basic principles of natural law.

The Taínos had a view of their origins that took no account of other peoples; they believed that mankind emerged out of a cave called the Cave of the Jagua Tree.[27] Their island world was a rather small one, surrounded by the waters, and they did not look beyond; it was inconceivable that Columbus and his men had arrived from a far-off continent. Nor was their view of their origins bound up with a sense of history, as Pané, in searching for their origin myths, imagined; their 'fables', as he called them, were not located in past time, but were timeless metaphors. Past and present were intertwined, just as the living and the dead, man and the animal world, were intertwined. They left no record of their history; there are no recorded stories about past rulers or natural disasters. However, they did imagine a primeval world located in and around their island, in which creatures were easily transformed from one state into another. Thus some of the cavemen of the early days of mankind went out to fish and the Sun metamorphosed them into hog plum trees.[28] Another of these cavemen was sent out to find a herb called *digo*, which was widely used in washing and bathing; the Sun then transformed him into a bird similar to a nightingale; and after that a friend of his, Guayahona, decided it was time to leave this dangerous place and led all the women in the cave on a journey in search of other lands. He told them to leave their little children behind to be collected later, setting them down by a stream; but the children became hungry, and the soft croaking sound they made as they begged for their mothers' teats transformed them into little frog-like creatures.[29] Guayahona then took all the adult women, even the *cacique*'s wife, and sailed with them to a separate island, Matininó, where they lived without men, and 'where they say today there are nothing but women'.[30] The name of this island actually means 'without fathers', and it is often thought to be Martinique, though the location is not really important. What matters more was the persistence of rumours about such an island, which immediately recalled, for Columbus, the legends of a land ruled by a queen, where all the warriors were women (perhaps with one breast removed in order to wield their weapons more easily – the word 'Amazon' was understood to mean 'without a breast' in Greek). As reports of this island accumulated detail, the story spread that the Amazons of Matininó were visited by Carib men once a year; only girls born as a result of these visits could remain on the island. Matininó became a source of great fascination, linking the New World to the imagery of Marco Polo and John Mandeville. For Columbus, it was 'the island of Matenico, where they are all women'.[31]

Of course, in Pané's account the result of the disappearance of the women to Matininó was that the men found themselves without female company; and, not surprisingly, the men on what the Taínos called 'Haiti' or 'Bohío' ('Home Island', that is, Hispaniola) wanted the company of women: 'they say that one day the men went to bathe, and while they were in the water it rained a great deal, and they felt a great desire to have women.'[32] However, while they were bathing, some strange creatures started to fall from the skies: 'these forms were neither men nor women, nor did they have the sex of male or female, and they went to seize them, but they fled as if they were eels.' They found four men with mangy, roughened hands, who were able to grab the creatures. 'After they had seized them, they took counsel on what they could do to make them women because they did not have the sex of male or female.' They then had a brilliant idea, and went looking for a woodpecker:

They took those women without the sex of male or female, and they tied their hands and feet, and they brought the aforementioned bird and tied it to their bodies. And believing they were trees, the bird began his customary work, picking and burrowing holes in the place where the sex of women is generally located. And in this way the Indians say that they had women, according to the stories of the most elderly. Because I wrote it down in haste and did not have sufficient paper, I was mistakenly not able to write down in that place what I had copied down elsewhere; but in any case I have not been in error because they believe everything just as I have written it down.[33]

Although the Taínos had forgotten the details of their northward migration, the sea played a significant role in their mythology. The inhabitants of the Cave of the Jagua Tree had been fishermen, and Pané heard tales about the creation of the sea as well as of man. Here the Taínos told of a man living long ago called Yaya. He had a son called Yayael, but, realising that Yayael for some reason wanted to kill him, he struck first. He placed Yayael's bones in a gourd, hanging it from the roofbeam of the house where he lived, in the manner described by the early European explorers. One day Yaya remarked to his wife, 'I want to see our son Yayael.' She turned over the gourd, intending to tip out the bones; however, rather than bones, fish of all sizes cascaded out, which they decided to eat.[34] Later four brothers, including a certain Caracaracol ('the mangy/scaly one'), arrived while Yaya was out inspecting his domain in the forests; these were the same men who had been so successful in catching the eel-like sexless creatures who had fallen from the skies. They too dined on fish from the gourd; but, hanging it up in a hurry, they caused it to drop and shatter, whereupon a massive stream of water, full of fish, flowed out: 'they say that so much water came out of that gourd that it filled up the whole earth, and many fish came out with the water; and thus it was, they say, that the sea had its origin.'[35] The fish seem to represent fertility: one young man had been transformed into millions of phallus-like creatures.[36]

Fertility was, indeed, the theme of many Taíno myths. Caracaracol was a favourite figure. One day he asked Bayamanaco for a piece of cassava bread, but Bayamanaco just held his nose and spat on his back in reply (for nose, read penis; for spittle, semen). His spittle was full of a chewed narcotic called *cohoba*; it made Caracaracol's back ache badly and he complained to his brothers about the pain. His brothers looked at his back and saw that a great lump was growing there, so they were forced to hack it open with stone axes, whereupon a female turtle came out, alive, 'and so they built their house and raised the turtle'.[37] Back in Spain, Peter Martyr, having read Pané, assumed this meant that the turtle turned into a young woman and that the four brothers all had children by her.[38] Pané, on the other hand, was mystified: 'I did not find out any more about this, and what I have written down is of little help.'[39] However, this myth was obviously important to the Taínos: a number of surviving *zemís* portray a figure who must be Caracaracol carrying the turtle on his humped back. The image of the scaly man was important in their culture, and there have been attempts to link these figures to specific diseases – for Peter Martyr, leprosy; for modern commentators, the syphilis that Columbus' sailors are often said to have brought to Europe, a relatively advantageous trade-off for the lethal European diseases that spread like wild-fire among the American peoples.[40] But at the root of these fertility myths lay ideas, now hard to recover, connecting mankind to the resources of the sea and the land, and celebrating both the miraculous growth of the cassava crop out of the earth and the wonderful wealth of the sea as a source of food. The Taínos observed a food taboo that excluded one type of freshwater turtle from their diet, apparently because it was associated with a disease like syphilis. And yet the round house that the turtle carried around all day could also be seen as a prototype of the round house or *caney* in which the *cacique* lived and in which the most important *zemís* of the village were enthroned on the *duho* stool.

Conversations with the Dead

Pané found it easier to make sense of the practices of the Taínos than of their beliefs, but here too he was full of disdain for their superstition. He conveyed a clear sense that the Taínos did not draw a sharp distinction between the world of the living and that of the dead. The dead wandered around, hiding by day, coming out at night, though they also had a special place on the edge of Hispaniola where they gathered together.[41] At night-time they would often try to mix with living people, and men would sometimes try to have sexual intercourse with these ghosts; but 'when a man thinks he has her in his arms, he has nothing because the woman disappears in an instant'.[42] Still, it was quite easy to recognise the walking dead as they had no navel. Since the dead came out at night, the Taínos were reluctant to wander about after dark. All these beliefs were (in Pané's view) shamelessly encouraged by their shamans or *behiques*, who learned their fables in the form of songs that were transmitted from generation to generation: 'in fact, just as the Moors, they have their laws gathered in ancient songs, by which they govern themselves, as do the Moors by their scripture.'[43] These songs were accompanied on strangely shaped drums, which las Casas later described as 'raucous'. Pané desperately needed a code of law or book of tradition, something like the Koran of the 'Moors', that would provide a framework for understanding these bizarre folk. Again and again he despaired of understanding how they thought and acted.

The shamans or *behiques* were intermediaries with the world of the dead and with the *zemís*, that is, not just the little idols every Taíno seemed to possess, but the gods represented by them. They were medicine men who professed to cure the sick. Here they had distinctive methods. Sick people were examined by the *behique*, who practised a sort of sympathetic medicine, eating the same food as the patient and even trying to look like someone suffering from an illness. But the shamans were only intermediaries; they would inhale *cohoba* powder (snorting tubes still survive, found on Taíno excavation sites); this would throw them into a trance, 'in such a fashion that they do not know what they are doing', though the *behiques* believed that they were able to converse this way with the *zemís*. The *behique* would try to draw illness out of the sick person: 'he pulls hard on him, as if he wished to pull something out.'[44] The shaman sucked on the patient's neck or chest or stomach, and he coughed and spat out a concoction of meat, bone or stone that he had put in his mouth, which symbolised the disease of which the patient was being purged.

These methods did not, of course, always work. Patients died and their families wanted to know why. In such cases, especially if the patient had been a member of a large or prominent family, the *behique* would be held to account. The Taínos would prepare a herbal infusion to which they would add the ground nails and hair of the deceased. They would then force this into the mouth or up the nose of the corpse, asking him whether the *behique* had caused his death, particularly by failing to follow the sympathetic diet he was expected to adopt:

> And they ask him this many times until at last he speaks as clearly as if he were alive so that he finally answers everything they ask him, saying that the *behique* did not keep the diet or that he was the cause of his death at that time. And they say that the physician asks him if he is alive and how he speaks so clearly, and he answers that he is dead.[45]

Guilty *behiques* faced a fate far worse than a hearing of a General Medical Council. They were beaten black and blue and left for dead; and if they revived the family of the deceased would pursue them, taking care to ensure that their testicles were crushed, for they were of the opinion that only *behiques* with crushed testicles could be killed.[46] Pané described all this in a deadpan manner, as if these conversations with the dead actually happened, though a little earlier he had castigated the Taínos as 'simple' and 'ignorant'. In fact, Columbus reported a variety of ways of dealing with the dead, which confirmed the sense that the living and the dead inhabited the same physical space. Bodies could be desiccated by heating (and Pané reports that on these occasions too a chance was seized to interview the deceased about his or her final illness); they could be left outside the village in a hammock with cassava water and bread, either already dead or dying. Those who were very ill, especially *caciques*, were sometimes strangled to help them on their way. But it was also, as has been seen, very common to hang up the bones of their relatives (particularly, it seems, children) in their huts, where the dead kept the living company. Small human bones were sometimes used as an adornment as well, strung on necklaces, and they were occasionally incorporated within the *zemís*, which could be made of cloth, beads, ceramics or wood as well as stone; this cannot have appeared so odd to the Spaniards, who were well acquainted with Christian reliquaries containing bits of human bone.

Many *zemís* survive in museum collections. Archaeologists consider that there was a significant expansion of the cult of *zemís* in the two or three centuries before Columbus arrived, though why this should have happened is unclear: there are no signs of a significant migration, bringing new ideas from outside, and the best explanation lies in fact in the lack of migration, as the population ceased moving and settled permanently in the valleys and villages where Columbus would find the Taínos. Taíno society was becoming more complex as it struck deeper roots in the soil of Hispaniola and the other major islands; agricultural cycles developed, and these were closely linked to the cult of *zemís*. By 1492, every household had one or more *zemís* – 'all or the majority of the people of the island of Hispaniola have many *zemís* of various sorts' – though there were also *zemís* that watched over the village, of whom the *cacique* or a lesser headman was the custodian.[47] The credulous Taínos, Pané averred, believed that these objects, which were no more than a 'dead thing', could make the wind blow, the rain fall, the crops grow, and that they could even speak. They were 'idols' or, better, 'demons'.[48] But they were highly prized: they were objects of trade and they were given as presents. The first fruits of the cassava crop were, las Casas said, dedicated to the *zemís*, and placed with them in the *caney* or round-house where the most important images were kept. They represented different gods, such as Itiba Cahubaba, who looked like a decaying corpse but was in fact a fertility goddess; the trapezoidal design that sometimes appears on the back of her head may, it has been suggested, be a diagrammatic world map.[49] Another, made of wood, looked like a dog and used to wander into the jungle at night, but ran away when the Christians arrived on Hispaniola and had not been seen since. Pané ironically commented that this was worthless nonsense, with the words 'as I buy, so also do I sell'.[50] There are plenty of representations of Caracaracol carrying on his back the turtle with which he fell pregnant. Another *zemí*, Corocote, was placed on top of the house of the noble Guamarete, but at night he would come down in human form and lie with the women; when the *zemí* was acquired by another *cacique* later on, exactly the same thing started to happen.[51] One tale related how a tree spoke to an Indian, asking to be cut down and made into an idol.[52]

For Pané, all these tales were simply proof of the idiotic superstition of the Taínos, which could only be set right by their conversion. The *zemís* were part of a seamless world in which gods, living humans, dead humans, animals, crops and the forces of nature existed side by side. Thus to convert the Taínos would involve changing their entire view of the universe and of mankind's part in it. The gulf between Taíno beliefs and Christian ones was wider than any the Christians had experienced in many centuries, wider by far than the relatively narrow gap between Christianity and Judaism or Islam, wider too than the gap between Christianity and Buddhism or the paganism of the Canary islanders or Lithuanians. The explorers had not found 'sects' or 'idolatries', in the sense of organised religious cults with temples and sacrifices, but something that was, as Pané testified, even stranger: a whole world view that was unfathomable.

CHAPTER 12

CUBA = CIPANGU = JAPAN, 1492

Going from Good to Better, October 1492

Columbus was certain that the simple people he had met in October 1492 must have neighbours who were more advanced in their technology, who lived in great cities and who were ruled by wealthy princes. It was this belief that led him from the Bahamas to Cuba in October and November 1492, under the misapprehension that it was Cipangu or Cathay. It stood to reason that a great civilisation flourished nearby: the Lucayan Taínos wore gold ornaments and, when asked, they pointed south to the source of the gold. They assured him that the natives of an island just to the south wore massive bracelets of gold on their arms and legs, though Columbus said, 'I actually believed it was a trick, so that they might get away.'[1] So Columbus did not wait but left San Salvador after a couple of days, feeling his way past the dangerous shoals and learning how to handle the unfamiliar currents; tacking southwards, he reached an island he named Santa María de la Concepción (generally identified as the modern Rum Kay) and anchored there, for he wished to take possession of each island individually, 'even though taking possession of one can be said to imply taking possession of them all'.[2] His arrival there gave one of the Taínos he had picked up in San Salvador the chance to jump overboard and swim away; the Spaniards gave chase but the Taíno escaped, and all the islanders 'ran away like chickens'. The crew made the mistake of trying to seize another Indian who had come in his canoe to trade some cotton with them; but at the admiral's command the Taíno whom they had just captured was sent back with his canoe and gifts of a red cap, green glass beads and little bells, 'which I put in his ears'. This appeased the islanders, who were troubled by the chase that they had witnessed earlier; the man who had been given the bells apparently was full of praise for the explorers, 'and really it seemed to him that we were good people'.[3]

Columbus was impressed by the green, fertile islands he passed, but his appetite for gold drew him rapidly down towards the bigger islands that (if he understood correctly the gestures of the natives) must lie to the south. How the Indians really reacted to his arrival is, of course, hard to judge; but Columbus' encounter with a Taíno who was paddling south towards Fernandina suggests that they were excited by his coming, and had a commercial instinct of their own. This man carried goods the Spaniards had only just been trading in Guanahaní: a string of glass beads and two silver coins. He also carried his own cassava bread, a gourd of water and what seemed to be a lump of red earth, powdered and kneaded, as well as dried herbs which Columbus had already been offered on San Salvador, and which he realised were obviously valued by the Taínos. 'I realised from those things that he was coming from the island of San Salvador, had gone to Santa María, and was going across to Fernandina', the third island of any size he had discovered, which he named after the king of Aragon.[4] Castilian truck had thus entered into the trade networks of the Taíno world almost overnight. Columbus ordered that the man be well treated, and the ships even gave him a ride to Fernandina, taking along his canoe for him. This way 'he will give good tidings about us' so that future visitors from Spain would be well received in the islands. This worked, because the natives of Fernandina proved very friendly, and surrounded the ships with their canoes, offering water and gifts. In return, to the delight of the Indians, Columbus' crew was ordered to give out laces, rattles and glass beads, and to feed those who came aboard, offering them *miel de açucar*, sugar molasses – the first encounter of the inhabitants of the region with the commodity that, in later centuries, would dominate the economy of the Caribbean world and fuel the hideous slave trade. To his excitement, Columbus found that the islanders wore gold everywhere, from their ears and noses to their legs; he was sure it was gold because he compared it with some in his possession (most likely it was the pale gold alloy *guanín*, which contains naturally alloyed copper and which was traded up the island chain from South America).[5] But frankly there was no reason to delay there, because the gold had evidently been brought from somewhere else, and that was the place to which he was heading: 'I cannot go wrong, with our Lord's help, or fail to find where it originates.'[6]

As he travelled so hopefully towards the court of the Great Khan, or Japanese emperor, Columbus was confident that he could see greater signs of

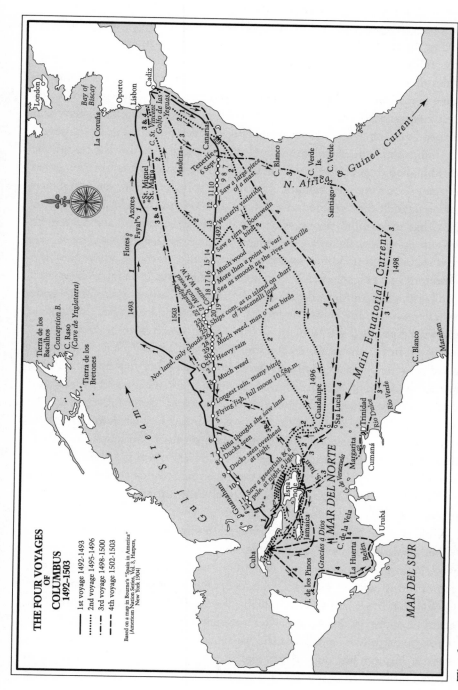

The four voyages of Columbus

civilisation. He thought that the further he voyaged, the more sophisticated the people he met were: 'I see that they have brought cotton and other things here to the ship, so they know better how to bargain for payment, which the others did not do.'[7] This was the voice of the merchant of Genoa. But there were other features that convinced him he was coming closer to civilisation. Some natives wore short capes made of cotton; he noted that women covered their genitals with small pieces of cotton, though not very effectively; then, further along, he observed that women wore fuller cotton pants or drawers.

At the same time, Columbus took a real delight in the colours of the world he had discovered – the brilliant feathers of the parrots, the rich green foliage of the shore, the brightly patterned fish: 'blue, yellow, red and multi-coloured, and others painted in a thousand ways, and the colours are so brilliant that there is no person who would not be astonished and take great delight in seeing them.'[8] Columbus had a businessman's eye for exotic products, rare commodities; and yet this insistence on the beauty of the New World also reveals genuine delight, a real love of nature. Later, as he moved south-eastwards through the islands, he said that 'he was going from good to better, both in the lands, the forests, the plants, the fruits, and the flowers, and in the people';[9] and sometimes 'the people' do seem to be lower on his list of exotica than the landscape and the flora. But the New World triggered his religious imagination as well: here were islands that had something of the character of Paradise.[10] Later he would ask whether the Garden of Eden itself was close by. This in turn reinforced his powerful sense that he was in the Spice Islands off the coast of China. For spices were known to originate in a semi-paradise, so that part of their attraction to a self-respecting burgher of Bruges or citizen of Siena was not just their taste and smell but the fact that this was the perfume of the lands bordering Eden, a perfume that Columbus said he could smell as it wafted on the breezes that came offshore.

Gold was the metal of Paradise, forged by the Sun, whose colour it took. When some of his men reported that they had met an Indian whose nose-piece looked like a minted coin, Columbus was upset that they had failed to carry off this precious proof that the court of an oriental emperor was nearby. On an island that he baptised 'Isabela', where he stopped on 19 October, he heard of a king in the interior who was rich in gold, but this did not make sense: the island was small and the natives were poor. Yet it was also a place of great beauty: 'nor do my eyes tire of seeing such beautiful greenery, so unlike our own.'[11] He was sure many of the plants and trees would produce valuable dyes and medicines, but could not recognise them; he would bring back specimens anyhow. 'The song of the little birds is such that it seems that a person would never want to leave here; there are flocks of parrots that block out the sun.'[12] There were also great reptiles seven spans long that slipped into the water; these must have been crocodiles, and his men soon managed to kill and decapitate one of them. The crocodiles were another reminder of the fact that he had reached the lands full of strange beasts described in the medieval bestiaries and by Marco Polo.

The crew traded with the natives on Isabela, exchanging broken glass and pottery for cotton balls and javelins. Meanwhile, Columbus waited for a suitable wind, and could not even sail round the island for lack of a good breeze. As the days passed he decided that the island had no gold mine, and that its delights were not great enough to detain him, 'since one should go where there is a lot of commerce'.[13] Still, the people of Isabela told him of another place, much bigger, not far off, called 'Colba' or Cuba, and beyond that Bohío, the 'Home Island'. This news resolved any uncertainties about where he was; a deft game of phoney etymology with the sounds *kuba* and *kipa* showed that Colba was surely 'the island of Cipangu of which such marvellous tales are told'. It was a very large island 'where there were gold, spices, large ships and merchants', and there was no doubt that it was there, because one only had to look at the globes and maps Columbus had studied. He would call there, present his credentials, and then perhaps move on to Hangchow to deliver his letter to the Great Khan 'and request an answer and return with it'.[14]

The Discovery of Cuba, October–November 1492

So, at midnight on Wednesday 24 October the ships raised their anchors and swung to the west-south-west, but the journey was slow, partly because of uncertainty about the route, despite advice from the Taínos they had taken on board, and partly because of stormy weather. Only on the evening of 27 October did the ships sight land. Cuba was thus the first of the major Caribbean islands that Columbus discovered, though it was not until nineteen years later that the Spaniards at last decided to launch an invasion of it. In fact, Columbus was favourably impressed by Cuba. 'He says,' las Casas reported, 'that that island is the most beautiful that eyes have seen.'[15] Columbus admired the mountains, comparing the landscape to that of Sicily; he identified many good harbours; and he found many clams, which suggested to him that the island would be rich in pearls, a view confirmed by the claims of the Indians on board his ships. 'The admiral understood that large ships belonging to the Great Khan came there and that it was ten days' journey from there to the mainland';[16] so there was no question – it must be Japan. However, it deserved to be named in honour of the king and queen of Castile, so he called it 'Juana', after the heir to the throne, the Infante Juan, and his sister Juana (the future Queen Juana the Mad of Castile). Columbus coasted along the low shores, and the ships entered a river mouth, where they saw palm trees, but of a different kind from those that grew on the Guinea coast of Africa: they had large leaves with which the natives covered their buildings. Columbus himself went ashore and into a couple of fishermen's huts, but the men had fled and all he found was a dog that could not bark, some nets and twine and other fishing gear, and many hearths, from which he concluded that many people lived together in these houses. He ordered his men to respect what they found and not to take anything away, though one is entitled to wonder whether he would have been quite so high-minded had they discovered golden artefacts.

Further down the coast, Columbus landed some of his men from a couple of boats, and even sent ashore one of the Taínos from San Salvador, 'for by now the natives understood something of, and showed themselves to be content to be with, the Christians'.[17] Columbus was unconcerned that the villages he and his men found were not full of golden palaces. Rather, in las Casas' paraphrase, 'the buildings, he says, were yet more beautiful than those he had seen, and he believed that the closer they came to the mainland, the better the buildings would be'.[18] They were made of palm trunks and branches. Probably because they had sharp-angled roofs, they reminded him of the tents that were erected during military campaigns, but they were laid out in a rather random fashion, without any sense of proper streets. They were very clean inside and well fitted out. The explorers found little statues of women and 'many heads shaped like masks'; Columbus remarked, 'I do not know if they have them for their beauty or if they worship them.'[19] Excitement at having reached 'Asia' was doubled the next day, when one of the Pinzón brothers reported on 30 October that the Indians who were on board the *Pinta* were helpfully directing the explorers to the city of 'Cuba', four days' journey down one of the rivers. As he heard these reports, Columbus found it impossible to make up his mind whether this was really a large island or part of the Asian landmass. He swung round to the view that (contrary to what the Taínos had been saying earlier) they had arrived not at an island but 'a very large continent which extended far to the north', ruled by a fabulous king of 'Faba', who was supposedly at war with the Great Khan. 'I found it to be so large,' he later wrote to the Catholic Monarchs, 'that I thought it could not be an island, but mainland, and that it could be the province of Cathay.' It was therefore time to send the messages of Ferdinand and Isabella to their rightful recipients. Ignoring talk of war between these peoples and the Great Khan, he would send a sailor 'who had travelled into Guinea on the same sort of errand' to the king of Faba, along with some of the Indians from Guanahaní; and he would then attempt to reach the Great Khan himself.[20]

Yet it was not easy to come in close to land; there were shoals, and in any case the natives fled in fear at the sight of the ships. Columbus sent one of his Indians ashore and instructed him to assure the natives that the newcomers were not part of the army of the Great Khan (quite what that piece of information meant to anyone is another matter); indeed, the Christians came with gifts. Since the natives were so wary of the explorers, Columbus' Indian friend had to shout his messages to the Cubans from the boat that was bringing him ashore. This Indian then swam ashore, and was seized by the natives and interviewed, but he bravely insisted that they had nothing to fear; so after that more than sixteen canoes came up to the ships, offering spun cotton and trinkets. Columbus, now determined to concentrate on the search for gold, ordered that none of this should be taken from the natives (though evidently a certain amount of truck was given to them as gifts). They were to be made aware that the ships had arrived in search of one item: gold. The sailors looked hard but found no one who was wearing gold ornaments. However, there was one man who had a silver nose-piece, so it seemed that Cuba contained silver at least.

> The Indians said by means of gestures that before three days passed, many merchants from inland would come from inland to purchase some of the things that the Christians bring there, and would give news of the king of that land, who, according to what could be understood from the gestures they made, was four days' journey from there, for they had sent many men throughout the land to let him know about the admiral.[21]

This reply is strangely reminiscent of da Mosto's account of trade on the Guinea coast; there too the natives spoke of merchants from the interior who would soon come and trade, and of kings who reigned several days' journey into the interior. In other words, Columbus knew the answer before he put the question. He had been to Guinea, he had seen trade conducted in this way. This was how things must be done in Furthest Asia, just as much as in West Africa.

However, Columbus was not only interested in business affairs. He did note down some comments about the customs and religion of the Cuban natives. He observed that the language they spoke was similar to that of the Lucayan Taínos, that they were naked like the Lucayans, and that the Cubans seemed to be on good terms with the other Taínos. He was coming round to the view that there was a host of islands all at war with the Chinese emperor, though he still inclined to the view that Cuba itself was part of the mainland.

> These people (says the admiral) are of the same nature and customs as the others found so far, with no religion [*secta*] that I may recognise, for so far I have not seen those whom I bring with me make any prayer, but they do say the *Salve* and the *Ave Maria* with their hands lifted to the sky as they are shown and make the sign of the cross.[22]

The time had evidently come to make contact with the local ruler. On 2 November Columbus carefully selected four people: a Taíno from Guanahaní; a Taíno from one of the Cuban coastal villages; a certain Rodrigo de Jerez; and the interpreter Luís de Torres, a former confidant of the governor of Murcia, a *converso* who 'had been a Jew' and understood the mother of languages, Hebrew, as well as Aramaic and some Arabic, all of which should surely fit him out well for a journey into Asia.[23] They were to spend up to six days exploring the hinterland, carrying beads which they could exchange for food, and spices which they could compare with the plants they found as they travelled. They were to search for information about this king, 'to learn about his situation, establish friendship with him, and favour him in whatever he might have need of from them'.[24]

While they were away Columbus received reports from Martín Alonso Pinzón that the natives were offering pieces of cinnamon bark in trade. The islanders also demonstrated knowledge of pepper when they were shown samples Columbus had brought from Europe (though what was cultivated in the Caribbean, and liberally used in Taíno stews, was closer to the *malagueta* pepper, later called *piri-piri*, collected by the Portuguese in Guinea than it was to the exotic peppers of the East Indies). This was all very satisfying to Columbus, and it was further proof that he was in the

Spice Islands: 'these islands are those innumerable ones that on maps of the world are placed at the edge of the Orient.'[25] As for gold and pearls, the natives, when shown samples, announced that Bohío to the east was the place where one found gold in infinite quantities, and where the inhabitants wore it on their arms, legs and necks. (*Bohío* meant 'home', but the word was also used for the large island later known as Hispaniola.) Most likely, the Indians simply wanted to please Columbus with a vague answer, and perhaps encourage his fleet to move on. They themselves did not greatly value gold, though items such as European shoelaces with brass tags seemed to them the stuff of heaven.[26] The admiral was fascinated by what he saw of the life of the villagers – how they harvested wild cotton, how they grew beans, rather different from those he knew, and root crops, which he called *mames*, probably a type of yam or sweet potato. His men found what appeared to be aloewood, used back home in the making of perfume and incense; they found mastic, and an Indian indicated that it was a good cure for stomach ache. Columbus already knew the value of this product, which was brought to Europe in vast quantities from the Genoese-controlled island of Chios; he said that he had seen it being produced there.[27] It was used in the fifteenth century as chewing gum and to clean one's teeth. So, not surprisingly, Columbus and his companions began to discuss the possibility of setting up a fort and harbour, for they had received more reports of big ships and merchandise to the south-west of where they stood, and the commercial opportunity could not be ignored.

An Imperfect Paradise, November 1492

On the other hand, this Paradise was not perfect. On 4 November Columbus began to hear the first tales of cyclopean people, and of dog-headed people who consumed human flesh, drinking the blood of their victims and cutting off their genitalia. To his wonderment and alarm, these tales were repeated as they travelled down the northern edge of the Greater Antilles. Since Columbus did not speak Arawak, the image of monstrous people says more about the admiral's expectations than about what the Taínos were trying to explain, although (as will be seen) these tales eventually merged with their tales of Caribs or *Caniba*, whose name conveniently seemed to incorporate the Latin word *canis*, 'dog'. Kings rich in gold, ports full of merchandise, but also strange peoples with dog-heads, were all part of the mental baggage Columbus had brought with him to the edges of what he believed to be Asia.[28]

The men Columbus had sent into the interior were not away for long; they came back during the night of 5 November. They had walked some distance (twelve leagues, they claimed, which was maybe as much as forty miles) and found a village with fifty houses, with about twenty people living in each house. They had been very well received; the natives touched them all over, believing that they had come from the sky, so that they were anxious to find out if they were made of flesh and bone. The guests were led to the main house of the village and seated on wooden *duhos*, while the villagers sat on the ground around them. Ferdinand Columbus, in his account of his father's first voyage, described these *duhos* very closely:

> They seated them on chairs made in one piece, strangely shaped and almost like an animal with short arms and legs and a tail as wide as the chair slightly raised for convenience to lean against; at the front it had eyes and ears made of gold. They call these chairs *duchos*.[29]

This exactly matches the appearance of surviving *duhos*. Then their Indian interpreter (Torres' Hebrew having proved useless) assured the Cuban natives that the Christians were good people, and did his best to tell them something about who they were and how they lived. The villagers offered food, begging the visitors to stay for five days or more. The visitors were shown spices, and the villagers confidently stated that there were plenty more to be found to the south-east, though they were unaware of any local sources. But they knew nothing of any great city, and no doubt did not even know what a city was, so the explorers thought it best to turn back. In fact, half the village tried to follow them, for they wanted to see the Christians return to the sky. In the end a headman, his son and one of their companions came on board the *Santa María* to visit Columbus, telling him about the many islands that existed round about. However, when night fell the natives began to panic, and asked to be put ashore – easily done, because the ships were beached for careening and repairs. Despite his promise to return, the Indian chief disappeared for good. Night, as Pané pointed out in his book, was an uneasy time for the Taínos, when the dead walked without their navels among the living. The natives wanted to get away. After all, what real evidence did they have that the Christians were living beings with navels?

Columbus' views on the Cuban Taínos became a mantra in his description of nearly all the 'good' peoples he encountered on his first voyage. He formed his view of them early; it was positive. He was firm in his opinions and liked repeating them. He wrote in his logbook that 'they are very much without malice, not warlike, all naked, men and women, just as their mothers bore them'; 'it is true that the women wear a cotton thing just big enough to cover their genitals and no more, but they are of good appearance and not very dark, less so than the women from the Canaries.'[30] He grappled with the question of their religious beliefs and practices:

> These people have no religion [*esta gente no tiene secta ninguna*], nor are they idolatrous; rather they are very gentle, without knowing what evil is, or what it is to kill or seize things; they are without weapons and are so timid that one of our people can make a hundred of them flee, even though our own people are only joking with them. They are believers, and recognise that there is a God in heaven, and they believe firmly that we have come from the sky.[31]

At the same time he had no doubt that 'Your Highnesses' would do well to make them into Christians – and, by extension, to assert dominion over them – because it would not merely bring a great multitude to faith in Christ, it would also bring Spain great riches and territories. The material and the spiritual were closely intertwined, not just in Columbus' thinking but in that of Ferdinand and Isabella. He urged that 'devout, religious persons knowing their language' should be sent to them.[32] Indeed, just after Ferdinand and Isabella had 'destroyed those who did not want to profess faith in the Father, the Son and the Holy Ghost' in Spain, and just as 'you will leave your kingdoms in a very tranquil condition, cleansed of heresy and evil', they found themselves in a position 'to bring such large nations to the Church and convert them'.[33] The expulsion of the Jews from Spain, the hunting down by the Inquisition of judaising *conversos* as heretics, the conquest of Muslim Granada had culminated in an opportunity to evangelise the peoples on the other side of the Atlantic.

Cannibal Tales, November 1492

Rather than trying to take possession of Cuba, an impatient and excited Columbus decided to head for an island called Babeque, where gold was so plentiful that the people went out to the beaches by candlelight to collect gold, which they then hammered into rods. That, at least, was what he understood the Indians who were travelling with him to say. He had to wait for a fair wind, but finally he set out on 12 November, a month after he had reached the region; and on the way east along the north coast of Cuba he kept seeing lush estuaries, which this time did not tempt him: he had a fair wind, and (he believed) if and when he came to a great city near the sea he would have no difficulty recognising that he was in its vicinity. He watched for good harbours; but what he wanted and expected to find was ports full of ships loading gold and spices. He kept watch for natives, though, and observed how they lived all along the shore. It was at this point that he noted in his diary that the cotton cultivated along the north shore of Cuba would sell very well in Cathay and Cipangu ('these parts') and would not need to be brought to Spain first.[34] His fertile imagination had leapt forward; he could see in his mind's eye the trading ships flying the flag of Castile, confidently setting sail for Hangchow after cornering the market in fine cotton. But he was especially pleased to win the confidence of some of the natives whom he took aboard his ships. He wrote that in the past, along the Guinea coast, men had been picked up and taken back to Portugal to learn Portuguese, but when they had then been sent back home they had vanished without trace. He thought that it made much more sense to bring both men and women to Spain, taking advantage of the fact that in Cuba men and women travelled together by canoe, which was not (he said) the case in Guinea. And this made even better sense because 'these women will teach our women a lot of their language, which is the same on all of these islands of the Indies', while in Guinea there were a thousand different languages.[35] The domestic setting in which this would most likely occur was, of course, one in which the Taíno women were servants or slaves of European women.

Columbus' journey through a few of the little islands that lay to the north of Cuba gave him further opportunities to claim land for Christendom. In each place where the admiral went ashore, he planted a cross; on an island off Cuba he constructed one from a pair of logs he found on a spit of land, next to a good natural harbour, for he was always alive to commercial possibilities, and always keen to map the places where trade forts could be established on the model of Arguim and Elmina in Guinea. If he visited quite as many islands as his logbook implied, he must have wandered rather aimlessly for a week on his way to Babeque and Bohío. This wandering irritated his ambitious colleague Martín Alonso Pinzón. Convinced by an Indian on his ship that gold was easily accessible on Babeque, Pinzón disobediently sailed off with his men in the *Pinta*, hoping to find the island and its riches; he did this 'for the sake of greed', as Columbus or his editor las Casas remarked, not that

Columbus himself can be acquitted of greed for gold.[36] In any case, even with quite favourable winds, contrary currents meant that neither the *Pinta* nor the *Santa María* and the *Niña* could reach land, and for some time Pinzón's ship remained within sight about sixteen miles ahead.

No less frustrating was the panic-stricken attitude of the Indians on board the *Santa María* when the ship coasted past north-eastern Cuba in late November. Tales of monstrous races began to surface again. Las Casas summarised what Columbus had written in his logbook about the land they were now passing:

> They said it was very large and that there were people upon it who had one eye in the middle of their foreheads and others whom they called cannibals, of whom they showed themselves to have a great fear. Once they saw that he followed this course, he says, they could not speak, for those people used to eat them and are very well-armed. The admiral says that indeed he believed that there was something in it, but that, since they were armed, they would be a rational people. He believed that these cannibals had taken some of them captive, and that, because the captives had not returned to their own lands, they said that they had been eaten by them. They believed the same thing about the Christians and the admiral, when some of them first saw them.[37]

Columbus reiterated this point three days later: 'all the people whom he has found up to today, he says, have the greatest fear of the people of Caniba, or Canima'; moreover, 'they say that the people here had only one eye each and dogs' faces, but the admiral believed they were lying'.[38] This account is rich in the imagery of the cyclopean monsters and man-eaters described by Mandeville and others.[39] Las Casas was scornful of such stories but typically laid the blame on the Christians rather than the Indians: 'whence it seems that the Christians had understood nothing, or almost nothing, because on this island there was never any one-eyed race or cannibals that ate people.'[40] His hero Columbus, on the other hand, naturally thought it was all lies and was not fooled. But las Casas revealed why Columbus was unconvinced: 'the admiral felt that the people who used to capture them must belong to the Great Khan's dominion.'[41] This was an elegant solution. What could *Caniba* be but *Khaniba*, the subjects of the Great Khan? For the moment the alternative and all-too-obvious etymology deriving *Caniba* from *canis*, 'dog', had no appeal, even if some of the peoples of the region were supposedly dog-headed. The fear of the Taínos matched the stories Columbus had heard six weeks before in Guanahaní, about raiders from the sea. Still, Columbus was keen to insist on the humanity of the *canibales*, and las Casas, for his part, could not let this evidence of Columbus' own humane approach pass without approval. Animals cannot reason and do not carry arms; therefore, according to Columbus' logic, carrying arms was a sign of having risen above the level of beasts. Later, as reports of the Caribs grew in detail, Columbus began to draw a sharp line between two types of Indian: the good, docile ones and the violent, cruel ones.

The region he had now found was very mountainous but 'walkable', with beautiful valleys full of fine tall trees.[42] One of the estuaries contained stones that glittered, which brought to mind the gold-bearing stones Columbus knew from the River Tagus in Portugal, though most likely he was only being shown pyrite or 'fool's gold' and was too enthusiastic to look carefully. On the beaches he saw other stones that seemed to contain iron and silver. But Columbus was puzzled that at first he did not encounter people or villages, only abandoned hearths. Eventually, on Tuesday 27 November, his two ships reached a large settlement in north-eastern Cuba, and a great mass of people, armed with javelins, came to meet him. He wanted to offer them gifts but they were hostile and made it plain that they would prevent the Christians from landing. All the same, three brave crewmen, who had learned Taíno words, disembarked from a lighter and tried to explain that the natives need have no fear of the newcomers. Rather than stand and fight, the islanders fled in terror, and the Christians were able to wander around their abandoned village. Gradually, however, as the ships worked their way up the coast, the explorers saw more and more settlements; they saw smoke rising through the forests; they saw well-tilled fields; they saw excellent harbours. They rode upriver, and Columbus told his companions to note all the wonders they saw so that those back home would realise that he was not exaggerating in his description of this world that had so enchanted him – the logbook uses this very word, *encantado*, to describe his sense of wonder.[43]

Spain's New Dominions, November–December 1492

The explorers planted crosses as they travelled, but it was clear that Columbus had no serious intention of establishing himself in the Bahamas or even Cuba if, as he was sure, richer lands could be found further along his route, lands containing either gold mines or flourishing ports of trade. Columbus exclaimed in his logbook: 'it is certain, my lords and princes, that where there are such lands, there must be innumerable things from which to profit.'[44] This was not just to the benefit of merchants, but of all Spain, since 'all must be subject' to Castile in these lands; 'and I say that your highnesses should not consent that any foreigner trade or even set foot here, except Catholic Christians – since this was the beginning and end of the project: that it should be for the growth and glory of the Christian religion.' But there were also great frustrations:

> I do not know the language, and the people of these lands do not understand me, nor do I, or anyone whom I have with me, understand them. Many times, with these Indians whom I am bringing, I understand them to say one thing, instead of something else that means the opposite; nor do I trust them much, for they have tried to run away many times.[45]

He insisted that there were, all the same, great dividends to be won, since by learning their language 'one will work to make all these peoples Christians, for that will be done easily because they have no religion and they are not idolaters'. If the king and queen had a city and a castle built in these lands, the people would be converted and the Spaniards could then benefit from the delights of this country, with its pleasant climate (he had still to experience hurricanes), its fertility and the pure water that ran in its rivers, especially by comparison with the foul waters of the rivers along the Guinea coast. In other words, what he had already found was far more desirable than the sun-baked lands the Portuguese were opening up on the route around Africa. After all, none of his crew had even suffered a headache since they had arrived! One old sailor who suffered from gallstones was better within two days. This image of lands where disease was absent and where it was possible to live long became a regular feature of European descriptions of newly discovered territories.

Scared of the explorers, the Taínos fled from their villages, which Columbus' men could thus explore at their leisure. On 29 November they found wax, which they brought to the admiral; but they also found a basket containing a human skull, hanging from a post in one of the houses. Columbus read nothing bad into this; he thought that these were the relics of important ancestors, and he noted that the houses themselves were very big, 'in such a way that many people can take shelter in only one of them, and they must all be descendants of a single person'.[46] He did not jump to the conclusion that the skulls were evidence of cannibalism. There were several reasons for Columbus' positive attitude. The cult of bones had little horror for a medieval Catholic accustomed to reliquaries. But what is really intriguing is his quick understanding that the houses they had found were inhabited by family clans. Genoa in the fifteenth century, like many other Italian cities, was dominated by noble families organised in *alberghi* or clans, who lived together in their own quarters of the city, in a close huddle of palaces. On this occasion a social model derived from the Old World really did help explain what he saw in the New World. Finally, he was still determined to show that the people he had discovered were fundamentally good folk who lived in accordance with the basic principles of natural law, exercising reason and avoiding bestial behaviour. It was this early sympathy for the natives that convinced las Casas of Columbus' heroic qualities.

The explorers were increasingly aware that they had come upon a well-populated land, even if they could find hardly any inhabitants. They admired the well-cultivated fields of Cuba. They were amazed at the fine craftsmanship of the canoes, one of which could carry 150 people; others had beautiful carvings. On 3 December Columbus arrived off a Cuban village full of people whom he urged (via his Taíno interpreter) not to rush away, and with whom he tried to trade, but he lost interest when he realised that they could not offer him any gold. He was not afraid of the villagers, for their only weapons were spears, hardened in the fire, which in any case he exchanged for small items of truck. He was convinced that 'ten men might make ten thousand flee, so cowardly and timid are they'.[47] But Columbus had underestimated the native Indians. They came in a great mass to the lighters that had been moored in the nearest river mouth, and one of the Indians started to make a long speech, which of course was totally incomprehensible to the Europeans. Every now and then the other Indians would lift their arms and cry out. Columbus was inclined to think it was a speech of welcome, until his Indian interpreter realised that the natives were threatening to kill the Europeans: Columbus 'saw that the Indian whom he had brought with him had changed expression, turning as yellow as wax'.[48] However, this trembling Indian showed courage after all. He pointed out a crossbow and unsheathed a sword, explaining to the natives that with these weapons the Christians could kill them all. At this news, the Indians melted away very fast.

Columbus was not discouraged by this surly welcome. He asked to be rowed up to the river bank, where many of the Indians had now gathered. Wielding whole handfuls of javelins, they were painted red, stark naked, but in many cases wearing plumes or tufts of feathers on their heads. Columbus offered to exchange the javelins for the little bells, brass rings and beads that he had brought, and this calmed the Indians. When his sailors killed a turtle, they cut the shell into fragments, which they gave to the Indians along with its claws and other pieces of the animal. Columbus decided that these people were much like the others he had met, and that they too thought the Europeans had descended from heaven. But what was unusual was a fine building with two doors, modest in size but beautifully decorated inside, 'in a certain way that I would not know how to describe' (as he disappointingly commented), and hung with seashells and other decorations. At first he assumed it must be a temple – 'I called to the natives and asked by means of gestures if they prayed in it; they said no' – and in fact they offered Columbus some of the objects he saw inside the building. It is likely that this was a *batey* in which the most important *zemís* of the village were kept, and in which the *cacique* perhaps resided. But a *batey* was not a house of prayer like a church, synagogue or mosque, and Columbus was again left with the impression that the Taínos had no religion, in the sense that they lacked a priesthood with elaborate rituals conducted in a temple.

It was only on 5 December 1492 that he bade farewell to Cuba and made the short crossing to Haiti. Columbus wavered over the question whether this was the mainland: he was impressed by its size and ready to jump to grandiose conclusions. The land he found was full of trees and plants that reminded him of Spain; the fish – mullet and sole – were those of Castile; even the blustery weather that he soon encountered was like a Castilian October day. Above all, he was captivated by the broad plains which, frankly, were even finer than those of Spain. So he had no hesitation in calling the island 'La Española', *Hispaniola*, 'the Spanish land'.

CHAPTER 13

LA NAVIDAD, 1492–3

The Second Spain, December 1492

Tacking back and forth, the small Spanish fleet worked its way towards Haiti and its outlying islands. The explorers saw many smoke signals; they decided that they came from watchtowers, and that they were evidence of war between local tribes; later, it became obvious that the signals were passing on messages about the Spanish ships.[1] Columbus saw no settlements along the coastline, but there were signs of cultivation, indicating that the island was thickly inhabited in the interior. The Indians on board were becoming nervous; they had expected to be taken back home and yet they were being carried into lands where they felt unsafe. On Wednesday 12 December Columbus sent his men out to capture some of the natives, not to enslave them but 'in order to show them honour and make them lose their fear';[2] he also wanted to give them presents, as a way of showing his own delight in the beauty of the land. A lovely naked young woman was brought to him and he presented her with clothes, beads, bells and rings made of brass. She was introduced to the Indian women the Spaniards had brought from Cuba, and was tempted to stay on board with them, but Columbus was determined to find out more, and sent her ashore with several of his crew and three of the Indians from his ships. The logbook reveals clearly enough what Columbus really wanted to learn from this young woman. She had a small piece of gold in her nose, 'which was a sign that there was gold on that island'.[3] So the old obsession was never far from the surface. Las Casas, as editor of the logbook, was well aware that Columbus' delight at what he saw and the people he met was constantly distorted by this greedy search for gold.

The men whom Columbus had sent ashore with the young woman returned the next day. Lacking the courage or energy to carry on, they had not reached the village, but they blithely promised that the woman would report their arrival and that the Indians would lose all fear of the Spaniards. They predicted that on the following day a mass of people would come to the ships. Columbus, 'so that the natives might acquire the desire to serve the monarchs', sent more men, some armed, into the hinterland. The effect was that all the villagers fled.[4] Still, they left their possessions behind, and the explorers looked around. They claimed to have seen one thousand buildings and decided that the village contained three thousand people – a rather low estimate of people per house. One of the Indians in Columbus' service managed to send a message to the fugitive Taínos that the Spaniards were 'not from Caniba' but from the sky, and were keen to give away many presents, with the result that two thousand Indians came back, but they were still fearful, trembling in the presence of the Europeans. Still, as they became more accustomed to them, their fear began to evaporate. They even went into their houses and brought them cassava bread and fish; they also learned that Columbus and his men had taken a fancy to parrots, so they brought some of those as well. They showered the explorers with gifts; they wanted nothing in return; in fact, nothing would please them better than if the Spaniards spent the night in their villages as their guests.

What really sealed this friendly relationship was the arrival of the young woman whom Columbus had honoured on board his ships, with her husband and many other Taínos. They were all impressed by the way Columbus had treated her, and carried her aloft; they wanted to thank Columbus for his great courtesy. Columbus, of course, was not present, and these events are only known at third-hand – through las Casas' edited version of the reports Columbus' men made to their admiral, which he then entered in the logbook. Still, he rejoiced in what they had discovered. 'The Christians told the admiral that these people were more beautiful and had a better nature than any of the others whom they had found up to that point'; Columbus replied that surely this was impossible, for all the native Indians they had met had shown themselves to have such good natures. The Christians also reported that these people were whiter than the Indians whom they had met before; indeed, a couple of women were just as white as Spaniards.[5] For Columbus, lighter skins were evidence that they were approaching Japan, for Marco Polo had insisted that the Japanese were white. Not just the people but the land was like, or better than, the countryside around Córdoba. Hispaniola really was a new Spain.

On 16 December Columbus found himself among another large group of
Indians, more than five hundred, who had already heard of his arrival on the
island, for news travelled fast in the Caribbean world. He was impressed by
the fact that the natives wore very attractive pieces of gold as ear- or nose-
rings, and easily persuaded them to give away these trinkets. 'They were very
sweetly spoken, without a religion', and so 'I have a great hope in the Lord
that Your Highnesses will make them all Christian, and they will all be your
subjects, so I consider them your people already.'[6] They were, he said, a little
plumper than the Indians he had met before, implicitly suggesting that they
could feed themselves well from the fertile land. Columbus wrote that the
marvellous fertility of the land meant that there was no real incentive to work,
or even to wear clothes. Everything seemed to be provided by Nature, but,
lacking useful artefacts for sale, Hispaniola was able to buy little gold from the
lands over the horizon that produced it in great amounts.[7]

Naked Kings, December 1492

Columbus' account of his first meetings with local *caciques*, or rulers, is occasionally repetitive. This suggests that he rewrote parts, relying on a confused
memory of the rapid succession of exciting and unprecedented events that he
witnessed. Whether Columbus entertained the Taíno ruler to a meal once or
twice does not, perhaps, matter, certainly not as much as his observations
about the way the *cacique*'s subjects showed their ruler respect, and about the
growing friendship between Columbus and this ruler. Columbus saw the
'king' of these people standing on the beach, a rather reserved young man who
was surrounded by his own people who were acting respectfully towards him
(a sign that this was a society with a proper hierarchy and political institutions). The day culminated in a visit by this king to Columbus' flagship; this
was a great success, although the king was reluctant to believe Columbus'
story that he was only the subject of an earthly king and queen, for it was
obvious that the Christians had arrived from the sky and that these Spanish
monarchs also lived in the sky. The explorers offered the king and his
courtiers some Spanish food, and they ate a little. All this gave Columbus
ideas about the policy that his king and queen should adopt towards the
native Indians. Hispaniola could easily be mastered if the Spanish established
a base there; only a very small number of men was required in order to establish mastery over the entire island, since the natives were unarmed (a mistaken
view), naked and 'very cowardly'. You could set three Europeans against a

thousand Taínos. 'And so they are good for being given commands and being made to till, to plant, and to do everything else that may be necessary, and you may build towns and teach them to go around clothed and adopt our customs.'[8] So Columbus believed that they needed to be introduced to the trappings of civilisation, for what he saw as their own good, and that their natural role was as subordinates.

Against them, though, were the other Indians, the Caribs, about whom evidence began to accumulate. The Taínos showed the explorers deadly Carib arrows made of long reeds into which sharpened wooden points had been fitted. Two Taínos even showed the Europeans wounds which they apparently blamed on the Caribs: great chunks of flesh had been torn out of their bodies, and the explorers were told that Caribs had bitten out the flesh, but Columbus refused to believe it. Still, the idea of good and bad Indians had by now been firmly planted. That these were good Indians was clear; the sailors went fishing and took along some Indians, who had a marvellous time. Then, on Tuesday 18 December, Columbus lured the young king back to his ship by decking out his vessels for a religious feast day and firing his cannons. The king came on a litter with a great retinue, and Columbus was deeply impressed by the respect his subjects showed for him, 'even though they all go around naked'.[9] Columbus was eating a meal at a table in the stern castle when the king arrived, but the latter insisted that he stay put and carry on eating, and that he should not come outside to receive him formally. The king signalled to his men, most of whom jumped to his command and arranged themselves on the deck outside, while a few close advisers were allowed to go with him into the stern castle. Columbus offered food. The king tasted a morsel before sending the rest out to his retinue. Columbus was impressed by his dignity; he said little, but his advisers 'watched his mouth and spoke for him, and with him, with great reverence'.[10] Then the exchange of gifts took place. First, the *cacique* (a term Columbus had learned by now) presented Columbus with a belt, quite similar in appearance to a Spanish one, but with some gold decoration; still, the gold was thin foil and confirmed the suspicion that the metal was not as plentiful as in Marco Polo's Japan. Columbus reciprocated with a hanging from his cabin that the *cacique* had admired, as well as a necklace of amber beads that he was wearing at the time. Columbus also gave him red shoes and a container of orange-flower water. Of course there was difficulty in communicating. The *cacique*'s advisers were unhappy about this, but the *cacique* seemed to be saying that Columbus could have whatever he wanted from the whole of Hispaniola. Columbus still had to realise that this *cacique* was only one of many; he did not understand the politics of Hispaniola, and was making guesses about its size and importance; but he began to see that it was over an island of this character, with extensive plains and mountains, well-watered valleys and a large native population, that Spain should try to establish itself as master. He realised that the island had tall peaks – he suggested that the mountains were even higher than Mount Teide in Tenerife, 'which is considered among the highest that can be found'.[11] There were still no signs of forts manned by Japanese or Chinese warriors, which he would not dare challenge. His instinct led him to see that this was the ideal base for Spanish operations in the Caribbean.

In fact, the time had come to show the *cacique* a picture of the new over-lords of this island, so he sent for his purse and took out a gold *excelente*, a coin minted by Ferdinand and Isabella, with the deliberate aim of portraying them as triumphant rulers of Spain. He showed the *cacique* the portraits of the king and queen on the coin, and boasted 'that your highnesses commanded and were lords over all the better part of the world, and that there were no princes who were as great'.[12] Then he had the royal banners unfurled, as well as banners bearing crosses, and the *cacique* was very impressed, naturally moved at the sight of the crosses, even if he had not yet heard the name of Christ. The *cacique* departed as the light failed, and a great procession wended its way back to the Taíno village; the *cacique*'s companions proudly carried the gifts Columbus had presented to their ruler. Columbus greatly enjoyed his first direct contact with Hispaniola, particularly since he gathered valuable infor-mation (much of it tendentious) concerning gold-rich islands off Hispaniola. An old man spoke of one island that was entirely made of gold. Misunderstandings of course abounded, and the Taínos were anyway only too happy to please the admiral with whatever fantasies made him happy. Columbus defended his decision not to carry off this old man so that he could help the Spaniards locate these gold-bearing lands: this man was a close adviser of the *cacique* and, even though he would probably have come will-ingly, Columbus now 'considered these people to belong already to the monarchs of Castile, and it was not right to offend them'.[13] In fact, the time had come to leave among them a sign that they had been visited by the Christ-bearer (*Christophoros*) Columbus. He therefore erected an enormous cross in the middle of the village plaza, with the enthusiastic help of the Indians. They started praying and worshipped the cross; as a result Columbus was full of hope that the islands would easily turn Christian. Later, his diary recorded his feeling that the people of Hispaniola were better subjects of the rulers of Castile than the Castilians: 'he already considers them Christians.'[14] If you told them to do something, they would eagerly run to do it: they were natural servants.

Heading eastwards, looking for harbours where the first Christian settlement could be established, he was carried away with enthusiasm for what he saw. He had seen all the great ports of East and West, he said, and he had sailed the Guinea coast, but 'the present harbour is superior to all the others'.[15] He began to notice variations in the native cultures. Along the north-west of Haiti he found people who, unlike the adult women in Cuba, did not even cover their genitals with pieces of cotton: 'here neither the young woman nor the old does so.'[16] Nor did the men hide the women away from the Europeans, as had happened further west. He admired their great beauty and their fulsome generosity; he found it impossible to believe that anyone had ever encountered such good-hearted people, 'so generous in giving and so timorous'. They brought gifts of cassava bread and fruit, but the admiral characteristically ordered his men not to take what they were offered without giving something in return, 'so the Christians paid for everything they received from the natives'.[17] European gifts were sometimes very modest – the metal tip of a shoelace or a broken bowl – but the Indians were willing to give all they had for these trifles.[18] Still, when he heard reports of gold mines in the interior, Columbus did begin to wonder whether he could have all the gold he wanted in return for nothing;[19] so his aim at the moment was not to annoy the native Indians, in the hope that they would, with God's help, point him towards something of far greater value than little bits of gold foil and balls of cotton. Local rulers began to vie with one another for Columbus' attention, still convinced he had alighted from the sky. One *cacique* sent a belt decorated with a mask in the form of a face with ears, a tongue and a golden nose.[20] Crowds of Indians converged on Columbus' party, offering geese, fish, bread and water in small clay jugs which they flavoured with spices and regarded as very healthy (proof, if any were needed, that the fleet was on the edge of the Spice Islands). Columbus seemed to have entered the borders of Paradise.

The First European Settlement, Christmas 1492

Columbus conceived the idea of a big Christmas celebration to impress the Indians. By 24 December his grand procession eastwards had reached the lands of a particularly important *cacique* named Guacanagarí. The crew was showered with gifts of cotton cloth, small pieces of the sort that the Taínos of this village wore, while whatever the Taínos received from the Christians was treated almost as a cult object. But there remained one puzzle that Columbus was desperate to resolve. Where was Japan? The natives of Hispaniola spoke of a place called Cibao, which Columbus now understood to be Cipangu; and they said that its ruler carried standards of hammered gold. But they also insisted that Columbus had to sail much further east to find this place. He thus assumed that he was in the Spice Islands to the south-east of Cipangu, a theory that was credible to him on the basis of some of the maps he had seen. In other words, he had overshot Cipangu. Cuba was not, after all, Cipangu; nor was Hispaniola. On Christmas Eve he reflected on what he had achieved, asserting that Hispaniola was a truly wonderful place, even if it was not a great oriental market of the type he still sought. He compared it with Cuba, which he now decided was much less attractive. So often he saw things in black and white: he now insisted that the two islands were as different as night and day.[21] He loved the sweetness of the people of Hispaniola, which one could deduce from the gentle way they spoke; the Cuban natives, on the other hand, had a threatening air when they spoke. There was a great contrast between the very wary reception accorded to the Spanish ships in eastern Cuba and the enthusiastic welcome they were receiving in north-eastern Hispaniola. The Cuban Indians were darker, he insisted, while those of Hispaniola were of good stature. He admired the way that the ordinary people readily obeyed their lords, and the dignified, reserved manner of the lords, who gave their commands simply by moving their hands. All this (he implied) made them ideal subjects of their Catholic Majesties in Spain. And this sharp contrast between Cubans and Hispaniolans was significant in other ways. The idea that Cuba was wilder and offered less, particularly less gold, delayed its conquest for nearly twenty years while the Spaniards consolidated their hold on Hispaniola.

Just as Columbus thought everything on his voyage was going from good to better, disaster struck his little fleet, before dawn on Christmas Day 1492. He was exhausted after two exciting days and a night without sleep, and he went to bed, leaving the tiller in the hands of a sailor who knew perfectly well that he should stay awake and not hand it over to a ship's boy, which is precisely what he did. The sea appeared to be dead calm; there was no sign of danger. In fact there were gentle currents that were carrying the *Santa María* towards the sandbanks off Hispaniola. Once beached on the sand, the *Santa*

María could not be shifted and began to break up. Columbus was determined to unload everything that was on the ship; and the *cacique*, Guacanagarí, willingly offered his help. Indeed, he seemed more upset about what had happened than the admiral. Every single movable item was taken off the ship, loaded on Indian canoes and taken to the Taíno village; nothing whatsoever was missing. Columbus acerbically commented that this would never have happened in Castile. Moreover, the *cacique* ordered some houses to be cleared so that Columbus' property could be stored under cover. Las Casas reported Columbus' words in his edition of the logbook:

> He and all the people were weeping, says the admiral. They are such loving people, without greed and amenable in everything, that I assure Your Highnesses that I believe there is no better people, or better land, in the world. They love their neighbours as themselves, and they have the sweetest way of speaking in the world: gentle and always with a smile. They go about naked, men and women, just as their mothers bore them, but Your Highnesses may believe that among themselves they have very good customs; and the king has a wonderful stateliness, so composed in a certain fashion that it is a pleasure to see it all. They have wonderful memories, and they want to see everything, and they ask what something is and what it is for. The admiral says all this just in this way.[22]

They lived, then, in a state of innocence, so their nakedness was not something scandalous; they were rational creatures, for they remembered things and had great curiosity; but the most important feature of their character was their selfless love of their neighbour as themselves – they already observed one of the 'two great commandments' of the Bible. They were quick learners; the *cacique* had begun to wear a shirt and some gloves with which he had been presented; in any case, he had impeccable table manners, and Columbus was impressed at the way he rubbed herbs into his hands before washing them after he had eaten. This concern with personal cleanliness was typical of many of the American Indian peoples, and was noticed by the Portuguese discoverers of Brazil a few years later. Someone who behaved with such 'decorousness' could only be of 'noble lineage'.[23] So Columbus and Guacanagarí became firm allies. They talked, insofar as it was possible to have a conversation, of the threat from Carib raiders, 'the people from Caniba', and Columbus made it plain that with his cannons and guns the Taínos had nothing to fear from the Caribs, who after all only had wood-tipped arrows.

The *cacique* was so grateful that he showered Columbus with what must have been quite splendid gifts: there was a mask with inset gold in its eyes and ears, as well as gold necklaces and other gold decorations. Columbus was ready to read a divine plan into everything that happened to him; he now understood that the shipwreck of the *Santa María* had been God's will: 'truly, it was not a disaster but great good luck.'[24]

He now determined to build a fort at this point, settling the excess crew who would not fit on the *Niña* and equipping them with all the supplies (including cannons, bread and wine) that they would need until his return. The fort would be called La Navidad, 'Christmas', in honour of the day on which the *Santa María* had been wrecked. For his return, to which he was beginning to give thought, Columbus could not be sure of being able to use the *Pinta*, which had gone ahead to search for gold, though he had news of it soon after Christmas: it stood not far off, and its crew had become extraordinarily excited by the discovery of rhubarb, which was still a rarity in Europe. The planks out of which the *Santa María* had been constructed would be used to build a tower and palisade for the fort. From here he would conquer the whole island, which was surely even bigger than Portugal (saying this must have given him some pleasure, since the king of Portugal had failed to support him when he had presented his original plan to cross the Atlantic).[25] He would leave behind craftsmen – a tailor, a carpenter, a caulker, a gunner, even a physician and a scribe;[26] but whereas previous expeditions along the coasts of Africa had sent craftsmen south to teach the native population the rudiments of Western technology, these men would be left behind to support the tiny community of Europeans, and to help discover where the gold mines and fields full of spices lay, with the result that when he returned from Europe, as he surely would, he would find a whole barrelful of gold waiting for him – not for nothing did he leave men skilled in the art of barrel-making behind. Then, within a mere three years, the Catholic Monarchs would have accumulated so much wealth that they could go and conquer Jerusalem: 'there is so much of it, in so many places, and on this same island of Hispaniola, the admiral says, that it is a wonder.'[27] 'Thus it is that everything has turned out perfectly,' said the ever-optimistic Columbus.[28]

Columbus was satisfied that he had reached the lands of a really important king. Guacanagarí was the overlord of five other rulers who came to see Columbus on 30 December. News of the Spaniards' arrival was thus spreading across northern Hispaniola. Columbus was keen that the Spanish king and queen should appreciate the dignified bearing and fine conduct of the Indian rulers. Guacanagarí seated Columbus on a platform made of palm bark. On Columbus' head Guacanagarí placed his own crown, probably a feather headdress. Columbus reciprocated by taking off something he was wearing, a collar made of bloodstones and coloured beads, which he placed around the king's neck; he also removed his scarlet cloak, and wrapped it around the king's shoulders. He had heard that the Indians were fascinated by a silver ring they had seen on the finger of one of his crewmen, so he now placed just such a ring on Guacanagarí's finger. The lesser kings had brought presents too, and Columbus was delighted to receive two large pieces of flattened gold. It is abundantly clear that the Indians and the Europeans had reached a ready understanding of each other's tastes and preferences.

Even so, Columbus was not entirely satisfied with Guacanagarí. He suspected that the *cacique* was actively preventing gold from reaching him unless it passed through his own hands first; the Indians wanted Columbus to trade only with them. Columbus the merchant conjured up images of trade monopolies more appropriate to his Genoese compatriots in the Mediterranean. Yet there was talk of regions in which gold was so common that it was not even greatly valued. Besides, there were the spices, which had to be sampled and taken home to Europe, so that the king and queen would see that this land produced spices more valuable than the black pepper or African *malagueta* pepper that reached Spain at the moment.

Columbus was becoming anxious to return to Spain. One important factor was his anxiety that Martín Alonso Pinzón and the *Pinta* would race back to Spain before him and claim all the credit for the discoveries.[29] He had collected enough evidence, he thought, to convince Ferdinand and Isabella that more expeditions to the lands across the Atlantic must be launched. He had an ally in Guacanagarí. So he went to take leave of the *cacique* and made sure that Guacanagarí was impressed by the show that he arranged. A cannon was fired, and the Indians saw, to their astonishment, how a great stone ball shot out of the side of the *Niña* and across the open sea. He asked his crewmen to stage a mock-battle, so that the *cacique* could see what formidable arms Europeans carried. And he discussed with Guacanagarí the recurring problem of Carib raids; he assured the *cacique* that he should not worry about Caribs, for even if they came to his lands, his lieutenants would be able to fend them off. 'The cacique showed great affection to the admiral, and a great deal of emotion over his departure, especially when he saw him go to embark.'[30]

First Encounter with the Caribs, January 1493

The first European settlement in the New World, at La Navidad, consisted of thirty-nine of Columbus' crew, under the leadership of three deputies whom he charged with the judicial powers granted to him by the king and queen. He left the trade goods that had been brought from Europe, in the hope that they would continue to barter such trinkets for yet more gold. He also left a year's supply of biscuits, seed for sowing, a good amount of wine and weapons. Columbus was keen that relations with the Indians should remain good; as such, his men were forbidden to vex Indian women or to seize Indian property.[31] On Friday 4 January Columbus raised anchor and the *Niña* headed east, catching up with the *Pinta* after two days. Martín Alonso Pinzón came aboard to make his excuses for travelling ahead of Columbus. He argued that his smaller, lighter ship was better suited for a visit to the island of Babeque, which was supposedly rich in gold, though in fact Pinzón discovered none there. Columbus was unconvinced: 'Pinzón had gone away out of great arrogance and greed', and his crew had traded their truck for substantial amounts of gold, half of which Pinzón had claimed for himself.[32] Reading the admiral's words, it is unclear who was greedier, Columbus or Pinzón.

Columbus' main concern now was to map the coasts he was passing, to identify river mouths rich in gold, and to press on. He began to realise that he had underestimated the size of Hispaniola, which meant that he had under-estimated its resources and value. The tone of his logbook became more prac-tical, and natural wonders no longer held his attention for so long. He saw some mermaids, by which he clearly meant manatees; 'but they were not so beautiful as they are depicted, for only after a fashion did they have human form in their faces.'[33] He also found that the natives were not all friendly. On Sunday 13 January he was becalmed close to a beach, and his men went ashore to trade their goods for the bows and arrows of the Indians. One naked Indian, 'very deformed in appearance', with his face coloured black all over rather than in the many colours Columbus had seen elsewhere, came aboard the *Niña*; his hair was very long, but it was plaited and hung down his back, with a tail of parrot feathers attached. 'The admiral judged that he must have been one of the Caribs, who eat people.'[34] Columbus decided that the word was *Caniba* further west, *Cariba* in these parts. More importantly, he began to accept that these were cannibals in the modern sense of the term, and from this followed a series of judgments about their human status and rights.

This fellow seemed to speak a different dialect from the Taíno Indians, but they discussed the inevitable topic of gold and the native gave the inevitable answer that a great deal could be found on those islands over there, along with an alloy of gold and copper, which was especially easy to find on the island of Guanín (a term that the Spaniards later used to describe the base gold alloy that was diffused across the Taíno world). The naked Indian also told of an island called Matininó, which was inhabited only by women, a place that was mentioned again by Ramón Pané in his account of native religion.

There were fifty-five Caribs on the beach, all with long pigtails decorated with parrot feathers; some were armed with heavy clubs.[35] The Christians attempted to trade, but the Caribs soon turned violent, trying to capture seven sailors who had come ashore in a longboat, and even running up with cords in their hands so as to tie them up. Columbus' men easily beat off the Indians, wounding a couple and forcing the rest to flee. Columbus had not been on deck to see all this happening, but his reaction when he was told about the skirmish was ambiguous. He thought it was good that the Caribs, if such they were, had been warned off, for if his men from La Navidad ventured along the coast, these Indians would be afraid of attacking them. These people were 'evildoers', and if they were not actually Caribs, they were their neighbours and had similar customs, 'a people without fear, unlike those of the other islands, who are cowards and without weapons, beyond reason'.[36] Columbus averred that the Caribs possessed 'many canoes, almost as big as galleys'.[37] He noticed that they were sending smoke signals across the island. It would have been good if some had been captured, in fact, and he thought of sending a raiding party against them the next day, but had to reckon with stormy weather and high seas. On balance, 'he believed they were the ones from Carib and that they ate people'.[38] If the king and queen decided they wanted him to bring slaves from the lands he had discovered, it was these people, who needed to be tamed, whom he would try to bring back to Spain.[39]

Over the next couple of days relations improved. There were exchanges of gifts; one of their rulers came aboard the *Niña* and was rewarded with the standard gift of a red cap. He and his companions also received some pieces of cloth, which could be interpreted as a reproof for their more savage condition: their nudity seemed to be that of wild and aggressive folk, rather than the innocent nakedness of the gentle Taínos. The Indian king sent him a gold crown. Even while he was hurrying home, Columbus was keen to acquire news of sources of gold, and thought that a brief visit to the women's isle of Matininó might be a good idea. It was a strange place and he really wanted to see it: he had heard that Carib men would come once a year to visit the women, and if the women then gave birth to a boy he would be taken back to Carib territory, while any girls would of course remain on Matininó.[40] There was supposed to be a great deal of copper or base gold there and on what he called 'the island of Carib'. But acquiring it would not be easy, 'because that nation, he says, eat human flesh'.[41] This region also produced a type of pepper that the natives ate with everything, more precious than the black pepper of the Indies; 'fifty caravels can be loaded with it every year in Hispaniola.'[42]

Columbus had made a fateful distinction. He did not like these 'Caribs'. The black face of their king symbolised the moral and spiritual darkness that the Caribs represented. They were wild and unpredictable, their king was ugly. Although he had no hard evidence that they ate human flesh, he associated their violence, and in particular their attempts to capture some of his crewmen, with the tales he had heard among the Taínos of man-eating savages in the islands. As for his description of their appearance, it has been seen that there are many similarities between the 'Caribs' and the Arawaks of the Guyana coast. It is quite likely that these were either Caribs or Taínos who had adopted Carib customs, bearing in mind the reluctance of modern commentators to draw as sharp a distinction between Taínos and Caribs as Columbus wanted to draw. He had established that there were good Taínos and bad Caribs. This dualism would dominate accounts of the New World for a long time. However, there was no time to explore these people and their lands further. From the seaweed he saw in the water, he knew that there were many more islands to the east, and he was even convinced that it was only four hundred leagues to the Canary Islands, which were therefore 'very near'.[43] It was time to set sail across the Ocean Sea and to bring news of his great discoveries to the king and queen in Spain and to the pope in Rome.

CHAPTER 14

FIRST NEWS OF THE NEW WORLD, 1493

Reports from Paradise, 1493

As he left Hispaniola, Columbus was already planning his return to the 'Indies'; but he was about to learn that the journey across the Atlantic posed massive risks. It is a tribute to his seamanship that he managed to steer through severe storms, making a landfall first in the Azores, on the island of Santa Maria, on 18 February 1493. Its Portuguese inhabitants were extremely hostile to Columbus and his crew, who had once again separated from Martín Alonso Pinzón. Columbus brandished his letters of safe-conduct from the king and queen of Castile, but the Portuguese were suspicious of interlopers. Still, in the end they let him go, consigning him to the horrible weather. For from the Azores, the *Niña* headed into further storms, and the ship was swept towards the mouth of the River Tagus, reluctantly limping into the port of Lisbon on 4 March. Meanwhile Pinzón's *Pinta* swung north and reached the European continent at Baiona in Galicia, in Castilian territory, and, had Martín Alonso Pinzón not died soon after landing, he might have been the first to reach the Spanish rulers with news of the discoveries. Columbus, for his part, was embarrassed to have to report his discoveries to the Portuguese court, which had rejected his plans several years earlier and which would not sit by quietly while Castile claimed new lands in the west.[1] King João II immediately insisted that anything he had discovered belonged to Portugal. Columbus showed some of the trinkets he had brought back, as well as his Indian companions, as proof that he had ventured far beyond the lands known to the Portuguese in the eastern Atlantic. Some courtiers murmured that the best way forward was to dispose of Columbus, but for once it was his good fortune that he had found so little – not barrels full of gold nuggets and black pepper, but thin pieces of gold foil, feathers and naked men. Relations with Castile were tense over issues such as Morocco and the Portuguese-Castilian border; but there was talk of a marriage alliance which would defuse tension, so the king decided that the best course of action was to release Columbus and let him make his way to the ports of Andalucía, from where, in any case, he would have to trail across Spain, since the king and queen were holding court in Barcelona. News of his arrival in Europe travelled fast, and the Catholic Monarchs sent him a message, bidding him to come to them and report on 'the islands he has discovered in the Indies'.

On the return trip Columbus had already been writing letters addressed to the king and queen, and to his backer Luís de Santángel, as well as preparing a version of his logbook that he could present at court. During the turbulent voyage he had despaired of reaching land alive, and – amid fervent prayers to God for his salvation – he had shut himself in his cabin to make a record of what he had seen, in the hope that it would somehow reach Spain even if he did not.[2] His great aim, he protested in his letter to Ferdinand and Isabella, was to enable them to pay for five thousand knights and fifty thousand infantry who could be sent eastwards to redeem the Holy Sepulchre in Jerusalem; meanwhile all of Christendom should rejoice 'at the finding of such a multitude of peoples gathered together, so that with little effort they can convert to our holy faith', and, by the way, an appropriate reward would be that Their Majesties obtain a cardinal's hat for his son Diego, aged about twelve at the time (Columbus pointedly mentioned similar honours for another somewhat grander Italian family, the Medici of Florence).[3]

News of Columbus' voyage spread extremely quickly: one of his letters, sent to a Spanish courtier from Lisbon, was rapidly translated into Latin and printed in Rome by the prolific publisher Stephan Plannck; and it appears to have seized the attention of Pope Alexander VI Borgia and his court. Latin versions also appeared from the printing presses of Antwerp, Basel and Paris, as well as a German version in Strasbourg; a popularised Italian paraphrase, in rhyme, was published in Florence in October 1493. These were just small pamphlets, mostly of four small folios, but their compact size made their diffusion even easier and more rapid. The most sensational news concerned the people Columbus had found. The version in Italian verse had a splendid cover, a woodcut showing the arrival of Columbus' three little ships at a wooded island; the picture is dominated by naked men and women who parade by the shore, carrying long bamboo staves; behind them can be seen their long-houses, open at the sides but with thatched roofs. The text concen-trated on the people of the newly discovered lands, and drew a distinction between those who were clean, tidy, gentle, meek and generous and the 'villainous race' who ate human flesh: 'they do great damage to our people, who are gentleness itself, so that others are wracked by envy of them. But I hope that Your Majesty will be able to purge them of the plague.'[4] Whatever the truth about the Caribs, there were also elements of the fantastic here: in his letters to his patrons, Columbus, just like Marco Polo, assumed that over the horizon there were people who were born with tails, even though he himself had never actually seen them, and he insisted that they were the only 'monsters' of which he had received news.[5] In the Italian verse account, the women of Matininó had become great archers, Amazons no less. All this was only to be expected. Columbus' reports fell on fertile soil. Medieval images of wild and exotic people and classical portrayals of the Golden Age had already moulded Columbus' response to everything he had seen. The Italian poem emphasised these antecedents still further. As far as the good Indians were concerned, the evils of possessiveness and materialism were simply absent. 'The things they have to eat and drink I never saw them call "mine" and "yours"; instead, they live their life in common, as is God's will.'[6] 'Nothing is lacking save manna from heaven.' They do not quarrel among themselves, but go around in peace, arm in arm: 'I think them so good-natured, upright and agreeable that God must have destined them for some good end.'[7] All this suited educated European expectations about the sort of people who lived on the edge of the world. Of course, they had a model already in the Canary islanders, and it is no coincidence that the Italian poem ends with the words *Finita la storia della inventione delle nuove isole di Canaria indiane*, literally, 'the history of the discovery of the new Indian islands of Canary is finished'. And, though these were only the words of the printer or translator, they expressed a fundamental idea of Columbus himself. He had been struck by the similar-ities between Canary islanders and Taíno Indians. And it was not simply a matter of appearance and customs, but also of Spanish political dominion: if these were more 'Canaries' as well as Indies, then Spain could claim them as its property, whatever King João (not to mention the Taínos) might say. They lay due west of the Canaries, for one thing; and there was a Spanish pope, Alexander VI of the house of Borgia, a Valencian from Xàtiva, who might be persuaded to share this view.

The Golden Age, 1493/1511

The news of Columbus' discoveries reached intellectuals, merchants, a wide range of common people. Peter Martyr was one of the most skilled Latinists at the court of Ferdinand and Isabella. Born in Lombardy in 1457, he had already written celebratory letters on the subject of the conquest of Granada, and he had taken great delight in the expulsion of the Jews. In 1511 his *De Orbe Novo*, 'On the New World', was printed. This collection included letters that were written (or that purported to have been written) at exact moments, as in the case of the first one, which carried the date 13 November 1493. Here he reported Columbus' discoveries to Ascanio Sforza, a powerful Milanese cardinal at the court of Pope Alexander VI. What he had to say aroused great excitement among the Venetian merchants in Spain, and in 1500 Peter Martyr graciously allowed his letter to be translated from Latin and sent to the Venetian chronicler Domenico Malipiero, along with a whole packet of information about the curiosities of the New World. Before long, a printer leapt at the opportunity to satisfy public demand for information, and the translation was printed in Venice in 1504 along with a work on navigation by the long-dead explorer of Africa Alvise da Cà da Mosto. Peter Martyr was furious when he discovered that his letter had been sent to press without his permission; knowing nothing of da Mosto, he inveighed against him as if he were still alive and had pirated his text.[8] But it is plain from comparison between the versions of his letter from 1504 and 1511 that Peter Martyr added considerably to the text as his knowledge grew and his opinions developed. There can thus be no doubt that the versions that have survived were polished and perfected over several years by a writer who was more than ordinarily self-conscious about his literary style. Thus information that came from later voyages to America here and there intruded itself into Peter Martyr's letters. Still, they provide one of the most extraordinary and influential assessments of the people of the New World; and their author wrote as if he himself has seen some of the items brought back across the Atlantic, notably the vividly coloured parrots.

In his letter of 13 November, Peter Martyr insisted that the motive for the voyage had been the 'increase' of the Christian religion and the winning of 'an unimaginable abundance of pearls, gold and spices'. But he also rapidly made the point that Columbus had sailed by way of the Canaries to the New World: 'the Canaries have, right up to the present day, been inhabited by men who are naked and who exist without any religion.'[9] They were *silvestris*, a word that has been translated as 'primitive' but that conjures up the image of the wild man of the woods. The final version of his letter pointed out that all had now been conquered thanks to the efforts of Alonso de Lugo, 'so all the Canaries were added to the dominion of Castile'.[10] Since Tenerife was still untamed in 1493, when this letter is supposed to have been written, it is clear that Peter added a reference to later events before the letters were printed; and he did this for good cause. He was keen to establish two basic facts. The people of the Canaries were somewhat similar to those of the Indies, so that the conquest of Hispaniola was simply a continuation of that of Tenerife; Columbus had sailed into the setting sun from the Canaries to reach the new lands. But Peter was also eloquent in his silence. Portugal's lengthy involvement with the Canaries found no place in his letter. It was Castile that had absorbed the Canaries, and it was Castile that had the natural claim to the Indies as well.

These islands were in fact the 'Antilles', the 'places opposite', for that is all the term really meant. Peter Martyr called them that, and the chains of islands in the Caribbean are still known today as the Greater and Lesser Antilles. Peter was convinced these lands were part of India; it was obvious, he said, just from Aristotle's works or the writings of Seneca, that 'no great stretch of sea separates the shores of India from Spain'.[11] Indeed, 'these islands taste of the soil of India, either through their proximity, or through their natural properties'.[12] He was enthusiastic about the spices that could be found there, while cotton abounded and 'fleeces are gathered from the trees, just as among the Chinese'. Some of the forty parrots that were brought back by Columbus looked just like Indian ones, suggesting that Columbus had been right about the small circumference of the world; others were green and yellow, and all most beautiful. On balance, then, Peter Martyr believed that Columbus had arrived in waters off China and the Indies; when he revised his letters for publication he left these comments in place, although by then he was well aware that the recently discovered lands looked more like new continents than integral parts of Asia.

Peter Martyr homed in on Hispaniola, and it was there, rather than in the Bahamas, that he placed the first significant meeting with the native inhabitants. They 'fled in a column for refuge in the dense woods, like timid hares fleeing from greyhounds'.[13] The Spaniards captured a woman and 'glutted her on our foods and wine', and they gave her clothes, 'for all those people, both sexes, live completely naked, content with nature'.[14] But these gifts convinced the natives that the Christian sailors had in fact come from the sky; the

Indians came and traded goods and information. The sailors celebrated the Angelus and when the Indians saw the Christians kneeling, they imitated them; when the Christians adored the cross, so did the Indians. This meant that they had a natural inclination towards Christianity; Peter did not need to spell out the implication that these were rational, convertible human beings – it was still unclear what their beliefs were, though they seemed to worship the sky, Sun, Moon and stars. Like rational creatures, they spoke clearly and Peter recorded an important word: *taynos, cioè nobili, et gentilhomini*, 'Taínos, that is, nobles and gentlemen'.[15] They had no knowledge of iron; but that did not mean they were lacking in fine craftsmanship, for the sailors were astonished at the quality of their buildings and of their canoes, all cut and carved with implements of sharp stone. They lived off *yuca* (cassava) bread, but the grated cassava had to be detoxified before it was baked, since it 'is more deadly than hemlock'.[16] Peter Martyr described accurately enough the process of extracting the poison from cassava. He also wrote of a grain crop that produced seeds the size of peas, white when young, but turning black, and out of this they also made a type of bread. 'They call this type of wheat *maizium*.'[17] They used gold, but in very thin sheets of foil, and it came from lands beyond the territory of 'this king' (that is, Guacanagarí), 'which later experience made clear' – further evidence that Peter constantly updated his letters. But the sailors soon saw that plenty of gold could be found in the riverbeds.

Peter Martyr also talked about other, less amenable Indians; he described *canibales* or Caribs, *huomini osceni*, 'obscene men', who ate human flesh and who terrified the other, good Indians.[18] In his version, the Caribs would catch boys, then castrate them and fatten them up with food, for they considered that the meat of these boys would then be more tender, just as in Europe animals were sometimes castrated when being reared for the table. Fully grown men were treated differently when they were captured. They would be killed and cut into sections; the internal organs would be eaten while still fresh, but the limbs would be salted and kept for later, just like hams in Europe.[19] But they had a taboo (to use a term that only became current later) against eating the flesh of women, so if they captured any women they would put them to work as slaves or, if they were young, they would use them to 'breed'; other writers insisted that the aim was to breed children who could be raised for eventual slaughter in a cannibal feast.[20] Unfortunately, there is something wrong with this account. It goes far beyond the vague rumours reported by Columbus in his letters and logbook. In fact, Peter Martyr's words are uncannily close to those in a letter by Dr Diego Álvarez Chanca, who accompanied Columbus on his second voyage to the Indies in 1493, proving that he read a later account of the Caribs and then worked it into his letter about the first voyage some time before 1501. Peter Martyr insisted that these Caribs were a genuine threat: ten of them could overcome a hundred other Indians without difficulty. In fact, Peter devoted about a third of his account of the native peoples to the Caribs, even though, as he admitted, the source of information was *fama*, 'rumour', 'hearsay'.[21]

What was forming in his mind was the image of a near-paradise, what he would later call a 'Golden Age', threatened by evil men of disgusting habits who seized these innocent folk and consumed their flesh – this fitted classical imagery of the violent end of the Golden Age very well. How marvellous it would be, he thought, if the gentle Indians could be brought to Christ, with Spain taking on the holy work of converting and defending them. Writing in 1501 to Cardinal Louis of Aragon, a member of the royal house of Naples and a relative of King Ferdinand of Aragon, Peter Martyr summed up his views:

> It has been discovered that with them the earth, like the sun and water, is common, nor do 'mine and yours', the seeds of all evils, fall among them. For they are content with so little that in that vast earth there is an excess of land to farm rather than a lack of anything. Theirs is a Golden Age: they do not hedge their estates with ditches, walls or hedges; they live with open gardens: without laws, without books, without judges, of their own nature, they cultivate what is right. They judge him to be evil and wicked who takes pleasure in inflicting injury on anyone.[22]

This was a society that followed natural law. Compare these words from the Italian poem mentioned earlier: 'The things they have to eat and drink I never saw them call "mine" and "yours"; instead, they live their life in common, as is God's will.'[23] Compare, too, the invective of Thomas More against those who possessively hedged and enclosed open land in his *Utopia* of 1516, a book that conjured up a just society, non-Christian, somewhere out in the Atlantic (even if it had cities and advanced technology).[24] More owed something to these learned accounts of the New World. Elsewhere, Peter Martyr added to his praise of Taíno society the comment that it was also a warlike society, and that this too was a trait of the Golden Age:

The islanders of Hispaniola, in my opinion, may be esteemed more fortunate than the Latins, above all should they become converted to the true
religion. They go naked, they know neither weights nor measures, nor that
source of all misfortune, money; living in a Golden Age, without laws,
without lying judges, without books, satisfied with their life, and in no wise
solicitous for the future. Nevertheless, ambition and the desire to rule
trouble even them, and they fight among themselves, so that even in the
Golden Age there is never a moment without war.[25]

In these letters and diaries it was always the man-eaters who excited most
fascination. The Sienese chronicler Allegretto Allegretti had read letters from
Tuscan merchants trading in Spain, and had spoken to other people who
seemed well informed. He noted on 25 April 1493 that Columbus had found
'some islands where men do no work, but live on what the land produces',
though they did travel the seas in boats made of tree trunks, carved using
sharp stones. These people thought the Spaniards were gods, and showed
them great honour and kindness. But against these inoffensive folk were
ranged others 'who eat other men from a nearby island, and they are great
enemies to one another'.[26] Writing around the same time, the Venetian
annalist Domenico Malipiero was, not surprisingly given his origins in a
mercantile republic, interested in the produce of these lands; he mentioned
the flowing rivers, 'such that one fishes for gold there'.[27] Giacomo Filippo
Foresti, from Bergamo, reported people with tails, repeating the rumours that
had reached Columbus; naturally everyone wanted to hear stories of weird
and wonderful people across the Ocean Sea, and this little nugget of rumour
attracted attention out of all proportion to its significance.[28] The ambassador
of the duke of Ferrara in Milan wrote excitedly to Duke Ercole II d'Este of
Ferrara in April 1493 to report the discoveries and to describe Columbus'
encounters with the timid, olive-skinned, naked people of those lands,
'according to what he himself writes in a letter, which letter I have seen'.[29]
For everything that was known went back to Columbus. He had a monopoly
on knowledge of the New World; his rival, Martín Alonso Pinzón, was dead,
and none of Columbus' crew on his first voyage is known to have put pen to
paper. So much for knowledge of the facts; but when it came to opinions there
was plenty of opportunity to embroider the information that was reaching
Italy and elsewhere. In June 1493 the bishop of Modena, twin capital of the
lands controlled by Ercole d'Este, wrote of the plans now being formulated by
Ferdinand and Isabella: they had assumed rule over the newly discovered

islands, each at least as large as Sicily; they would send flocks of animals and craftsmen of every sort 'to give measure and rule to these island-dwellers, who lead a life like beasts and in the same way as savages [*siluestres*]', going around naked, though quite comely in appearance, 'as those who return from there relate'.[30]

A Borgia Divides the World, May 1493

These intriguing scraps of information set off intrigue in different quarters. The king of Portugal continued to seethe.[31] The Treaty of Alcáçovas of 1479 seemed to be a dead letter now that Castile laid claims to lands across the Atlantic. There was still uncertainty about how deeply Columbus had penetrated into the empire of China or Japan. But the new lands needed to be properly assigned. Ferdinand and Isabella had granted Columbus massive privileges, had claimed the right to rule in those lands, and were proclaimed as rulers by Columbus whenever he reached a new island. Still, in the face of competing claims, the authority of the pope as vicar of Christ had to be invoked; and Ferdinand and Isabella sent him a detailed account of what had been found and how Columbus had discovered so many 'fortunate lands, teeming with inhabitants'.[32] Since he was a Valencian there was good reason to hope the pope would be generous to Spanish interests. Alexander VI, a much-maligned figure, had an acute political sense and framed his response to the ambassadors sent by the king and queen in characteristically deft terms, issuing two papal bulls entitled *Eximie devotionis*, 'Extraordinary Devotion', and *Inter Caetera* I and II, 'Among Other Works', on 3 and 4 May 1493.[33] Portugal, he pointed out, had been granted generous rights by earlier popes in Africa, Guinea and the trading fort of Elmina; 'moved by a similar impulse', he felt it was entirely appropriate to honour the Castilian monarchs in the same terms. So, if Portugal complained, Alexander could always say that King João had benefited from this bull by having his own standing in Africa publicly confirmed by the present pope, while what he was granting to the Spaniards was no greater than what he had already granted to the Portuguese. In any case, he was rewarding Castile for its excellent work in searching out 'lands and islands, both distant and undiscovered, for the honour of Almighty God and the extension of the empire of Christendom and the exaltation of the Catholic faith'. As las Casas wrote: 'a world that for so many hundreds of years had lain undiscovered teemed with countless nations of people who would come to swell

Christ's empire.'[34] This work would lead to 'the fulfilment of the final prediction of the Gospels'.

> Christ's vicar on earth thereupon stretched forth his apostolic hand to assist the cause with all the power at his command, confident that He who holds all the realms of the earth in his hand and whose powers he exercises in this world through his apostolic office and role as Supreme Pontiff would ensure that a task as critical and noble as the conversion of such a vast multitude of newly-discovered infidels and the establishment of the Holy Church throughout the vast swathe of lands that is the Indies, begun to some degree by our glorious monarchs, would go ahead in due fashion.[35]

These were also the Catholic rulers who had achieved 'the recovery of the kingdom of Granada from the tyranny of the Saracens'.[36] The Granada war had held them back, but the pope knew that these monarchs had been aiming for some time to search out lands 'not so far found by others, so that you might bring the inhabitants to worship our Redeemer and to profess the Catholic faith'.[37] These inhabitants were naked, peaceful and vegetarian (an unfounded claim that was no doubt based on descriptions of their reliance on cassava bread and similar crops). Rather than repeating the phrase 'they have no religion', the pope emphasised that they were said to believe in a single Creator God in heaven, and so 'they appear to be well prepared to embrace the Catholic faith and to be instructed in good morals'.[38] This emphasis on the missionary side to Columbus' voyage is striking, especially when it is remembered how many priests were on board his fleet – none. Probably prompted by representations on behalf of the Spanish Inquisition, the pope thought it important to ban any excommunicated people from travelling to these lands, for trade or any other purpose.

Thus Ferdinand and Isabella were granted 'all distant and unknown mainlands [*terras firmas*] and islands existing to the west in the Ocean Sea which have been discovered or are yet to be discovered by you or your emissaries', along with all their cities, castles, jurisdictions and so on.[39] Columbus had (the pope said) already built a 'well-fortified tower' in one of the main islands, so the conquest was under way. The pope left the exact identity of these places open, showing less confidence than Admiral Christopher in the notion that they formed part of Asia. Still, Alexander implied that these lands were connected to the Indies in some way, for Columbus had found them while 'sailing westward toward the Indies in the Ocean Sea with divine aid'.[40] In the third of these letters, *Inter Caetera* II, Pope Alexander went one step further by drawing a line across the globe, from the North Pole to the South Pole (both of which were, of course, in totally unknown regions). This line would run one hundred leagues 'to the south and west' of the westernmost Azores or Cape Verde Islands, and beyond that line Castile would exercise dominion, while any land already ruled by a Christian king before Christmas 1492 would remain in that ruler's hands. No one, not even people of royal or imperial blood, should dare to sail into these waters without the express permission of the Spanish monarchs.[41] Later, on 25 June, the pope set out his instructions to the friar, Bernat Buyl, who would lead the first mission to the lands in the west, charging him to convert the native Indians, to conduct Mass, to build churches, chapels, bell-towers and convents (for some reason the pope even specified the right to build garden sheds), and to look after Christian settlers.[42]

All this activity in Rome was overshadowed by international politics. The French king, Charles VIII, was vigorously planning the conquest of the kingdom of Naples, and was likely to be an unwelcome visitor to Rome. The Turkish threat continued to obsess the Venetians and others, with reason, though it was hoped that revenues from the new lands in the west would pay for the decisive war of all wars against the Turks; meanwhile the impossibly ambitious French king insisted that the conquest of Naples would provide him with a springboard from which he would capture Constantinople and Jerusalem.[43] At that level, Alexander was one player among several in the game of Italian and European politics, and certainly not the most powerful one. The news from the Atlantic came as a relief from all this. It provided a golden opportunity to assert the pope's claim to dominion over all creatures, as vicar of Christ. The papal bulls uncompromisingly asserted the authority of the See of St Peter over all the lands that had been and that were yet to be discovered. This has sometimes been seen as a claim to automatic authority over all detached islands, from Sardinia and Corsica close to Rome, to England, Ireland and Scandinavia (which was thought to be an island), and then to more distant lands such as Greenland, and now the 'Indies'.[44] In fact, Alexander VI's claim went further than that: it was an assertion of authority in mainlands as well, for Columbus had expressed the view that one of the lands he had visited, Cuba, was somehow connected to the mainland of Asia (or was Japan, or near Japan, and so on). It was an assertion of authority over the whole globe, 'by the authority granted to us by Almighty God through St Peter and the vicariate of Jesus Christ which we exercise on earth'.[45] It was an assertion of papal authority over the gentle, naked, unconverted peoples of these lands, whose future destiny must be that, by divine will, they would soon enter the Catholic faith. The pope acted boldly; he did not take the view that inoffensive pagan peoples had a right to live unmolested so long as they lived according to natural law. Rather, the peaceful innocence of the American Indians made them ideal converts; the question why the Word of Christ had not yet reached them was left to one side, for the important point was that the opportunity had arisen now and could be confided to princes as trust-worthy as the Catholic Majesties of Spain. In this way, then, Alexander Borgia seized the opportunity to express papal dominion *in orbe*, in the world, as well as *in urbe*, in Rome.

CHAPTER 15

INTO THE CARIBBEAN, 1493–4

Columbus Visits the Cannibals, November 1493

At the same time as seeking the enhancement of their authority in the new lands by papal grant, Ferdinand and Isabella also sought the extension of their power in those lands by means of a new, larger expedition. Papal theory had to be matched by hard practice. Columbus had come before them in Barcelona and had not been able to amaze them with heaped piles of gold, pearls and silk cloth; but what he had produced, not least his Indian companions, had convinced them that there was more to be found, and that an armada was now needed. Seventeen ships were fitted out, under the supervision of the archdeacon of Seville, Juan de Fonseca. Fonseca's involvement reflected a feeling that the whole enterprise was becoming too big for the boastful Genoese admiral. But Columbus detested having to share his glory with anyone outside his immediate family, and relations with Fonseca soon deteriorated. Aboard these ships (which included once again the reliable *Niña*) were several priests and friars, under the direction of Father Buyl, among them Ramón Pané. There was also the physician from Seville, Diego Álvarez Chanca, who left a vivid memoir of his travels in cannibal country, preserved in a sixteenth-century manuscript alongside a Castilian translation of Peter Martyr's writings about America.[1] As the copyist, Fray Antonio de Aspa, wrote, 'the one relates that which he heard and he of Seville that which he saw'.[2] Though Chanca addressed his letter only to the city of Seville, it had an enormous impact elsewhere and was read among others by Bernáldez, the leading court chronicler of the day.[3]

Columbus had promised to return to La Navidad in Hispaniola. However, he set out this time on a more southerly route, hoping to reach the Indies faster, but also hoping to reach gold-rich lands more easily. He left Cádiz on 25 September 1493 and reached the island he now named Dominica, in the chain of the Lesser Antilles, on Sunday 3 November 1493; the name commemorated its discovery on *Domingo*, 'the Lord's Day'. It seemed to be uninhabited. This was the region that was being penetrated most persistently by Carib raiders; but, undaunted, Columbus seized an opportunity on the next island he reached, which he named María Galante after his flagship, and, raising the royal standard, 'with all appropriate solemnity he reconfirmed the possession of all the islands and mainland of the Indies that in the name of the Catholic Monarchs he had taken on his first voyage'.[4] He then rapidly explored this area of the Lesser Antilles, arriving in Guadeloupe, where the captain and men from one of his caravels landed and explored a village from which all the adults had fled, leaving their children and possessions behind. The sailors took nothing of substance away, and gave the children little bells in the hope of reassuring their parents.[5] Chanca said that they saw cotton, some spun and some ready for spinning, in the houses. But as they explored, the captain and his men also found more sinister evidence. 'Especially he brought away four or five bones of the arms and legs of men. As soon as we saw this, we suspected that those islands were the Carib islands which are inhabited by people who eat human flesh.'[6] So far, Chanca had not set foot on the island; the evidence before his eyes was human bones brought to the ships from the village. Were these the bones of ancestors hung up in the huts of the Indians, as was traditional among the Taínos, or were these the remains of a feast? Everyone was well aware of the reports of man-eaters that Columbus had gathered; all must have been aware, too, of the expectation that one would find man-eating human beings in the farthest reaches of Asia – 'they go quite naked except for a little cloth round their privy parts . . . if they capture any man in battle they eat him,' as Mandeville had observed of the Cynocephales, the dog-headed people of the Nicobar Islands.[7] *Cynocephales* meant 'dog-headed' in Greek; and, as has been seen, the words *canibales*, *Caniba* and *Cariba* recalled dogs as well.

Columbus was nonetheless keen to make direct contact with the inhabitants. They were naked and looked from a distance, when seen running away, much like those he had met on his first voyage. Chanca wrote that Columbus wanted 'to learn what people they were' – *que gente era* – and to find out whether these were the dreaded Caribs. The admiral needed to know how far away Hispaniola lay, and in what direction. So he sent a couple of skiffs to shore, and Ferdinand Columbus related that each boat picked up an Indian and bore him back to the flagship. As it happened, the first adults the Spaniards met were well able to provide this information. They were young men from Boríquen, now known as Puerto Rico, lying immediately to the east of Hispaniola and to the north-west of Guadeloupe.[8] They were prisoners of the Caribs, who had been raiding along the chain of islands towards Boríquen; and Columbus' men then discovered six women who were also desperate to escape from the Caribs and who begged to be taken away.

Michele da Cuneo provided an eyewitness account of events. He was a gentleman from Savona, a trading city not far to the west of Genoa; a good friend of Columbus, he was in a sense the first tourist to cross the Atlantic. He wrote that the Spaniards seized 'twelve beautiful and very fat females, aged between fifteen and sixteen, with two boys of the same age whose genital members had been cut away clean to the belly'; and on Sainte-Croix they later found two boys who had been castrated so recently that they were still quite ill.[9] The *Cambali*, as Cuneo called the Caribs, simply referred to their prisoners as *schiavi*, 'slaves'.[10] Meanwhile a few crew members headed deeper into the forest and became lost, so that those who had stayed on the ships 'had already given them up for lost and eaten by those people who are called Caribs', since they were expert navigators who surely would not lose their way.[11] The Spaniards tried to encourage those Indians whom they saw on the seashore, calling out to them in Arawak '*Tayno! Tayno!*', the word for 'good' or 'noble' (i.e. Taíno). Many female captives of the Caribs came to the Spanish ships, which stood off the island for eight days; boy captives, some of them fleeing from the Caribs, clamoured to be taken aboard, while a few other natives were captured. Since the Caribs were understood to eat male flesh only, raising male children for the pot, the boys' attempts to flee from Guadeloupe were perfectly comprehensible.

Chanca explored the island further. 'We went on land many times,' he said, and the villages along the coast were closely inspected. 'There we found a great quantity of men's bones and skulls hung up about the houses like vessels to hold things.'[12] There were women in the villages, but few men – no doubt this was why so many captives were able to reach the shoreline and escape to the ships. The reason for the lack of men was that ten canoes had gone away to raid other islands. The houses, even if made of straw, were well constructed and were full of equipment and supplies, while both the men and the women seemed to be very productive: Chanca was especially struck by the quality of their cotton cloth, just as good as anything one saw back home in Spain.[13] The Spaniards were anxious to win the confidence of the women: they made plain their disgust at the eating of human flesh, and the women were delighted. They said that the men were *Caribes* and every time an islander was brought into their company by the Spaniards, they would signal whether or not they were Caribs. Athough some of the Caribs were women, the men were easier to identify because they wore two cotton garters on each leg, one below the knee and one above the ankle, in order to make their calves swell and so look more attractive, at least according to their standards of elegance. The explorers were, then, emphatic that the Taíno Indians genuinely believed that the Caribs regularly ate Taíno flesh.

For 'the customs of this race of Caribs are bestial'.[14] They were concentrated on three islands (Chanca gave the Arawak names; their exact identity is uncertain, especially since Guadeloupe, with its two high peaks and small connecting isthmus, may have counted as two islands). The Caribs showed great solidarity among themselves, 'as if they were of one family'.[15] With their wooden *canoas* they would travel as much as 150 leagues to raid other lands, carrying their bows and arrows, which were tipped with serrated fish bones or slivers of tortoiseshell. Chanca called them an 'unarmed people', for he thought that these weapons were no match for the steel and guns of the Europeans. But they were clearly sufficient for the purpose of the Caribs, which was to carry off young, good-looking women from the other islands. 'They keep them in service and have them as concubines, and they carry off so many that in fifty houses no males were found, and of the captives more than twenty were girls.'[16] They were treated 'with a cruelty that appears to be incredible'.[17] The Carib men did not touch the boys who were born to women of their own people, but the male children of their captives were raised for the pot, after being castrated. Three boys, all castrated, had fled to the Spaniards. The Caribs would not eat the flesh of women or boys, which in their view was not good, so these male children were put to work as servants for several years and then, 'when they wish to make a feast they kill and eat them'. As has been seen, this letter, or one on the same lines, made a strong enough impression on Peter Martyr for him to modify his letter about Columbus' first voyage and to work into it a chilling account of the same Carib customs (the fact that Chanca's letter survives in the same manuscript as a copy of some of Peter's letters suggests a close kinship between the two accounts). Chanca offered an eyewitness description:

As for the men whom they are able to take, they bring such as are alive to their houses to cut up for meat, and those who are dead, they eat at once. They say that the flesh of a man is so good that there is nothing like it in the world, and it certainly seems to be so for, from the bones which we found in their houses, they had gnawed everything that could be gnawed, so that nothing was left on them except what was too tough to be eaten. In one house there a neck of a man was found cooking in a pot.[18]

The way the bones were described excludes the possibility that they were the bones of close relatives hung from the rafters; they had bits of sinew still adhering. The image is of animal-like humans who 'gnawed' (*roer*) the flesh on the bone, even if they sometimes cooked some man-meat in a cauldron as well. The Sicilian humanist Scyllacius, writing in 1494, insisted that the 'cannibals' admitted to eating human flesh.[19]

Chanca's letter and other accounts of cannibalism have been vigorously challenged by modern commentators, some of whom categorically deny that cannibalism has ever existed on a significant scale in human societies. (Similar stories would soon emerge from Brazil, however, following its exploration by the Portuguese and the French.) Occasionally writing under a thick veil of jargon, post-modernist, post-colonialist writers see Chanca and his contemporaries as apologists for Spanish imperial ambitions in the Indies – but perhaps there is something patronisingly 'colonialist' about the assumption that the native peoples would follow Western standards and understand that human flesh is disgusting to eat.[20] The explorers did certainly wish to show that some of the native peoples followed revolting habits. Columbus had speculated about enslaving some of the natives in the letters he wrote at the end of his first voyage. He was looking for suitable victims, and he identified them among the Caribs: 'when Your Highnesses order me to send you slaves, I expect to bring or send the majority of them from these people.'[21] Thus it was vital to him to draw a sharp line of distinction between the good, meek, mild Taínos, who were the obedient if uncomprehending subjects of the king and queen, and the violent, disgusting Caribs who refused to live in peace and whose main motive in raiding Taíno lands was not even to take their goods – it was to seize their persons as food. In an inversion of roles, the Taínos were made to become the cattle of the Carib rustlers, bred for food (as with animals in the field, females could be kept back for breeding while males were the source of the best beef). But the real animals were the Caribs, whose behaviour was not that of rational human beings living in a well-ordered society that operated according to natural law. They, their lands and their possessions were thus seen as the legitimate target of the Spaniards, who could present themselves as defenders of the unarmed and excessively peaceful Taínos. This interpretation attributes to the Spanish conquerors a more developed strategy than they could possibly have had in 1493; but it rightly underlines the way Columbus and his men divided the Indians into good and bad ones, Indians who were white (Taínos, fairer than you might expect) and others who were black (ugly, covered in face paint).[22] However, these were early days. Columbus oscillated between different ideas of how to treat the peoples he had discovered. He speculated about enslaving Taínos and in the same breath praised them as fine, dignified subjects of the Crown. All the same, in the coming years these sharp distinctions between 'good' and 'bad' Indians would do much to mould their fate.

Violence in Paradise, 1493–4

Violence recurred again and again during Columbus' second voyage. The image of Paradise continued to fascinate the admiral, but this was a flawed Paradise into which evil elements had intruded. As the fleet sailed up the chain of the Lesser Antilles past Montserrat and Sainte-Croix, the explorers met suspicion and hostility. Chanca described a confrontation off the shore of one island where the natives in their canoes were dumbfounded by the sight of the armada. Surrounded by Columbus' men, women and boys took up their bows and wounded a couple of sailors. More would have been injured in the rain of arrows had the crew not carried wooden and leather shields. Still, these arrows could be lethal, however simply they were made, and in the end one man was mortally wounded when an arrow passed through his shield and penetrated deep into his chest.[23] The sailors caught one Carib with the ship's grapple and 'pulled him over the ship's edge, where we cut off his head with a hatchet'.[24] Some Caribs, and some of the Taínos they had enslaved, were later sent back to Spain. But the Europeans had other ideas about how to treat the Caribs as well. Michele da Cuneo had his own craving for human flesh:

> While I was in the boat I laid my hands on a gorgeous [*belissima*] Cannibal woman whom the Lord Admiral granted me; when I had her in my quarters, naked, as is their custom, I felt a craving to sport with her. When I

tried to satisfy my craving, she, wanting none of it, gave me such a treatment with her nails that at that point I wished I had never started. At this, to tell you how it all ended, I got hold of a rope and thrashed her so thoroughly that she raised unheard-of cries that you would never believe. Finally we were of such accord that, in the act, I can tell you, she seemed to have been trained in a school of harlotry.[25]

Columbus therefore saw the captured Caribs as possessions who could be handed out to his friends. He can have had no real doubt that Cuneo would rape the woman; and Cuneo was proud of the way he mastered her.

The fleet edged along past Puerto Rico, which Columbus named San Juan in honour of the saint and of the heir to the Castilian throne, and the explorers saw well-laid-out fields that reminded them of the *horta* of Valencia. By late November, the fleet had reached the northern coast of Hispaniola, and was approaching the lands of Guacanagarí, or Guacamari, as Chanca called him. The explorers had begun to realise that Hispaniola was a large island divided into several petty realms. But as they approached the river mouth near La Navidad they uncovered a mystery. There were a couple of dead bodies in the water; one had a rope around his neck and the other had a rope round his feet. Then the next day, twelve leagues away from La Navidad, they found two more bodies, and were able to see that at least one of the men had a beard. This was worrying. The Indians did not have beards. The suspicion grew that these were men from La Navidad, whose bodies had floated downriver. Two days later Columbus brought his ships up close to the site of La Navidad. He carefully avoided the shoals on which the *Santa María* had broken its back eleven months earlier. Ignoring some Indians in a canoe, for his doubts about what had happened were growing, he fired off some shots to see if his men in La Navidad would reply with shots from their own cannon. But there was no response from the settlers. The Indians, however, did make contact, and a relative of Guacanagarí came to one of the ships bringing two golden masks. He assured Columbus that the Christians were all well, though some had died of illness and others had been killed in a violent quarrel among themselves. As for Guacanagarí, he had been wounded in his thigh during a war with the neighbouring *caciques* named Caonabó and Mayreni. The nearest village had been burned to the ground in the fighting, and Guacanagarí was recuperating in a village a little distance away.

So they went to the place where they had left the sailors and found their stockade wrecked, with old clothes thrown around and the buildings burned;

there was no sign of life within the colony; there were a few Indians creeping about, but these carefully avoided the Europeans. One of the Indians who had been taken back from the first voyage was serving as an interpreter, and he learned from his own conversations with the natives that the men were all dead but, said Chanca, 'we had not believed him'.[26] There were different views about what might have happened. Some argued that Guacanagarí was the real villain, but it was pointed out that his own village had also been burned. However, Columbus and his men found many of the possessions of the crew who had been left behind at La Navidad in the damp and mouldy houses of the Indians who lived nearby: 'a very handsome Moorish mantle, which had not been unfolded since they brought it from Castile', and even an anchor Columbus had lost on the first voyage. In a wicker basket, tightly sewn up and hidden away, they found the head of a man. But this was not the head of one of the lost sailors; it was the mother or father of someone in the household.[27]

They also began to interview the Indians. The natives showed the explorers the graves of eleven Christians, and 'all with one voice said that Caonabó and Mayreni had killed them'.[28] Michele da Cuneo reported seeing dead bodies with their eyes gouged out; the explorers thought that the Indians had eaten their eyes, 'for as soon as they have killed anyone, they immediately gouge out his eyes and eat them'.[29] It looked as if they had been dead for two to three weeks, though opinions differed about this. The Europeans were also struck by the way the Indians immediately began to complain about the misconduct of Columbus' colonists: 'but with all this they began to complain that the Christians had taken, one three, another four women, from which we came to believe that the evil which had fallen on them was the result of jealousy.'[30] According to las Casas, some of the Spaniards who had been left behind had gone into the interior with their women; 'the admiral felt in his heart of hearts that they must all be dead but he kept his thoughts to himself for the moment', and even sent trinkets to Guacanagarí and his people.[31]

Columbus vainly searched for papers among the wreckage of La Navidad, hoping that there might be some document that would tell the story of its dramatic end. Finally he was able to extract the truth from the local Indians, some of whom had learned a certain amount of Spanish and knew the names of the colonists. It was all about women and gold. In the *Libro Copiador*, a newly discovered collection of letters attributed to Columbus, the admiral concluded: 'I believe this Ocanaguari [*sic*] is not to blame for the death of our people.' He felt that the best course was to continue to work closely with

1 Cipangu or Japan, from Martin Behaim's globe of *c.* 1492. Behaim saw Japan as a stepping stone across the Atlantic, lying midway between the Portuguese Azores and the coast of China. Columbus held a similar view of Japan.

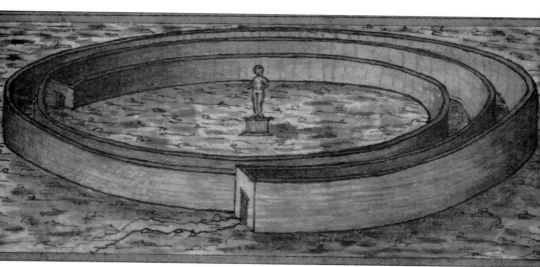

2 *Fquenes* or temple of the Majoreros of Fuerteventura, drawn by Leonardo Torriani in the late sixteenth century. While the spiral shape is more or less credible, the classical statue at the centre is clearly a conceit, for nothing similar survives from the Canary islands; it bears comparison with Boccaccio's story of a similar statue, found in 1341.

3 High place to which Canary islanders can be seen wending their way, drawn by Leonardo Torriani. The use of mountain tops for religious ceremonies is reported by several writers.

4 Contest between inhabitants of Grand Canary, drawn by Leonardo Torriani. The islanders duelled on foot with staves, on level platforms.

5 A man and a woman from La Gomera in the Canary islands, drawn by Leonardo Torriani. The simple kilt worn by the man matches early descriptions of the Canary islanders, while the woman's cape corresponds to clothing found on mummies. The exposure of her breasts is also credible.

6 A man and a woman from El Hierro in the Canary islands, drawn by Leonardo Torriani, the man in rough skins and the woman in a transparent shift.

7 A man and a woman from Grand Canary, by Leonardo Torriani. Although the cape, headgear and kilt on the man are verified by other sources, including archaeological finds, the care to cover so much of the body seems to reflect Christian influence.

8 Gadifer de la Salle and Jean de Béthencourt set out for the Canaries. Illuminated page in Bontier and Le Verrier's early fifteenth-century chronicle *Le Canarien*, from a manuscript originally owned by the Valois Dukes of Burgundy. In this shorter version of the chronicle, de la Salle is the hero.

9 A king and his nobles attend Mass following the conquest of Lanzarote and Fuerteventura led by de la Salle and Béthencourt. At this point the text sets out what Christians ought to believe, while the illustration portrays the ideal outcome of the expedition: the acceptance of Christianity by the native peoples. This manuscript of *Le Canarien*, from Rouen, was prepared for Béthencourt's nephew and retells the story from Béthencourt's perspective. Drawn around the time of Columbus' first voyage, these simple illustrations were the work of someone who had no direct contact with the islanders. What is interesting is the way in which the artist has translated what he read in *Le Canarien* into images.

10 Inhabitants of La Palma, as shown in the Rouen manuscript of *Le Canarien*. The inhabitants are prasied in the text as *belles gens*.

11 A group of Gomerans wearing kilts, from the Rouen manuscript of *Le Canarien*. The text discusses their strange type of speech, apparently the 'whistling language' which still survives on the island.

12 Armed natives of the island of Enfer, 'Hell' (Tenerife), with a European ship approaching from the left. The text notes that the islanders are brave and have resisted all attempts to force them into submission. From the Rouen manuscript of *Le Canarien*.

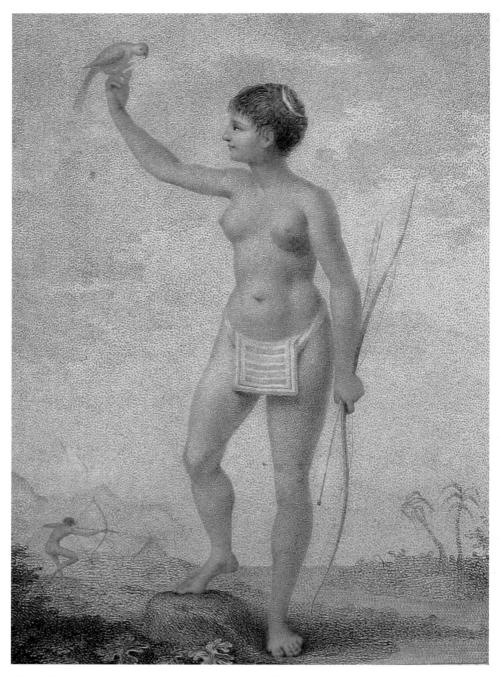

13 An Arawak woman carrying a bow and arrow; the blunt head of the arrow was intended to stun rather than to kill birds, which were prized for their feathers. Although married, she wears no more than a tiny apron. These Arawaks were close cousins of the Caribs and Taínos of the Caribbean, with whom they shared many features of their society. From a late eighteenth-century account of Surinam by J.G. Stedman.

14 Wooden *duho* or ceremonial stool from Hispaniola, unusually in the form of a creeping man. The figure may represent a shaman in a trance. He appears to wear garters on his calves similar to those attributed to the Caribs, though these also appear on Taíno wooden sculptures. This object was discovered in a cave near Puerto Plata in 1870, and its discoverers assumed it was about five hundred years old at the time. It is too small and too oddly shaped to have served as the throne of a *cacique* or petty king; it would probably have carried a *zemí*, or idol, instead.

15 Three-pointed zemí or idol from Hispaniola. Made of stone, measuring 27 by 15 cm, it carries on its back the outline of a serpent. The exact significance of the three-pointed zemí is unclear, though Columbus thought that such objects were believed to promote fertility.

16 The same zemí from a different angle.

17 Hawk's bell from La Isabela, Hispaniola. These are typical items of truck employed in trade between the first European settlers and the American Indians; it is made of copper alloy and measures 1.3 cm diameter.

18 Early printed edition of a letter by Columbus describing his first voyage, showing merchants (whether Spanish or oriental) trading with the naked inhabitants of Hispaniola. The galley, with its strange animals, may be intended to represent an oriental junk rather than a European galley. This version of the letter was printed in Basel.

19 Cover illustration of an Italian verse translation of Columbus' letter concerning his first voyage. The figure on the left represents the Spanish monarchy, claiming dominion in the newly discovered islands; the three ships are the *Santa María*, the *Niña* and the *Pinta*; and in the background the artist has tried to represent the *bohíos* or huts in which the Taínos, who are shown in their nakedness, lived. The island is lush and further land lies suggestively on the horizon. A mirror image of this tableau was used to illustrate one of Vespucci's letters.

20 German woodcut of about 1505 inspired by Vespucci's account of South America, showing feathered Indians, their bodies decorated with stones, with a woman preparing a cannibal feast on the left in the background. Human limbs hang from the rafters of the hut. Portuguese ships stand off the coast.

21 Vespucci's *Mundus Novus* in a Leipzig edition of 1505, portraying the inhabitants of South America as naked and warlike, but living in a lush land. Mermaids or manatees can be seen behind the Portuguese ship.

22 A family of Tupí Indians from Brazil. This image appears in John White's portfolio of images of the New World from the late sixteenth century; it did not originate with White, who was chiefly interested in the English settlements in Virginia, but was based on images printed in the accounts of Brazil by the Protestant missionary Léry and the Catholic missionary Thevet.

23 A Tupí war dance illustrated by Theodore de Bry. Some of the Indians wear feather capes and head-dresses, but others appear to have covered themselves with a fine felt made of feathers.

24 Crudely drawn woodcut of Hans Staden's experiences among the Tupí Indians; here he is seen protesting at their cannibal feasts. From his *Warhaftig Historia* of 1557.

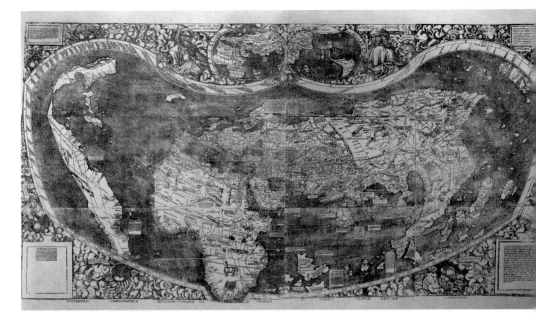

25 The *Universal Cosmography* of Martin Waldseemüller, 1507, produced at Saint-Dié in Lorraine, and ascribing the name 'America' to part of the New World.

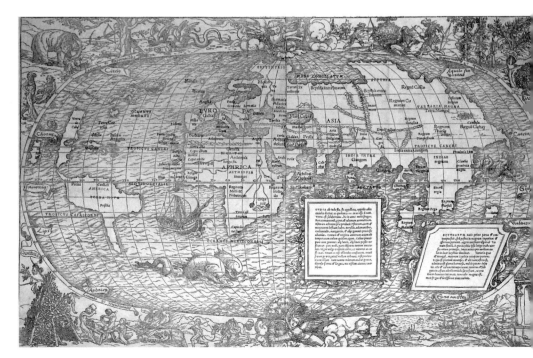

26 Hans Holbein's world map of 1532, indicating continuing uncertainty about the shape of parts of the Americas. Cuba has been confused with the North American mainland.

Guacanagarí, whom he still saw as an ally and who was likely to be the best source of information about where to find gold.[32] Las Casas knew two slightly different versions of the details, and was always keen to show that it was the Spaniards, rather than the Indians, who were the shedders of blood. One of the leaders of the settlement, Pedro Gutiérrez y Escobedo, had murdered a rival and marched with his supporters into the lands of Caonabó with the women they had seized and with animals left behind by Columbus. But Caonabó defeated and killed every one of them, before descending on La Navidad, which was now defended by a mere six men. One night, after the invaders torched the palisade and the houses where the Europeans were sleeping, the remaining colonists fled to the sea in a great panic and drowned. In another version recorded by las Casas, the colonists divided into factions, one consisting of men from Biscay; gold and women were the great issues, and if they had simply stayed under the protection of Guacanagarí all would have remained well. Las Casas implied that they were responsible for their own fate, but also that the Indians had indeed put them to death, and justly so: 'they were killed for the sins and crimes they had committed.'[33]

These sins included heresy. One of the men had told Guacanagarí and his followers 'certain things injurious and derogatory to our holy faith'.[34] Columbus instructed the *cacique* in correct belief and insisted that he should wear round his neck a silver image of the Virgin Mary, though Columbus did not demand that he should accept baptism at this stage. It is certainly possible that the colonists included men with unorthodox beliefs, such as half-hearted *conversos*. Still, there was a lingering suspicion about Guacanagarí. Dr Chanca related that he himself unwrapped the *cacique*'s bandages in the light of day and saw no sign of a thigh injury;[35] and Father Buyl even recommended that he be seized. Columbus understood that this would be a disastrous move. The king and queen had sent him to evangelise the Indians, and it made no sense to antagonise them, since there would be other *caciques*, perhaps related to Guacanagarí, who would raise armies and march against the Spaniards.[36]

Dr Chanca was very struck by the appearance of the naked Indians. He thought their black, red and white body paint was quite a comical sight, and he was also amused by the strange haircuts of the Taíno Indians, some of whom had their hair shaved, and some wore it tangled and long.[37] These were not savage Caribs; but they were a simple people, easy to master. He was convinced that once the Indians and the Spaniards could understand one another, the Taínos would rapidly be converted. They seemed to want nothing less, though he was disconcerted by their *figuras*, that is, their *zemí* idols, and considered them to be 'idolaters'.[38] When he picked up some *zemís* and pretended he was about to throw them into the fire, 'they took it so ill that they were on the point of tears'.[39] They were convinced that the goods the Spaniards exchanged with them had come from heaven itself, just like the explorers. The explorers, for their part, felt they had found heaven in Hispaniola. But the first glimmerings of the idea that the Taínos were a suitable workforce who could be employed looking for gold can be found in the concluding pages of Chanca's remarkable letter. Chanca predicted that much more gold would be found, for what had been discovered so far was surface gold, picked up in riverbeds. By digging down, one would find not just small nuggets but whole shiploads of gold. The problem was that the Indians, despite the great elegance of their stone tools, had no idea how to dig into the soil. Clearly, though Chanca did not say this, the time would soon come when they would have to be recruited to mine for gold.

The Spanish Stockade, 1494

Columbus now began to develop his wider strategy for Hispaniola. Conversion still remained a priority, if not as high a priority as las Casas liked to think; Ramón Pané would soon be sent into the interior to investigate native beliefs and practices. The location of La Navidad had been determined by the shipwreck of the *Santa María*. In fact, it was a muddy, damp place. A new settlement needed to be created, and on a site a hundred miles east of La Navidad Columbus set in train the building of La Isabela, which soon turned out to be little better located than La Navidad. Its site has been excavated and closely studied, and its history can now be closely reconstructed from the material remains.[40] It was founded on 2 January 1494, though it was abandoned after four years, by which time a new settlement at Santo Domingo, in the south of the island, had begun to develop as the main Spanish base on the island. La Isabela was founded not as the capital of a pan-island colonial government, as Santo Domingo would rapidly become, but as the main trading centre of the Spaniards in the New World. Columbus was keen to create a *feitoría* or 'factory', modelled on Elmina in West Africa. Just as Elmina functioned as a funnel through which great quantities of gold from the interior were channelled to Portugal, so La Isabela would be the collection point for the gold and spices of the Indies.[41]

Archaeologists at La Isabela have detected a contradiction. The immediate success of Elmina after 1482 was not matched at La Isabela. The settlers needed to eat as well as to trade, and their numbers were much larger than the small team who kept the Elmina trade station functioning. La Isabela was built with defence in mind, as one might expect after the experience of La Navidad; it was constructed mainly of packed earth, but the builders used a limited amount of stone as well, and the building that has been identified as Columbus' own house had a stone doorway. Many colonists had to make do with thatched huts similar to shepherds' shelters in the Spanish countryside, and not totally dissimilar to the houses of the Taínos. But the Spaniards tried to be as self-reliant as possible: from the material remains, it is clear that there was a sizeable community of artisans, not just masons but workers in wood and metal, makers of tiles and bricks and boat-builders. Some people lived on a second, satellite site, at Las Coles, on the opposite side of the river.[42] This was more of an agricultural settlement, and it was also a centre of pottery production; the settlers quarried for stone nearby and found the clay and other raw materials they needed for their bricks and pots, while the soil was better than that around La Isabela itself. The archaeologists who have dissected the brief history of this site have suggested that the masterplan of Columbus always included not just a fortified settlement, a *castillo*, but satellites such as Las Coles which would ensure the self-sufficiency of La Isabela. Chanca's account of the settlement laid some stress on the produce of the soil: there were to be watermills, as well as land sown with vegetables, 'and it is certain that they grow more in eight days than they do in twenty in Spain'.[43] Chanca was very partial to these root vegetables, which could be bought for beads, pins and broken plates.

What was significant for the relationship between the Spaniards and the Indians was that the Spaniards did not seek to create a mixed or *mestizo* society, though it is certain that Spaniards had Taíno women as mistresses: there must have been children of mixed ancestry, but their fate remains a mystery. A mixed society would develop elsewhere in the New World during the sixteenth century, notably in the great conquered empires of Peru and Mexico. But in the very first years of European contact with the native Americans, when the scale of what had been discovered was unclear and the islands were still assumed to be linked somehow to Asia, other strategies were developed and sharp lines were maintained between the communities.

The other striking feature of La Isabela is the presence and character of Taíno artefacts on the site.[44] Some were probably pre-Columbian, that is, objects that found their way into the soil before 1492, left in a midden or dump that stood on this site. The use of Taíno pottery by the Spaniards was

limited; they seem to have had little interest in Taíno products. The proportion of Spanish pottery found on the site of La Isabela is actually higher than
one would expect to find on a contemporary archaeological site in Spain,
where plenty of Italian and other foreign goods would appear. The style of
Spanish goods found on the site is typical not just of Andalucía but of the
arabised culture of southern Spain, and includes plenty of glazed maiolica.[45]
The crucial point, however, is that La Isabela was not a place where Spanish
and Taíno culture mixed freely. As for the small items of truck – hawks' bells,
beads and bracelets – that the Spaniards regularly exchanged with the Taínos,
the quantities that have been excavated are quite small, apparently because
what there was was carried into the interior by the Taínos; in addition,
Columbus attempted to place all trade with the Indians under his own
control, acting in the name of the Crown.[46] No gold objects have been found:
any golden artefacts or nuggets of gold passed quickly through the colony to
the Old World. On the other hand, over a hundred Spanish coins have been
found, mainly low-value coins made of the heavily debased silver alloy known
as billon; real silver coins were a rarity. The coins themselves were not just
from Spain but from Genoa, Sicily, Portugal and elsewhere, palely reflecting
the trading world of late medieval Seville.[47] So it is clear that the residents did
business among themselves, operating a modest money-based economy, but
mixing little with the Taínos. La Isabela was indeed an enclave, a fortified
settlement with some of the characteristics of the African trading station at
Elmina, as Columbus had intended all along. The settlers existed separately,
on the edge of a land whose contours were still uncertain and which,
Columbus still insisted, lay not far from Cipangu or Cathay.

CHAPTER 16

MISRULE IN HISPANIOLA, 1494–6

Fleeting Glimpses of Cathay, 1494–5

The later history of Columbus' rule over Hispaniola is a depressing story of rebellion, exploitation and maladministration. The admiral's compulsive search for the Asian mainland quickly took him away from La Isabela, along the southern shore of Cuba and back to Hispaniola by way of Jamaica. His captain-general Pedro Margarit was placed in charge of the pacification of Hispaniola, and Columbus set out in April 1494. There was a constant conflict between his role as governor of the new lands claimed by Castile and his function as Admiral of the Ocean Sea, charged with the duty of making contact with the Great Khan. Should he be governing or exploring? He was certainly better at exploring. And he, just like those who stayed behind on Hispaniola, was greedy to find the source of gold. The court chronicler Bernáldez believed he was looking for the province of 'Catayo', a land of idolaters and necromancers, fabulously rich in gold, though Bernáldez later told Columbus that the journey was impossibly long.[1] Far from deterring him now or later, the idea of pressing on and on took Columbus' fancy, and he began to speculate about how he would enter the Indian Ocean, and then reach Arabia and Jerusalem (throwing in Ethiopia for good measure), conveniently returning home to Cádiz on the next passage from the port of Jaffa in the Holy Land. At the time of his third voyage, this grew into excited speculation about meeting Vasco da Gama and the Portuguese in India. Ferdinand Columbus said that his father was discouraged from attempting a circumnavigation of the globe because he was short of supplies, rather than because he thought it was an impossible feat.[2]

But Columbus simply did not find the evidence he expected of high civilisations. On Jamaica he was confronted by hostile Indians, 'painted a thousand colours', naked apart from their feathered headdresses and breast-plates made of nothing more solid than palm leaves; 'they made the greatest howling in the world', according to Bernáldez, who subtly replayed the image of the more aggressive Indians as honorary dogs.[3] But, if they were dogs, they were mere poodles, for a single dog from one of Columbus' ships terrified them into flight: 'a dog is the equal of ten men against the Indians.'[4] This angry reception was not what Columbus needed; he was trying to collect water and supplies, so he made every effort to mend fences with the Taínos, and before long he had made friends with the local *caciques*. Yet he remained very puzzled. On Cuba he asked the natives whether this was the mainland, *Tierra Firme*, and they repeatedly gave him the answer he wanted to hear, that the land went on and on to infinity, or at least for forty months of travelling by canoe, and that the sea was full of islands.[5] He now found the Cuban Indians more friendly and courteous than before. This was a small world, and he fell in with a *cacique* who actually knew one of the Indians he had taken back home on his first voyage and who had heard already about Columbus, for, as has been seen, news spread easily in the island world. The natives refused to believe that the ships had not descended from heaven, so when they were told that they had actually come from Castile, they concluded that heaven and Castile were one and the same. In some respects it was no worse an error than Columbus' insistence that he had touched the shores of East Asia. But there was also an element of humour. Despite his close reading of Mandeville, Columbus grew suspicious of stories that further to the west there lived people who had tails. It seemed to be a local joke: those who went around naked teased those who wore clothes by suggesting that they had something to hide.[6] Hard reality and ancient fantasy intermingled; the footprints of a large animal, perhaps an alligator, were supposed to be those of a griffin. Peter Martyr was aware of the wider significance of this: large animals, it was understood, only occur on continental mainlands. Word games were played with ever more frantic zeal to prove that the places mentioned by Marco Polo matched the names given to them by the Taíno Indians.

What Columbus wanted to find was people who were fully clothed, preferably in rich silks. So it was very exciting when one of his men who had gone a short distance into the jungle stumbled upon a troop of thirty Indians among whom were three men in tunics, one with a tunic right down to his feet which made the Spaniard think he was a Christian friar, all the more so since they were 'as white as us'.[7] The Spaniard was in fact so alarmed that he turned and fled, but the man in the long tunic tried to catch up with him.

Columbus finally decided that this man must have been the local *cacique*. But the admiral was becoming tired and ill, and, aware that he could easily become stuck without provisions, he turned back to Hispaniola. In the last stages of his journey through the Greater Antilles, he could not find time to sleep; he had a high fever and even lost consciousness. His men thought he was at death's door. He was certainly confused about his objectives: whether to carry on the search for the lands of the Great Khan; whether to go back to La Isabela and organise the life of the new colony; or whether to launch a war of extermination against the cannibals. Las Casas had seen a copy of a letter by Columbus and was taken aback by the last option; he wondered whether there had been a copyist's error and the word 'destroy', *destruyr*, had been written in place of the word 'discover', *descubrir*, so that all his hero intended was to explore further the cannibal islands. Columbus wrote to Ferdinand and Isabella, asking for supplies of cattle and other necessities to be sent to Hispaniola; in return he would send payment in the form of slaves – 'from among these cannibals, a people very fierce and suitable for the purpose, and well-proportioned, and of very good understanding, who, having abandoned their inhumanity, will be better than any other slaves, which inhumanity they will lose when they are outside their land'.[8] So they were human in respect of their appearance and intelligence, inhuman in respect of their behaviour; but they could be turned into ideal servants. Las Casas found a moral in all this:

> It may be that what the admiral says about going off to destroy the islands of the cannibals, where there lived people widely reputed to eat human flesh, did not please the Lord who had created these people and redeemed them with his blood, and that killing them was not the way by which the Lord intended they should be saved.[9]

In fact, las Casas insisted, God must have intended some at least of the cannibals to be saved, and Columbus' illness was perhaps God's way of stopping him from making such an attack. And so the ailing admiral went back to Hispaniola after all.

Pacification by Means of War, 1494

Here he found that everything was in chaos; but he decided he could turn this chaos to his advantage. A bitter war was being led by four *caciques*, Caonabó,

Behechio, Guarionex and Guatiguaná, against Guacanagarí and the Spaniards. Guacanagarí was still loyal; but two of his wives had been seized by Behechio and Caonabó (who had already been blamed by Guacanagarí for the destruction of La Navidad). Caonabó appears to have been a regional overlord of other *caciques*, and he may have been a successful outsider, born in the Bahamas.[10] One of Guacanagarí's wives had been killed, the other was a prisoner. Guacanagarí was tremendously pleased, therefore, to see Columbus again. And Columbus was pleased, too, for he believed that 'with discord among the *caciques* he could more easily subjugate the country and punish the rebellion of the other Indians and the death of the Christians' who had been left behind at La Navidad.[11] Still, optimism was no substitute for arms and men. Ferdinand Columbus estimated that his father had two hundred Europeans under his direct command, some of them ill, along with a mere thirty horses and thirty dogs. The Indians were thought to have raised a hundred thousand men. Already, then, many of the Taínos had ceased to be convinced that the explorers were gods who had come down from heaven.

The Indians were divided; but so were the Spaniards. Columbus had asked Pedro Margarit to tame the island. Margarit went into the interior with four hundred men, into the great plain of the Vega Real. Here, las Casas lyrically wrote, there were very peaceful folk who lived as free a life as could be imagined:

> The people were unarmed and naturally very meek and humble and entirely given over to the kind of life that is typical of men who have time on their hands, are surrounded with sensual delights that are readily available and have no law, nor have ever had, which might suggest that there was any reason to change their mode of existence or to place limits on the absolute and unconditional liberty they enjoyed. These Indians were not accustomed to working and required no more by way of food than what they needed for themselves and their households.[12]

This was in great contrast to the way the Spaniards consumed food. One Spaniard would eat in a day what a Taíno household would eat in a whole month. This was a favourite image of las Casas, which he magnified by commenting: 'and just think what four hundred of them would consume.'[13] The Spaniards had no compunction about beating the Indians, even threatening and abusing the *caciques*. Las Casas conjured up a dramatic image of what the Indians thought of the Europeans, after two years of increasingly brutal treatment:

> It seemed to the Indians that, as well as being intolerable, ferocious, cruel, and entirely devoid of reason, these visitors must have been placed on the earth simply as consumers of food and that they can have had no foodstuffs back home in their own country but had made their way to these islands simply to save themselves from starving to death.[14]

Las Casas tried to imagine himself in the position of the Indian men who saw their wives and daughters raped 'with no consideration for social rank or distinction or state nor for the bonds of matrimony nor for any other imped-iment to the violation of chastity, the only thought in their minds being which of the women they fancied and found the most attractive'.[15] Nor did the native males fare well: Indian boys were seized and made into servants by the Spaniards. This ingratitude turned the Indians against the Christians; the Indians began to flee, for they knew that they did not have the strength to resist European arms. Margarit not merely sowed distrust between native Indians and Europeans; he also began to quarrel with his fellow counsellors while Columbus was away in Cuba and Jamaica. Everything was falling to pieces. When ships arrived from Castile, Margarit decided to go back home and tell the court that the whole enterprise in the Indies was a waste of time and money, 'declaring publicly that there was no gold to be had here, nor anything else of value, and that everything the admiral said was a pack of lies'.[16] Along with him went Father Buyl and several other churchmen who had been charged with the spiritual care of Hispaniola.[17] Ramón Pané remained somewhere in the interior; but the conversion of the Indians, and even the spiritual needs of the Europeans, were almost totally neglected.[18]

Las Casas wrote his account of these events in his *History of the Indies* much later, between 1527 and 1559. His anger at the inhumane treatment of the Indians shines through every page. He had sailed for the Indies in 1502, aged only eighteen, and he had lived in Hispaniola for ten years among the growing class of Spanish landlords, until, moved by the preaching of the Dominican friar Montesinos, an early defender of the rights of the Indians, he vowed to devote his life to their cause. He took the cowl as a Dominican friar and proclaimed the rights of the Indians before Emperor Charles V and King Philip II with all the fervour of Moses in the presence of Pharaoh. But there was no Moses to lead the Indians to safety. The islands of the Caribbean were a lost cause by the time las Casas wrote. Very few Taínos were still alive in the mid-sixteenth century. Still, las Casas knew that the 'destruction of the Indies' that had already occurred in the islands was not complete, though it was proceeding at a frightening pace, on the American mainland; and his message had a worldwide appeal as well, as Espinosa's defence of the Guanches of Tenerife would later prove. At the very foundations of what historians rather pretentiously like to call the 'Lascasasian' approach to Indian rights lay the argument of the greatest Dominican of all, St Thomas Aquinas, in the thirteenth century, which took further the views of Pope Innocent IV. Pagan governments were not intrinsically evil. Those pagan rulers who followed the principles of natural law, showing respect for a Creator God and regulating their affairs justly, were entitled to live unmolested. The Indians did have a natural right to self-government without interference from Christian masters; the duty of all good Christians was to win the Indians to the faith of Christ by gentle persuasion, love and good example. The Christians should thus have been the caretakers of the souls of the Indians, but frankly those who governed the Indians were not competent to perform the task. The native Indians were mild and gentle; they had committed no sin against the Christians; and if the Indians had ever been difficult, that was no worse than the behaviour of boys of ten or twelve years of age: 'I know by certain infallible signs that the wars waged by the Indians against the Christians have been justifiable wars and that all the wars waged by the Christians against the Indians have been unjust wars, more diabolical than any wars ever waged anywhere in the world.'[19] The violent and greedy treatment of the Indians at last gave them the courage to 'take the remedy into their own hands, each in his own territory or district as prescribed in natural law and the law of nations and each in his own jurisdiction as defined under canon law'; for, said las Casas, the law of nations dictates that all peoples should be permitted to live in peace in their homes.[20] Ironically these non-Christians were truer to the spirit of Christian law than the Christian conquerors. In ordering their subjects to kill the Christians, the *caciques* were simply enacting the good law of any upright ruler who has 'proper jurisdiction'.[21] 'Where in the world,' las Casas plaintively asked, 'is there a people, however barbarian, or meek, or forbearing, or untouched by civilisation, who would not do exactly the same?'[22]

Las Casas was aware, however, that Guacanagarí remained on good terms with Columbus. He visited the sick admiral when Columbus returned to Hispaniola, and insisted that he was not implicated in the killing of

Christians (including the thirty-eight men at La Navidad), nor had he tried to mobilise the Indians against the Spaniards. In fact, he had shown every consideration to the hundred or so Spaniards who remained in his lands. As a result, he earned nothing but hostility from the other *caciques* who saw him (to use a modern term) as a collaborator. Columbus apparently believed him or, if he did not, he knew that he had to appear to do so, for it would be extremely helpful to find allies among the Taínos. Working with native troops was standard practice, as in the conquest of the Canaries and of Muslim Granada. The fact that Guacanagarí was so willing to work along-side Columbus did not, however, impress las Casas. Given the choice, las Casas would side with the majority of the Taínos, even against Columbus and Guacanagarí. He acerbically remarked that the law of nature requires all men to do their duty and to preserve their country and the common good. This, he said, was a fundamental principle of natural law, just as it was a principle that one must show obedience to God in matters of religion or to one's parents within the family. It was a mortal sin that Guacanagarí committed in betraying his fatherland: 'all the other rulers and chiefs and peoples of those kingdoms had justice and right on their side when they pursued him and waged a just war against him and his kingdom as a capital public enemy to them all', for he was 'a traitor and threat to his fatherland and nation'.[23]

Ferdinand Columbus took a far more positive approach to the conflict with the *caciques*. He insisted that his father's clever tactics enabled him to defeat the Indians without difficulty. Guatiguaná came under attack, for he had ordered the killing of twelve Christians; five hundred of his people were enslaved and packed off to Spain in a fleet that set sail from Hispaniola on 24 February 1495, 'a move undertaken without doubt without the consent of the king and queen'.[24] As reports filtered through to the royal court, arriving on the same ships as the slaves, perplexity grew. Columbus' letters were full of assurances that all was under control; but there were also very disturbing reports of the breakdown of order. Father Buyl was one of those who returned with plenty of complaints, as did a certain Juan Aguado, who impressed the court with his knowledge of conditions in Hispaniola. The Spanish court decided that Columbus' colony needed to be properly inspected, and in October 1495 Aguado was sent out again to conduct a full investigation. Ships were beginning to move back and forth: the journey across the Atlantic was no longer Columbus' monopoly.

Handcuffs from Heaven, 1495

Another person who went aboard a ship bound for Spain, though he may well have died before crossing the ocean, was Caonabó. Alonso de Hojeda, who would later play a major part in the government of Hispaniola, was sent on a secret diplomatic mission to Caonabó, along with nine other men. Everyone knew Caonabó was one of the most powerful *caciques* and a great warrior, so it seemed better not to attack him directly. Hojeda brought as a gift some very finely wrought, highly polished handcuffs, made of brass: these always fascinated the Indians, who used the same word for brass, *turey*, as for heaven. Archaeologists excavating a series of burials from a contact-period site in north-eastern Cuba have been able to show that European shoelaces with brass tags (made in metal workshops in southern Germany) were favoured as grave goods above objects of gold or silver, and were probably used in daily life as pendants, garters and bracelets.[25] So the Taínos were under the misapprehension that brass goods offered to them by the Spaniards were a gift from heaven. Caonabó and his men were very excited when Hojeda announced that he had arrived with gifts of brass. They had already been very impressed by brass church bells, whose sound they understood to be some sort of heavenly language. Hojeda convinced Caonabó that the handcuffs were ceremonial bracelets that the Spanish rulers wore during public dances or on other grand occasions. Hojeda suggested that the *cacique* should go and bathe in a large river a short distance from the village, and once he had bathed Caonabó asked Hojeda to show him the handcuffs. Hojeda took him a little way off and then, with his Christian companions, they grabbed him and fastened his wrists; they bound him with rope, threw him on the back of Hojeda's horse, and Hojeda cantered off. Meanwhile the other Christians threatened Caonabó's companions with their swords until they had quietened down and the captain and his captive were well on the road to La Isabela.[26]

Las Casas admitted that this was a much-told story with many variants. He also reported that Caonabó was kept captive in Columbus' house. When the admiral came in and they saw one another for the first time, Caonabó did not stir, and the Spaniards were irritated at this lack of honour to Columbus, who was an imposing figure, six feet tall; yet when Hojeda entered, he stood up as a mark of respect for his captor. Las Casas concluded that this was proof that Hojeda was indeed his captor.[27] Caonabó confessed (Ferdinand Columbus related) that he had been behind the killing of the Christians at La Navidad. Columbus also interviewed Caonabó at length about Taíno beliefs, adding to the material Ramón Pané was gathering on his behalf. Caonabó told him about native beliefs concerning the fate of the dead. Columbus found him 'a mature man of great knowledge and very sharp intelligence'.[28] Even so, Columbus was convinced he was a troublemaker and decided to send him back to Spain, though, as stated before, whether he reached there alive is doubtful. In some versions the ships that were due to carry him and five or six hundred Taíno slaves back to Spain were caught in a hurricane and sank like stones; the Spaniards on board managed to reach land, but the captives who were chained to the deck, including Caonabó, could not escape and drowned.[29] This was not the only such disaster. Las Casas took mischievous delight in the fact that a ship on which the *cacique* Guarionex was sent to Spain later foundered, not merely with loss of life but also with the loss of 3,600 *castellanos* worth of greedily gathered gold nuggets.[30]

Tribute in Gold, 1495–6

Ruthless repression of rebellion now followed. Las Casas said: 'how can anyone who is not a subject be guilty of rebellion?', but the Spanish view was uncompromising: these were the subjects of Castile.[31] Dogs were unleashed against the Indians, who had nothing to protect their naked bodies against the teeth of savage hounds. The Indians simply did not know how to deal with the Spaniards. One problem was that they had difficulty counting to high numbers, so their scouts could never provide accurate information about what sort of forces they faced.[32] Bartolomé de las Casas testified, much later, to the scale of devastation: 'huge massacres, and the extermination of whole villages', notably in the lands formerly ruled by Caonabó, and he asserted that his evidence was taken directly from the writings of Columbus himself.[33] Hispaniola was turned upside down: in the interior, the Vega Real submitted and an important fort was built at Concepción de la Vega; many Taínos fled into the mountains; it amounted to 'the violation of their whole way of life and the annihilation [*anichilación*] of their nation'.[34] Overwork led to the death of many; lingering illness, already widespread among the Christians, turned into an unstoppable plague among the Indians, who lacked all resistance to European diseases.[35] Food crops failed as the Indians deserted their fields and fled into the mountains, where they could find enough root crops to feed themselves.[36] Las Casas insisted that in 1496 the Indian population was one-third of what it had been two years earlier. He bewailed not just the horrific slaughter by bloodthirsty Spaniards, the enslavement of Indians, and their death through disease and overwork, but also the loss of souls in need of salvation. To the causes of death among the Taínos one more must be added. Families were increasingly broken apart as the men were sent off to the gold fields, so that they spent little time with their wives and the birth rate fell dramatically.

It was now time to capitalise on this victory. Columbus decreed that four times a year every adult in the highlands of Cibao, supposedly rich in gold, must pay tribute in gold dust to the king and queen of Castile. This tribute was to consist of a container the size of 'a large Flemish hawk's bell' filled with gold dust; elsewhere on Hispaniola, where gold was scarcer, tribute was to be paid in cotton instead.[37] Columbus introduced a system of tax discs; the Indians would receive as a receipt a small disc of copper or brass which they were expected to wear round their neck as a sign that they had paid their dues; new discs of a slightly different design were issued quarterly, so it was impossible to escape the tax. It was, las Casas said, a demand that went beyond reason, for the Indians could not satisfy this lust for gold and were not a strong people; lacking proper equipment, the best they could do was trail their fingers in the water of the rivers in order to catch small golden nuggets, 'squatting on the banks of rivers and streams and scooping up the aggregates'.[38] They knew no more than that about how to find gold. These demands exceeded anything the Huns, Vandals, Turks or Moors had asked of those they had conquered: 'they had always enjoyed absolute freedom and knew nothing of care, and they should have been won over to the faith and to the Christian religion with love and gentleness and sweetness and by honeyed words.'[39] Guarionex begged the admiral to take vast tracts of land and cultivate them in whatever way he wished, if only he would drop this absurd demand for gold. Later, Guarionex told tall stories about gold-rich lands in the south of the island in the hope of ridding himself of the crushing tax demands of the Spaniards.[40] Before long Columbus had to halve the tax, since it was impossibly optimistic about the gold reserves on Hispaniola and about the possibility of making the Taínos find the metal.[41]

Certainly, las Casas argued, the blame for this policy fell in significant measure on the shoulders of Christopher Columbus, who, as a foreigner, believed that the only way to secure his position in the eyes of the Catholic Monarchs was to provide them with great quantities of gold. Las Casas had the advantage of knowing Columbus personally ('I know all this from conversations with the admiral').[42] He took the view that Columbus had good enough intentions, for he thought that, by discovering the New World, he had opened the door to its Christianisation; but he had no grasp of law and believed that he could simply strip the local kings of their own legal titles to rule.[43] Yet Columbus could see well enough that the island was out of control. The arrival of the inspector Juan Aguado was troubling: normally an inspection would only take place when a viceroy or other high official left office, though since Columbus held his office for life it was hard to see how this could be done while the admiral was alive. Whatever the case, Columbus claimed plenipotentiary powers and thought the inspection was a humiliation. He decided that the time had come to leave for Spain, where he would ask the king and queen for further support and would make sure that his detractors, whose numbers grew by the week, were challenged. Typically, he placed his trust in his close family: he left his brothers in charge in Hispaniola, Bartholomew as captain-general, able to exercise the admiral's powers on his behalf, and Diego as second-in-command. A certain Francisco Roldán was appointed chief justice and governor of La Isabela; he had already served Columbus well. So, on 10 March 1496, the much-travelled *Niña* and another caravel set out by way of Guadeloupe for Spain. In Guadeloupe, Columbus' reception was hostile; a fleet-footed Canary islander serving in Columbus' crew was wrestled to the ground by a native woman whom he was chasing. Columbus was so impressed by the vigour of the local women that he was convinced they were just like the Amazon women he knew from legend. But Columbus exercised his charm, sent gifts and even persuaded the local queen and her daughter to sail for Spain with him. 'God knows why she should have done so!' las Casas remarked.[44]

Las Casas was always keen to distinguish between the Columbus he admired, an inspired explorer who was a divine agent in the opening up of the New World to Spain, and the Columbus who, consumed by vanity, greed and wrong-headed zeal, had in fact opened up the New World to brutal conquerors. In his *Short account of the destruction of the Indies* las Casas delivered a devastating assessment of Spanish behaviour in Hispaniola, before passing on to Cuba and then the mainland: 'there were countless people that I saw burned alive or cut to pieces or tortured in many new ways of killing and inflicting pain.'[45] Although the inhabitants of the Caribbean lived much simpler lives than those of Aztec Mexico or Inca Peru, with their very complex city-based civilisations, the colonial methods developed in Hispaniola provided a model for all of Spanish America. It was, largely thanks to Columbus, a model based on gold. The lust for gold was allowed to dominate all other considerations.[46] It will be seen how a whole labour system (the *encomienda* system) was soon to fall into place, which nicely avoided the terminology of slavery, but which also made demands greater than those that would have been made on slaves in Seville, Madeira or Genoa at this time. It is a horrific story of mass murder, cruelty and fear. No one can read las Casas' denunciation of Spanish policy without being intensely moved. Contact with the Americas would have come sooner or later: John Cabot was planning his first expedition under the English flag, which took place in 1497; the Portuguese were to discover Brazil by accident in 1500. Disease would have spread. Millions would have fallen victim. But the Spaniards put in place a way of managing the native population that made all this inevitable damage far worse; the Spaniards also, to do them credit, agonised about what they had done, and las Casas was the most prominent agoniser.

His *Short History of the Destruction of the Indies* looked back from the 1540s and stressed that God had made the peoples 'as open and innocent as can be imagined', though their simplicity and lack of assertiveness exposed them to danger, since these qualities made them obedient and submissive, even to violent Spanish masters. Las Casas paired their meekness and gentleness with their physical frailty, which meant that hard work exhausted them, and what would have been mild sicknesses in Europe became deadly diseases in the New World. They were portrayed as 'pure in mind' – their nakedness was a sign of innocence; they were intelligent; they were, in short, ideal recruits to the Catholic faith, if only they were given the chance to convert. Millions of souls had been denied the right to exchange their earthly paradise for a heavenly one; European greed for gold, war and disease had carried away twelve to fifteen million Indians. They were not treated like humans; they were not treated like animals; they were treated like excrement left in the middle of the road; and this was ironic, for they had at first thought of their cruel Spanish masters as gods. Whether or not las Casas' estimate of Taíno mortality is accurate, the Taínos did disappear rapidly in the early sixteenth century. A certain Pedro de Isla went through the Bahamas a few years after Columbus died, looking for native Indians: he found eleven. And yet the Bahamas had not even been occupied following their discovery by Columbus; they were raided with impudence to provide extra manpower in the gold mines as the native population of Hispaniola dived downwards. On Jamaica and Puerto Rico there were only two hundred Taínos left by 1509, las Casas claimed, though there are grounds for rejecting such a low figure.[47] Las Casas remembered atrocious acts of cruelty: *caciques* being roasted alive; man-eating dogs being set on the Indians; the wife of Guarionex being raped. No gratitude had been shown to co-operative *caciques*: Guarionex had offered to provision the Spanish settlements, but the Spaniards only demanded gold; the lands of Caonabó had been given over to sugar production; Guacanagarí, Columbus' first ally, died destitute, having fled from the Spanish massacres of his people. In Cuba, invaded in 1511, las Casas witnessed the massacre of three thousand Indian men, women and children who had come to meet the Spaniards with friendly intentions. To compensate for the severe labour shortage hundreds of thousands of black Africans were bought from Portuguese and other slave traders, who had generally acquired them from compliant black rulers in Africa, a situation las Casas accepted with equanimity for much of his life, seeing them as unfree aliens and not as free natives, as were the Taínos. The history of human misery in the Caribbean did not end with the extinction of the Taínos.

Las Casas was a polemicist, and he exaggerated the peacefulness of pre-Columbian Hispaniola. He was not scared by tales of cannibalism or human sacrifice, in respect of the Caribs first of all and the Aztecs later. He thought these peoples could be weaned away from these practices, and he vigorously turned the argument upside down, arguing that the real violence and cruelty were to be found among the Spaniards rather than the Indians (though he seems to have heartily approved of the burning fires of the Inquisition in Spain itself). He insisted on the meek, mild nature of the Taínos, even if this occasionally led him to compare them with young children, implying that they were in need of guidance. But that guidance had to be moral guidance, through faith in Christ. He thus shared with Columbus the sense that the discovery of the New World had been an opportunity for evangelisation, a truly historic moment, a sort of Second Coming of the apostles, if not just yet of Christ (and both Columbus and King Ferdinand thought that the Second Coming of Christ was not far distant). Was it instead a holocaust or genocide? For all las Casas' blood-curdling tales of cruelty, there was no actual policy of extermination singling out certain ethnic groups for mass slaughter. This was therefore not 'genocide' as defined in the U.N. Convention on Genocide: 'acts committed with intent to destroy, in whole or in part, a national, ethnical [*sic*], racial or religious group'. When las Casas spoke of 'annihilation' he meant that the policy of the Spaniards had resulted in the destruction of the Taíno communities, culturally and then demographically. But this is not to say that the Spaniards sought to wipe out the Taínos, though they may have had stronger views on how to deal with the Caribs. In fact, the loss of Taíno labour was a disaster, a sign that the Spanish policy had failed:

Hispaniola was a mess. Columbus argued consistently that the Taínos were human in form, behaviour and character. He had no doubt that they formed part of the family of mankind. The Caribs, the Amazons or the humans with tails were perhaps another matter; it remained to be seen. But under the pressure of temptation he started to treat the Taínos as a subject labour force whose *raison d'être* was simply to dig for gold. They had been dehumanised not on the grounds of Indian behaviour or appearance, but on the grounds of Spanish cupidity and utility.

CHAPTER 17

THE PROJECT UNRAVELS, 1497–8

A Pear-Shaped World, 1498

T he unravelling of Columbus' great project had begun. In part this was because it was not one project but a mixture of dreams, expectations and unplanned responses to unexpected discoveries. The story of his third and fourth voyages has been told many times, and what needs to be extracted from those events, sometimes tragic, sometimes burlesque, is the reaction of Columbus, of his agents on Hispaniola and of people back home to the peoples of the Caribbean world. One matter that was rapidly resolved was the Spanish claim to dominion over the lands Columbus had discovered. Portugal had good reason to feel that the papal bulls of 1493 had been over-enthusiastic in their support of Spain, and had neglected Portuguese interests in the Atlantic. Pope Alexander VI mediated further agreements: Spain and Portugal agreed to divide their interests, drawing a line down the middle of the Atlantic, 370 leagues west of the Cape Verde Islands. This would be defined by a team of experts who would sail westwards in two caravels, measuring every degree they travelled; islands and mainlands on one side would be assigned to Portugal and on the other to Castile.[1] The final agreement was enshrined in the Treaty of Tordesillas of 7 June 1494. The new line was later found to have sliced through the still-unknown eastern edge of South America, which gave Portugal its claim to sovereignty over what came to be known as Brazil. But for the moment the Treaty of Tordesillas acted as a spur for Portuguese exploration along the eastward sea route to India, and (having already discovered the southern tip of Africa in 1487–8) the Portuguese at last began to plan the triumphant series of voyages that would bring their ships to Calicut. They hoped to reach India before Columbus found a way to the Asian mainland through the maze of islands that he supposed were the East Indies.

Gradually Columbus managed to convince Ferdinand and Isabella that he was worth supporting yet again. Ferdinand Columbus hinted that this was because his father was able to produce nuggets of gold, some the size of chickpeas or pigeon's eggs, as well as gold masks and other artefacts made by the Taínos.[2] Ferdinand was now a page in the royal household, so his account of events has the advantage of being an eyewitness one. The admiral also pressed the argument that his discoveries would enable Christendom to attack Islam from the rear. But the king and queen delayed and deferred; an advance sailing under Pedro Fernández Coronel set out in February 1497, but this time it was not possible to gather together a sizeable armada at a few months' notice, even with the backing of the Genoese and Florentine businessmen who now saw an interesting opportunity in the voyages to the west.[3] Columbus had to trail around behind Ferdinand and Isabella, from Burgos to Medina del Campo, in the north of Spain; his persistence paid off, as it always did in the presence of the king and queen, and he was rewarded with enlarged privileges. This was quite an achievement at a time when the Genoese in Spain were attracting some of the opprobrium that had earlier been directed at the Sephardic Jews.

The enforced delay gave Columbus plenty of time for soul-searching. He read widely, not just works of geography but biblical texts, and became increasingly convinced that he was God's messenger, the 'bearer of Christ' or *Christophoros*. He left Sanlucar de Barrameda in southern Spain on 30 May 1498, skirting round a French fleet – for France and Spain were at war over the kingdom of Naples – and arrived in the Caribbean on 31 July. He took advantage of the peace with Portugal to set out across the open ocean not from the Canaries but from the Portuguese Cape Verde Islands, which he thought an unpleasant little territory (one of its islands functioned as a leper colony).[4] But the islands were on the same latitude as the gold-bearing lands of West Africa; therefore it stood to reason that a route along the same latitude would bring him to lands of the same general character, also gold-bearing (taking into account the assumed link between strong sunlight and gold, the sun-coloured metal). This took him across the ocean to an island in what he judged to be Carib territory, from which three mountains rose into the sky, so he named it 'the island of the Trinity', Trinidad, as it remains. The sailors saw houses and found evidence that there were fishermen in the villages, but everyone had fled. They then coasted along what they thought was another island, to the south of Trinidad, though in fact it was the South American mainland. There they saw beautiful countryside and many hamlets.

As they moved along the fast-flowing waters they encountered a canoe carrying twenty-four or twenty-five men, described by Columbus himself as 'well-proportioned and not black, but whiter than the others who have been seen in the Indies, and very graceful and with handsome bodies, and hair long and smooth, cut in the manner of Castile'.[5] But what really excited Columbus was that they wore cotton turbans, 'worked elaborately and in colours, which, I believe, were *almaizares*', a word for the head-covering worn by Spanish Muslims.[6] They also wrapped a similar piece of cloth around their loins. This, then, was proof that the ships had reached the edge of the Orient: Columbus had probably seen quite similar costumes when he travelled as a young man down the coast of Islamic West Africa. The explorers attempted to make contact but no one could understand the language of the Indians. So they tried to lure them to their ships by displaying trade goods – brass bowls, mirrors, all the items they knew the Indians liked to have. Then a cultural misunderstanding took place:

> To attract them with merry-making and encourage them to approach, the admiral ordered the drummer-boy and another man who sang with a drum to go up on to the poop-deck, and some other young men to start dancing. As soon as the Indians saw this, they assumed a warlike posture, raising their shields to their arms, and began to shoot with their bows and arrows at the men who were dancing. At the admiral's orders the men stopped dancing and began to shoot back with their crossbows, so that the Indians' effrontery should not go unpunished and they should not lack in respect for the Christians.[7]

The Indians then beat a tactical retreat. However, the pilot of another caravel was brave enough to visit the canoe and gave them presents; 'he reported that these were very handsome people and whiter in colour than those of the other islands, only they wore their hair long like women, tied with little cords, and that they covered their private parts with little cloths.'[8]

Columbus' excitement grew as he sailed along what later explorers would realise was a long projection sticking out of the northern flank of South America. He wanted to call it the 'Land of Grace', *Gracia*, but the locals, he discovered, called it 'Paria'. Columbus, though, would remember it for its pearls; he observed that the natives wore gold pieces on their breasts and pearl-encrusted strings around their arms, 'like a rosary' and 'made up of large and small pearls threaded together'.[9] (As the Indians in due course testified, these pearls were brought from the rich pearl fisheries further west, since the gulf itself is not a source of pearls.)[10] Columbus was having serious problems with his eyes and was in great pain, and he did not go ashore himself. Instead he sent a landing party which was very well received. The people, whitish like those of Trinidad and wearing similar coverings (including the bright turbans), led the landing party to a rectangular house with many seats, where the men sat at one end and the women at the other, while the sailors were offered fermented drinks made from maize and various fruits. They had a good meal, and the Indians were so determined to treat them well that they were then taken off to the house of the son of their first host, in order to eat another grand meal. But everyone was upset that they could not understand one another. The canoes in this part of the world were more sophisticated than those Columbus had seen in the northern Caribbean: they were lighter and better made, with cabins amidships that were used by the chieftains and their wives.[11] Yet beyond this region there was, as ever, a land whose inhabitants were said to be more sinister. The Indians pointed out a lofty land to the west, 'but all told me that I should not go there, for there they ate men, and I understood then that they said that there were cannibals there, and that they were like the other cannibals'.[12] Columbus wondered whether in fact they meant that there were large wild animals out there. In any case, he felt sure that he had at last found a route into the lands of civilisation. He began to talk about the *Tierra Firme*, the mainland, though it was hard to be sure whether this was actually the mainland of Asia or some other coastline, presumably sticking out of Asia – the southern continent about which d'Ailly and others had mused.[13] Moreover, 'all the Indians in the cannibal islands had told him that there was a great continent to the south of them'.[14] That he was near Asia he could not doubt.

Columbus was nevertheless confused by the rush of water coming through the straits between Trinidad and the mainland of South America, and he was also troubled by the way his compass seemed to be going out of control. The water was a mixture of fresh and salt water, and he correctly identified the mouth of a great river system, the Orinoco, pouring millions of gallons of water into the Gulf of Paria and stirring up its surface. But he was convinced that this was only part of the answer. The river beckoned him in a special direction. After long months studying prophetic texts in Spain while awaiting permission to depart on his third voyage, he had become obsessed by the sacred as well as the natural history of these lands. He decided that he was approaching a point that stuck out of the globe; the world, he argued, was not round but pear-shaped, with a small projection sticking right out like a stalk, 'and on one part of it is placed something like a woman's nipple', which brings this part of the world nearest to the sky.[15] The seas themselves sloped upwards at this point. Where then could he be but on the outskirts of the Garden of Eden itself? The Garden of Eden was not accessible, but was guarded by an angel with a flaming sword; so much was clear from the account in Genesis of the expulsion of the first man and woman from its bounds.[16] This 'nipple' must be the point from which the four great rivers described in the Bible flowed. That meant that there was a route, whether along these rivers or across the open sea, which would take him to the very heart of Asia. But before he could go there, as had happened on his second voyage, other duties intervened. He knew he had first to set sail for Hispaniola and find out what his brothers and Roldán had achieved; on 30 August 1498 his ships therefore entered the harbour of Santo Domingo, the new capital of Hispaniola, on its southern shores. He had plenty of surprises awaiting him.

'In Their Demeanour Like to Brute Beasts', 1497–8

On every front there were competitors seeking to take away Columbus' monopoly in the New World. There were problems in the Caribbean: in Hispaniola, Roldán turned against the Columbus brothers, presenting himself, perhaps hypocritically, as the defender of the persecuted Indians; more of this in a moment. Shipping was beginning to move back and forth between the Old World and the New, bringing supplies and returning with disaffected men, Taíno or Carib slaves and trade goods; Columbus had lost his monopoly on movement. There were problems on a global scale as well: if the Portuguese reached Asia by following a sea route around Africa, they might (on Columbus' globe) find themselves before long in the waters he had discovered, competing for access to the spices and gold of the East, and for favours at the courts of China, Japan and India. Moreover, other European rulers were beginning to examine the idea of opening a route to Asia. This was partly thanks to Columbus himself. He had sent his brother Bartholomew to the court of Henry VII of England in 1488–9, anxious to secure support from any quarter at a time when no one believed his arguments about the westward route to the Indies.[17] Although generally an ally of Ferdinand and Isabella, with whom he contracted a fateful marriage alliance, and although careful with his pennies, Henry VII began to realise that there was a good opportunity to capitalise on England's position to the north of Spain, looking due west from the British Isles across the open Atlantic.[18] King Henry was advised by John Cabot, a Genoese who had taken Venetian citizenship and had worked for Ferdinand of Aragon on the port installations in Valencia.[19] Henry, Cabot and indeed Columbus were well aware that the men of Bristol had come back from voyages in search of cod full of tales about misty lands to the west, and there was a succession of voyages in search of the 'island of Brasylle' in 1480 and 1481.[20] Greenland appeared on a map of 1467, though with fanciful place-names attached; but when the Portuguese sea captain Corte-Real explored it in 1500 he and mapmakers back home assumed it was part of north-east Asia.[21] In any case, no products from the New World, apart perhaps from cod fished off Greenland and the Labrador Grand Banks, reached Europe before 1492.[22] More importantly, there were no reports of strange people met by the English explorers.

Cabot's voyage on the *Matthew* in 1497 was designed to show that the Spaniards had been sailing too far to the south in their search for Asia, a route partly determined by the lust for the gold that was thought to lie in these latitudes. The Milanese ambassador in London reported that Cabot was searching for the real Cipangu, for he was unconvinced that Cuba or any other land Columbus had found was Japan. The ambassador wrote: Cabot 'believes that all the spices in the world have their origin' in Japan, and Cabot knew about this because he had already intrepidly penetrated to Mecca and had asked there where spices originated.[23] If Cabot's hunches were correct, London stood to become a more important spice market even than Alexandria. In March 1496 King Henry blithely granted Cabot extensive rights of conquest, trade monopoly and dominion in the lands he would discover; typically, though, he left it to others to finance the expedition. As for the natives of these lands, they only received a brief mention: 'whatsoever islands, countries, regions or provinces of heathens and infidels, in whatsoever part of the world placed, which before this time were unknown to all Christians'.[24] The fact that the king specified these were to be previously unknown lands avoided a direct clash with the interests of Columbus and the Crown of Castile. No mention of the papal division of the world into Spanish and Portuguese spheres was made. It was simply assumed that Christian discoverers could raise the flag of England in whatever non-Christian land they visited, without reference to the native inhabitants.

John Cabot was only able to obtain one ship, the faithful 'shippe of Bristowe' known as the *Matthew*.[25] After a first try in 1496, when he was defeated by the weather and the pessimism of his crew, his first full voyage, in 1497, apparently took him to the 'New-found-land', and possibly to Labrador.[26] Spices were not found; but there was an astonishing amount of cod, and one would never need to go to Iceland for it again. It was widely assumed that Cabot had found more islands, rather than a continent – the duke of Milan was told by his agents that Cabot had found the Island of the Seven Cities.[27] The Englishman John Day wrote to 'the Lord Grand Admiral', almost certainly Columbus (then back in Spain, between his second and third voyages), with a description of Cabot's voyage; he patriotically claimed that 'the cape of the said land was found and discovered in the past by the men from Bristol who found "Brasil", as your Lordship well knows'.[28]

Day reported that Cabot had found a grassy land, 1,800 miles to the west of the tip of Ireland.[29] This discovery happened on 24 June 1497.[30] Cabot and his men disembarked, carrying a crucifix and banners with the papal and English royal arms. The men followed a trail that led inland, and found a place where a fire had been laid. They saw what seemed to be the droppings of domestic animals and a carved stick painted red, with holes at each end. 'By such signs they believe the island to be inhabited.'[31] Assuming this was Newfoundland, this was the time of year when the local Mic-Mac Indians moved inland for hunting, so it would have been surprising if they had encountered many people. But as they coasted along the shore they did sight 'two forms running on land one after the other', though they could not tell if they were human or animal.

Another, larger expedition set off under Cabot in 1498; it seems to have headed towards Newfoundland, with the idea that the ships would strike southwards towards the tropics, in search, perhaps, of a passage to India, or at least Japan and China. Cabot himself disappeared, though it is possible that some of his sailors made their way back to Europe with three Indians. For the *Great chronicle of London* reported that in 1501 or 1502 there 'were browgth unto the kyng iij men takyn In the Newe ffound Ile land'; 'these were clothid In bestys skynnys and ete Raw fflesh and spak such speech that noo man cowed undyrstand theym, and In theyr demeanure lyke to bruyt bestis.'[32] The king kept two of them at court and soon they were dressing like 'Inglysh men': a chronicler who saw them then could barely tell them apart from other people, except that they knew not a word of English.

A Venetian writer described how the Portuguese navigated the waters off Newfoundland around 1501:

These men resemble Gypsies [*Cingani*] in appearance, body and height; they have marks on their faces in various places, some more than others, some less; and are clad in the skins of various animals, but mostly of otters; their speech is entirely different from any other which has been heard until now in this kingdom, nor is it understood by anybody; their limbs are well-made, and they have very meek faces, but bestial manners and gestures like wild men.[33]

They were wild men of the forests, then, true *silvestres* or 'savages'. Actually, in the words of John Cabot's son Sebastian, 'it is a very sterile land', inhabited by polar bears, moose ('large stags like horses'), sturgeon, salmon, soles a yard long and an infinity of codfish.[34] It was not, then, the semi-paradise about which Columbus and Peter Martyr enthused so poetically, in which seasons were of little importance and crops almost shot out of the soil.

The English failed to capitalise on the discovery: King Henry VII was not really interested in the sea, and his son Henry VIII was much more interested in building a fleet that would outrank that of France (one can imagine his annoyance when the French king built a ship with a tennis court and windmill on board, and his delight when it proved too heavy to float). As far as England was concerned, the American lands only came into focus in the second half of the sixteenth century, when Spain was a bitter enemy, and serious colonisation only began when Jamestown was founded in 1607.

The Virgin and Child of Calicut, 1497–8

The year of John Cabot's voyage saw yet another expedition in search of the Indies. In July 1497 Vasco da Gama set out with four ships, at first following the classic Portuguese route along the west coast of Africa and past the Cape Verde Islands.[35] The voyage nearly ten years earlier of Bartholomew Dias, as far as the Cape of Good Hope, had mapped out the coast of south-west Africa, but da Gama had also learned enough about the winds and currents in the South Atlantic to realise that his best chance of rounding the Cape lay in choosing what at first appeared to be a wildly eccentric route: from the Cape Verdes he swung out into the ocean, describing a route that traversed three times the distance covered by Christopher Columbus in 1492. It was a risky undertaking: his ships were swept along, arriving somewhere along the coasts of modern Namibia and South Africa, where they met tawny-coloured people dressed in skins, whose menfolk covered their penises with sheaths, and who carried wooden poles. These bushmen knew metals: they had little beads of copper in their ears, and they appreciated gifts of small Portuguese copper coins.[36] Spices, gold and pearls were new to them. However, further south, Vasco da Gama's chronicler described people who possessed arts and crafts familiar from other parts of Africa: they had sheep and oxen, they were skilled pipers, and they danced prettily in the manner of the black Africans known from much further to the north.[37] The Portuguese bought an ox for three bracelets and dined well off it, for it was full of fat and as tasty as anything back home.

The sense that they were not so far from home despite the distance travelled was reinforced by other events. They followed the coast, marking their route with crosses or *padrões*: these were direction-finders, but they were also a signal that Christ had reached these shores. Da Gama and his crew noted the presence of iron, for the people carried spears with iron blades and covered their bodies with copper ornaments.[38] They were glad to buy linen cloth in exchange for generous amounts of copper, though some of the people they encountered wore nothing more than loincloths; the women, who were good-looking, wore larger loincloths; this was understood as an indication of their relative modesty.[39] These people were not isolated from the world; one man had travelled from far up the coast, where he had already seen big ships. For the Portuguese, this meant that the lands they aspired to reach could not be far away. The recorder of da Gama's voyage found the people handsome and 'well-made', not monstrous by any stretch of the imagination; their blackness was expected, while the broad similarities to other Africans rendered this world less strange than the Caribbean, or even the Canaries.

The further they coasted into the Indian Ocean the more the Portuguese were reminded not of the Christian but of the Muslim world. Da Gama reached towns along the coast of Mozambique where the ruddy-skinned inhabitants included Muslims.[40] Many spoke Arabic. They dressed finely in linen and cotton, and wore silken turbans embroidered with gold; they were active in trade with the 'white Moors' to the north, and in fact Arab vessels were in port, piled with gold, gems, pearls and spices, including the much-desired pepper of the Indies. The merchants boasted that pearls and jewels were so abundant in the lands towards which the Portuguese were heading that one simply gathered them, without any need to exchange goods for them.[41] This was a different, more material, paradise from the one Columbus sought as he identified the route to the Garden of Eden. The Portuguese absorbed all the rumours they heard like sponges: there were Christian kingdoms to the north, at war with the Moors; there was the Ethiopian realm of Prester John, still busy in defence of Christendom after three centuries.

By the time he reached Mombasa, da Gama had entered a much more familiar world and was convinced that he had already made contact with Christians. Two merchants of Mombasa proudly showed the Portuguese an image of the Holy Spirit drawn on paper.[42] With the help of a willing pilot, da Gama was able to make his way to Calicut in India, where he arrived on 20 May 1498. Here again he was entering a world that had close links to home. He found a couple of Moors from Tunis, who spoke Spanish and Italian, and who unenthusiastically greeted the Portuguese with the words: 'May the devil take you! What brought you here?'[43] The Portuguese were, nonetheless, convinced that they had reached a Christian land. The chronicler was less attracted by the appearance of the Indians than by that of the Africans, finding the Indian women gaudily dressed; for once the reaction to all the gold that they wore in the form of bracelets and rings was that there was simply too much of it. The Portuguese were impressed by a building they identified as a church; it was made of stone and was the size of a monastery, with a great bronze pillar at the entrance. Within there was an imposing chapel, access to which was reserved to the *quafees* or 'deacons', and 'within this sanctuary stood a small image which they said represented Our Lady'.[44] The figure carried a child, so the identification was as certain as could be. Therefore Vasco da Gama entered the compound with some of his companions, and they said their prayers. The local priests threw holy water over the Portuguese visitors and presented them with 'white earth' made of cow dung, ashes and sandalwood, with which the local Christians were accustomed to anoint themselves.[45] The local Christians were also devotees of any number of saints, whose images were painted on the walls of the church, some with several arms or with giant teeth.[46]

It was all, of course, a great mistake. Their first encounter with the Hindu gods was transmogrified in the fertile imagination of the Portuguese into an encounter with the Virgin and Child. The panoply of gods painted on the walls was read as a cycle of Christian saints.[47] The Virgin and Child was probably an image of Krishna being suckled by his mother Divaki. The Portuguese knew these people were not 'Moors', whose places of cult had no images and whose language and practices were easily recognisable – it was only in the year that da Gama left Portugal that Islam was banned in Portugal. (Indeed, it is possible that the image da Gama saw in Mombasa, and the 'Christian' merchants he met there, were also Hindu.)[48]

India was a land of kings, of scheming Moors, of undoubted wealth, in which the Portuguese were not really welcome. Still, da Gama was able to leave well loaded with pepper, and to reach Lisbon again in September 1499. The route to the Indies, the real Indies, had been opened; this was indeed the land rich in spices of which Marco Polo had spoken, and it had all the accoutrements of high civilisation, including great cities, flourishing markets, skilled craftsmen and, last but not least, men and women who clothed themselves, if not as fully as Europeans.

CHAPTER 18

COLUMBUS ECLIPSED, 1498–1506

Roldán's Rebellion, 1498

Columbus was a talented navigator but a disastrous administrator. When, at the end of his second voyage, he elevated Francisco Roldán to the office of *alcalde mayor*, chief judge, he failed to define the relationship between this office and that of his brother Bartholomew, who carried the title *adelantado*. Ferdinand Columbus said that Roldán had been given 'so much credit and authority over both the Indians and the Christians, that he was obeyed by them as much as the admiral himself'.[1] Ferdinand portrayed Roldán as a ruthless man who had only his own interests at heart, as a conspirator whose aim was to kill Columbus' brothers, and as a rebel against the Crown, whose intention was to keep for himself the tribute in gold that should have been sent to Spain. Brandishing his staff of office, which represented his right to act on behalf of the Crown, he stirred up the Spanish settlers and made them believe that the Columbus family had one aim, 'to remain masters of the country and to keep the others in perpetual subjection'.[2] In any case, the Spaniards should not allow themselves to be ruled by a bunch of Genoese foreigners. What the Spaniards wanted (according to Roldán) was to use the Indians in any way they liked, and that included taking Indian wives. They were being forced against their will to observe vows of poverty, chastity and obedience.[3]

But relations with the Indians were even more complex. The Indians were the source of all the tribute; and they had begun to rebel. Roldán himself was sent by the Columbus brothers to the settlement at Concepción, in the interior, to suppress an Indian revolt. Far from being weak and passive, the Indians had found a political voice. They aimed to seize the fort at Concepción from the Spaniards; at the same time, Roldán arrived with forty men, and was later accused by Ferdinand Columbus of also planning to seize the fortress.[4] Bartholomew Columbus tried to strip Roldán of office, but Roldán insisted that only the king could do this. There was an impasse, and the situation became graver still when Roldán and his men, who had now swollen in number to sixty-five, were accused of trying to break into the storehouses at La Isabela in search of arms, food and clothing, right under the nose of Columbus' other brother, Diego, whom some, in any case, suspected of collusion with Roldán. All of this suggests an almost complete breakdown in authority within Hispaniola. No one knew who was in charge, or rather no one was in charge.

Nonetheless, it is possible to read between the lines of Ferdinand Columbus' account of events, and to see that his portrayal of Roldán as the enemy of Spain and of the Indians does not really fit the information he himself provided. His account is full of contradictions, and at times Roldán does seem to have friends among the Indians. We are told that Roldán set off for the province of Jaraguá, in the west of the island, because it was fertile, because the native inhabitants were regarded as more intelligent than other Taínos, and above all 'because the women were more beautiful and pleasing than they were elsewhere'.[5] And yet the same Roldán was said to have presented himself to the Indians of Jaraguá as their 'defender and protector'.[6] He encouraged them to stop paying tribute; he stirred up the *cacique* Guarionex, who decided that the time had come to kill the entire Spanish garrison at Concepción. Roldán's dream was a co-ordinated rebellion against the Columbus family and its allies, and the *caciques* agreed that they would rise up against their oppressors at the next full moon. This date was set 'since the Indians had no way of counting except on their fingers'.[7] Apparently the skies were cloudy and one of the *caciques* miscalculated, launching an attack too early and spoiling these well-laid plans, to the fury of Guarionex. The Spanish rebels, having missed the chance for a large-scale Indian rebellion, withdrew to Jaraguá, 'proclaiming all the while that they were the protectors of the Indians', but 'each one stealing whatever he could'.[8] While telling the *caciques* that they should not pay tribute to the Columbus brothers, Roldán supposedly levied taxes that were even higher than those demanded by the legitimate governors of Hispaniola, and, to guarantee compliance, he held hostage members of the family of one *cacique*, Manicaotex, from whom he demanded particularly large amounts of gold: three marks each quarter, or nearly 700 grammes.[9]

There was nothing Christopher Columbus could do about this: it happened while he was still in Spain, planning his third voyage, which, as has been seen, in any case first took him along the coast of South America, far from Santo Domingo. When the admiral sent supply ships from Spain, some of them accidentally touched land in Roldán's territory, and some sailors defected to him, bringing much-needed supplies.[10] And then Columbus himself arrived in September 1498 and, over the weeks that followed, adopted a conciliatory policy which suggests that the admiral was desperately disappointed that the government of the island, and above all its tribute system, was disintegrating. What would he have left to show his king and queen if half the gold tribute was secreted away by rebels? And he was enough of a realist to see that his brother Bartholomew had made the Columbus family even more unpopular. The admiral issued a safe-conduct to Roldán; they met, and eventually, in November 1498, an agreement was hammered out according to which Roldán and his supporters would leave the island for Spain, even carrying a letter of recommendation to the king and queen from the admiral. What is striking about the agreement is that it went into great detail about many issues, including the number of pigs and piglets owned by Roldán that were to be left behind (and paid for by the Crown).[11] And yet there was one matter that received scant attention: the Indians. There were some brief clauses that dealt with slaves owned by Roldán's men, who must have been Indians, and with pregnant women, clearly Indian – their children were to be free. But it was simply taken for granted that the tribute system would continue. Columbus had by now had time to reflect on the reasons for the rebellions among both the native population and the Spanish settlers. He made no effort to change his policies; and the losers were not Roldán's supporters but the fast-diminishing Taíno population of Hispaniola. Columbus even appointed a captain who was to range through Hispaniola, 'pacifying the Indians and compelling them to pay tribute', though other events prevented this harsh policy from being put into effect.[12] Roldán proved strangely reluctant to leave, and Columbus was reluctant to try to force him to do so. Columbus was fully aware of the hostility of the settlers to non-Spanish governors. He needed to conciliate the settlers. He also knew that the best chance of stability on the island was a working agreement with Roldán. So after another year of protracted negotiations Roldán emerged as *alcalde mayor* for life.[13] He even conducted campaigns on behalf of Columbus.[14] In the end, this did not help Roldán, who began to have trouble with his erstwhile supporters. One of his lieutenants decided that he wanted to marry the daughter of a *cacique*; in principle this was not a problem, but the Indian woman was already Roldán's mistress. Finally, in 1502, Roldán was put on board a ship bound for Spain, which foundered with all hands.

Columbus had barely resolved his differences with Roldán when he found a new rival. Alonso de Hojeda had accompanied him on his second voyage and acquitted himself well. In September 1499 he arrived in Hispaniola. Acting as the agent of Columbus' old rival Fonseca in Seville, Hojeda spread word that the era of the Columbus dynasty was nearing its end. Queen Isabella, he said, was mortally ill, and the admiral would be left without defenders once she was gone. Dealing with Hojeda seemed more urgent than subduing the Indians, and Columbus sent none other than Roldán against him. Hojeda knew that he was not strong enough to resist Roldán's men, so he met him and explained that what he really wanted to do was to report to Columbus on his own voyage along the coast of Paria, which he had discovered to be full of large land animals such as deer and 'tigers' (jaguars).[15] This posed another threat to Columbus: his monopoly on the exploration of the seas had been broken, with the full support, it must be said, of Fonseca and, above him, of Ferdinand and Isabella. The king and queen were made aware of the settlers' complaints; some, who had returned to Spain, camped in the courtyards of the Alhambra, where the king and queen were staying, and sat eating grapes as a sign that this modest food was all they could afford.[16] The crowning insult was the appointment of a rather dubious figure, Francisco de Bobadilla, in 1499 – though he only arrived in August 1500 – to inspect Columbus' performance as viceroy in Hispaniola. Columbus' third voyage ended in public disgrace for the Admiral of the Ocean Sea. Bobadilla arrested Columbus and despatched him back to Spain in chains, along with his brother Diego, while (it was later said) taking a handsome share of the revenue from the Indians for himself.[17]

Columbus' extraordinary privileges and rights were thus being closely questioned. Among them, the exclusive right to explore the newly discovered lands in the 'Indies' was perhaps the right about which he cared most. Others might find the route to the sources of gold about which he dreamed; others might argue that these lands were not the Indies at all; but he, as the bearer of Christ's name, had no doubt about the mission to which God had called him.

Towards the Lands of the Mayas, 1502

The first few years of Columbian rule in Hispaniola had brought chaos and misery for the Indians. A rudimentary colonial regime had been set in place, with a line of forts linking the north of the island, around La Isabela, to the new centre of operations at Santo Domingo on the south coast. Back in Spain in November 1500, and freed from his chains (which he had worn throughout the voyage and right up to the moment he appeared before his monarchs, in an act of high theatre), Columbus defended himself against his detractors by insisting that Hispaniola was not like 'Sicily or some province or city under settled government'.[18] What he dangled in front of his king and queen was the prospect of a route to Calicut; the Portuguese were now friendly, and he confidently expected to greet their sea captains in the Indies. How could the sordid concerns of the settlers, dominated by the cost of keeping an Indian woman, compare with the high ideal of opening up the East and blazing a trail to Jerusalem? His humiliation by his enemies and increasing problems with his health only encouraged Columbus to think of himself as the scorned and suffering servant of God. Columbus became more and more convinced of his divine mission; with the help of some equally enthusiastic collaborators he compiled a *Book of prophecies* in late 1501 and early 1502, consisting of quotations from biblical and later writings. The Psalmist said: 'they shall come before You, and all the ends of the earth shall be converted to the Lord';[19] the baptised former rabbi Samuel of Fez, whose works Columbus raided, foresaw the conversion of Gentile peoples;[20] and the Calabrian abbot Joachim of Fiore, writing three hundred years before Columbus, knew that a man would come out of Spain and that he would 'recover the fortunes of Zion', which could only mean that he would open the road to Jerusalem.[21] Even the Koran was mobilised to demonstrate Columbus' mission to convert the peoples of the world to Christ.[22] The *Book of prophecies* culminated with a mass of biblical references to the conversion of the peoples of the islands: Isaiah wrote that 'the islands shall wait for his law' and, even if in strict historical terms he must have meant the islands of the Mediterranean, Columbus' imagination leapt forward to see in the prediction the islands of the Ocean Sea.[23] All this appealed enormously to Ferdinand and Isabella. They too were caught up in this apocalyptic view of their times; they too were impressed by the discovery of heathen peoples who needed to be brought to the knowledge of the Christian faith before the last days of mankind could be inaugurated.

Delicately the king and queen separated two problems. Columbus the Christ-bearing admiral could still wander the seas and look for his routes to China, Paradise or wherever.[24] However, though he was allowed to retain his notional authority in Hispaniola, another governor was despatched there to represent the interests of the Crown; among his staff was an official who would make sure that Columbus received his cut of the profits from the island, while also ensuring that profits from salt and the valued dyestuff brazilwood would reach the Crown. This governor was Nicolas de Ovando, who was sent out with thirty ships, the largest fleet to cross the Atlantic so far.[25] The king and queen were shocked at Columbus' treatment by Bobadilla, who also needed to be carefully investigated, along with Roldán. So they were willing to let Columbus set out on a fourth voyage, on condition that he did not go to Hispaniola, and on condition that he did not bring back any slaves, for several small slave-raiding expeditions had caused great annoyance at the Spanish court.

The fourth voyage did not get under way until May 1502, and the fleet consisted of a mere four ships, compared to Ovando's thirty.[26] But one of the ships' boys was Ferdinand Columbus, and this gives added importance to the descriptions of native peoples and new lands in the account he later offered of Columbus' very turbulent and dangerous fourth voyage. Off Santo Domingo, the weather was foul and the admiral asked for permission to enter the harbour. He was refused. In fact, thirty-two ships bound for Spain set out in the growing hurricane, with Roldán, Bobadilla and the *cacique* Guarionex aboard, and nearly all the vessels were swept to the bottom of the sea with massive loss of life.[27] Three ships turned back and only one limped across the Atlantic to deliver four thousand *pesos* of gold mined by the Taínos to the Castilian treasury.[28] Las Casas remarked:

And this was the end of King Guarionex on whom those calling themselves Christians had inflicted such grave affronts, violence, injury, and insult, and who even now suffered the gravest insult of all, stripped as he was of his kingdom, his wife, and his children, and on the point of being shipped back to Spain in irons for no fault of his own, without any reason or just cause, when he was to all intents and purposes murdered by drowning.[29]

The same hurricane demolished much of Santo Domingo: 'it seemed as if the whole host of demons from Hell had been unleashed upon the face of the earth.'[30]

Columbus rode out the storm and tacked past Jamaica westwards through the Caribbean, on his way to find a passage to India. He had no idea that he was heading towards the coast of central America, and when he reached the island of Guanaja his ships stood just north of the Mosquito Coast, near what became known as Cape Honduras.[31] While they were off this island, the explorers came across a massive canoe, eight feet wide and as long as a galley, with a large central awning full of people and goods; 'the admiral gave orders to take whatever seemed to be most noteworthy and precious.'[32] This was a departure from his normal practice of trying to win confidence among newly encountered people by trading small items of truck with them. The reason must lie in las Casas' insistence that 'the admiral still persisted in his belief that he might obtain news of Cathay and the Great Khan'.[33] He was looking for evidence that these people were Asiatic. And to Columbus the signs were plain. Some covered themselves with shirts, jerkins and breech-cloths; the women covered their faces and bodies with sheets, in the manner of the Moorish women of Granada.[34] They seemed different from other peoples he had met. Even the shape of their skulls was different, for they had narrower foreheads. They drank maize beer, which was, Ferdinand Columbus said, rather like English beer. Already struck by the use of sharp stone axes among the Taínos, Columbus was now impressed by the fact that these people possessed both sharp swords with stone cutting-edges and axes made of copper. These were copper objects they themselves produced. The sailors saw little crucibles which showed that they knew how to work copper.[35] For Columbus was unwittingly drawing near to another world. He was right that he had entered a different cultural orbit from that of the Taínos; he was even right that a few hundred miles away there lay great cities fabulously rich in gold. The people he had encountered lived on the outer edges of the lands of the Mayas, who had reached the apex of their civilisation between the third and the ninth centuries. But, in his thinking, the first signs of copper indicated that he was slowly but surely climbing the ladder of civilisation.

Columbus was aware from his third voyage that a large mainland existed to the south but, his son recorded, he now wanted to find a way through the straits that must surely exist between the southern continent and Asia; this would lead him to the Indies. He began to think of the southern continent as a detached part of Asia rather than as an entirely separate New World. In other words, he still had no idea that a neck of land separated the Caribbean from the sea beyond, nor, of course, that there existed a vast Pacific Ocean which must be crossed in order to arrive in Cipangu and Cathay.[36] He was still trying to reconcile his assumptions about the size and shape of the world with what he found; and, not surprisingly, he experienced some frustration.[37] The coppersmiths of Guanaja, he decided, were really of no interest in themselves, and he was no more impressed by the inhabitants of the central American mainland, along which he now coasted southwards. In northeastern Honduras he found ugly, dark, naked folk, 'very savage in every way', of whom it was said by an Indian interpreter that they ate human flesh and raw fish straight out of the sea, clear signs of their beast-like status. They had massive holes in their ear lobes, so large that you could pass a hen's egg through them; therefore he named the region 'Coast of the Ears', *Costa de las Orejas*. The Indians who lived along this coast had elaborate tattoos on their bodies, with designs of what looked like lions, deer and castles, the last of which surely proved that great cities lay not too far away. This, then, was another example of the way in which the explorers classified the people they met as either 'good' or 'bad', which sometimes also meant light-skinned or dark-skinned. Columbus was also struck by the fact that the language spoken along this shore was quite different from that of the Taínos, making interpretation extremely difficult. Despite the conviction that these people 'seem truly to be devils', Columbus and his men landed to hear Mass on Sunday 14 August 1502, and they were impressed by the richness of the land, which, they said, was full of deer and leopards; they won the confidence of the natives, and the next day they were offered as gifts not human flesh and raw fish but roasted geese and fish, as well as red and white beans.[38] 'There is no indication that they have any religion,' Ferdinand Columbus reported.

Further down the coast the explorers met a strange people who at first wished to trade with the Christians, but were then struck with fear when the ships' scribes began to record the replies they made to questions put through an interpreter. They thought that writing was some sort of bewitchment (around the same time the inhabitants of Brazil marvelled at messages written by European explorers on paper, which seemed to make the paper 'speak'). In fact, the Indians were the real magicians, for when they came close to the Christians they would throw a strange powder in the air towards them, and would make clouds of incense out of it as well. Their fear of the Europeans became such that they returned all the gifts Columbus' men had offered them.[39] But the curiosity of the explorers had been aroused; a party went inland and found the burial site of these people, a *palazzo grande* made of wood, which contained embalmed bodies and, over each tomb, a carved panel

showing human or animal figures, to which jewels, pieces of alloyed gold
(*guanín*) and other objects were attached. Ferdinand Columbus or his translator oddly described some of these ornaments as Ave Marias, so they must
have looked like rosaries.[40] This, at least, was evidence that the people who
lived along the coast did after all observe religious rituals. All the evidence he
possessed convinced Columbus that these were the Indians most gifted with
reason (*di più ragione*) he had encountered on this voyage, so he ordered that
two of their leaders be seized, and gave the Indians to understand that he
needed their services as guides. The Indians did not believe this: they recognised the greed of the Europeans and thought that Columbus intended to
ransom the men for gold and jewels.[41]

Columbus had reason to feel satisfied as he made his way down the coast:
gold seemed plentiful. The admiral encountered naked folk, painted white,
black and red, who wore a single item, a gold disc or mirror around their
necks, or sometimes an eagle made of *guanín*. Pedro de Ledesma, a pilot on
this voyage, told las Casas that eighty canoes loaded with gold had
approached the Spanish ships. Columbus ordered that two Indians be seized
and interrogated; one wore a mirror that weighed as much as fourteen gold
ducats, and the other wore a gold eagle that weighed twenty-two.[42] 'The
two insisted that there were huge reserves of this metal, which they
appeared to be fixated upon, within a day or two's journey from that spot.'[43]
The real fixation was of course among the Spaniards. And even further
down the coast, as they approached the mouth of the Veragua River, they
found a king who sat under a great leaf to shelter himself from the rain, and
busily bartered more of these mirrors, nineteen in all, for the goods the
explorers had brought. But what was really impressive was the evidence that
these people knew how to build in something other than wood: 'This was
the first place in the Indies where we saw signs of building, a large mass of
plaster that appeared to have been worked with stone and lime, and the
admiral gave orders to take a piece of it as a reminder of the ancient edifice
[*antichità*].'[44] It is striking that the explorers recognised this structure as
something old. With its stone and plaster, it sounds like something left by
the Maya Indians.

Hints of high civilisation somewhere in the interior accumulated.
Columbus wrote a letter to the king and queen in which he briefly described
the fourth voyage; he told of his excitement on hearing of 'the province of
Ciguare, which, according to them, lies inland to the west nine days'
journey'.[45] Here there were infinite amounts of gold, and everyone wore

massive coral bracelets and decorated their furniture with coral as well. The Indians Columbus encountered said he would be happy if he had one-tenth of the riches of Ciguare:

> In Ciguare they are accustomed to trade in fairs and markets; so these people related, and they showed me the way and manner in which they carry on barter. Further they said that the ships carry cannon, bows and arrows, swords and shields, and that the people go clothed, and that in the land there are horses, and that the people are warlike and wear rich clothing and have good houses.[46]

Ciguare was said to be a land surrounded or washed by the sea, ten days' journey from the River Ganges. It lay in relation to Veragua as Pisa lies in relation to Venice. In other words, there was a neck of land, and it lay on the other side. Some have seen this as the first reference to the Pacific shores of America. But Columbus' words were an amalgam of his fervent expectations, his attempts to make sense of languages he could not understand, and reports of lands in the interior that still were (in the case of Aztec Mexico) or had been (in the case of the Maya states) the seats of rich, warlike and highly organised civilisations. To him, of course, all this meant he was closer than ever to the Far East. He could not imagine that this was another continent, with its own high civilisations.

In December, January and February the ships worked their way past the modern Costa Rica and into northern Panama (the region known to the Indians as Veragua).[47] The weather was atrocious; they had an encounter with a fearsome water-spout, and there were worms everywhere – in the planking of the ships, but also in the food, which was best eaten at night so that you could not see the worms that were being cooked along with the ship's biscuit.[48] Once the worst of the weather was over (as he thought), Columbus went in search of gold mines, and sent a party into the interior, without finding anything. The obsession with collecting gold mirrors remained, though the explorers were unimpressed by the local practice of chewing coca, 'which seems a very unpleasant thing to do' and rotted the Indians' teeth.[49] The natives also had the odd practice of turning their backs on one another while having a conversation. Still, the country was attractive, rich in fish and maize (from which red and white 'wines' were brewed), and the reports of well-stocked gold mines in the interior did not go away, so this seemed to be the place in which to establish a settlement by a river mouth, to be called

Belén, 'Bethlehem', in memory of the three Magi who had reached Bethlehem on the same day in January.[50] Naturally, as Admiral of the Ocean Sea and viceroy of all these lands, Columbus claimed the right to create a settlement. But what his plan principally revealed was that he was thinking of starting afresh: Hispaniola was out of his hands and was widely regarded as a failure. He would thus leave his brother Bartholomew here with eighty of the men and return to Castile to arrange for further men and supplies to be sent.[51] A dozen houses were built of wood and thatch, and the colonists tried to regulate relations with the local population by the drastic policy of attempting to capture the chieftain or *quibian*. The latter was accused of plotting to destroy the colony and to kill all the settlers.[52]

Las Casas, typically, sided with the person he called 'Quibia', and argued that the Indians were justifiably upset to see a colony being built on land the Spaniards had taken without asking: no one who had the use of reason could possibly disagree that the Indians would try to prevent this happening, even if that meant a resort to arms.[53] The Indians, he said, were by now familiar with the 'insolent behaviour' of the Spaniards. Anyhow, the *quibian* escaped from his captors, and he and his men attacked the colony the moment Columbus' ships had left the shore. The Christians were badly mauled, and in the end Columbus had to return and try to rescue the survivors. This was rendered more difficult by the state of his ships, which were rotting away and taking on water. For a time Columbus despaired of bringing his men out; one of his ships was trapped in the river mouth, in constant danger of attack, with his own brother on board. He felt himself to be in enormous danger and, as often happened when he was under great stress, he ran a high fever.[54] He made his way to the highest point on the ship and called out for help to the captains of the other vessels, but he heard no reply. After a time, exhausted, he dozed off, and then he did hear a voice:

'O fool and slow to believe and to serve your God, the God of all! What more did He do for Moses or for his servant David? Since you were born, He has always had you in His most watchful care. When He saw you at an age with which he was content, He caused your name to sound marvellously in the land. The Indies, which are so rich a part of the world, He gave you for your own; you have divided them as it pleased you, and He enabled you to do this. Of the mighty barriers of the Ocean Sea, which were closed with such mighty chains, he gave you the keys.'[55]

His second attempt to found a colony had failed within days.[56] His ships were so badly damaged that by the time he reached 'the province of Mago, which marches with that of Cathay' – the southern coast of Cuba – in May 1503, only two were left.[57] And yet he did not stop seeing himself as a specially chosen agent of God. Nor had he yet experienced the worst tests of this disastrous voyage.

The Moon Turns to Blood, 1503–4

The two remaining ships limped on their way to Jamaica, the sailors working day and night at the pumps to keep the vessels afloat. Strong currents made it impossible to reach Hispaniola, and in the end the ships were beached on the Jamaican shore. Even then the below-deck quarters were waterlogged; the castles fore and aft were fitted out so all the men could have somewhere to sleep. Columbus had learned some lessons and was keen to prevent his men from raiding into the interior of what was still a little-known island.[58] He did not intend to build a settlement; he would not even let his men leave the ships without special permits, because he knew (his son said) that the Spanish sailors would raid the villages and abuse the Taíno women.[59] Fortunately the Indians were friendly and keen to barter with the Europeans. What was vital was to secure supplies of food, such as cassava bread. This was paid for with trinkets such as laces, beads and bells. Still, this was an impossible situation. Neither ship was in a fit state to be relaunched, neither ship could be careened and made ready for the sea. The obvious course was to send some of his men to Hispaniola in Indian canoes; there they would ask for a ship to be sent so that the Admiral of the Ocean Sea could be rescued. Again, the Indians were co-operative. The canoes set out in July 1503, carrying a letter from Columbus whose contents survive. It was addressed to the king and queen and told in suitably harrowing terms of his terrible experiences, of his certainty that his discoveries were opening the way to the Indies, and of his faith in God who had sent him to these lands.[60] The canoes, under the captaincy of Diego Méndez and Bartolomeo Fieschi (a Genoese), reached Hispaniola despite running out of water in the middle of the open sea, and Méndez himself wrote a report of his own colourful adventures.[61] But no one in Hispaniola was interested in rescuing Columbus.

This left Columbus in Jamaica in the company of increasingly unruly sailors, some of whom fell sick, while others murmured, rightly enough, that

Columbus was not welcome in Hispaniola. They said that that his real intention was to remain in Jamaica while his agents secured the best terms for his rescue and restoration to power from the king and queen. The months slipped past and there was no sign of ships coming to rescue the castaways. Columbus himself was ill with gout. The murmurings developed into mutiny, and a group of men seized ten Indian canoes, aiming to reach Santo Domingo on their own. The mutineers took food from the Indians, telling them to go to see the admiral if they wanted something in return. They also seized more than twenty Indians and made them paddle the canoes, but when the weather turned against them they realised that the canoes were overloaded and solved the problem by killing most of the Indians, throwing some into the water after stabbing them to death, while others simply jumped overboard in fear. Defeated by high seas, these sailors then returned and became a thorough nuisance in Jamaica, wandering through the villages and taking food by force from the Indians.[62] All this seriously damaged Columbus' attempts to foster good relations with the Indians: 'the Indians were to be so well treated that out of friendship and the desire to have our trade-goods they would continue to bring us the food they brought us.'[63] He did not seek gold, for once, nor did he intend to settle and conquer the island; his aim was simply to survive while awaiting help from Hispaniola, which seemed strangely slow in arriving.

Columbus' policy worked well at first, but the Indians gradually lost interest in the increasingly unwelcome visitors. The admiral had arrived at the end of June 1503; he was still there at the end of February 1504. For one thing, the visitors were very demanding, eating twenty times what the Indians ate. For another, the novelty of the trinkets they had been offering had worn off. Local prices rose: that is to say, you now had to offer ten times as much truck to obtain the same amount of food that the Indians had exchanged in the early months. Columbus knew that without supplies from the Indians his situation would be even more desperate than it was already. He came up with a brilliant solution to the problem. His astronomical tables showed him that there was to be an eclipse of the Moon on the night of 29 February 1504. So he told the Indians that God punished the wicked and looked after the good, and that God would send them plague and famine if they failed to bring supplies to the Christians; He would send them an angry sign in the sky that would prove God's wrath against them. Columbus invited them to look carefully at the moon as it rose that night, and, when they saw the blood-red disc of the eclipsed Moon rising above the horizon, the Indians were struck with fear; they at once began to run to the beached ships with food, and they begged Columbus to speak to God and urge Him to relent. Columbus artfully retired to his cabin, apparently to speak with God; in fact he watched the eclipse carefully through the port-holes, waiting until it had passed its apogee before re-emerging to tell the Indians that God had indeed relented, and that they would see the sign of His favour in the sky: the Moon would soon lose its fiery cast. These tactics triumphed. Thereafter the Indians were only too happy to bring supplies and to praise the God the visitors worshipped, though there is no suggestion that any effort was now made to convert the Taínos.[64] Columbus' manipulation of an eclipse has been imitated several times in fiction – by Rider Haggard's heroes in black Africa, and by Tintin among the Indians of the Andes. And yet Columbus' act of theatre was not simple trickery. As a man obsessed by portents, he had in mind the biblical prophecy of Joel, which he had already cited word for word in his *Book of prophecies*, compiled shortly before his fourth voyage: 'the sun shall be turned to darkness, and the moon to blood, before the great and terrible day of the Lord comes.'[65] Moreover, after his return to Spain he added a note to his *Book of prophecies* in which he gave a detailed astronomical description of the Jamaican eclipse.[66]

Nicolas de Ovando, in Hispaniola, took a mischievous pleasure in Columbus' misfortunes. He realised that the admiral's enforced absence offered him his best chance to pacify Hispaniola without interference from rivals. Eventually, a single caravel was sent to Columbus, bringing Ovando's polite good wishes, a barrel of wine and a side of salt pork; but the captain regretfully refused to take the stranded men on board and even declined to carry any letters to Hispaniola.[67] In the end Columbus made his escape on a privately chartered ship obtained by Diego Méndez, the messenger he had sent eleven months before. Finally, in August 1504, he arrived in Santo Domingo, where Ovando made a great show of receiving him with honour.[68] The admiral lingered for a month; Columbus then chartered another ship with his own money, and set sail for Spain. He would never return to the New World. He continued to fantasise about his plans for the future, despite being wracked by gout, and died two years later in Spain, still unconvinced that he had reached a totally new continent. His patron (and the patron of the Taíno population) Isabella died in 1504. Ferdinand was still anxious to extract gold from the Indies; but his major preoccupations lay in Italy, following his acqui-sition of Naples under the nose of the French in 1503. Even so, the Columbus family continued to occupy an important role in the government of Hispaniola; Christopher's son Diego would eventually become governor, claiming the right of succession, but he was no better suited to the task than his father had been.[69] Endless legal challenges to the rights claimed by the Columbuses proved a constant distraction, not just to the family but to the good government of the Caribbean islands.[70]

Encomienda Tribute

These legal disputes would determine how much wealth remained in the hands of the Columbus family; but there was still plenty to go round – Christopher's illegitimate son Ferdinand was able to lead a leisured life as a collector of books and prints. Columbus grumbled that he was entitled to one-tenth of the profits from the Indies, but what he was given was one-tenth of the fifth the king and queen received. All the same, the balance sheet was favourable enough. There is another balance sheet that needs to be considered, that for Hispaniola itself. The evolving tribute system, the *encomienda*, formally guaranteed the legal freedom of the Taínos while at the same time placing on their shoulders heavy burdens in tribute, and leaving them at the mercy of callous and greedy settlers. This *encomienda* system was derived from medieval Castilian practice: the king would draw up a division (*repartimiento*) of conquered lands and assign the parts to his vassals, who would be liable for tribute but were expected to manage their own estates independently. In the New World the system underwent swift and significant adaptation, so that it was now the governor, not the king, who assigned rights to his followers (*encomenderos*), and these were rights not over land but over a workforce whose task was to produce tribute in gold or possibly cotton.[71] As for that workforce, it was not legally owned by the *encomendero*. The Taínos were free in the sense that they had their own leaders (though many of those had been persecuted out of existence); while working in the gold fields they lived in their own reserved areas. Theory – in Spain – and practice – in the Indies – could be far removed from one another. Only in 1512, with the Laws of Burgos, was an attempt made, many thousands of miles away, to guarantee the position of the Indian workers; the laws seem to have been honoured mainly in the breach. Few settlers cared whether these people were legally free, 'natural slaves' or indeed unfree. These distinctions meant nothing to the greedy, ambitious men who sought their gold.

PART IV

SOUTHERN HORIZONS
*The Peoples and Shores of Atlantic
South America*

CHAPTER 19

VESPUCCI'S TABLOID JOURNALISM, 1497–1504

A Florentine Publicist

Columbus was a capable self-publicist; but in this respect he was far surpassed by his friend Amerigo Vespucci, who had the added advantage of recognising South America for what it was, and of breaking with the assumption of Columbus and Cabot that the 'Indies' were part of Asia.[1] This meant, of course, that the natives of the newly discovered lands were not the Asiatic peoples mentioned by Marco Polo or their neighbours; it gave them a new identity, as the teeming inhabitants of an isolated continent or continents utterly disconnected from the spheres of Christendom and Islam. Vespucci's voyages, or rather his accounts of his voyages, therefore marked a crucial moment in the European encounter with 'primitive' peoples, especially since he insisted that the number of these newly discovered peoples was truly enormous. The Genoese Columbus, whose world view was rooted in the assumptions of the Genoese mercantile classes, was a very different figure from the Florentine Vespucci. Though a man of modest means, Vespucci was a product of the humanist culture of Renaissance Tuscany; he was also connected to patrician society, partly through his beautiful cousin Simonetta Vespucci, a star of high society, and partly through links to branches of the Medici family.

With his obsessions, ambitions and fantasies, Columbus is a puzzle; but no more so than Vespucci, whose claim to have travelled four times (some have even argued five times) across the Atlantic has to be questioned, and whose writings, in the form they have come down to us, are sensational and at times unbelievable. One view is that Vespucci's editor or printer became so carried away by the extraordinary material he received from Vespucci that he 'improved' it – some writers have even spoken of a 'pseudo-Vespucci' created by contemporary publicists.[2] Another view is that Vespucci was the first tabloid journalist, who polished his stories for public consumption; yet another, that he became confused about what he had seen in the New World and began to mix together his own experiences with those of other travellers, producing a brilliant but artificial account of the native peoples of South America which exaggerated his own role and offered descriptions of people and things he had not himself seen. His letters survive in a mixture of printed versions and manuscripts by various hands; and, as far as they go, the hand-written letters tell much the same story, so it does seem that Vespucci himself began the process of embroidering his tales even before his work was printed. Later, his translators added more frills, for what he wrote in Italian was turned into Latin, and then into other languages as well, even back into Italian. One of his admirers was Thomas More. In 1516 More introduced readers of *Utopia* to the fictitious Raphael Hythloday, who 'accompanied Amerigo Vespucci on the last three of his four voyages, accounts of which are now common reading everywhere'.[3]

Underneath Vespucci's frills, however, lay a more pragmatic observer than Columbus, not very scientific in his attention to detail, but lacking the mystical turn of mind that propelled Columbus across the Atlantic. His detractors have insisted that he claimed to have achieved far more than his modest role would have allowed; the first of these detractors was las Casas, who was infuriated by the fact that Amerigo gave his name to the New World (in fact it was not Vespucci but a mapmaker in Lorraine who invented the name 'America' in his honour but without his knowledge). It was not just the naming of America but the claims Vespucci had made about the novelty of what he saw that upset the passionate friar. Las Casas strongly felt that Vespucci had stolen the glory from his hero Columbus.[4] 'He attributed to himself the discovery of the greater part of that Indian world, when God had conceded that privilege to the Admiral.'[5] Vespucci did in fact claim to have taken a circuitous route around the Caribbean in 1497 during a first voyage that was probably an invention based on his later experiences, on those of Columbus and on sources as distant as Mandeville's travel book and as recent as Dr Chanca's letter.[6] When describing the wealth and resources of new lands, it made no sense to be over-scrupulous. Vespucci was a Renaissance man who admitted that he sought fame. In this he was no different from contemporary Renaissance historians who attributed brilliant and bold decisions to war captains in Italy who, as we know from more reliable sources, had acted hesitantly and unimpressively.

Two printed letters are particularly famous. One survives in a Latin translation of 1502 or 1503, apparently set to type in Florence. This is known as the *Mundus Novus* or 'New World'; it was extremely popular throughout Europe, especially in Germany, where it was reprinted several times (in Augsburg, Cologne, Nuremberg, Rostock and Strasbourg), and in Venice, Paris and Antwerp; it was also translated into German, Flemish, French and Italian, and back into Latin from the Italian, all within twelve or thirteen years.[7] Vespucci had originally sent the letter to his patron Lorenzo di Pierfrancesco de' Medici in Florence (this Lorenzo was a junior but wealthy member of the family of Lorenzo de' Medici, 'the Magnificent'). In it, Vespucci described a voyage in Portuguese service that had begun in May 1501.[8] In the title of the letter, the idea of a 'New World' was loudly proclaimed, though it has to be said that this term was already being used by others, such as Peter Martyr. Still, it is not necessarily the first person to say something who acquires a reputation for saying it. The other letter that had an enormous impact was apparently sent from Lisbon in September 1504 to the most powerful figure in Florentine politics, Pietro Soderini. It was printed a few months later. Here, at rather greater length than before, Vespucci (or a ghostwriter) set out all the voyages that he claimed to have made, and brought together his account of the native peoples he had encountered. It was reprinted in 1507, in conjunction with the world map of Martin Waldseemüller that attached Vespucci's name to America.[9] His eyewitness accounts of native peoples tell one more about what he thought his audience wanted to hear than about what he actually saw. This was sometimes true of Columbus too, especially when he wrote to his king and queen. Columbus benefited from the way news of his voyages was rapidly diffused by printers. But it was Vespucci who was the real bestseller, taking by storm the book-buying public north and south of the Alps; it was Vespucci who lodged in the minds of his readers a dramatic image of the New World, with its cannibals and other marvels – not simply the outer edges of Marco Polo's Asia, but something fabulous in its own right, and totally new.

Vespucci was born in 1454. He came from a line of notaries, well trained in the art of expressing themselves in writing. His uncle had a strong interest in Platonic philosophy, and Amerigo received a good classical education; one of his school exercise books survives. After a modest start in business, in 1489 Vespucci was asked to look into some bookkeeping irregularities in the Seville branch of one of the Florentine business houses. He was living in Seville between 1492 and 1496, as reports of Columbus' first two voyages spread.

Though less obvious a presence than the Genoese in Seville, these Florentine houses were an important source of funding for merchants trading into the Atlantic, and they also gave their support to Columbus in later years, when he was short of ready cash.[10] And they were also an important source of information for their employers and colleagues back home. Just as the Florentines of Seville had alerted Boccaccio to the remarkable discovery of naked folk in the Canaries 150 years earlier, they now sent letters back home to Italy describing the people of the newly discovered lands; sometimes it was the news of cannibalism that fascinated the writers; on other occasions it was the fact that these peoples were naked and had no knowledge of Christ.[11]

A Voyage of the Imagination, 1497

Vespucci claimed that he was not satisfied with the reports from the lands to the west; he wanted to see them for himself. In his letter to Soderini he related that he had already developed a strong interest in 'the world and its wonders';[12] so when he heard that a fleet of four ships was due to depart from Cádiz for the New World in May 1497, he leapt at the opportunity to go west – but it has to be said at once that the general view is that he did not actually travel on this voyage, and that the Soderini letter recounted a journey of the imagination. Even so, the account of his supposed first voyage incorporated observations from his later travels, transposed back in time, for it is generally accepted that he did travel west in 1499. In addition, the first voyage was built out of other accounts of strange lands and of the New World. If one were writing a biography of Vespucci all this would matter a great deal.[13] What matters here is the way readers in Europe reacted to Vespucci's reports, rather more than the accuracy of his claims: both Thomas More and las Casas accepted that there were four voyages. Strictly, one should read Vespucci's claims about the peoples and places of the New World in the Soderini letter as part of a composite picture of America not in 1497 or 1499, but in 1504, the date it was sent to press. However, some ships did sail west in 1497: Alonso de Hojeda had been entrusted by Fonseca with the command of the first small fleet to break Columbus' monopoly on exploration – a good reason why las Casas viewed this expedition with grave reservations.[14] The argument against Columbus' monopoly was that these ships were heading into areas that were not part of the area opened up by Columbus' first and second voyages, and were therefore not automatically part of the massive grant of dominion and rights of exploration that had been made to him by the

Catholic Monarchs. Basing himself on the Soderini letter, las Casas snob-bishly speculated that Vespucci too was some sort of merchant or investor who hoped to make a profit out of Hojeda's ventures.[15] Possibly (in 1499 at least) Vespucci was drawn across the Atlantic by news that there were pearl fisheries in the southern Caribbean, and he may have fancied himself as a jewel merchant.[16] But it became clear that the real source of profit was to be found not in pearls but in human bodies: the crew carried off more than two hundred slaves.[17]

In the Soderini letter, then, Vespucci claimed to have seen things in 1497 that he probably only saw in 1499, as well as things he never saw. However, this account of his first voyage needs to be pursued. It is full of rich imagery describing the peoples of the New World. This is how Vespucci described his arrival in 'a land that we judged to be mainland', attributing these events to the voyage of 1497.[18] The ships had arrived in Paria, where the line of the Lesser Antilles met what Vespucci would later understand to be the continent of South America. This irritated las Casas, who wanted it to be made plain that it was Columbus, not Hojeda or Vespucci, who was the discoverer of Paria and the Pearl Coast.[19] Vespucci reported that the first people they saw were naked and were frightened of the Europeans, who were bigger than they were; but eventually the sailors found people with whom they could trade in small items of truck. All this sounds very much like the world Columbus knew, and yet, when Vespucci went on to describe their social life, he conjured up some start-ling images, which he or his publisher borrowed partly from his later encoun-ters along the coast of South America, and partly from the news that had been circulating in Europe since 1492, for instance in letters sent from Cádiz and Seville to commercial houses in Florence, Venice and Genoa.[20]

His readers, including Soderini, needed some titillation. Vespucci thus described people who were completely naked, not even covering their geni-tals, going about 'exactly as they emerged from their mothers' wombs'.[21] They had reddish skins, darkened by the sun, he said, because he thought that underneath their tan they were actually white. They had no body hair, except for long dark hair on the head, and they removed their eyebrows and eyelashes, because they thought body hair was very ugly; but their faces were rather broad, Asiatic-looking, 'somewhat reminiscent of the Tartars' (echoing what Italian observers had said when they heard of the Caribs: 'many brown men with wide faces like Tartars').[22] The women were 'well-shaped', which for Vespucci meant that they were quite well covered with flesh, so that their genitals were generally not too visible, though they had no shame in showing them: 'they are no more shamed by their shameful parts than we are in showing our nose or mouth.'[23] Their bodies remained firm even in old age, so that their breasts did not sag.[24] They were very agile, with both men and women running and swimming great distances; in fact women were better swimmers than men.[25] The toughness of the women was put to use in wartime, for these Indians were cruel and indefatigable warriors. Women carried the equipment into battle, and they carried massive loads no man could bear. Even pregnancy did not interrupt their routine; and, since giving birth was so easy for them, they would start work again the very next day after the birth.[26] On the other hand, when they were angry with their husbands, they callously drank a potion of herbs that made them abort the foetus. These women lacked the ability to love and had a cruel, vindictive side.

There were other great differences between the way they fought wars and the way wars were fought in Italy. For one thing, they had no iron, using the teeth of fish or animals to tip their arrows, and wooden spears tempered in the fire. Vespucci added that 'they are not accustomed to having any captain, nor do they march in battle order, for each man is his own master'.[27] Without captains in war, they also functioned without kings or lords in peacetime, 'nor do they obey anyone, for they live in their own liberty'.[28] They had no system of justice, but they rarely seemed to quarrel among themselves. This lack of a legal system and of proper political structures raised the question whether Indian society was regulated by the principles of natural law; the lack of a political system could be used to argue that they should be brought under the control of Christian monarchs capable of imposing order, thus creating a proper society. The Indians spoke a great variety of languages. They had a very different sense of value from Europeans. They prized feathers and beads made from coloured stones, which they would hang from their lips and ears; they were not interested in gold or pearls.

Frankly, though, 'their way of life is very barbarous'.[29] The explorers were puzzled by their lack of a religious life: 'We do not encounter among these peoples any who had a religion, nor can they be called Moors or Jews, and are worse than heathens, because we never saw them perform any sacrifice, nor did they have any house of prayer: I judge their life to be Epicurean.'[30] Vespucci was alluding here to the idea that not merely does mankind have a natural knowledge of God but it expresses this through worship in temples and through cult activities such as sacrifices, an idea that, as will be seen, was expressed by Thomas Aquinas. Once again, some readers would have questioned whether these folk lived according to natural law, and therefore whether they deserved to be regarded as fully human in status. In his 'New World' letter, which described a later voyage in Portuguese service, Vespucci made this point again, learnedly adding the Stoics to the Epicureans as classical models for these tribes who lived without a code of religious law: 'they have no temple and no religion [*legem*, 'law'], nor do they worship idols.'[31] While Columbus had expressed some puzzlement at the lack of 'religion', for the admiral this had been a sign that these people were ready to be converted easily to the Christian faith. Vespucci's guide was the classics rather than God, and so he classified these people as Epicureans who simply lived a life of pleasure (actually this was a misunderstanding of Epicurean philosophy, but it was an almost universal misunderstanding). But he did observe that they had a variety of death rituals: one way of saying goodbye to the dying that shocked him was the custom in some areas of taking a sick man into a forest, putting the patient in a hammock along with a supply of food, dancing around the hammock for a day, and then leaving the sick man to see if he could find his way back to the village: 'but few survive in that fashion.'[32] Vespucci did not report the shamanistic practices witnessed by Ramón Pané in Hispaniola; he said, though, that he saw attempts to cook the illness out of patients by placing them by a great fire, or bleeding them, or giving them herbal concoctions which they drank and vomited up. It is quite possible that his account here was based not on observation but on a reading of Pané, Columbus or someone who had recycled Pané's words not very carefully.

Vespucci was determined to emphasise how bizarre the New World was in comparison with the Old. Thus the Indians ate whenever it took their fancy, without set mealtimes, and they did so on the ground without napkins or tablecloths. These people did not know wheat and other grains, even though the flour they made from cassava was good; they lived off roots, fruit, fish and herbs, and were only fond of one type of meat, of which more shortly. Marriage meant nothing to them, he maintained, for 'each man takes as many wives as he wants' and discards them when it pleases him to do so, without disgracing the divorced wives, who in any case 'were inordinately lustful'.[33] In his 'New World' letter he added that he had met people who lived just like animals, for they permitted sons to mate with their mothers, brothers with their sisters, 'and in general men with women as they chance to meet'. He played on the fantasies of his readers by claiming that 'they showed themselves to be very desirous to copulate with us Christians';[34] and 'when they were able to copulate with Christians, they were driven by their excessive lust to corrupt and prostitute all their modesty'.[35] Vespucci's self-declared sense of

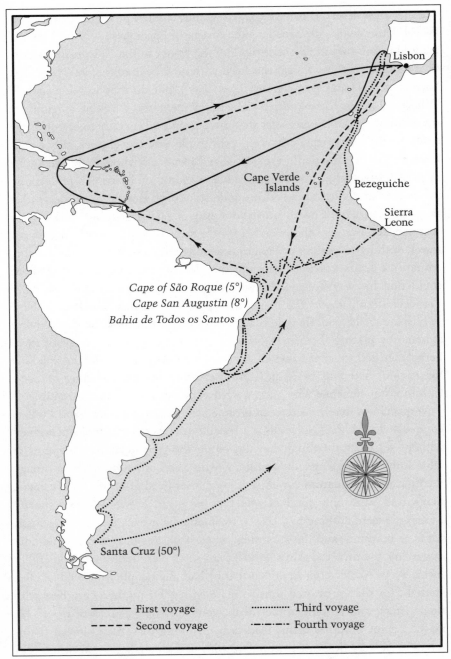

Lisbon

Cape Verde
Islands

Bezeguiche

Sierra
Leone

Cape of São Roque (5°)
Cape San Augustin (8°)
Bahia de Todos os Santos

Santa Cruz (50°)

——————— First voyage

- - - - - - Second voyage

·············· Third voyage

—·—·—·— Fourth voyage

The four voyages attributed to Amerigo Vespucci [after Formisano, *Letters from the New World*] decency did not allow him to say more; rather, he left all this to the imagination of Soderini, Lorenzo de' Medici and other readers. The firmest sign of friendship was when they offered their virgin daughters or other women in the family to visitors for the night, an image he may have derived from tales about other parts of the world, such as Zurara's reports about La Gomera.[36] In fact, in one of his manuscript letters, describing a later voyage, Vespucci wrote instead of how uncles deflowered virgins before they were married, which seems to be a misunderstanding of the 'avunculocal' family structure among the Taínos.[37]

They urinated in public: you could be conversing with one of them, man or woman, and the Indian would simply 'release that foulness' without even turning aside. On the other hand, they did have some good habits: they would pass their bowel motions out of sight if at all possible; they were fastidious about keeping themselves clean, washing themselves continually (this was true of many South American Indians). They also impressed Vespucci with their sleeping arrangements. He liked the hammocks he saw: Vespucci tried them and found them more comfortable than European beds. This, at any rate, is a credible detail, as is Vespucci's description of the massive huts in which the Indians lived, made of wood and covered with palm leaves, capable in some cases of safely sheltering six hundred people.[38] In one village there were only thirteen of these long-houses, but there were about four thousand inhabitants.[39] Vespucci maintained that the Indians kept on the move, and every eight or ten years they displaced the whole village, for they believed that after a time the soil became filthy and that this would cause illness; this matches the practice of the Tupí Indians of Brazil, whom he probably met on what he claimed to be his second voyage. Altogether, then, Vespucci offered a mixture of reasonably exact detail and fantasies about sexual life or eating habits that owed more to traditional texts such as Mandeville than they did to careful observation.

As the ships coasted along the southern shores of the Caribbean, they entered a land where the natives lived in villages built above the water, just like Venice: this was the origin of the name 'Venezuela', which means 'Little Venice'.[40] Admittedly, the houses were not Venetian *palazzi* but huts; however, they were raised on top of great poles that reached down into the water, and they were linked to one another by drawbridges which could be raised in the event of danger. Indeed, when they saw the Europeans, the natives raised their drawbridges for fear of the newcomers.[41] They turned hostile, and Vespucci reported that it had been necessary to massacre their attackers, though the explorers resisted the temptation to burn down the village, 'since it seemed to us something that would burden our consciences'.[42] The goods they found in the village were not worth much, and they pressed on, to find another group of Indians living a little way inland who were roasting meat, fish and what looked like a dragon, except that it was without wings; they found many more of these animals (iguanas) alive and bound in the huts, and decided they were very dangerous.[43] The people in this area were quite friendly, offering food to the visitors, performing dances for them, and finally 'there we spent the night, where they offered us their women, and we were unable to fend them off'.[44] Vespucci and his colleagues were taken on a grand tour of the local villages, and then more than a thousand of the natives accompanied them to the shore, swarming over the four ships, 'marvelling at our instruments and our equipment and the size of the ships'.[45] As a joke the Europeans fired some cannons, which scared the Indians out of their wits; they jumped overboard like frightened frogs. These Indians were thus presented to the world as simple, generous, even helpful, for they offered food when they saw the travellers repairing their boats.[46] Nor was it just the people who impressed the Europeans. This was a fertile land, rich in wild animals such as lions, deer and pigs, even though they were rather different in appearance from the animals of the Old World.[47] But they possessed no domesticated animals. They were also astonished by the Europeans. They found the whiteness of the explorers very odd; they were convinced by the story put about by Vespucci's companions that they were visitors from heaven who had decided to look around the world. The idea seems to have been planted by the explorers, then, rather than to have been the natives' immediate reaction as Columbus had reported when he sailed through the Bahamas and the Greater Antilles.[48]

Further west the welcome was distinctly less cordial. Vespucci had already been warned that the docile people of Paria suffered regular raids from cruel folk who arrived by sea, 'and by treachery and force killed many of them and ate them', raiders against whom the natives could barely defend themselves.[49] When they sailed up towards an island called 'Iti', somewhere in the Lesser Antilles, naked, painted and plumed warriors shot their arrows at the ships to prevent the sailors from landing.[50] But they were easily enough beaten off by the explorers' far superior weapons; 222 were captured. The sailors, after more than a year at sea, were now anxious to turn homewards, enriched by their cargo of slaves.[51] Las Casas later fulminated against Vespucci and Hojeda:

Although these natives are without faith, yet those with whom Amerigo went had neither just cause nor right to make war on the natives of those islands and to carry them off as slaves, without having received any injury from them, or the slightest offence. Moreover they were ignorant whether the accusations of those of the mainland against the islanders were just or unjust.[52]

The impression, however, is that there were some basic rules of engagement. Contrary to las Casas' assertion, slaves were only taken in great numbers when the natives turned hostile. On the other hand, at least in Vespucci's account, the explorers made a consistent effort to act in a friendly way towards the natives, guided, no doubt, by the hope that they would be led to supplies not of slaves but of gold. Still, if gold was not to be had, slaves were a good substitute.

Vespucci's Cannibals, 1499

Vespucci's account of his second voyage in his sixth letter is in part corroborated by his other letters. This may not appear to be the best supporting evidence, but it is all we have; and the crucial issue is, in any case, not what Vespucci actually saw but what he said he saw, and what made an impression on the imaginations of the inhabitants of the Old World. Proof that the other letters reflected Vespucci's earlier outlook can be found in his comment in the first letter that he believed the land they were visiting was 'continental land – which I esteem to be bounded by the eastern part of Asia'; he had still to work out the distinct identity of the New World.[53] Three or four ships set out from Cádiz in May 1499. They headed south-west from the Cape Verde Islands and reached the coast of South America; in fact, they crossed the equator and were the first visitors to the territory of modern Brazil, though only its northern flank. As they sailed along they caught sight of a large canoe, whose passengers, hemmed in between a large Spanish caravel and its longboats, jumped into the sea in fear; but the explorers found that four boys 'not of their race' were still on board. These were captives who had been freshly castrated, as one could see from their wounds, and who were being taken away to be eaten. 'Then we knew that these were a very fierce people known as Cannibals [*Camballi*], who eat human flesh.'[54] In his first letter Vespucci described in slightly less sensational terms how the majority or all of this naked, beardless race of cannibals lived off human flesh, preying on neighbouring islands in their canoes, and eating only male captives, while they kept the women as slaves.[55] As proof, Vespucci could cite the 'bones and heads of some of those they had eaten', which he had often seen, though the cannibals were quite courteous and offered tasty food to the visitors – evidently not human meat.[56] On the other hand, these descriptions do betray the influence of the letters by Dr Chanca and Michele da Cuneo, or of other early accounts of the Caribs. In significant measure, Vespucci saw what he had been told he would see.

Making their way into the region of Paria and 'Little Venice', they reached the islands of the southern Caribbean, one of which was inhabited by very strange people:

> We found there the most bestial people, and the ugliest we had ever seen, and this is what they were like: they were exceedingly ugly in face and demeanour, and they all had their cheeks stuffed with a green grass, which they chewed like beasts, so that they could barely speak; and each of them bore two small dried gourds around his neck, one filled with that grass which they kept in their mouth, and the other with a white flour that resembled powdered chalk: and every so often, having wetted with their mouth a certain spindle they carried, they put it in the gourd containing the flour, and then they would put it in their mouth on both sides of their cheeks.[57]

Vespucci was at a loss to understand why they did this. But there was no mistaking the way he implicitly compared the natives of this island to cattle that mindlessly chewed the cud. Their human credentials were cast into doubt. Another strange feature of this island, he said, was the lack of fresh running water, though they found that the natives drank the sweet dew that gathered on the leaves of a particular plant that looked like donkey's ears.[58] They would go fishing, taking along a great leaf under which they would stand to protect themselves from the sun. Apart from good fish and large tortoises, there was 'nothing of value' to be had here, so the ships headed east towards an island inhabited by giant men and women, massive and fine-looking people who carried big bows and enormous clubs: this was probably the modern Curaçao. An attempt to kidnap a female giant led to trouble, and the Europeans often had to defend themselves against the Indians. But they did collect some pearls and mapped a little more of the coastline of the New World, accentuating rather than resolving the puzzle about the identity of these lands.

Vespucci had become obsessed by the novelty of the New World, and revelled in his role as Florence's overseas correspondent across the Atlantic. He had also come to the attention of the Portuguese royal court, and he now moved from his base in Seville to Lisbon. As a Florentine, his ties to Castile were entirely voluntary, and he was intrigued by the news that the second fleet bound for India, under Pedro Álvares Cabral's command, had found land in the South Atlantic in 1500, 'where there lived a white and naked people'; this land was some way beyond the coastline he claimed to have visited when he crossed the equator on his second voyage.[59] Cabral's men thought this was an island, but Vespucci would show that it was part of the great southern continent, 'the very same land which I discovered for the Sovereigns of Castile'.[60] He encountered two ships from Cabral's fleet, which were returning from India, as he passed through the Cape Verde Islands in June 1501, and sent an excited report of the (real) Indies back to Florence with their crew.[61] If he is to be believed, his third journey was the most ambitious of all. His task was to give expert advice on the route, for he was beginning to acquire a reputation as a skilled navigator, which may appear odd in someone who did not actually captain ships (though later in his life, from 1508 to his death in 1512, he became Pilot Major of Castile, setting up a school for pilots and dreaming up avant-garde schemes for sturdy armour-plated ships able to weather the Bay of Biscay).

Bound for the coast of South America, the ships left Lisbon in May 1501 – the exact date varies from one letter to another, which does not inspire confidence in the details Vespucci offered, any more than does the fact that large amounts of information about the American Indians in his accounts of the third voyage are almost identical to the information provided in his accounts of his first and second voyages.[62] So we hear about women who gave birth and then went off into the fields to wash themselves; he repeated his points about incest and polygamy, claiming this time to have met a man with ten wives.[63] He added that virgins were always deflowered by the closest relative after their father, presumably meaning their uncle; 'once thus deflowered, they are married off.'[64] The women were, of course, 'very lustful', and they had a method for making a man's penis swell and thicken until it looked gross and distorted. The medicine they used to achieve this, which was derived from animal venom, had dangerous side-effects: many of these engrossed penises rotted and fell off, leaving the men to all intents and purposes as eunuchs.[65] In describing the sexual abandon of the people he met, Vespucci undoubtedly satisfied the curiosity of his readers in Europe; at a more serious level, he was trying to show that these folk, even when 'gentle and tractable', lived lawless lives governed, if that is the right word, by bestial instincts.[66] This was not the world conjured up in Peter Martyr's letters of pristine simplicity, a Golden Age untrammelled by fights over property. Rather, they had no property because they had no law, government or religion, and they had no clothes not just because 'they need none' in the heat, but because they were lacking in shame and modesty.[67] Living according to nature did not mean living according to a system of natural law that reined in their vices.

Vespucci offered a little more detail about the stones the natives inserted in their cheeks and lips. They fitted them into large holes they had made in their faces, which were consequently badly disfigured:

> The men are accustomed to make holes in their lips and cheeks, and in those holes they put bones or stones, and you must not think they are small ones, for most of the men have no fewer than three holes (and some seven, and even nine), in which they place stones of green and white alabaster, which are half a span long and as big as Catalan plums, so that they appear something utterly unnatural: they say that they do this in order to appear more fierce; all in all, it is a bestial thing.[68]

That was the real point: the inhabitants of the South American coastline lived like beasts. He called them 'rational animals', a somewhat ambiguous term that was surely intended to stress their intermediate status between beasts and humans.[69] Living 'as nature dictates', without law or religion, they knew nothing of the immortality of the soul; hence Vespucci's comparison of them to the ancient Epicureans who, it was thought, just lived for this world.[70] They had no knowledge of the calendar, though they had the custom of setting down stones each time there was a new moon. On this basis it was possible for the explorers to calculate the age of some of the natives, one of whom Vespucci believed to be 132 years old.[71] Apart from death in battle or as the victims of feasts of human flesh, all these people lived long, for there was no disease; this was proved by the fact that during ten months spent on these shores not a single sailor died (which was probably a very unusual fact on a long voyage) and few even fell ill for a while.[72] Vespucci thought that a physician would be better off avoiding this place: there would be no work.

Ignorant, naked and savage, these people were also warlike. It was far from clear why they fought one another: Vespucci met with no success in his attempts to make them explain this, and he was puzzled by the fact that the normal reasons for war – conflicts over property, claims to kingdoms and so on – did not apply in this world. He said that they 'have no notion of greed, that is, either greed for things or for power, which seems to me to be the cause of all wars and all acts of disorder'.[73] All they valued were feathers and bones, and they had no interest in gold, silver or genuinely precious stones (as opposed to the coloured stones that they put in their cheeks and lips).[74] Vespucci made his point about the causes of war several times in his writings, having already observed during his account of his first voyage:

> And the cause of their wars is not the desire to rule, or to extend their boundaries, or any inordinate greed, but merely an ancient enmity which has existed among them since olden times; and when we asked them why they warred, they could give no other reason than that they did it to avenge the deaths of their ancestors and their fathers.[75]

This wish to avenge their ancestors was another 'bestial thing' – a surprising comment from a native of Renaissance Tuscany where feuding between the greater families over matters of honour and past insults was a constant feature of daily life – 'they knew nothing but that in ancient times their forefathers had done so', and maybe the real motive was simply the need to find supplies of human meat.[76] These natives went into battle naked, but that did not prevent them from acting with very great cruelty, armed with their bows, spears and stones. The victorious side would celebrate the end of a battle by eating the bodies of their dead enemies, though, Vespucci added, they took care to bury members of their own community who had been killed in the fray. Another Italian visitor to South America, Antonio Pigafetta, who accompanied Magellan's fleet in 1519–20, offered a more detailed explanation of cannibal practices:

> An old woman of this land of Verzin [Brazil] had an only son who was killed by his enemies, and some days later the friends of this woman took one of the said enemies who had caused her son's death, and brought him to the place where she was. She, seeing the man who was taken and remembering her son's death, ran incontinent upon him like an angry bitch and bit him in the shoulder. But he managed to run away and escape. And he told how they had tried to eat him, showing the bite which that woman had made in his shoulder. After that, those who were captured on one side or the other were eaten. Whence came the custom in this country of eating one's enemies.[77]

He maintained that they would eat their victims bit by bit, putting pieces of the dead man in their chimney to dry; and then they would cut off a slice every day and eat it with their meal, so that they could remember their enemies. It thus had something of the character of a ritual of vengeance, and something of the character of the sort of simple meal Pigafetta must have observed in north-eastern Italy, where farmers would place a Parma ham in the chimney and cut it away a slice at a time. Whatever he saw with his own eyes, it is hard to escape the impression that he was influenced by what he had read in the works of Vespucci and others.

As for the captives, Vespucci related that their fate depended on their gender. Males were enslaved and married to their captors' daughters, while females were treated as concubines.

> And at certain times when a diabolical fury comes over them, they invite their relatives and the people to dinner, and they set them out before them – that is, the mother and all the children they have got from her – and performing certain ceremonies kill them with arrows and eat them; and they do the same to the aforesaid male slaves and the children that have come from them. And this is certain, for in their houses we found human flesh hung up for smoking, and a lot of it, and we bought ten creatures from them, both males and females, who were destined for sacrifice, or, better said, sacrilege; on this we strongly reproached them: I do not know if they will mend their ways.[78]

One man claimed to have eaten human meat from more than two hundred bodies (elsewhere he said three hundred: the story grew in the telling).[79] There was clearly some demand for a more explicit account of cannibal feasts, and Vespucci willingly obliged: 'the meat they most commonly eat is human flesh, as we shall tell.'[80]

In the Soderini letter, Vespucci or his ghostwriter described how the ships made their way south-westwards down the coast of South America, and how they tried to make contact with the suspicious inhabitants of the coastal plains and forests. Their ships stood a little to the north of the elbow of Brazil (Cabo San Agostinho). Two sailors went ashore close to the foot of a mountain, with a plan to go inland and see whether they could find spices. But they failed to return. So, after waiting for a whole week, several other explorers went ashore and tried to persuade a group of women to come and speak with them, but the women were evidently uneasy. Then a courageous young man from the

Portuguese fleet approached the women, while the others retired to their longboats. The women were amazed by him, feeling him and looking at him with wonder. But another woman came down from the mountain with a large club, and with a single blow killed him. The other women then hauled the body by its feet up the mountainside, while the native men, who had held back, came forward and started shooting arrows at the Europeans in their longboats. They were dispersed by cannon fire; however, what the explorers could see happening on the mountainside disgusted them. They could make out the native women clearly; they were chopping the dead young man to pieces and roasting his flesh on a great fire; they joyously displayed the meat which they then ate, while the native men gesticulated in a way that Vespucci understood to mean they had already feasted on the two sailors who had landed a week earlier.[81] This distressing set of events completely dominated the account of the voyage in Vespucci's letter to Soderini; but in his other letters concerning the same voyage he wrote instead about the life of the Indians of South America, repeating points made in the accounts of other voyages and including data – for instance, the description of the stones native men inserted in their cheeks and lips – that particularly applied to the Indians who lived along the coast of Brazil.[82]

Is the account of the killing and eating of the young man reliable? It bears little relation to the way the South American Indians conducted their cannibal feasts; the elaborate rituals of cannibal feasts were reported in Vespucci's third letter.[83] So it seems that the purpose of this account was to titillate European readers, imagining a cannibal dinner that the Europeans could not possibly have witnessed. The horrific story conveyed a message of the utter barbarity of these people. It also satisfied the ghoulish interest of European readers in ceremonies that lay a very long way from their experiences (setting aside the regular human sacrifices conducted by the Spanish Inquisition, but these were taken for granted). A German woodcut of about 1505 portrayed 'the people and island found by the Christian king of Portugal or his subjects', *das Volck und Insel die gefunden ist durch den christenlichen Künig zu Portugal oder von seinen Unterthonen*. Vespucci's story had obviously caught the imagination of Europeans. In the woodcut, two Christian ships stand out to sea as witnesses, while a group of Indian men, splendidly arrayed in feathers and carrying bows, stand on the shore. A woman suckles a child, but behind her other women are enjoying a cannibal feast: one is chewing a human arm, while from the rafters of their hut hang a head and some limbs.[84]

The caption to the illustration also revelled in the description of the incestuous, warlike people of this part of the New World.

In Vespucci's account, the sailors were deeply unhappy at the decision of the captain not to land a force in order to punish these savages, but to sail away instead. The explorers headed further and further south, possibly reaching the shores of modern Argentina, and touched 'new land', no doubt another extension of the South American coast, before heading back to Portugal in April 1502. If Vespucci is to be believed, they had travelled far into the land of the Southern Cross (a constellation he seems to have noted), and they observed that the seasons had reversed, so that in the southern hemisphere winter was now closing in. His description of this part of his journey is confused and even contradictory – if he was genuinely in charge of navigation, it is a miracle he and his companions ever returned. Knowledge of the southern hemisphere was only acquired piecemeal during Vespucci's seagoing career. Nor, in 1499, is it at all likely that Vespucci thought the mainland they visited was anything other than an extension of Asia; his views about the nature of the New World developed over the next few years. A further attempt to explore the South Atlantic in 1503–4, and to mark out a route westwards to Malacca in the Indies, was defeated by bad weather; there is plenty of doubt whether Vespucci really took part, as the Soderini letter claimed, and if he did join the expedition Vespucci's fourth voyage was even less productive than Columbus'. The crew saw no one in the regions they visited.[85] If anything, it became obvious that America was not the gateway to the Spice Islands, but no one could guess as yet at the sheer extent of the ocean dividing America from Asia. This would not become clear until Ferdinand Magellan wintered in the far south of South America in 1520, and then found his way past Tierra del Fuego into the Pacific. Magellan, too, had difficulty finding people when he first arrived in the deep south of South America, perhaps because the inhabitants of Patagonia were less wedded to the sea than was the case further north.

Slavers and their Victims, 1499–1504

Others came to the conclusion that these lands were not Cathay or Cipangu with the help of their mercenary instincts: the silks and spices of the East were simply not to be had. Slaving expeditions became more and more frequent, however. Slave raids were repeatedly mentioned in depositions made by opposing parties in the long-running legal dispute between the

Crown and the Columbus family about the latter's rights in the New World.[86] Vicente Yáñez Pinzón, the brother of the turbulent Martín Alonso Pinzón, had captained the *Niña* on Columbus' first voyage; now he set out under royal licence for the New World in 1499. He was ordered not to bring back Caribbean natives as slaves, though Africans would be acceptable if he entered eastern Atlantic waters. In fact he took thirty-six slaves from the New World, and then toured the smaller islands of the Caribbean, finding them deserted as a result of Carib or European predations; he also discovered the first marsupial encountered by Europeans, the opossum, one of the few species to live outside Australia.[87] But the most persistent slavers were the Guerra brothers. Luis Guerra and a colleague went to Brazil in 1500–1, taking slaves from 'Topia', the land of the Tupí Indians; they sold one girl named Sunbay in Spain for six thousand *maravedís*, though this was an exceptionally high price. (It was not a good deal – Sunbay then fell ill.) The Guerras raided into Topia with impunity, because this land lay in the Portuguese sphere and therefore the natives could not be classified as notional Castilian subjects.[88] These captives were called *indios bozales* – the term *bozales* indicated that they were primitive, even savage, and was also used of untrained black slaves from West Africa:[89] 'in the case of *indios bozales* who come from a distant land, they undergo so much change and such trials, that the vendor is not obligated and cannot be held responsible for anything that may affect the health and frame of mind of the slave.'[90] This is a revealing recognition that the journey and subsequent life in Iberia entailed both physical and psychological damage. Both Guerras were back again soon after, once again looking for slaves, but they were reprimanded on their return for taking Caribbean ones, 'the said Indians being our subjects' and therefore immune from enslavement. In 1504, the Guerra brothers were allowed to go slaving anywhere except the lands of Columbus and the king of Portugal, which concentrated their efforts in Carib territory. The Spanish historian Oviedo wondered about this: 'I do not know if these merchants were authorised to enslave the people of that land because they are idolaters, savages, sodomites, or because they eat human flesh.'[91] In other words, a sad routine of slave raiding developed, to the horror of las Casas.

At the same time, knowledge of the peoples of South America was growing: Juan de la Cosa met the Tairona people on the north coast of South America, observing the first signs of more elaborate buildings made of stone and other heavy materials – aqueducts, temples, paved roads – and then, further west, visited the Sinu or Zenu who went around naked, though the men wore penis sheaths, sometimes made of gold.[92] The explorers managed to obtain some gold, but when the natives asked for it back they wisely consented; it was important, after all, to build trust, and rumours that reached the Europeans of a great temple with gold-plated idols suggested that the real riches lay a little further inland. These rumours would accumulate over the next decade and re-emerge as the story of a great kingdom rich in gold: El Dorado.

America is Born, 1507

On balance, then, the land was attractive, but the people were not. The land would provide Portugal with useful assets and ought to be exploited; there was brazilwood in vast quantities, there were spices, there was rock crystal. There were moments when Vespucci enthused about the land in language more typical of Columbus: 'I thought I must be near the Earthly Paradise'; but while Columbus intended his statements about the Earthly Paradise to be understood literally, in the hands of Vespucci such a comment was only metaphorical.[93] And for Vespucci it was only a description of the land: it was in no sense a description of the people, for the natives had often proved to be very aggressive towards the Europeans, just as they were towards one another.

Eventually Vespucci concluded that this was the southern continent. 'We learned that the land was not an island but a continent, both because it extends over very long, straight shorelines, and because it is filled with count-less inhabitants.'[94] Vespucci was convinced these were the Antipodes, a new continent that had little or nothing to do with Asia, though this difference of opinion did not prevent Columbus from regarding him as 'a very respectable man', who offered his services to the admiral.[95] This was a brand-new world, but it was also very densely inhabited: 'I have discovered a continent in those southern regions that is inhabited by more numerous peoples and animals than are in our Europe, or Asia or Africa.'[96] In fact, the idea of a southern continent was not so new: it had been mooted in several medieval works of geography. What *was* striking was the existence of so many untamed inhabi-tants. Vespucci, unlike Columbus or the Portuguese who reached Brazil in 1500, did not preach about the conversion of these peoples or their place in God's plan for humanity. Indeed, he appeared to question their humanity by insisting on their barbarous practices, their lawlessness and their ignorance, ignorance of material things such as iron as well as spiritual matters such as the soul; and, worst of all, there was their cannibalism, already verified among the Caribs, as well as their practice of incest. When he thanked God in his letters, it was not for revealing these peoples and for giving them the chance of salvation, but for bringing his ships to land when they were short of water and supplies.[97]

In 1507 Amerigo Vespucci received an extraordinary accolade from the mapmaker Martin Waldseemüller, who was part of a team of scholars based at Saint-Dié in Lorraine that was trying to reconcile the old geographical orthodoxies of Ptolemy with the new discoveries in the Atlantic and the Indian Ocean. Their patron was the duke of Lorraine and titular king of Sicily, René II. Waldseemüller circulated a new edition of Vespucci's sixth letter and also provided some comments of his own about the continents, of which he was still convinced there were only three: Europe, Asia and Africa. But there was also a great, inhabited island, which constituted the 'fourth part' of the world, and which had been discovered, he said, by Amerigo Vespucci.[98] So it was after him that it should be named: 'America' (which was originally pronounced with the stress on the 'i').[99] In addition, Waldseemüller produced a world map that carried a portrait of Vespucci holding a pair of dividers to represent his skill in mapping the world. The image of South America on the map was fragmentary, providing some detail for its northern and eastern shorelines, but offering only a very rough guess about its western flank, the 'unknown land beyond' or *terra ultra incognita* – though, as it happened, it was not a bad guess. Central America appeared; most of North America was absent. To the west of central America, less than halfway to Cathay, stood the island of Cipangu, a rectangle looking like an elongated Sardinia. There was a sea passage between South America and the much smaller landmass to the north, giving access to the seas around Cipangu. But two legends lay across South America: 'all this land was discovered by command of the king of Castile', *tota ista provincia inventa est per mandatum Regis Castelle*, and, further south, 'America' to match 'Affrica' and 'Asia' in their respective places. The injustice is not that Vespucci received this accolade for identifying (rather than discovering, in the modern sense) South America, but that none of those who explored and identified the continent of North America received any similar recognition; and so, by a strange twist, he gave his name to the most powerful nation of the modern world and to its people. The question that now has to be asked is what the relationship might be between his sometimes fantastic portrayal of the South American Indians and the peoples of the seaboard around 1500; and also what other observers – native Portuguese and French – thought they saw in the land that became known as Brazil.

CHAPTER 20

THE LAND OF THE HOLY CROSS, 1500

The Lands of the Tupinambá

It may seem odd to separate the landfall of the Portuguese admiral Pedro Álvarez Cabral in Brazil in 1500 from the explorations of Vespucci along the same coast, especially when Vespucci travelled in the service of the king of Portugal and showed a strong interest in Cabral's achievements. But there are good reasons to do so. In the first place, Cabral was bound for Calicut in India by way of southern Africa and the Cape of Good Hope, following in the wake of Vasco da Gama three years earlier. He had not, as far as can be seen, set out to discover land in the western Atlantic; and, when he did so, he surmised that what he christened 'the Land of the Holy Cross' was an island rather than part of a great continent linked to the places revealed by Christopher Columbus. In the second place, the discovery of Brazil by Cabral is traditionally seen in both Portugal and Brazil as the moment of the birth of Brazil – rather oddly, since there was no serious attempt to colonise Brazil for several decades – and the rich description of the Tupinambá natives of Brazil by a Portuguese knight in his service, Pero Vaz de Caminha, which survives in Lisbon, is seen as 'the founding charter of the Brazilian nation'.[1] In reality, the founding charter of Brazil was the Treaty of Tordesillas, which ensured that a large slice of eastern South America lay on the Portuguese side of the line that divided the Atlantic, and the world, into Spanish and Portuguese spheres of influence.

Vespucci's descriptions of the Indians of South America singled out several features of their appearance and customs that can be verified from other evidence, archaeological as well as historical; elaborate descriptions of the native peoples of Brazil were provided in the mid- to late sixteenth century by Protestant and Catholic missionaries in French service. They did insert large stones in their faces; they did live in long-houses and they did go around naked; and, as the French missionaries testified, they did feast on human flesh. At some stage in his travels Vespucci crossed into the lands inhabited by the Tupí Indians. Had he penetrated down the Amazon to Marajó Island, which is about the size of Switzerland, he would have encountered a high culture that produced elaborate pottery, particularly burial urns with ornamentation in the shape of birds and animals.[2] Artisans such as potters seem to have formed one social group in a society that was quite well stratified, and that – not unusually in Brazil – possessed links to the outside world, including, possibly, links down-river to the complex societies of the Andes region. But along the coasts of Brazil life was simpler and lines between social classes were not clearly drawn. The Tupí Indians were on the move: they had come down from the interior, prob-ably from the Guaraní region in Paraguay and eastern Bolivia, and they had displaced the indigenous Gê peoples of the coastal plains during the century or so before the arrival of the Europeans. Those whom the explorers encountered were the Tupinambá, a branch of the larger Tupí-Guaraní ethnic and linguistic group. But they were not simply migrants from the heartlands of the continent: they were constantly on the move, even within the coastal plains. Their economy was based on slash-and-burn agriculture: they farmed an area, used up its resources and then moved on. Often this generated wars with neigh-bouring tribes as they competed for resources, though it was not a question of laying claim to a particular territory, for, like the Indians of the Caribbean, they had no sense of hard territorial boundaries.

The earliest visitors such as Vespucci and Caminha insisted, as ever, that these people had no religion, and Vespucci denied they had any chieftains or system of rule; but André Thevet, a Catholic missionary, and Jean de Léry, a Protestant missionary, were more fully informed. The natives had a godhead called Monan, who had created the sky and animals, though not the sea. The Tupís did not actually worship Monan: early man had shown no gratitude to his creator, and Monan turned his back on human beings. But there were plenty of shamans and prophets who peopled their myths. Maira-pochy or 'the bad great one' had arrived in a village all covered in filth (the Tupís were obsessively clean) and had presented the local chief's daughter with a fish, whereupon she became pregnant. Her child was later asked to identify his father and did so by handing Maira-pochy a bow and arrow.[3] One does not need the elaborate theories of structural anthropology applied to Brazilian myths by Claude Lévi-Strauss to decipher at least some of the symbolism here. Another prophet was known as Sumé, and he was supposed to have

taught the Tupí Indians how to till the soil. This aroused enormous enthusiasm among the missionaries; by deft etymology it was possible to identify
Sumé with none other than São Tomé, St Thomas, the apostle of the Indies,
proving after all that the whole of the Americas had been evangelised soon
after the Crucifixion (though in Spain Oviedo argued this case, and then
concluded that the Indians were worthless beasts because they had forgotten
what they had been taught and had returned to savage practices).[4] Another,
later view reflected puzzlement that the New World was not really 'India': this
proposed that the natives were originally not *indios*, Indians, but *iudios*, that
is, Jews, because *iudios* and *indios* share all but one letter, which often looked
identical in handwriting – the Ten Lost Tribes of Israel were always lurking
somewhere on the mental horizon.[5] Contrary to Vespucci's testimony, the
Tupinambá did have a concept of the afterlife, and received messages from
ghosts who used cuckoos as intermediaries. Their cannibalistic practices also
proved that they had a concept of an afterlife: the spirits of dead ancestors
needed to be appeased or honoured by taking revenge on those who had killed
them. As in Taíno society, there were shamans, who exercised a considerable
amount of influence, for example over when to go to war, and lay chieftains,
who were treated as the first among equals. The power of the chieftains
depended on success on the battlefield, but most decisions were made
communally, in village meetings which might take place every day. The
shamans, as elsewhere in the Americas and in Asia, were physicians, who
developed ways of sucking disease out of their patients; with the help of
tobacco and narcotics they would experience trances and make contact with
the world of spirits beyond.

The Tupí Indians went around naked, and the explorers were eloquent
about the way even women exposed their genitalia. They spent the whole day
and night uncovered, living in long-houses that acted as home to whole
groups of families. They slept naked, and the long-houses were like furnaces
with so many people inside; more worrying was the fact that there was no
privacy between and within families, and European observers thought that
this could promote sexual licence and even incest.[6] Although they were
naked, they did paint their bodies red and black, and the women painted
images of birds or waves on the bodies of the men. Their men might wear a
bold headdress of yellow feathers, which fitted the shape of the head almost
like a wig.[7] In some cases their leaders plastered themselves with a sticky
solution and rolled themselves in a fine felt made of tiny soft feathers, so that
it seemed they were covered in brightly coloured velvet. Feathers were their

greatest treasure; they had no great interest in gold, and no knowledge of other metals. Their main tools were, predictably, stone axes inserted in wooden shafts, with which they built their impressive long-houses and the defensive palisades that surrounded their villages.[8] Nevertheless, their archers were highly skilled and would shoot down parrots and other birds whose feathers were particularly prized, often stunning them with their arrows rather than actually killing them. They wore necklaces of shell, fish-bone and sometimes human bones too. The large stones that men inserted in their cheeks and lips were described by Vespucci: 'beautiful stones, cerulean, marble-like, crystalline, or alabaster'.[9] Pero Vaz de Caminha, in 1500, noticed that the presence of large plugs of stone or bone in their lips made it difficult for Tupí men to speak clearly; plugs of this sort are still worn by tribes in the Amazon forest. For European explorers the Tupinambá idea of beauty was completely incomprehensible, especially since the explorers often admired the physical grace of these Indians. Why then did they deform their faces? The Canary islanders had seemed strange, as had the Taínos, but the Tupís were even more extraordinary.

The Great Blemish

John Hemming, a stalwart modern defender of the Brazilian Indians, has stated that there was 'one great blemish' in Tupinambá society: their passion for war, in the form of raids, at dawn or dusk, on nearby villages – to which another blemish, closely related, has to be added: their passion for human flesh.[10] Vespucci had been mystified about their motives for fighting, but his answer that they fought over ancient vendettas seems to have been correct. Hemming has taken the view that the aim of their battles was to capture men who would be taken back to the village and, in due course, eaten. But they did not fight as a means of obtaining protein; it was more a question of humiliating their enemies and satisfying those ancestors who had themselves been captured, eaten and thus humiliated.[11] The killing, cooking and eating of their victims was not a casual matter, like broiling some newly caught fish. As has been seen, Vespucci's account of the almost casual eating of the Christians who had ventured on shore during his second voyage is simply not credible. Captives were kept within the community, often for years; as Vespucci else-where admitted, they might even be offered wives who would give birth to children, themselves destined for slaughter. They could probably move freely within the village, until the time came to fatten them up for food; they did not escape, because they had no right to do so once they had been captured, and nowhere to go – it is not clear that the village from which they had come would have welcomed them back. They accepted their fate.

One who did not was Hans Staden. A German gunner in Portuguese service, he was captured by a Tupinambá tribe in 1552; because he was fighting on the Portuguese side, the native warriors took him for a Portuguese. By now, the enemy Portuguese qualified as much as rival Tupí tribes for cannibal consumption. This particular tribe had linked its fortunes to the French, who were trying to create their own colony, *La France Antarctique*, in this region. Staden tried to convince them he was actually French, in the hope of being released. The Tupinambá were wise to this: other Portuguese troops they had captured and eaten had tried the same trick. Staden later claimed that he survived because he developed such severe toothache that he could not eat; he thus lost weight just when he was supposed to be gaining it. Gradually he won the confidence of the natives and even became an honoured figure (he says that he was regarded as something of a prophet). But he could not wean the Indians from their love of human meat. When he tried to intercede with the chieftain for some victims, his pleas were gently rejected, and he was offered as a present a cooked human leg. Later he escaped to tell his story (no doubt with a certain amount of exaggeration), and he and the French missionaries recorded the cannibal rituals of the Tupinambá.[12]

The victim was expected to play his role in the ceremonies that led up to the cannibal feast. He would promise that his own kin would come and avenge him in due course. Michel de Montaigne recorded a song chanted by one of these victims, in which he taunted those he dared to kill and eat him:

> They should all come boldly and gather to dine off him, for they will be eating at the same time their own fathers and grandfathers, who have served to feed and nourish his own body. 'These muscles,' he says, 'this flesh and these veins are your own: poor fools that you are. You do not recognise that the substance of your ancestors' limbs is still contained in them. Savour them well; you will find in them the taste of your own flesh.'[13]

He would continue to spit and defy his enemies as they danced elaborately around him. Then suddenly he would be repaid for his taunts: his brains would be knocked out with a great club (here Vespucci's description had some merit, accidentally or otherwise). Every part of him except the brains would be eaten or otherwise employed, for his bones were kept – his tibia could be used to make a flute, his skull might adorn the staked fence that surrounded the village.[14] The feast was thus an elaborate ritual, and it was not a daily event. For some, such as Hemming, what matters most is that these practices, which he does not seek to deny, were used by European observers to justify their conquest and enslavement of the Brazilian Indians.[15] One could certainly argue that the Europeans did not occupy all the moral high ground: the Spaniards, though not as yet the Portuguese, were guilty at home of practices that were in their own way rituals of human sacrifice – the principal victims of burning by the Inquisition being secret Jews, secret Muslims, witches and eventually Protestants.

Later in the sixteenth century Montaigne, himself descended from Spanish *conversos*, had a servant who had lived for ten or twelve years in the French settlement in Brazil, and this led him to reflect on the morality of Tupí cannibalism.[16] His first point was that 'each man calls barbarism whatever is not his own practice'. The only standard for truth or reason is the example of the place where you live: '*there* is always the perfect religion, the perfect government.' If these people are wild, it is in the sense that wild fruit is wild, but that, after all, is just a product of nature; real wildness is a degenerate turning away from 'the common order'. These distant people in fact live in pristine purity and original simplicity, in a true Golden Age. Montaigne wondered what classical authors who speculated about mankind's Golden Age, such as Plato, would have made of them. It is true, he said, that they have neither property nor (he asserted) agriculture, no metal, wheat or wine; but they also lack deceit, avarice, envy and treachery, and live – as so many visitors to Brazil had earlier insisted – long lives in the best of health. Montaigne knew a good deal about their long-houses, their food (he had tasted cassava bread), their dances; and he, unlike Vespucci, emphasised that 'they believe in the immortality of the soul and that those who have merited well of the gods, are lodged in that part of the heaven where the sun rises, and the accursed in the west'. He knew that they were very warlike, and he even commented that they treated prisoners well, until, that is, the moment when they killed them and ate them, sending some pieces to absent friends. They do this, he reported, not because they depend on human meat in their diet, but because it is a form of revenge against their enemies. With an eye on current atrocities inside France and Spain as well as in the Americas, Montaigne asked whether the practice of eating one's dead enemies was worse than that of tearing apart a living human body on the rack, of 'roasting a man bit by bit', or setting ravening dogs on one's living enemies.[17]

The problem of cannibalism was debated elsewhere. One issue was the relationship between cannibalism and the consumption of the Host in the Mass, which was understood by Catholics to be the real body and blood of Christ: 'Take, eat, this is my body.'[18] The Host itself became the focus of energetic cults in the late Middle Ages, notably in northern Germany; its identity provoked deep anxiety, and the rejection by the Protestants of the idea that it really was Christ's body and blood stirred up further debate, in which the Protestant missionary Léry took some delight: were the 'most barbarous, cruel and dreaded' Waitaca Indians of Brazil so much worse than the Catholics? The Catholics 'wanted not only to eat the flesh of Jesus Christ grossly rather than spiritually, but what was worse, like the savages named Ouetaca . . . they wanted to chew and swallow it raw'.[19] In 1537 the great doctor of Salamanca University, Francisco Vitoria, considered whether it was permissible to eat human flesh.[20] He observed that doctors sometimes prescribed the drug known as *momia*, which was made of ground mummies obtained in Egypt; but the anthropophagy described in accounts of savage peoples, he pointed out, was always the result of murder, and was classified by Aquinas with buggery of animals and sodomy between males among execrable crimes.[21] It was also legitimate to fight a war against peoples who practised cannibalism and human sacrifice, because these peoples were guilty of a manifest injustice even involving the killing of children.[22] He said this while defending the right of non-Christian peoples to exercise dominion without interference – in normal situations. Meanwhile, contemplating Aztec human sacrifice, las Casas argued that this too had to be understood in relation to the values of the society in which the Aztecs lived. They understood the religious value of sacrifice and erroneously thought it right to sacrifice the most precious of living beings, man, to their gods. But it was done with sincere intentions. He did not pause to consider the burning pyres of the Spanish Inquisition.

Cabral's Landfall, April 1500

Nearly all that is known about the arrival of the Portuguese in Brazil on 22 April 1500, and their subsequent exploration of part of the coastline, is derived from the short but vivid report sent by the knight and scribe Pero Vaz de Caminha to Lisbon, and addressed to the king of Portugal. It was no doubt

read with fascination – it was certainly read, because further expeditions soon
followed. But it was not printed or widely disseminated; it was only identified
in the Lisbon archives in the late eighteenth century.[23] However, an
'Anonymous Narrative' written by someone who sailed with Cabral all the
way to India summarised several of the points made by Caminha, and was
printed in Venice as early as 1507.[24] The discovery of this new land was
considered important enough to warrant the despatch back to Lisbon of a
small ship that was accompanying the fleet bound for the Indies; it carried
letters by Caminha and one or two others, and objects acquired in Brazil; but,
for reasons that will be explained, no Indians were placed on board. Admiral
Cabral and his officers well knew that this territory could be claimed by
Portugal. The question that has obsessed a certain class of historians is
whether, in addition, Cabral was merely making public a discovery that the
Portuguese had actually made years earlier but kept secret to ensure interlopers did not arrive. It is, of course, hard to see what use Brazil could be to
the Portuguese while knowledge of its existence was suppressed. The main
motive behind this argument is the determination to prove that the
Portuguese discovered America before Columbus, as if discovering the shores
of Africa and the route to India were not enough to satisfy national pride. In
fact, Cabral had chosen a route through the Atlantic that brought him far to
the south-west, in search of the Roaring Forties, which would blow him
towards the Cape and the Indian Ocean.[25] It was brave, even foolhardy, to
venture so very far out of sight of land, though da Gama had done the same;
and when Cabral misjudged the winds and the distances he arrived on the
opposite shores of the Atlantic, accidentally and unexpectedly. Caminha
endorsed his letter to the king in a way that should really settle this argument:
'Letter of Pero Vaz de Caminha concerning the discovery of the new land
which Pedro Alvarez made.'[26]

Pero Vaz de Caminha's report is uncannily reminiscent of Boccaccio's
report of the Portuguese arrival in Grand Canary almost 160 years before. A
month out of the Cape Verde Islands, the Indies fleet had arrived in the
modern province of Bahía, within sight of a high, round mountain that they
named, for the time of year, Easter Mountain, *Monte Pascual*. The land itself
they named the 'Land of the Holy Cross' or 'True Cross'. Almost at once they
caught sight of 'dark brown and naked' people on the beach and in a river
mouth close by, carrying bows and arrows.[27] Nicolão Coelho, one of the
captains in the fleet, who had already served with distinction under Vasco da
Gama, was sent to parley with them, and persuaded them by signs to lay

down their weapons; they then began to trade European goods – a red cap and a linen cap that Coelho was wearing – for the Tupí equivalent, a head-dress of red and grey feathers and a necklace made of low-grade pearls. These were to go to the king in the same package as the letter from Caminha. After this the fleet made its way northwards, hoping to take on wood and water. Finding a good harbour and an interested band of Indians, the ships came closer to shore; they also picked up a couple of Indians in a canoe, and these men were greeted on board with great delight. This was the first opportunity to take a close look at the Tupí Indians, who were judged to be reddish in colour and 'well shaped'.[28] Later, Caminha observed that many Tupís coloured their bodies, which were divided into halves or quarters, using black and red dyes; and they even covered themselves in chequered patterns.[29] They reminded Caminha of Arras tapestries, so complex were some of the designs of body paint.[30] Not surprisingly, their shameless nakedness caught the attention of the voyagers, who realised that these people thought no more of showing their genitals than they did of showing their faces. 'In this respect,' Caminha commented, 'they are very innocent.'[31] This remark set the tone for a sympathetic and observant account of the Brazilian Indians. In the next few days, he would record how he saw pretty young girls with long hair and no covering over their private parts, a theme he could barely leave alone in his report.[32] He also saw a girl painted from head to toe and thought that she was so comely to look at that Portuguese women would be jealous of her well-rounded figure.[33] Another young woman had black paint all over her knees, calves and ankles, while her genitals were left completely exposed, 'with such innocence that there was not there any shame'.[34] That was the important point. These people excited Caminha for two reasons: he took a voyeuristic interest in the naked women, it is true; but he was also impressed by the natu-ralness and innocence of their nakedness. He did not see them as creatures who lived in an animal-like state of licentiousness, but as women who simply had no knowledge of the reasons for covering their private parts – who lived, in some sense, in a prelapsarian condition.

On the other hand, he was also capable of describing them as 'bestial people and of very little knowledge' and 'rather like birds or wild animals, to which the air gives better feathers and better hair than to tame ones', clean folk who, he surmised, lived completely in the open, without houses (for at that point he had seen no houses, though he did a little later on).[35] Reconciling these two views might appear to be difficult, but it is in fact quite easy to see what was happening in Caminha's mind. From the fact that he referred first to their lack of houses, and later to the presence of houses, it becomes clear that his letter was written in sections, day by day most probably; and it is all the more precious for recording such fresh reactions. His own views oscillated, as had those of other observers of the newly discovered peoples of the western Atlantic. He had carried with him across the Ocean Sea existing assumptions about the bestial nature of primitive peoples, but in the light of his own experience he modified these views so that it was no longer an aggressive, violent, licentious bestiality, of the sort Vespucci delighted in describing; and if they were animal-like, the people of the Land of the Holy Cross had the qualities of timid and graceful animals, not of wild beasts.

He was, of course, amazed by the pieces of white bone the men wore in their lips, perhaps four inches long, but presenting no difficulty when they drank or ate. Some men had inserted in their lips 'wooden plugs which looked like stoppers of bottles'.[36] Later in his exploration he met an old man with a hole in his lip large enough for a thumb to be inserted; in the hole there was a green stone. The Tupí Indians valued these green stones highly, but Caminha rated them as worthless.[37] Still, Caminha's captain decided that it had curiosity value and traded it for an old hat, with the idea of sending it back to Lisbon. Caminha observed how the men shaved the hair above their forehead, but one man was wearing a tight-fitting wig of yellow feathers, glued to his hair, made in such a way that he could wash himself without having to remove it.[38]

Cabral among the Tupí Indians, April 1500

That evening, two Indians were invited on board ship, including the man with the yellow wig. Cabral decided that he should dress grandly for the occasion, sitting enthroned, wearing a golden collar and with a fine carpet spread at his feet, on which Pero Vaz de Caminha and his companions seated themselves. The Portuguese even lit torches, to add extra grandeur to the occasion. This show of magnificence contrasted as sharply as could be with the simplicity of the visitors, whose reaction clearly defied all expectations. Since they had never seen a captain in his finery, they did not bother to greet him or anyone else; but they did notice his golden collar and made signs that there was gold in the land from which they came, or at least that was what the Portuguese understood their gestures to mean. When one of them saw a candlestick made of silver he made similar gestures, whetting the appetite of the Europeans for supplies of silver as well. In fact, the Tupí Indians were quite well acquainted with silver and even copper, which was traded down from the spine of the Andes across the vast tracts of South America, though it was not found in the lands they inhabited. Just to confirm what these gestures meant, the explorers displayed a grey parrot that was on board, and again the Indians pointed to the land, as if to indicate that these parrots could be found there too. But after this the two parties found they had less in common:

> They showed them a sheep, but they paid no attention to it. They showed them a hen; they were almost afraid of it, and did not want to touch it, and afterwards they took it as though frightened. Then food was given them: bread and boiled fish, comfits, little cakes, honey and dried figs. They would eat scarcely anything of that, and if they did taste some things they threw them out. Wine was brought to them in a cup; they put a little to their mouths, and did not like it at all, nor did they want any more.[39]

They were even reluctant to drink the water they were offered. Caminha observed that the Tupís did not possess any domestic animals, even chickens, and insisted that they lived off manioc roots, seeds and fruits, but that they were still healthier than Europeans (he knew nothing of their taste for human meat, reported by later visitors).[40] It is, of course, easy to understand their confusion when presented with Portuguese pastries, which were apparently as rich and sweet then as they are now. The Tupí were fascinated by the sight of a white rosary, and appeared to beg to be given it along with Cabral's precious collar; the Portuguese made a good show of not appearing to understand what seemed to be quite clear gestures. It was late, and so the visitors simply lay down on the carpet to sleep; their genitals were clearly visible and Caminha noted that they were not circumcised, so clearly they were neither Moors nor members of the Ten Lost Tribes of Israel.[41] But it seemed right to throw cloaks over them, and they did not object. They were given pillows for the night, and the man who had a feather headdress made sure that his feathers were not ruffled.[42]

   The next morning, a Saturday, the Portuguese ships moved into a safer anchorage and Bartholomew Dias (the captain who had reached the Cape of Good Hope in 1487–8) went ashore, releasing the two Indians and giving them rosaries, red hats and shirts. Cabral also sent ashore a servant named Afonso who had been convicted of serious crimes. There were twenty such men on board, who could earn a pardon by serving in the fleet. All the same, Afonso may not have been entirely glad to hear that he was being left alone among the Indians, 'to stay with them and learn their manner of living and customs'. The Indians did not want him to remain among them.[43] Caminha himself went ashore with another prominent figure, Nicolão Coelho, and this means that his account is enormously precious – unlike Columbus and Vespucci, he was not mixing second-hand reports with his own observations. But the Tupí Indians proved to be suspicious of the Portuguese. Two hundred naked warriors, armed with their bows, stood on the shore and were only willing to lower their arms when the two who had visited the ship signalled to them to do so. Gradually confidence grew, and before long the Indians brought water in gourds, and even took the kegs offered by the sailors and filled them with water. They were even keener to do this when Coelho offered the traditional gifts of European explorers: bells, bracelets, hats, linen caps.[44] Later the Indians were even given sheets of paper, in return for which they offered feather caps, which were sent back to Lisbon.[45] In fact, the Indians became very friendly and, although they did not want Afonso to stay with them, they looked after him; an elderly Indian who helped Afonso was so covered with feathers that 'he looked pierced with arrows like Saint Sebastian'.[46]

On the Sunday the Christians celebrated Mass in the shadow of the banner of the crusading Order of Christ. This took place on an offshore island; but on the beach opposite the Indians began to blow horns made of bone and danced excitedly as the Mass came to an end. The Portuguese then began to deliberate about how they should gather information about this land and its inhabitants. There were two alternatives. They could capture a couple of natives and send them to Lisbon; but it was argued that this would be counterproductive – the captives would simply say what they thought would please their interlocutors: 'it was the general custom that those taken away by force to another place said that everything about which they were asked was there.'[47] Moreover, no one would understand a word of what they said, and they would take a while to learn Portuguese properly. And, finally, it would only cause a 'scandal' among the Indians, who would be concerned at such treatment of their fellow men. This was an extraordinarily sensitive series of thoughts about the disadvantages of carrying away specimen natives (that seems the right phrase to use) in the way Columbus and others had recently been doing, and as the Portuguese had done in the past in the Canaries and West Africa. There was an alternative: to leave a couple of Portuguese convicts among the Tupís, who 'would give better and far better information about the land'. Meanwhile, the captains met in conference (with Caminha closely observing) and decided that a supply ship should be sent back to Lisbon with news of the discovery, 'so that you might order it to be better reconnoitred, and learn more about it than we could now learn because we were going on our way'.[48] It was on this ship that Caminha's letter to the king was despatched, while Caminha carried on to India, where he met his end.

Caminha was an acute observer. When large numbers of Tupís came to Cabral, he realised that they had not come 'to recognise him for their lord, for it does not seem to me that they understand or have knowledge of this'.[49] Caminha's idea that the Tupís had no chieftains was a misunderstanding that other observers would soon contradict. However, he learned as he continued to observe, and was soon able to see that he had been wrong when he claimed that the Indians lived freely in the open air. In fact, they had villages made up of ten or so large huts, which he was able to visit: 'all had one single room without any divisons', and walls made of wooden boards, with doors at each end.[50] Inside, he could see posts to which hammocks were tied. The huts contained thirty or forty people each, and had fires burning within them. This seems to be an accurate description of the often hot and dark long-houses in which the Tupís spent the night. But Caminha did not witness any cannibal feasts. Maybe this was because the Portuguese were only there for a week and a half, and these feasts were certainly not daily events; maybe it was because some Tupís simply did not eat their fellow humans, for, as will be seen, a French report only five years later mentioned cannibalism among some tribes, but not the tribe among whom a group of Frenchmen spent several months.

An Innocent People, May 1500

Caminha also recorded the reaction of the Indians to European technology. On the Tuesday of their visit, the Portuguese began to load brazilwood on their ships – this was to become the most prized asset of early Brazil, a wood that produced a strong red dye and that, in conjuction with long-standing tales of the 'isle of Brazil', gave the land its permanent name. The Indians gladly helped carry the logs. Meanwhile, two carpenters decided to make a large cross out of a piece of wood they had set aside for this purpose. The Tupís were fascinated by what they saw; they crowded round, 'and I believe that they did this more to see the iron tools with which they were making it than to see the cross, because they have nothing of iron'.[51] So Caminha did not suggest that they had an instinctive awareness of the significance of the cross. Colleagues had already reported to him that they had seen Tupí tools in their long-houses, stone hatchets that were, nonetheless, quite strong.[52] On Thursday 30 April Cabral suggested that some of his companions should go down to where the cross was leaning against a tree, waiting to be erected the next day, and pay their devotions to it by kneeling and kissing it. There were about a dozen Indians present, and the Portuguese invited them to do the same, which they willingly did. Caminha was impressed: 'they seem to me people of such innocence that, if one could understand them and they us, they would soon be Christians, because they do not have or understand any belief, as it appears.'[53] Once again European explorers were puzzled by the lack of a formal, organised cult among the people they had discovered, jumping to the conclusion that they had no 'religion' or even beliefs. However, this did the Tupís no harm in Caminha's eyes. It proved that they were a *tabula rasa* on whom Christianity could be written quickly and easily:

> For it is certain this people is good and of pure simplicity, and there can easily be stamped upon them whatever belief we wish to give them; and furthermore our Lord gave them fine bodies and good faces as to good men; and He who brought us here, I believe, did not do so without purpose. And consequently, Your Highness, since you so much desire to increase the Holy Catholic Faith, ought to look after their salvation, and it will please God that, with little effort, this will be accomplished.[54]

Just as Columbus had trumpeted the discovery of new peoples who could be converted to Christianity by monarchs who had secured fame by suppressing Jews and later Muslims, so Caminha advertised to King Manuel the opportunities for the further spreading of the Catholic faith after the suppression of Judaism and Islam in Portugal in 1497.

It was on this note that the Portuguese visit to Brazil drew to its climax. On Friday 1 May 1500, a great celebration of Mass was held in the presence of the Indians. The newly made cross was carried in procession by a group of priests and friars who were on board the ships. Over two hundred Tupís gathered to watch as it was raised and set in the ground, adorned with the arms of the king of Portugal. Fifty or sixty Tupís joined the

Europeans, kneeling during the Mass itself, 'and when it came to the Gospel and we all rose to our feet with hands lifted, they rose with us and lifted their hands, remaining thus until it was over'.[55] They showed a similar quiet reverence during the elevation of the Host. One young woman stayed throughout the Mass.

> She was given a cloth with which to cover herself, and we put it about her; but as she sat down she did not think to spread it much to cover herself. Thus, Senhor, the innocence of this people is such, that that of Adam could not have been greater in respect to shame.[56]

After the service was over, a man of about fifty stayed with the Portuguese and impressed them by pointing to the altar and then upwards to the sky, 'as though he was telling them something good'.[57] He even remained for the sermon. After that, Captain Coelho produced a pile of tin crosses, and these were strung around the necks of forty or fifty willing Tupís. The Indian who had been pointing to the sky was rewarded with a 'Moorish shirt'. All this was regarded by Caminha as enormously encouraging: 'And as it appears to me and to everyone, these people in order to be wholly Christian lack nothing except to understand us, for whatever they saw us do, they did likewise; wherefore it appeared to all that they have no idolatry and no worship.'[58] A priest must be sent to baptise them, especially since the two convicts who were being forced to remain would spread the Word among them. 'Now Your Highness may see whether people who live in such innocence will be converted or not if they are taught what pertains to their salvation.'[59] It was only at the end of his letter that Caminha turned back to the question of gold and silver, remarking that the climate was temperate and reminded him of the region between the Douro and Minho rivers in Portugal. No doubt it would make a useful stopover for ships bound for Calicut. Everything can grow there. 'But the best profit which can be derived from it, it seems to me, will be to save this people, and this should be the chief seed which Your Highness will sow there.'[60] On this note Caminha finished his letter on 1 May 1500, stating his location as 'your island of the True Cross' and begging the king to release his son-in-law, who had been sent as a convict to the dreaded island of São Tomé in the armpit of Africa.

Whether or not King Manuel agreed to that, he did write to the Catholic Monarchs in Spain, mentioning very briefly the discovery of the Land of the Holy Cross: 'In it he found the people nude as in the first innocence, gentle and peaceable. It seemed that Our Lord miraculously wished it to be found, because it is very convenient and necessary for the voyage to India, because he repaired his ships and took water there.'[61] King Manuel had therefore read Caminha's letter, which these words echo. An anonymous narrative of Cabral's voyage, written by someone who accompanied him to India, makes similar points – 'women likewise go nude without shame and they are beautiful of body, with long hair' – and even referred to Caminha's report, thereby helping to fix the image of the Tupí Indians as simple and friendly.[62] Italian observers, in Venice and elsewhere, were mainly interested in the amount of pepper and other spices Cabral had managed to bring back from India, and the effect that this might have on the spice trade through Alexandria.[63] In the eyes of the Portuguese, it was their success in repeating Vasco da Gama's achievement that really counted; Brazil was a curiosity of entirely secondary interest.

CHAPTER 21

THE REALM OF KING AROSCA, 1505

Brazilwood and Black Slaves, 1501–11

Portugal did not ignore the new land across the Atlantic to which it was entitled under the terms of the Treaty of Tordesillas, but its priorities lay in Africa and India. The 'Land of the Holy Cross' would provide a foothold in what until now had been primarily Spanish territory, a point King Manuel deliberately failed to make when he wrote to the Catholic Monarchs announcing his men's discovery of land in the south-western Atlantic. It has been seen that Castilian ships did venture into these waters occasionally at the start of the sixteenth century, looking for slaves from 'Topia'. Not to protect the Tupinambá so much as to protect Portuguese interests, a small series of commercial ventures was launched in the direction of Brazil. An expedition in 1501 reported that, frankly, there was little to be loaded apart from brazilwood. But this was a prized dyestuff, so a royal licence was granted to Fernão de Noronha (or Loronha), a wealthy convert from Judaism, who agreed to send six ships each year to Brazil to collect brazilwood and slaves; parrots too were brought back, at least in 1504. On his first outward journey Noronha discovered a beautiful offshore island which still carries his name. He was to explore three hundred leagues of coastline each year as well and to set up a small fort, subject to a sliding scale of royal taxation, from zero in the first year to one-quarter in the third year. It has been estimated that these ships were soon bringing back about thirty thousand logs each year, weighing 750 tons. The ships often carried black slaves and other labourers, whose task was probably to prepare the brazilwood. However, a detailed account that survives from 1511, concerning a ship named the *Bertoa*, indicates that, as Caminha had already hinted, the Indians themselves gave extensive help in preparing and loading the logs, though there is no suggestion that anything like an *encomienda* system of forced labour was introduced; rather, they were rewarded with knives and other small metal goods, though arms were deliberately excluded.[1] Thus those who lived along the coast became familiar with and keen to obtain the European tools that they were unable to manufacture for themselves. They also became increasingly familiar with chickens. Slowly, without the imposition of a colonial regime, significant changes were taking place in their technology and daily life.

A Lost French Ship, 1503–4

Over the next decades, the Portuguese discovered that they needed to defend themselves neither from the co-operative Tupinambá nor from rival Castilians, but from envious Frenchmen, who also took an interest in brazil-wood; by the mid-sixteenth century, France would be planning the creation of *La France Antarctique* in the lands claimed by Portugal. But the history of French involvement began by accident, in 1503, when a single Norman ship, the *Espoir*, was blown off course towards Brazil. This was not another logging expedition; the foolhardy Norman captain, Binot Paulmier de Gonneville, ambitiously intended to round Africa and to reach the Indies in the wake of Vasco da Gama. Like Cabral, he reached Brazil first, but, unlike Cabral, he never managed to enter the Indian Ocean. He even secured the services of two Portuguese pilots, who had been out to India and who therefore risked extreme punishment for giving away state secrets if they were arrested by the Portuguese. They may have been surprised to find that there was only one ship, and that this was a 120-ton vessel that had never sailed further than Hamburg.[2] Nevertheless, the ship was loaded with a good supply of armaments, to fend off enemies in the Atlantic or the Indian Ocean, including cannons, harquebuses and muskets; there was enough salted fish, dried peas, local cider and water for over a year (and enough ship's biscuit for two); and then there was the merchandise – scarlet cloths, fustians, a velvet cloth, a cloth embroidered with gold, but also simpler goods such as fifty dozen little mirrors, knives, needles and other hardware, as well as silver coins.[3]

Paulmier de Gonneville hailed from a very respectable family in Gonneville-les-Honfleur, quite near Rouen, and he had the financial support of a group of investors from Honfleur. This was not a royal but a private expedition. Within Normandy, it became something of a *cause célèbre*, because Gonneville brought back from Brazil the son of a Tupí chieftain, whom he married to his daughter. One hundred and fifty years later, his great-grandson wrote to Pope Alexander VII asking for funds so that he could teach the Christian faith in the southern hemisphere, bringing knowledge of Christ to those peoples from whom he himself was descended. This led him to enclose an account of Gonneville's voyage, based on a formal declaration Gonneville and his companions made on their return to Normandy; they had been despoiled by pirates at the end of their voyage, and needed to register an account of what had been lost and what they had been doing. In later decades, all his family possessed was second-hand statements, copying and summarising with bewildering variants an earlier account of what was supposed to have happened; and when they read what records they had managed to preserve, Gonneville's descendants assumed that the Norman ship had ventured far beyond the Cape of Good Hope, for no memory of Brazil itself had been preserved in the family, but rather the awareness that Gonneville was aiming for India by the Cape route.[4] This supposed route caused excitement among geographers: not unreasonably, one eighteenth-century explorer, seeking to redeem French claims to lost lands uncovered by Gonneville, suggested that he had landed in Madagascar. And then, in 1869, a seventeenth-century copy of the formal declaration made by Gonneville himself was discovered in the Arsenal Library in Paris, taken from long-lost Admiralty records in Rouen. This leaves no doubt that Paulmier de Gonneville and his crew sailed south-west, not south-east, and were the first people to witness important features of Tupinambá daily life.

The *Espoir* set out from Honfleur on 24 June 1503; avoiding a landfall in the Spanish Canaries, the ship hugged the African coast and was fortunate to pass the Portuguese Cape Verde Islands without challenge. They spent ten days at Cape Verde itself, on the African coast; there, they traded some of their iron goods with the native Africans, buying chickens and *couchou*, 'a sort of rice', in other words couscous.[5] The ship then swung out to sea, hoping to catch the Trade Winds and to be swept eastwards in the wake of da Gama. Instead, it was caught by fierce gales, and was swept westwards, as Cabral had been, though they were convinced that they were in the right latitude to pass the Cape of Good Hope – they saw *manches-de-velours*, 'velvet sleeves', or penguins, which someone, no doubt the Portuguese pilots, identified as birds that lived on the southern tip of Africa. For weeks they were tossed about, and then they drifted. Another pilot, a Frenchman, fell ill and died. However, on 5 January 1504 'they discovered a great land', which reminded them of Normandy itself.[6] The sailors felt they had gone far enough and that the ship would bear no more; they persuaded Gonneville that it was pointless to try to recover their route to India.

In any case, it became clear that the land was inhabited, and they managed to strike up a good rapport with the natives. It is generally assumed that these were a branch of the Tupinambá Indians, but it is worth stressing that a few features of their life, as described by Gonneville, do not match other descriptions of the Tupinambá at this period, and that Gonneville did also visit other Indians whose customs were more similar to those described by Caminha and even Vespucci. As Léry later made clear, there were other peoples who lived alongside the Tupinambá.[7] Whoever these Indians were, the Normans won their trust by giving them presents. They saw the Indians as 'simple people, asking only to lead a happy life without a great amount of work'.[8] For they lived by hunting and fishing, and from what the soil produced of its own accord, though they did cultivate some vegetables and roots. The land itself was well provided with birds, fish, trees and wild animals; one of Gonneville's party made drawings of these wonders.[9] These Indians went round half-naked, while some others wore coverings made of skin or feathers, rather longer in the case of women. Women wore coloured strings made of vegetable matter in their hair, as well as necklaces and bracelets made of bone or shell; men carried spears of fire-hardened wood, and bows and arrows, and their headdresses bore long, brightly coloured plumes.[10] The colour of these plumes varied from one man to another: the 'vassals' of a particular king wore plumes of a single colour; those subject to the king Gonneville knew best wore green feathers.[11] Gonneville's party also observed closely the villages in which the Indians lived: hamlets of thirty to as many as eighty long-houses, full of hammocks, with holes in the roof through which smoke could escape, and with doors that could be bolted shut with wooden staves, just as in stables in Normandy (though why these Indians should wish to bolt their doors is a puzzle – perhaps for defence). They used wooden utensils, and even boiled their food in wooden pots, which were so thick that they did not themselves catch fire.[12]

All this adds a little detail to Caminha's description of their customs. Spending very much longer in Brazil, Gonneville's men were more observant than the Portuguese in matters of 'government':

They say that the said land is divided into little cantons, each of which has its own king; and, although the said kings are hardly better lodged or dressed than the others, even so they are very revered by their subjects; and no one is so brave as to dare to refuse their commands, since they have power of life and death over their subjects.[13]

In fact, the sailors witnessed an extraordinary demonstration of this authority. A young man of eighteen years of age had casually insulted his mother; when the chieftain by chance heard about this, he refused to listen to any pleas for mercy, even those of the mother herself, but ordered the youth to be thrown in a river with a stone tied around his neck, so that he drowned. The local king was a dignified Indian of medium stature named Arosca, and seemed to be about sixty years old; his domain appeared to stretch over about a dozen villages, and was a day's journey in extent. He and his six sons often came to visit the *Espoir*, and a warm relationship developed between Arosca and Gonneville. He was at peace with his immediate neighbours, some of whom also came to visit the ship; but Arosca was at war with other Indians in that land, and he very much wanted the Normans to accompany him on one of his expeditions and show off their artillery; but they made their excuses and declined to do so.[14]

The Indians were fascinated by everything they saw in the ship: 'had the Christians been angels who had come down from heaven, they could not have been more loved by these poor Indians.'[15] Simple items of truck like knives and mirrors meant as much to them as gold, silver or even the philosopher's stone meant to Christians.[16] They were particularly fascinated by the sight of written words on paper, for they could not understand how paper could be made to 'speak'. They were delighted to exchange food for the truck the sailors had brought along. But the spiritual dimension was not neglected by the visitors. In an act reminiscent of Cabral's conduct four years earlier, they built a great cross for Easter 1504, and this was carried in barefoot procession by Gonneville and his senior crew, joyously accompanied by Arosca and his sons. When they heard these men singing the Easter litany, the Indians were also mightily impressed. Cabral had ensured that the Portuguese cross carried the arms of King Manuel; but Gonneville inscribed his with the names of King Louis XII of France and the pope, adding also the names of the entire crew for good measure.[17]

Cruel Eaters of Men, 1504

After several months it was time to leave; the Normans had stayed in Brazil the whole time from early January to early July 1504. Arosca was so reluctant to see them go that he made them promise to return in twenty months, *dans vingt lunes au plus tard*; and he entrusted to Gonneville his son Essomericq and a companion named Namoa, to take them with him to the lands of Christendom, on the understanding that Gonneville would return with artillery with which Arosca could defeat his enemies. Meanwhile the Indians promised to look after the cross; and, as the ship set sail, they even made signs of the cross with their fingers to show the departing Normans that they would look after this treasure.[18] The report, which has a formal, official character, did not follow in Caminha's tracks by insisting that this was proof that they had an instinctive appetite for the Christian religion. But the implication that they were capable of being won to the faith was clear.

The *Espoir* had no better fortune on its return journey than on its outward journey. In fact, foul weather forced the ship to put in twice on the coast of Brazil before it was able to cross the Atlantic. Namoa fell seriously ill, and there was debate as to whether to baptise him; since he knew nothing of the creed but was already an adult in his late thirties, it was decided not to do so, and he was allowed to die unbaptised. The officers were unhappy about this, so when Essomericq too fell ill, Gonneville and his companions stood as godparents for him. He was given the name Binot, which was the baptismal name of Gonneville himself.[19] The crew thought that this worked wonders, for he soon recovered from his illness and survived the whole journey. But meanwhile the weather forced the ship to put in at another point on the coast of South America – where it is now impossible to say – and here they found Indians whom they regarded as more primitive than Arosca's followers. They were reddish in colour, and they went around naked, so one could see their private parts; they painted their bodies black, and they inserted green stones in their faces; they ate bread made of roots. They seemed to have no kings over them, but were agile hunters, fishermen and swimmers, as well as skilled bowmen. But above all they were cruel eaters of human flesh: *au reste, cruels mangeurs d'hommes.*[20] This accusation was not levelled against Arosca's people. No less extraordinary was evidence that these man-eaters had had some contact with Christians in recent times; they possessed some trinkets that must have come from Europe, and they were not very surprised to see the ship, though they were well aware of the threat posed by European artillery. Gonneville had probably arrived in the areas visited by the slave raiders in the last few years. A few Normans who went on shore without proper arms were attacked: a ship's boy was killed, and two men were carried off into the forest.[21] Nicole Le Febvre, who had made drawings of what he had seen in Brazil, was also killed.[22]

The Normans were desperate to leave, and sailed off as soon as they could; but their next landing took place on a shore inhabited by similar folk, though these caused the sailors no harm. The Normans caught two Indians with the intention of taking them back to France, but the men jumped overboard about nine miles out to sea; Gonneville did not doubt that they were good enough swimmers to reach land.[23] Still, it was pleasant to set out again across the ocean; the voyage past the Azores was slow, but it was easy enough until they came within sight of home. For as they entered the waters off Jersey and Guernsey the ship fell prey to two pirates, Edward Blunth of Plymouth and Mouris Fortin, a Breton corsair. The *Espoir* was in no condition to escape. The pirates caught up with and pillaged the ship; they sank her, with the loss of the logbook as well as the drawings made by Le Febvre. Many of the sailors were massacred. Only twenty-eight men reached Honfleur alive; but among them were Gonneville and Essomericq, who aroused considerable wonder 'since there had never been anyone in France from such a distant land'.[24] In view of the loss of all their documents, Gonneville and his colleagues registered a complaint against the pirates in June 1505;[25] but what was remarkable was the emphasis they placed not on the horrific act of piracy that they had come to report, but on the experiences they had had in South America and, in particular, the life of the people they met there.

There is no reason to disbelieve that this account recorded Gonneville's experiences. It was much more than a sailor's yarn. Essomericq was a real person whom Gonneville cherished as his son-in-law. A return to South America was out of the question for Gonneville; after twenty moons Arosca was left waiting for his son and for the French artillery. Of course, Gonneville assumed that native Indian society was in certain essential respects like his own, and his account of kingly power may have owed as much to his idea of the functions of a French king as it did to his observation of how Arosca exercised his authority: for example, he thought that Arosca's power had a territorial dimension. As in so many accounts of the New World, there were good and bad Indians; the cannibals whom he met later played the necessary role of villains in his story. It is possible, too, that by 1503 a good many Normans with an interest in the sea had heard of the Caribs and even of Vespucci's graphic tales of cannibal butchery. So it cannot be assumed that Gonneville's account was untainted by those of others, or by expectations of how the native peoples of the New World would conduct themselves.[26] However, Caminha and Gonneville, unconnected men, with different backgrounds, reacted with a similar sense of wonder and perplexity to what they saw in America. And this was part of a wider pattern. The explorers did not share a learned knowledge of past debates about pagan peoples; there was no single great lineage of ideas derived from Columbus, let alone Aristotle, Aquinas or Boccaccio, that determined how one responded to native peoples; there was no template. But nonetheless there was a surprising degree of uniformity in the way individual Europeans responded to the wonders they uncovered.

CHAPTER 22

A COMPULSORY VOLUNTARY 'REQUIREMENT', 1511–20

The Church in the New World, 1492–1516

It took twenty years from Columbus' first discoveries for an official policy to be formulated in Spain that determined how newly conquered peoples should be treated. During this long delay, the *encomienda* system continued to develop and expand, and the Indians continued to die. Little was done, meanwhile, to spread the Catholic faith among the Indians. Ramón Pané had no successors. Queen Isabella, however, hoped that the areas under Spanish rule could be properly divided up into Indian parishes; this would enable missionaries systematically to target Indian communities. But even ten years after Columbus' first voyage there was only a trickle of arriving clergy. By 1503 there was a thatched Franciscan friary at Santo Domingo; the Franciscans in Europe agreed that they wanted to create a 'Province of the Holy Cross' in the New World, and twenty-three friars were sent out in 1511; so there was progress, but at a snail's pace.[1] For instance, the friary had begun to gain some stone buildings by 1508. But the Franciscans turned inwards, looking after themselves and the Spanish colonisers, and turning their backs on the Indian population. For there were worries about the Christian faith of the Europeans: King Ferdinand despatched some Dominican friars, the arch-heresy hunters of his day, in search of unorthodox opinions that were said to be spreading in Hispaniola, even among priests; nor is this a surprise, for crypto-Jews and other dissidents saw the overseas colonies, whether the Canaries or the Caribbean, as promising places of refuge. Rather than rooting out dissent, the Dominicans actually succeeded in creating it, in unexpected quarters: in December 1511 the friar Montesinos mounted his pulpit in the New World, to denounce with exceptional force the ill-treatment of the Indians. Among his audience was the young and impressionable Bartolomé de las Casas. When Ferdinand of Aragon died in 1516, there was still no resident bishop in the Greater Antilles, though there had been one for a time at Caparra in Puerto Rico – he was upset when the Caribs burned his thatched cathedral, and he went back to Spain in 1515.

The question that remained unanswered in the twenty years after Columbus' discovery was whether the Indians had what would now be called rights. In the two decades after 1492, the situation on the ground did most to determine how the Indians were treated. Spanish (and Portuguese) explorers did not come fully armed with the scholastic texts that argued for and against the autonomy of non-Christian peoples. Columbus, Roldán, Ovando and others were mainly guided by greed for gold, rivalries among themselves, and the practical problem of inserting themselves in a society where the *caciques* were already at war with one another and sought outside support. On the other hand, warnings and advice from the royal court did reach the governors of Hispaniola: for instance, instructions to Ovando in 1501 stressed that the Indians 'are our subjects and vassals', and that they therefore could not be enslaved. The emphasis, while Isabella was alive, was on the free status of the Indians, which, even in the *encomienda* system, was formally recognised: the gold the Indians had to provide was a tax or tribute, and indeed precisely because it was a tribute it confirmed that they were not slaves but subjects with obligations.

There was a further problem: there was not a single answer to the question about the status of unconverted native peoples, since not everyone agreed with Thomas Aquinas' argument that they had the right to govern themselves if they observed the basic principles of natural law. Nature could be seen as brutal, or it could be seen as ennobling. This was the constant dilemma. Taínos could be painted in glowing colours as men and women who lived a simple existence, in harmony with one another and with the natural world, as in the writings of Columbus and Peter Martyr; Caribs could be painted in black as brutal and bestial warriors whose taste for human flesh was clear proof that they were savages from the forest. In addition, South American Indians could be portrayed as people who had no instinctive understanding of the rules of incest, no modesty – or the effective opposite, a pure innocence that would lead them instinctively to Christ once they had set eyes on the cross. Similar distinctions can be seen in the way the Canary islanders were observed and treated. The variety of views became a positive clash of views when las Casas and Sepúlveda passionately argued their cases in the presence of Charles V and his morose son Philip II of Spain. These issues were also argued passionately in the works of the early sixteenth-century historians. Las Casas called his contemporary Gonzalo Fernández de Oviedo a 'vain trifler'; but he knew the New World very well, and was a real expert on its natural history. He saw the Indians as to all intents lapsed Christians, whose ancestors had been blessed like all peoples at the ends of the earth with a visit from St Thomas the Apostle. Then, out of their fundamental stupidity and ignorance, they had lost their knowledge of Christian truth: 'Because these people of the Indies, although they are rational and descended from the family of Noah, had become irrational and bestial with their idolatries and infernal ceremonies and sacrifices, so the Devil had control of their soul for centuries.'[2] They were therefore in a sense rebels against the Christian Church, but in any case their limited capacity for understanding meant that they would always have to serve. They were also in a sense rebels against Spain, for Oviedo related an absurd tale of the conquest of the Americas by a prehistoric and pre-Christian king of Spain named Hesperus 3193 years earlier, meaning that Spain was only reviving a standing claim to rule the peoples and lands of the New World, a claim that clearly could be contested by nobody: 'God returned the sovereignty of the Indies after so many centuries', decreeing that they should join Granada and Naples as the perpetual possessions of Spain.[3] In sum, they were *indios bestiales*, 'bestial Indians', consumed by their vices and immersed in incest.[4] By Oviedo's time, of course, the debate had become wider, for it now embraced the peoples of the American mainland. Though he knew Hispaniola particularly well, his awareness of Aztec human sacrifice coloured his account of Indian religion.

Aristotle and the American Indians

It was not historians and naturalists but lawyers who set the agenda for the treatment of the American Indians around 1512. The fundamental problem they believed they had to face was whether the Indians were as human as Spaniards. Was humanity something absolute, so that a sharp line divided human beings from animals? To a reader of the Bible this might have seemed self-evident: man was created in the image of God and had been given dominion over the animals, as Genesis related.[5] But there was another approach, for late medieval writers experienced a constant tension between the authority of Holy Writ and that of the classical philosophers. Anthony Pagden has examined the use of images derived from Aristotle's *Politics* and *Nicomachean Ethics*, which became known to readers in the Catholic world in the thirteenth century and had an enormous influence on Aquinas and on the teaching of philosophy, law and theology in the universities. What Aristotle conveyed was the idea of degrees of humanity.[6] He presented a powerful image of the 'barbarian' as someone who possesses a natural cruelty. Cruelty is characteristic of beasts, not humans; therefore a barbarian who acted cruelly could be said to have lost the right to be called human.[7] Eating human flesh was one sign of animal-like barbarity.[8] Or, put differently, men (this is not the place to consider Aristotle's view of women)[9] must learn to control their animal nature, using 'reason'; this will enable them to realise their potential. 'Reason' was not simply a tool of philosophers; it can be understood here as 'intelligent thinking', an ability to calculate, in the broader sense of that word. (It was seen earlier in this book how medieval Jews were accused of lacking 'reason' when they denied the Christian faith, which Christians argued to be transparently true.) In the thirteenth century, Albert the Great, Aquinas' teacher, mentioned barbarians who lived in societies that were not based on justice and had no laws; this was in contrast to the idea that Aquinas himself expounded of a society based on 'natural law', in which certain fundamental practices and ideas could be found, such as knowledge of one Creator God, a horror of incest and a system of justice. While missions should be sent to such a society, there was no automatic right of conquest if it caused no offence to Christians – a view whose lineage can be traced down to las Casas.[10] On the other hand, humans who did not associate with one another but lived asocial lives, rather like Petrarch's Canarians, or 'wild men of the woods', failed to create a society based on justice. Their behaviour could descend to that of animals, living off raw meat, drinking out of skulls, refreshing themselves with draughts of blood. For Aristotle, living in Greek cities provided the essential conditions under which human beings could reach their full potential and cast off barbarity.[11]

If there were barbarian people whose humanity was not fully developed, then it followed that they should not exercise dominion over Aristotle's Greeks, for their natural condition was to serve those who were fully human. Only by being mastered would barbarians like the American Indians, 'who, it is said, are like talking animals', reach a full state of existence, according to the Spanish legal scholar Gil Gregorio.[12] The concept here is that of the 'natural slave'.[13] Someone who is a natural slave may or may not be a legal slave, for the natural slave may not yet have come into the power of his master. And the legal slave may simply be a captive of war, a Greek who has suffered misfortune and is fully rational.[14] Natural slavery, as Pagden has stressed, is a psychological condition:[15] the natural slave benefits from being under the control of his master, performing mechanical or 'banausic' tasks such as, in the years around 1500, the heavy labour required in a Madeiran sugar mill or the tiresome task of panning for gold in the riverbeds of Hispaniola (slaves were 'living tools', Aristotle said, 'just as a tool is an inanimate slave').[16] Thus the Taínos might be seen as slaves by disposition, though legally, of course, they were the free subjects of Queen Isabella. One writer, Mesa, insisted that they were natural slaves, lacking full mental capacity, and in the same breath said that they were the subjects of the Crown and that therefore they could not just be traded on the slave market like merchandise.[17] So they were natural slaves but not legal slaves; where this left the *mestizos*, those of mixed parentage, who were increasingly common by now, is a moot point. Debates about these problems gathered pace at the beginning of the sixteenth century: King Ferdinand called a meeting of theologians and lawyers, a *junta de letrados*, in 1504, and debate raged over the speeches of Montesinos in 1511.[18] While the very fact of debate indicates that the Indians had their stalwart defenders, there was an increasing emphasis on the idea that the American Indians were 'talking animals': barbarians, natural slaves, legitimately subject to the exercise of harsh corrective authority. The main issue for many of those involved in the debates was not so much the rights of the Indians as the rights of the Castilian Crown in the New World.

What King Ferdinand needed was a reasoned argument by a highly skilled lawyer, a tract that would set out clearly the case for Spanish dominion across the Ocean Sea. The papacy, it is true, had granted those rights of dominion; but Pope Alexander VI had never spelled out the details of how authority was to be exercised (even though, as has been seen, he had taken an interest in the garden sheds his missionaries would build). Nor did Ferdinand wish to leave the resolution of the problem to the pope: the Valencian Alexander VI had on balance been friendly, but Pope Julius II, the 'warrior pope' (1503–13), had a very different agenda and would hand no prizes to Spain while he was trying to manipulate Italian politics in his own favour and that of his Italian family. There was a lawyer named Dr Juan López de Palacios Rubios who had been a warm supporter of King Ferdinand, writing in defence of his ruthless seizure of Navarre in 1512; he was also an expert on Aristotle's *Politics*, on which he had written a commentary and which had had great influence on contemporary thinking about 'barbarians'. Between 1512 and 1516, most probably in the first half of this period, he wrote his 'Book about the Ocean Islanders', *Libellus de insulanis oceanis*.[19] He was also most probably the author of the strange document known as 'The Requirement', which set out how conquering Spaniards should proclaim the authority of the Crown in the lands they occupied. Palacios Rubios' book was highly conservative, written in the mode of a late medieval scholastic tract, full of references to biblical and legal texts, and to major classical authorities, especially Aristotle; it did not seek to find a novel answer to a novel problem – the discovery of what would prove to be many millions of unbaptised people in an unsuspected corner of the world – but to tease out of these older texts an answer to the question of Spain's rights in the New World. Like so much of the early literature about the American Indians, it offered a combination of positive and negative images, but it was the negative images that prevailed, much to the irritation of las Casas, who read and annotated with colourful remarks the only surviving manuscript of the book. Las Casas lost his temper when Palacios Rubios described the Indians as 'at liberty and free' (*liberi et ingenui*), which might seem a favourable comment, but not to someone who saw in such words the roots of massive hypocrisy.[20] Some of his angry marginal notes read 'absurd', 'false', 'heretical'.[21]

Palacios Rubios remarked very early on: 'In these islands, according to what I have learned from trustworthy accounts, they have met rational men, tame, peaceful and capable of understanding our Faith. Among themselves they do not have private property.'[22] His account of what they ate and culti-vated surely owed much to Peter Martyr and other enthusiasts for their way of life: they ate fish but no meat apart from an animal rather like a hare (this would be the agouti; there is no reference to cannibals); they would not eat domestic animals because they regarded them as part of the family (this seems to be an agreeable fantasy); they did not experience avarice, for they had no sense of property. This lack of property also meant that the question of whether the Castilian Crown had the right to assume control over their property following the conquest of the Greater Antilles was in many respects a non-question.[23] But then there were the negative traits. They went around naked and felt no shame; they lived all together in one big house; the *caciques* took many wives; worst of all, this was a society in which there was no real institution of marriage and in which there seemed to be total sexual abandon, and women would give themselves just like that to any man, even thinking it wrong to deny themselves. So no one really knew who was father to whom, with the result that succession passed through women – a bizarre misreading of the complex 'avunculocal' system of kinship among the Taínos.[24]

In the realms of religion there was also a balance sheet, with some positive but many more negative features. 'Seduced by demons', many adored their *zemís*, while others were closer to Vespucci's Epicureans, for they immersed themselves in idle pleasure. But a minority 'observe the precepts of natural law and, venerating and worshipping a single God, recognise naturally, illuminated by a certain light of reason, the obligation to practise good and to avoid evil.'[25] They even have some idea that 'no evil is without punishment', which suggests an implicit belief in a God who remunerates Good and punishes Evil and points them on the road to the belief that mankind is saved by Christ's Incarnation. They do not need to prove that they are already believers in Christ: 'it is enough for our proposition to know that these islanders, to whom no one has preached our faith nor shown them its articles, are not obliged to believe explicitly. It is enough if they believe implicitly.'[26]

Palacios Rubios used evidence about Taíno customs; but Aristotle was never far away, and he soon turned in his book to the question of their right to be free. As Aristotle and Aquinas had indicated, 'some were marked out from birth to serve and others to rule'.[27] It is also the case that different people have different levels of intelligence, and this gave some the right to dominate others. No man of letters (*letrado*) in early sixteenth-century Spain could be expected to assert anything else: the *letrados* exercised great influence at court and in wider society, forming a new elite whose power resided in their brains rather than their swords. All this was particularly applicable when one looked at groups of people who were so inept that they had no idea how to govern themselves, though Palacios Rubios accepted that non-Christian peoples were entitled to govern themselves so long as they caused no offence to Christians or so long as the lands they inhabited had not once been in Christian hands, like the kingdom of Granada and, he insisted, the 'Fortunate Isles' or Canaries.[28] But, once the islands in the Ocean Sea were brought (legitimately, of couse) under Spanish rule, the Crown's subjects were obliged to perform the same services and duties as any other subjects of the Crown anywhere else.[29] Had not Emperor Augustus imposed tribute throughout the Roman Empire, tribute that had to be paid in gold, silver, iron and salt?[30] In other words, the Spanish Crown had a perfect right to levy the taxes it required. As for the effects of this on the Indian population, this was not an issue on which Palacios Rubios chose to dwell.

The Laws of Burgos, 1512

There was a second area where Palacios Rubios and the Spanish lawyers attempted to determine the fate of the Indians. Around the time Palacios Rubios wrote his tract on the islanders of the Ocean Sea, the first set of laws concerning the treatment of the Indians was issued, the 'Laws of Burgos' (*Leyes de Burgos*) of December 1512. Again, there was a mixture of positive and negative aspects. The Indians were to be properly fed, though one might see this as an attempt to make sure they were strong enough to do what was demanded of them; the Indians were to be adequately clothed, though one might see this as a challenge to their custom of going around naked;[31] the Indians were in future to be paid wages for their work – the subject of old complaints – for if they were legally free why were they made to work for nothing? The Indians were to be sent preachers; though this was a tacit admission of how little had been done in the twenty years since 1492, it was dressed up as a denunciation of the obstinacy and idleness of the Indians: 'It has become evident through long experience that nothing has sufficed to bring the said chiefs and Indians to a knowledge of our Faith (necessary for their salvation), since by nature they are inclined to idleness and vice, and have no manner of virtue or doctrine.'[32] In the traditional spirit of respect for established native authority, the authority of the *caciques* as headmen in their communities was recognised, and they were even assigned better clothes and their own servants.[33] But the majority of Taínos found themselves locked into the *encomienda* system in squads of between forty and 150 workers; thus the existence of the *encomienda* was now formalised.[34] There were some humane clauses: women more than four months pregnant were excused labour in the mines, though they were still expected to perform domestic tasks.[35] Indians were not to be physically punished: 'we order and command that no person or persons shall dare to beat any Indian with sticks, or whip him, or call him dog, or address him by any name other than his proper name alone.'[36] Spaniards who ignored this law were, at least in theory, to be fined. On the other hand, there was an attempt to regroup Indian settlements close to Spanish ones, which was very destructive of the social and economic life of the Taínos, breaking up the villages in which their families had lived for generations and depriving them of access to their cassava plantations (they were commanded to plant new ones, and it was simply assumed the fresh locations would be good ones). This was excused on the grounds that they would be converted much more easily if they lived close to Christian settlements; if they live too far away, when they return home, 'because of the distance and their own evil inclinations, they immediately forget what they have been taught and go back to their customary idleness and vice, and when they come to serve again they are as new in the doctrine as they were at the beginning'.[37] It was also argued that transferring the Indians would benefit them, because if they fell ill they would be able to find medical help more easily; while this clause recognised that very many were falling ill, it was little more than sophistry to justify a harsh policy. Further, it was argued that these arrangements would ensure that newborn infants were baptised. In fact, a high proportion of the laws consisted of pious plans for the conversion of the Indians and the building of churches.

The creation of Indian villages close to Christian settlements was partly negated by the demand that Indians should travel to the gold fields for five months at a time, to be followed by forty days of rest at home; 'and the day they cease their labour of extracting gold shall be noted on a certificate, which shall be given to the miners who go to the mines.'[38] The application of these laws was not rendered easier by the political conflicts that continued in the New World; while the laws were being issued, Ovando and Diego Columbus battled for supremacy not just in Hispaniola but across the water in Puerto Rico. In other words, the Laws of Burgos regulated relations between the Spaniards and the Indians in theory, but did little to change what was happening on the ground. It is not necessary to take the same stance as las Casas to see that the remedy had come much too late to save the patient. The Taínos were in terminal decline.

The Doctrine of Submission, 1511–13

A third area where Palacios Rubios made a very distinctive contribution was in helping to draw up 'The Requirement', *El Requerimiento*, a document that was required to be read publicly to those who were about to have their lands brought under Spanish rule.[39] It began with a clear but uncompromising statement:

> On the part of the King, Don Fernando, and of Doña Juana, his daughter, Queen of Castile and León, subduers of the barbarous nations, we their servants notify and make known to you, as best we can, that the Lord our God, Living and Eternal, created the Heaven and the Earth, and one man

and one woman, of whom you and we, all the men of the world, were and are descendants, and all those who come after us.

The text then stated that God had called to his service 'one man, called St Peter', whom all should obey as 'head of the whole human race, wherever men should live'. God 'gave him the world for his kingdom and jurisdiction'. Thus he and his successors had the right 'to judge and govern all Christians, Moors, Jews, Gentiles, and all other sects'. This was a classic claim to over-arching papal authority. However, the pope did not exercise direct power over all humans; one of Peter's heirs 'made donation of these isles and the main-land to the aforesaid king and queen and to their successors, our lords, with all that there are in these territories'. If those hearing the document read out were in any doubt about this, they could ask to see written proof (the fact that they could not read was irrelevant; the standards of evidence were naturally those of Christian society). In fact, the document insisted, some lands have already willingly fallen under the sway of the king and queen, and have accepted Christian preachers who have converted some of the inhabitants, who acted out of their own free will. Ferdinand and Juana 'have commanded them to be treated as their subjects and vassals; and you too are held and obliged to do the same'. Really, then, there was no choice: God had endowed St Peter with authority and St Peter's heir had endowed the Castilian monarchs with that same authority.

There was a faint acknowledgment of communication difficulties when the Indians were told: 'as best we can, we ask and require you that you consider what we have said to you, and that you take the time that shall be necessary to understand and deliberate upon it.' How long this was to be was not made clear; but it cannot have been very long, because the native peoples were also warned against 'malicious delay' in making up their minds. The final demand was clear:

that you acknowledge the Church as the Ruler and Superior of the whole world, and the high priest called Pope, and in his name the king and queen Doña Juana our lords, in his place, as superiors and lords and kings of these islands and this mainland by virtue of the said donation.

At the same time, the natives must accept the right of Christian preachers to spread the faith among them: 'if you do so, you will do well.' There was a valu-able reward: 'we in their name shall receive you in all love and charity, and

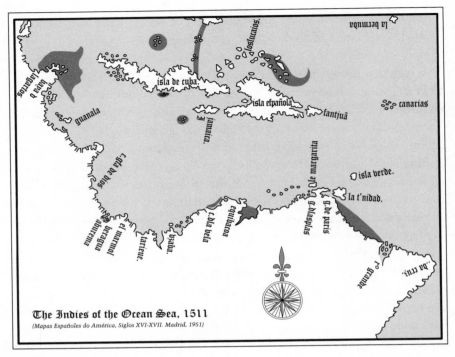

The Indies of the Ocean Sea, 1511
(Mapas Españoles do América, Siglos XVI-XVII. Madrid, 1951)

The Indies in 1511

A Spanish map of the Caribbean; islands probably intended to represent the Lesser Antilles are marked as 'canarias', indicating the way in which the idea of the Caribbean islands as 'New Canaries' survived well after 1492

shall leave you, your wives, and your children, and your lands, free without servitude', and you will be able to act as 'you like and think best'. This, then, was the way in which the Indians and other conquered peoples could guarantee their status as free subjects rather than as slaves of the Crown. The king and queen promised many privileges and benefits to those who accepted their rule, but did not define what these were. There was no actual obligation to accept baptism: 'they shall not compel you to turn Christians, unless you yourselves, when informed of the truth, should wish to be converted to our Holy Catholic Faith.' But 'The Requirement' ruthlessly set out the alternatives for those who did not comply, expressing with startling clarity the two extremes of the Spanish reaction to native peoples:

But, if you do not do this, and maliciously make delay in it, I certify to you that, with the help of God, we shall powerfully enter into your country, and shall make war against you in all ways and manners that we can, and shall subject you to the yoke and obedience of the Church and of their Highnesses; we shall take you and your wives and your children, and shall make slaves of them, and as such shall sell and dispose of them as their Highnesses may command; and we shall take away your goods, and shall do you all the mischief and damage that we can, as to vassals who do not obey, and refuse to receive their lord, and resist and contradict him; and we protest that the deaths and losses which shall accrue from this are your fault, and not that of their Highnesses, or ours, nor of these cavaliers who come with us.

All this would, of course, be announced in due legal form, and a notary would keep a formal record that the proclamation had been read and witnessed. By 1513 the document was in use; whether reading it from the poop of a ship or on an empty beach, or to Indians who did not understand a word of what was being said, fulfilled the command to read it out was a moot point.[40] Some Spaniards viewed it with horror: las Casas said he did not know whether he should laugh or cry at the absurdities of 'The Requirement', and outside observers such as Walter Raleigh and Montaigne thought it was a very bad joke indeed.[41] The Portuguese did not adopt anything like it at this stage. Even Oviedo, no admirer of the Indians, could not understand how anyone thought the Indians would make sense of the document. Contemporary Spanish theologians too, such as the Dominican friar Matías de Paz, had their doubts, for they were aware of the argument that non-Christian peoples had a right to govern themselves so long as they gave no offence to Christians: 'an infidel prince possesses, strictly speaking, legitimate dominion.'[42] Matías de Paz had worked alongside Palacios Rubios when the Laws of Burgos were being drawn up, but he began to see that the Indians were being severely mistreated.[43] It was a highly paradoxical requirement voluntarily to accept the authority of the Crown and of the Church. The Indians could also choose to reject the authority of Crown and Church; but to do so would be to call up the full force of the Spanish Empire, which would engage in a 'just war' against these rebels. It was a stark choice; indeed, it was no choice. It was gibberish to the Indians, who often did not understand what a written text was and, as has been seen, thought that in some sense it 'spoke'.

The roots of 'The Requirement' lay not just in papal doctrine about the authority of the successors to St Peter. Patricia Seed has traced its origins back to Islamic and even ancient Israelite practices in time of war.[44] Islam had left a heavy imprint on the Iberian kingdoms; and biblical examples were closely studied by Palacios Rubios and Matías de Paz. Seed has compared the statement in 'The Requirement' that natives shall not be required to accept Christianity with the Koranic view that 'there is no compulsion in religion'.[45] The great Spanish Muslim philosopher of the twelfth century, Ibn Rushd, or Averroes, described how a message had to be sent to the enemy, requiring them to submit. 'Islam' itself means 'submission'; but this submission had taken two forms since the early Muslim conquests in the Middle East: submission in the political sense, submission to the caliph, allowing what was often a minority of Muslims to rule over subject Christians and Jews; and submission in the religious sense, for pagans were expected to submit to Allah, while increasing numbers of Christians did the same. Those who submitted politically were subject to a poll tax, the *jizyah*, from which Muslims were exempt; the Christian conquerors of Muslim Spain knew about this, and imposed similar taxes on the Muslims who had once taxed their ancestors. So there was some similarity between the tribute in gold demanded by the Spaniards in the New World and the tribute in money or kind demanded by Muslims from Christian and Jewish subjects. By 1518 this tribute had settled at three pesos for each Indian man aged twenty and upwards, unless they were unmarried, in which case they contributed only one peso.[46]

The continuing role of the *caciques* as heads of their communities resembled the self-government permitted by the Muslims to Jews and Christians, allowing them to administer their own laws. Once the Christians gained the upper hand in Spain, from the thirteenth century onwards, a comparable practice was enshrined in many of the 'surrender treaties' which allowed the Moors to submit to Christian rule on what both sides agreed were honourable terms.[47] Thus in the late Middle Ages, the *aljama* or community of Moors or Jews in cities such as Valencia was self-governing, and communities were often obliged to live in defined areas, just as the Indians had to move to special villages close to the Spanish settlements in the New World.

Finally, Spanish lawyers and theologians thought back to the words of Deuteronomy, which were themselves clearly based on the practice of far more powerful neighbours in Assyria, Babylonia and Egypt; these provisions were intended, the Bible stated, to apply to 'all the towns that are very far from you, which are not towns of the nations here'.[48] It is far from clear that the militarily feeble ancient Israelites would ever have had an opportunity to apply these rules, but, in respect of places 'very far from you' across the ocean, they seemed to apply very well:

When you draw near to a town to fight against it, offer it terms of peace. If it accepts your terms of peace and surrenders to you, then all the people in it shall serve you in forced labour. If it does not submit to you peacefully, but makes war against you, then shall you besiege it; and when the Lord your God gives it into your hand, you shall put all its males to the sword.[49]

Palacios Rubios cited these very words in his book on the islanders of the Ocean Sea.[50] He understood them to mean precisely that you must offer peace; in the same way, Jesus had said: 'as you enter the house greet it. If the house is worthy let your peace come upon it; but if it is not worthy, let your peace return to you.'[51] Predictably, las Casas read the passage from Deuteronomy very differently, writing in the margins of Palacios Rubios' manuscript: 'therefore, you must not start a war first.' When Palacios Rubios went on to say that it was lawful to launch a war against infidels if they did not allow Christian preachers into their land – a typical medieval argument beloved of crusade theorists – las Casas responded that this was 'absolutely false'.[52]

Thus what was really new about 'The Requirement' was the absurd way it was to be proclaimed to native peoples in a language they could not understand, speaking of a faith they did not know and popes and kings whose existence they did not suspect. But within the document there was nothing particularly novel, and that was why it commanded so much assent in Spain, well away from the front line of the encounters with native peoples. Whether derived from biblical theory and practice, or from Islam, or from the methods of the Christian conquerors of Muslim Spain, the choice between peace and war presented by 'The Requirement' was deeply rooted in the thinking of European Christians around 1500. In fact, it was a universal phenomenon: similar practices existed among the Aztecs and Incas; the Mongols had made similar demands as they swept across the plains of Asia into Europe nearly three centuries earlier. 'The Requirement' became a standard part of the baggage of Spanish conquerors in the decades that followed – in Peru and across the Americas, in the Pacific islands opened up by Magellan's voyage.

Theory and Practice in Cuba, 1511–13

The Laws of Burgos were not all theory. Their earliest test came with the conquest of Cuba, which started in 1511 (Jamaica was occupied in 1510);[53] the treatment of the conquered Taínos shows that some attempt was being made to apply the new rules by 1513. The invasion of Cuba was led by Diego

Velázquez de Cuellar, a man of high social standing; according to Hugh Thomas, 'he was obviously an engaging man', who enjoyed lively conversation and feasting, and became one of the earliest enthusiasts for smoking tobacco with his friends.[54] He gained experience of the New World by acting as deputy governor of western Hispaniola, which brought Cuba, sixty miles to the west, virtually into his sights. Diego Columbus was now governor of Hispaniola, and wanted to maximise his power in the region.[55] He was also the prime mover in the conquest of Cuba, which was justified by the fact that a *cacique* from Hispaniola, Hatuey, had escaped there; the conquest began, then, as hot pursuit of this *cacique*. Las Casas related how Hatuey warned the puzzled Taínos of Cuba what they could expect from the Spaniards: the Spaniards were indeed cruel by nature, but that was not the only motive for their violence, since they also wanted the Indians to worship their God. If the Cuban Indians wanted to see the God of the Christians, then Hatuey could show them that God: 'he had a basket full of gold and jewels and he said: "You see their God here, the God of the Christians."'[56] Archaeological discoveries have confirmed that the Cuban Taínos had no great fascination with gold; indeed, following contact with the Europeans, it was European brass that was in greatest demand, and members of the Taíno elite were buried with their precious brass pendants made out of old German shoelaces.[57] Las Casas accompanied the Cuban expedition, which confirmed him in his deep distaste for his compatriots' conduct. At first, all went well for Velázquez: Hatuey was captured and sentenced to burn. In the grand tradition of the Spanish Inquisition, a Franciscan friar came up to him at the stake and offered to instruct him in the Christian faith, for if he accepted Christ he would benefit in this world by being garrotted before the pyre was set alight, and in the next by gaining access to the delights of Heaven.[58]

> The cacique, who had never heard any of this before, and was told he would go to Hell where, if he did not adopt the Christian faith, he would suffer eternal torment, asked the Franciscan friar if Christians all went to Heaven. When told that they did he said he would prefer to go to Hell. Such is the fame and honour that God and our Faith have earned through the Christians who have gone out to the Indies.[59]

Already in holy orders, and already moved by Montesinos' sermons attacking the mistreatment of the Indians, las Casas actively defended the Indians from the mindless savagery of the invaders, who seemed to think that they needed to terrorise the Indians into surrender. He said that he saw three thousand men, women and children massacred for no reason at all.[60] He told one of the Spanish commanders that the Spaniards were in effect serving the Devil, and he began to sympathise more than ever with the Indians; he witnessed mass rapes and the destruction of communities. Once, though, he was charmed to find that a cult had developed around a statue of the Virgin Mary, left on shore after a shipwreck; he even offered a better one in exchange, but the Indians were happy with what they had.[61] This proved that they were of the right disposition, at any rate, potential Christians who could be drawn to the faith – the parallel with Espinosa's Virgin of Candelaria on Tenerife is striking. By 1514 las Casas had had enough of the Cuban war of conquest; he left the island in disgust and embarked on his career as the great defender of Indian rights.

Velázquez's approach to his Indian subjects was pragmatic, but it did show the influence of the Burgos laws. As in Puerto Rico and Jamaica, some Spaniards realised that the harsh policy adopted in Hispaniola had provoked fierce internal tensions followed by a dramatic decline in native numbers, endangering productivity. Las Casas later said that many Indians fled into the mountains to avoid the Spaniards, or even hanged themselves, though the relentless, ruthless Spaniards eventually caught up with the survivors.[62] It was not easy to find replacement labour, so it was important to make sure that the Taínos were treated reasonably well, and this chimed with some provisions of the new laws – the appointment, for instance, of inspectors to examine Indian welfare, and the bonding of *caciques* to individual Spanish landlords, who had to ensure that the *cacique* and his followers were properly fed and clothed, and had the chance to hear Christian preachers. But much was still demanded of the Cuban Indians; *encomiendas* of up to three hundred Indians were created, twice the normal maximum on Hispaniola; las Casas charged Velázquez with working them to death: 'at the end of three months all but thirty of them had died of the hard labour in the mines.'[63] Equally awful, he said, was the fate of their children: while their mothers and fathers were searching for gold, seventy thousand helpless children died of famine.[64]

It is always difficult to know how far las Casas was exaggerating, especially when he produced numbers; Hugh Thomas has interpreted the rule of Velázquez much more positively. Velázquez aimed to create a European colony in the New World. This was to be achieved by supplying Cuba with domestic animals such as horses and pigs: in three years a hundred pigs are said to have multiplied into thirty thousand. The governor also took an interest in the local sources of meat such as turtles, and there were even attempts at turtle-farming. Rice was introduced from Spain; but Velázquez understood the importance of traditional Taíno crops as well, and cassava and maize cultivation was reorganised.[65] Towns were built; Santiago, in the south-east, not far from Hispaniola, became the seat of government. Some gold was extracted, but it was soon realised that Cuba offered less gold than Hispaniola, as Columbus had suspected. Genoese businessmen with know-ledge of the Canary sugar plantations began to appear, and sugar was intro-duced;[66] but it was not until the nineteenth century that Cuba was transformed into a great centre of sugar production, taking the place of Haiti. Clearly it would be a mistake to idealise the way Velázquez governed Cuba, but a few lessons were being learned, very late indeed, about how to exercise authority over the Taínos. The permanent problem was that back home in Spain King Ferdinand wanted and needed a flow of gold, and without native Indian labour, or that of imported black slaves, the gold could not be obtained.[67]

Mexico, a New New World – But Strangely Familiar, 1520

Cuba was the starting point for an adventure that transformed the Americas and Spain's role in the New World. Hernán Cortés had participated along-side Velázquez in the settlement of Cuba; he served as Velázquez's secretary, had been appointed a city magistrate, and made himself rich from the gold mines; he was closely involved in Velázquez's project of founding new towns.[68] But he also knew that expeditions in 1517 and 1518 had sailed northwards along the coast of central America, and had brought back from the lands of the Maya Indians not just rumours of a great empire beyond the mountains, but astonishing trophies such a a statuette of a man made of gold and precious stones. Columbus and others had already seen the first signs of a more complex civilisation when they visited the coasts further south, but here were even grander temples, paved streets and stone houses, and evidence of human sacrifice as well. Peter Martyr wrote of the remark-able illuminated books that had been seen; 'annually they sacrifice an uncountable number of children, girls and even slaves bought in the market.' Lured by these scraps of evidence, Cortés set out from Cuba on a private expedition, against the wishes of his patron Velázquez. He marched into the heart of what proved to be the Aztec Empire, negotiating with its ruler

Montezuma (Motecuçoma, Moctezuma), and eventually overthrowing him.[69]

There was an extraordinary contrast between the people and places Cortés encountered as he crossed the Mexican highlands and the societies that had been visited by Spaniards, Portuguese and others in the Atlantic islands and on the coast of Brazil. In the same years, Ferdinand Magellan fulfilled Columbus' dream in one respect, by taking his ships westwards and not eastwards to the Spice Islands; Cortés in Mexico, and after him Pizarro in Peru, fulfilled it in another, by showing that rich, well-organised civilisations existed across the Atlantic, ruled from great cities with magnificent temples and busy trade networks. The Mexicans lacked iron, though not several softer metals, and they did not make use of the wheel (a less obvious failing to a Spaniard, for in Spain mule transport was the norm); but they had great palaces stocked with gold and coloured textiles, and built solidly and on a grand scale out of finely dressed stone. The Mexicans also possessed writing and recorded their own history, for they had a powerful sense of time in a tradition that went back to the time-obsessed Maya civilisation several centuries earlier. These lands were not Cipangu and Cathay, but they were the seat of great empires (a term the conquistadores used to describe Mexico), and their fate, as Cortés insisted, was to be subjugated to the greatest empire of all, the Christian, Roman, Spanish and German empire of Charles of Habsburg.[70]

The discovery of high civilisation in Mexico transformed the way Europeans looked at the New World. The territories discovered and settled by Columbus became the outer edge of a far more complex New World, in which prelapsarian simplicity was much harder to find amid the bloodletting of Aztec human sacrifices at the top of pyramid temples, or indeed amid the sheer prosperity of the marketplaces of the Mexican cities. Less than four hundred men under Cortés' command stood on the heights above the great lake in which Tenochtitlán, the Aztec capital on the site of modern Mexico City, appeared to float, surrounded by satellite cities, and they were dazzled by what they saw:

Gazing on such wonderful sights, we did not know what to say or whether what appeared before us was real, for on one side in the land there were great cities and in the lake ever so many more, and the lake itself was crowded with canoes, and in the causeway were many bridges at intervals, and in front of us stood the great City of Mexico.[71]

Later, after he and his men had entered Tenochtitlán as the guests of Montezuma, the Aztec ruler invited Cortés to climb the steep steps to the top of a temple platform where human sacrifices were regularly conducted; 'then Montezuma took Cortés by the hand and told him to look at his great city and all the other cities that were standing in the water and the many other towns and the land around the lake.'[72] From this high point Montezuma pointed out the great marketplace, from which the great hubbub of voices reached them, even though it was three miles distant; and they also saw the great profusion of temples and shrines, and the canoes taking food and merchandise back and forth. It was a 'marvellous sight'. Soldiers who had seen Rome and Constantinople said that this market surpassed those of both cities; and Cortés' companion Bernal Díaz described in detail what he saw when he walked through the market – slaves (as many as the Portuguese bring from the Guinea coast), axes made of bronze, copper and tin, cotton cloth, sandals made of sisal, food cooked and uncooked, and stalls selling chocolate, as well as gold, some of which was threaded inside goose quills, which were then used as currency. There were three judges who sat in the market, and they had deputies who inspected what was on sale, all of which would remind any Iberian traveller of the *almoxarifes* and other market officials back home whom they had inherited from the Muslims.[73] All this reinforced a powerful sense that this was an efficiently controlled empire and, therefore, a highly desirable acquisition for Spain.

The conquerors of Mexico were at first more inclined to see the Aztecs as 'Moors' than to describe them as something totally new and different. Cortés said of the cotton market: 'it seems like the silk market of Granada.'[74] He also wrote about the palace of the Aztec emperor Montezuma in the language he might have used to describe the palaces of the Alhambra: 'he had another very beautiful house, with a large patio, laid with pretty tiles in the manner of a chessboard. There were rooms nine feet high and as large as six paces square. The roofs of each of the houses are half covered with tiles while the other half is covered by well-made lattice-work.'[75] Anthony Pagden has commented: 'the whole thrust is to suggest a familiar barbarian empire.'[76] Those who arrived from Spain could not escape the analogy between conquering this empire and conquering the Moors of Granada. Tenochtitlán was, Cortés averred, as large as Córdoba or Seville.[77] He was deeply disgusted by the practice of human sacrifice; but he also wrote in praise of the well-organised society he observed:

I will say only that these people live almost like those in Spain, and in as much harmony and order as there, and considering that they are barbarous and so far from the knowledge of God and cut off from all civilised nations, it is truly remarkable to see what they have achieved in all things.[78]

Similar impressions would be left by the highly ordered Inca Empire, seized by Pizarro from 1532 onwards, with the help of half the number of men available to Cortés. He too had travelled from lands where the Indians lived simple lives (having been governor of Panama City), impelled by rumours of a fabulously rich civilisation on the Pacific side of South America. But the basic framework for governing these alien societies had been created as a result of the discovery of the less complex, village-based societies first encountered in the Canaries, the Bahamas, the Caribbean and Brazil, societies that lacked books, a strong awareness of the passing of time, great temples or indeed a sense of territorial power. Despite these radical differences, the *encomienda* system, which had had such disastrous results in the Caribbean, was introduced to Mexico and then to Peru, Chile and beyond. Las Casas had no doubt that the violence of the conquest of Mexico was just another ghastly chapter in the tragic history of Spanish oppression of the American peoples. Cupidity had taken the place of cure of souls.

THE RENAISSANCE DISCOVERY OF MAN

The True Discoverer

The great Swiss historian Jacob Burckhardt wrote his *Civilisation of the Renaissance in Italy* in the middle of the nineteenth century. One of its most striking themes is 'The Discovery of the World and of Man'.[1] But he devoted only a very small amount of space to the themes of this book. He noted the role of the Italians in the great voyages, and the 'superiority' of geographical knowledge in Italy over that in other lands, pointing to the works of Pope Pius II in the mid-fifteenth century, above all his description of the Tyrol and of Scotland, and his aesthetic appreciation of the landscape, which was 'genuine modern enjoyment'.[2] Burckhardt was deeply impressed by Columbus:

> Yet ever and again we turn with admiration to the august figure of the great Genoese, by whom a new continent beyond the ocean was dreamed, sought and found; and who was the first to be able to say: *il mondo è poco* – the world is not as large as men have thought.[3]

For Burckhardt, 'the true discoverer, however, is not the man who first chances to stumble upon anything, but the man who finds what he has sought'. Burckhardt said very little more, perhaps because Spain and Portugal rather than Italy led the great wave of exploration at this time; even so, he hardly mentioned Amerigo Vespucci, and he ignored the Italian humanist Peter Martyr.

Burckhardt only looked at Columbus in the traditional context of the discovery of land, of information about the physical condition of the world. What interested him more in his book was the discovery of the individual, which he saw as the central theme of Renaissance civilisation; it was expressed in the writing of biography and autobiography, in the description of daily life (often rather more artificial than he supposed, and including plenty of fantasies of pastoral simplicity). Man possessed a dignity, or at least the potential to develop and express that dignity. Of course, Burckhardt's 'man' was a literate, cultured Renaissance intellectual, a courtier at the palace of the duke of Urbino or a member of the salon of Lorenzo de' Medici. Historians now insist that an earlier 'discovery of the individual' took place among the scholars of medieval Europe, in the so-called 'twelfth-century Renaissance'.[4] Still, no one would deny that the late fourteenth and fifteenth centuries, the period of the 'classic' Renaissance, saw a new emphasis on human dignity and autonomy, on the capacity of the individual to mould his fate and fortune, an individualism that can be observed in the great portrait painters of the fifteenth century. This book has indicated that there was another, parallel 'discovery of man' that took place within the period of the Italian Renaissance. The history of this discovery began with the reaction of the two great Renaissance pioneers Boccaccio and Petrarch to the news of the first encounters with primitive peoples in the Canary Islands. Another Italy, the Italy of commerce, also left traces, in the reaction of da Mosto to the peoples of West Africa, and then in Columbus' accounts of the riches of the New World.

Italy left many other traces in Columbus' response to what he saw, notably his joy in nature; but the Italian author who influenced Columbus most strongly was not Pope Pius II, from Siena, in the fifteenth century, but Marco Polo, from Venice, in the thirteenth. For Columbus often placed written authority above experience, or rather constantly sought to reconcile his experiences with written authority, as when he insisted that he was on the edges of Cathay or that the Amazons of classical legend lived just over the horizon. He was constantly made aware that what he had found did not fit his expectations; even if he was convinced that he was near Asia, he recognised the novelty of what he saw and those he met, and at the same time kept trying to revert to his original assumptions about what and who would be on the other side of the Atlantic. This tension between expectation and experience was something he could never resolve, though other explorers managed to do so more successfully, in Vespucci's case by eventually recognising that the New World was not in fact Asia. The discovery of the American landmasses, it has been pointed out, can be seen as a gradual mental process, and not just as events in 1492, 1497, 1500 and other points in time when particular areas were first identified.[5] To this one can add that the discovery of the peoples of the Americas was also a gradual, at times difficult, mental process, or series of processes, in the minds of the first observers and their readers.

But medieval myth was a powerful force in the thinking of all the explorers, determining their expectations. What interested Columbus was geographical and ethnographic information; he did not seek to make himself into an expert on theories of natural slavery, but he knew enough about the great scholastic debates to realise that there were unresolved questions about the right to dominion of non-Christian peoples, especially those who had some notion of a Creator God, of justice to fellow humans and of the need to avoid incest and other bestial behaviour. The authority of classical and medieval authors as sources of exact information was thus gradually undermined as the Europeans realised that they had uncovered new peoples, and that these new peoples lived in a New World. The eyewitness accounts of Columbus and Caminha, though influenced of course by the intellectual climate within Europe, were added to day by day, and have an immediacy that expresses very well the sheer surprise they experienced. It was a surprise that was shared by readers of Columbus' letters in Europe, and by the perhaps gullible audience Vespucci reached.

The Wonder of Discovery

The aim of this book has been to recover something of that sense of wonder, first of all in the Canaries and then in the two decades after Columbus' first voyage. Even in the Canaries, which were mistily known to classical writers, there were enormous surprises, not just in the way of life of the partly naked islanders, but in the way Christ had apparently left them outside the lands to which news of his coming had extended. This was partly resolved by the story Espinosa repeated of the visit of the Virgin Mary, in about 1400, in the form of the statue of Candelaria. And then there was the question of title to ownership, which the papacy was keen to address but which could only be resolved by the efforts of armed fleets, sent by one Iberian kingdom after another. But the problems that had been broached first of all in the islands of the eastern Atlantic turned critical once it was plain that the 'New Canaries' far to the west contained much larger and (from the Christian perspective) more isolated populations, and once it became obvious that they were only the edge of a whole New World containing many millions of unconverted peoples, some of whom ate one another, most of whom went around naked, and many of whom seemed to have no public cult with priests and sacrifices. With the

European discovery of Mexico, it became clear that complex civilisations did exist across the Atlantic, and that they not merely consumed human flesh but made holocausts of war captives. From 1520, therefore, the Spaniards found themselves dealing with another category of humans, who seemed to combine order and organisation with frightening violence, not that the Spaniards were innocent of acts of horrendous violence. While they knew that they were dealing with a different type of society, the Europeans continued to assess the status of the peoples they met within the framework laid down in the twenty years between Columbus' arrival in the New World and the promulgation of the Laws of Burgos. The charter of privilege that entitled them, as they believed, to treat the native peoples they encountered in the way that they did was 'The Requirement'; and the system they adopted to exploit their new, 'free' subjects was the *encomienda*.

The conflict between expectation and experience that left Columbus confused about what he had found also left him confused about how to treat the people he had found. His delight in their free and simple life, as expressed in his letters to readers in Europe, was without doubt an attempt to 'sell' the New World, to prove that his expeditions were great successes and that he had been led across the Ocean Sea by God, who had opened the way to the conversion of the Indians – all of which had been predicted by the Hebrew prophets about two thousand years earlier. However, he soon turned against the Indians, angry at the response of the *caciques* to his attempts to establish dominion across the island and to exact tribute in gold. Columbus undoubtedly had a major role in introducing the *encomienda* system to the New World, even if it only evolved gradually during his lifetime and after his death; the attempts in the Laws of Burgos to alleviate some of the worst abuses still left the system in place, and ready to be imposed in a broadly similar form in Mexico and Peru.

The Crown and the Church back in Spain slowly and carefully began to reconcile what and who had been discovered with ancient and medieval arguments about the status of conquered peoples. These discoveries forced the Spanish court to think about how it should govern those who had been placed under its control by papal grant. It was now that the legacy of classical and medieval thinking about 'barbarians' and 'infidels', derived from Aristotle and Aquinas in particular, became important. Fine lines were drawn: in law, the conquered peoples were subjects, not slaves; but maybe they were 'natural slaves' who were incapable on their own of fulfilling what human potential they had, and needed to be mastered and to serve, in the way Aristotle had argued in the *Politics*. These arguments were profoundly rooted in the scholastic tradition of late medieval scholarship – in points of canon and civil law and theology, in a close reading of the authorities of past time – and they were clearly reflected in 'The Requirement'. Even then there were vigorous opponents, and las Casas spent half a century pricking the conscience of Spanish rulers about the fate of the Indians, though he seems never to have cared about the victims of the Inquisition in Spain itself, at worst roasted alive, at best shamed and dispossessed. His objections had some effect: the New Laws of Charles V, issued in 1542, with las Casas' approval, tried to protect the Indians from abuse by the *encomenderos*, but only after the event – *encomenderos* who abused their Indians could lose them to the Crown. However, strong opposition from Spanish interest groups ensured that most of these laws were revoked within three years.

So neither las Casas' protests nor the extinction of the Canary islanders and Taínos led to a radical change in attitudes among those claiming dominion. There was massive mortality on the mainland once the Spaniards and others had penetrated central and South America. Spanish viceroys happily associated themselves with the Aztec and Inca elites; but the conquerors remained to a large extent a privileged caste. Greed for gold rapidly became the prime motive for conquering first Mexico and then Peru, to be followed by the frantic search for a land even richer in gold, El Dorado, in which Spaniards, Italians and Germans all took part.[6] These were searches for rich civilisations, and Cortés had already hinted that city-dwelling emperors, rich in gold, owning handsome books, were more like the Moors than the Taínos and Caribs, even if they did sanction human sacrifices and eat the victims. Aristotle, if any of the conquistadores cared to read him, had insisted that living in cities was a condition of civilisation.

The Encounters Continue

Elsewhere, history seemed to repeat itself when Europeans encountered 'primitive' peoples whose way of life was so very different from their own, who almost invariably lacked writing and whose technology was far less developed (meaning they were easy to master). In 1513, hoping to find the Fountain of Youth for his ageing master Ferdinand of Aragon, Juan Ponce de León encountered Calusa Indians in Florida, marking the first Spanish contact with tribes of North American Indians; the Calusa Indians lived in large communities and were great engineers of mounds, ramps and causeways.[7]

Magellan's voyage around South America in 1519–20 introduced the gigantic, hardy Patagonian Indians to European explorers; but when the Vicenzan gentleman Antonio Pigafetta wrote a memoir of this great voyage, he clearly conveyed the contrast between the primitive Indians of the New World and the cultured Indians of the Old World. In Patagonia the natives chewed raw meat, even unskinned rodents;[8] but across the Pacific, in the Spice Islands, kings dined off porcelain plates and ate delicately prepared meals of fish and pork spiced with ginger.[9] Here, at last, was the outermost edge of the world of the Indies described by Marco Polo, which Columbus had been unable to reach. But there was always hope of finding new marvels within the Americas. Encounters between native Indians and Spaniards in search of the magical island of 'California' took place in Baja California from the 1530s onwards, and then further up the coast in the modern State of California.[10] Pizarro's conquest of Peru was followed by the invasion of Chile in the 1540s, against a background of constant rebellion among the Mapuche Indians; although much of Chile had been notionally under Inca sovereignty, the land was inhabited by peoples who were closer in style of life to many of the 'primitive' peoples examined in this book. Cabeza de Vaca's epic journey right across southern North America between 1528 and 1536 brought him into contact with large numbers of unsuspected peoples in the interior, whose way of life he reported in a matter-of-fact way.[11] European readers were hungry for tales, including tall tales, about the astonishingly diverse American peoples.

Spanish arrogance, as it was seen by Spain's rivals, occasionally encouraged counter-arguments. In the late sixteenth century, the French attempt to gain a foothold in Brazil led the Catholic missionary Thevet and the Protestant missionary Léry to describe the life of the Tupí Indians, including their cannibal feasts. In *The Great Voyages*, printed between 1590 and 1634, the artist Theodore de Bry and his sons tickled the fancy, including the erotic fancy, of Europeans with their copperplate prints depicting the native peoples of America. There was one that showed Columbus arriving on the shores of the New World and claiming for Spain the right to dominion over a naked, submissive female figure who represented America; the illustrations were attached to reprinted texts by Peter Martyr, Vespucci and others, but it was the illustrations that took charge. De Bry used his prints as propaganda for the Protestant cause: he included an adapted version of Léry's description of Brazil in his series, and was happy to include an illustrated edition of some of las Casas' writings, which presented Catholic Spain in the worst possible light.[12] Since the de Bry prints were copied again and again in the seventeenth century, they helped to fix a mental image of the American peoples. But the enduring image was still one of exotic peoples, savage in their ways, addicted to cannibalism, naked like animals, charged, though, with what readers might see as an alluring sexual energy, ready, indeed, to be mastered. England too began to claim its share, a century after John Cabot's voyage. A set of drawings and watercolours by John White, produced in the 1580s, included images of Floridan and Brazilian Indians, though the artist's main purpose was to advertise the way of life of the Algonquin Indians in North America. His pictures were copied by de Bry and other engravers, and offered information and encouragement to investors in the English ventures to America around 1600. White's pictures show how the physical appearance, religious rites and daily life of the naked peoples of the New World continued to exercise an irresistible fascination a century after Columbus' first voyage.[13]

In other quarters of the globe, other conquerors than the Spaniards, even without the dubious help of 'The Requirement', showed a similar set of assumptions: that it was right to claim dominion in lands inhabited solely by primitive peoples; that these peoples, even if legally free, could not enjoy the status of the conquerors, though exceptions might be made for a few leaders; that these peoples were a source of labour and of sexual gratification. The Pacific, already penetrated by the Spaniards and the Portuguese in the sixteenth century, in later centuries became the theatre for a new wave of encounters and conquests by the Dutch and the English. Australia came to be seen by the British conquerors as a *terra nullius*, a vast no-man's-land, for they misunderstood the Aborigines' territorial sense. Many European settlers treated the Aborigines as wild beasts, extirpating completely the native population of Tasmania. Similar stories can be told of the colonisation of large tracts of North America. Admittedly, there were some observers who saw dignity and heroism in their opponents, notably Alonso de Ercilla, the author of a late sixteenth-century epic poem recording the Spanish conquest of the Araucanian Indians of Chile, whom he endowed with chivalric qualities. However, the history of these often violent encounters is not over yet. Atrocities have continued in remote parts of Brazil, where native tribes live lives not so very different from what was described by Caminha and Gonneville. Again, greed for material resources has pushed aside any sense that these peoples are rational, sentient human beings with rights.

The age of the Renaissance did, then, see another 'discovery of man' than that which has been identified in the culture of the Italian Renaissance.[14] In one sense, it was an incomplete discovery, for not all observers accepted that the newly discovered peoples were fully human. Often they drew sharp lines between good people who could be redeemed by being shown the arts of civilisation, and (importantly) by becoming Christian, and bad folk who were fundamentally evil, ignorant, bestial. And yet it was precisely the demotion of some or all of these peoples to a lower status than Europeans that moulded European relations with the wider world. The discovery of man in the Atlantic transformed the world, laying the basis for the great empires of Spain, Portugal and eventually England, France and Holland. It transformed the Americas, by mortality and conquest, and Africa, as demand for slaves to work mines and plantations in the Americas grew exponentially. But it also jolted Renaissance Europe: Christians, Jews and Muslims were only part of God's Creation. Were these new men and women Adam's children? Did they have souls that needed to be saved, or had they been set in place simply to serve the greater cause of Christendom? On balance, it was the second explanation that won the argument. Few heeded the words of the prophet Malachi: 'have we not all one father? Has not one God created us? Why do we deal treacherously, every man against his brother, profaning the covenant of our forefathers?'[15]

ABBREVIATIONS

Book of prophecies: West, D.C., and Kling, A., *The* libro de las profecías *of Christopher Columbus*, Gainesville FL, 1991.

Cabot voyages: Williamson, J.A., *The Cabot voyages and Bristol discovery under Henry VIII*, Hakluyt Society, 1962.

Cabral's voyage: Greenlee, W.B., *Cabral's voyage to Brazil and India*, Hakluyt Society, 1938/1995.

Col. It.: Davies, M., ed., *Columbus in Italy: an Italian versification of the Letter on the Discovery of the New World*, London, 1991.

Da Gama: *Journal of the first voyage of Vasco da Gama, 1497–1499*, ed. E.G. Ravenstein, Hakluyt Society, 1898.

Da Mosto: Cà da Mosto, Alvise da, *The voyages of Cadamosto and other documents on western Africa in the second half of the fifteenth century*, ed. G.R. Crone, Hakluyt Society, 1937.

De Canaria: Pastore Stocchi, M., 'Il *De Canaria* boccaccesco e un "locus deperditus" nel *De insulis* di Domenico Silvestri', *Rinascimento*, 10 (1959), pp. 153–6.

Espinosa: Espinosa, Alonso de, *The Guanches of Tenerife*, Hakluyt Society, 1907.

Four voyages: Jane, C., ed. *The four voyages of Columbus*, 2 vols, Hakluyt Society (and later one vol. edition; English translation on even pages), 1929–32.

Gerald of Wales: Gerald of Wales, *The history and topography of Ireland*, trans. J.J. O'Meara, Harmondsworth, 1982.

Glas: Glas, Captain G., *The history of the discovery and conquest of the Canary Islands translated from a Spanish manuscript, lately found in the island of Palma, with an enquiry into the origins of the ancient inhabitants*, 1st edn, London, 1764.

Gonneville: d'Avézac, M., ed., *Relation authentique du voyage du Capitaine de Gonneville ès nouvelles terres des Indes*, Paris, 1869.

Hemmerlein: *Felicis Malleoli vulgo Hemmerlein Decretorum Doctoris Iureconsultissimi, De nobilitate et rusticitate Dialogus*, 1497.

L. Am.: Ife, B.W., *Letters from America: Columbus's first accounts of the 1492 voyages*, King's College London School of Humanities, 1992.

Laws of Burgos: Simpson, J.B., ed. and trans., *The Laws of Burgos of 1512–1513: royal ordinances for the good government and treatment of the Indians*, San Francisco, 1960.

LC, *DI*: Briffault, H., trans., *The devastation of the Indies: a brief account*, Baltimore MD, 1992.

Le Canarien: *Le Canarien: manuscritos, transcripción y traducción*, ed. B. Pico, E. Aznar and D. Corbella (Fontes Rerum Canariarum, vol. 12), La Laguna, Tenerife, 2003.

Lettera: *Lettera di Amerigo Vespucci delle isole nouamente trouate in Quattro suoi viaggi*, Florence, 1505.

Libretto: Pietro Martire d'Anghiera, *Libretto de tutta la nauigatione de re de Spagna de le isole et terreni nouamente trouati, Venice, 1504: a facsimile from the only known perfect copy, now in the John Carter Brown Library, of the famous little book of the King of Spain's voyages*, ed. L.C. Wroth, Paris, 1929; also reproduced from the same text in Alvise da Cà da Mosto, *Questa e una opera necessaria a tutti li naviga[n]ti (1490)*, ed. F. Fernández-Armesto, Delmar NY, 1992.

Mandeville: Mandeville, John, *The Travels of John Mandeville*, trans. C.W.R.D. Moseley, Harmondsworth, 1983.

Matías de Paz: Zavala, S., and Millares Carlo, A., eds and trans, Juan López de Palacios Rubios, *De las islas del mar Océano*, Fray Matías de Paz, *Del dominio de los reyes de España sobre los indios*, Mexico City and Buenos Aires, 1954.

Mundus Novus: *Mundus Novus. Albericus [sic] Vesputius Laurentio Petri de Medicis salutem plurimam dixit*, Rome, c. 1502.

NRC: *Nuova Raccolta Colombiana*, English edition.

Palacios Rubios: Zavala, S., and Millares Carlo, A., eds and trans, Juan López de Palacios Rubios, *De las islas del mar Océano*, Fray Matías de Paz, *Del dominio de los reyes de España sobre los indios*, Mexico City and Buenos Aires, 1954, and Biblioteca Nacional Madrid, MS 17641.

Pané: Fray Ramón Pané, *Relación acerca de las antigüedades de los Indios*, ed. J.J. Arrom, 8th ed., Mexico City and Buenos Aires, 1988; Fray Ramón Pané, *An account of the antiquities of the Indians*, ed. J.J. Arrom, trans. S.C. Griswold, Durham NC, 1999.

RC ii: Nader, H., and Formisano, L., eds, *The Book of Privileges issued to Christopher Columbus by King Fernando and Queen Isabel*, Repertorium Columbianum, vol. 2, 1996.

RC iv: Dotson, J., and Agosto, A., eds, *Christopher Columbus and his family*, Repertorium Columbianum, vol. 4, 1998.

RC v, *PM*: Eatough, G., ed., *Selections from Peter Martyr*, Repertorium Columbianum, vol. 5, 1998.

RC vi, DB: Lardicci, F., ed., *A synoptic edition of the log of Columbus' first voyage*, Repertorium Columbianum, vol. 6, 1999 [text 'DB' and text 'LC'].

RC vii, *LC*: Griffin, N., ed., *Las Casas on Columbus: background and the second and fourth voyages*, Repertorium Columbianum, vol. 7, 1999.

RC viii, TCL: Phillips, W.D., ed., *Testimonies from the Columbian lawsuits*, Repertorium Columbianum, vol. 8, 2000.

RC ix, *Oviedo*: Carrillo, J., *Oviedo on Columbus*, Repertorium Columbianum, vol. 9, 2000.

RC x, *LD*: Symcox, G., ed., *Italian Reports on America 1493–1522: letters, dispatches, and papal bulls*, Repertorium Columbianum, vol. 10, 2001.

RC xi: Symcox, G., and Carrillo, J., eds, *Las Casas on Columbus: the third voyage*, Repertorium Columbianum, vol. 11, 2001.

RC xii: Formisano, L., *Italian reports on America 1493–1522: accounts by contemporary observers*, Repertorium Columbianum, vol. 12, 2002.

RC xiii, *FC*: Caraci Luzzana, B., Symcox, G., and Sullivan, B., eds, *The history of the life and deeds of the Admiral Don Christopher Columbus attributed to his son Fernando Colón*, Repertorium Columbianum, vol. 13, 2004.

Scyllacius: Baldacci, O., ed., *Delle Isole del Mare Meridiano e Indiano recentemente scoperte*, Florence, 1992.

Telde: Rumeu de Armas, A., *El Obispado de Telde: misioneros mallorquines y catalanes en el Atlántico*, 2nd edn, Madrid and Telde, 1986.

Torriani: Torriani, L., *Descrição e história do reino das Ilhas Canarias antes ditas Afortunadas, com o paracer das suas fortificações*, ed. J.M. Azevedo e Silva, Lisbon, 1999.

Vespucci: Formisano, L., ed., *Letters from a New World: Amerigo Vespucci's discovery of America*, New York 1992 [ep.: Letter; app.: Appendix].

Vitoria: Vitoria, F. de, *Political Writings*, ed. A. Pagden and J. Lawrance, Cambridge, 1991.

Wild majesty: Hulme, P., and Whitehead, N., *Wild majesty: encounters with Caribs from Columbus to the present day*, Oxford, 1992.

NOTES

Many of the primary sources I have used exist in several editions, some of which include both original texts and translations, not necessarily on facing pages. Most of the references to primary sources in the notes, especially to the collection known as the Repertorium Columbianum, are therefore to documents and paragraphs rather than pages, in the hope that they will then be useful to those with access to different editions such as the lavish Nuova Raccolta Colombiana, which itself exists in Italian and English versions; I have also mentioned a number of editions of the Caminha letter and other widely published sources. In some cases, such as the editions of Ramón Pané's tract and several Hakluyt Society volumes, translated texts are especially well annotated and useful. References to pages rather than sections are prefaced by 'p.' or 'pp.'. Notes that mention items without date of publication are referring to items in the list of primary sources (pp. 346–51), and many of these titles have been abbreviated – see my list of abbreviations on pp. 314–16. In the list of secondary literature (pp. 351–67), books and articles are listed by author and date, to match the brief references in the notes. Spanish authors are listed in accordance with convention under the first element in their surname (e.g. Carlos-José Hernando Sánchez is under Hernando); this includes books in Catalan and Galician. Portuguese names are conventionally listed under the final name (e.g. Felipe Themudo Barata is under Barata). Since the emphasis in the notes is on primary sources, some items in the list of secondary literature do not appear in the notes but have been included because of their relevance and importance.

Chapter 1: Finding People from Other Worlds

1. Trinkaus and Shipman (1993), pp. 402–9.
2. Trinkaus and Shipman (1993), pp. 278–83, 312–22.
3. Augustine, *City of God*, xviii, c. 8.
4. Fernández-Armesto (2004).
5. Hanke (1959); Hanke (2002); also Tierney (1997).
6. Earle and Lowe (2005); Blumenthal (2007).

7. Merediz (2004).
8. *Daily Telegraph*, 5 October 2005.
9. Davies (1995), esp. pp. 28–33.
10. Mark 16:15–16; cf. Matthew 28:19–20; also *Book of prophecies*, pp. 152–3.
11. Davies (1995), p. 29.
12. Davies (1995), p. 21.
13. Davies (1995), pp. 31–2.
14. *Daily Telegraph*, 5 October 2005.
15. Pagden (1986).
16. Cf. Neandertal 'cannibals': Trinkaus and Shipman (1993), p. 105.

Chapter 2: Wild Men and Wanderers

1. RC vi, DB c. 1.
2. Greenblatt (1991).
3. RC vi, DB c. 1.
4. Flint (1992a) and (1992b), pp. 56–61.
5. Flint (1992b), p. 59; cf. Greenblatt (1991), p. 68.
6. Fernández-Armesto (1991).
7. Gil and Varela, *Cartas*, pp. 217–23.
8. RC ix, *Oviedo*, 3.3.2; cf. Flint (1992b), pp. 42–3.
9. See RC iv; Taviani (1985).
10. Cf. Kayserling (2002).
11. *Libretto*, f. 1r; RC xiii, *FC* c. 3; RC ix, *Oviedo*, 3.3.3.
12. RC xiii, *FC* c. 4.
13. *Book of prophecies*, pp. 224–7.
14. RC ii.
15. RC x, *LD*, no. 43.
16. Mandeville, c. 29.
17. Cited in Bernheimer (1952), p. 5.
18. Bartlett (2006), p. 132.
19. Pym (2007), pp. 3–9; Geremek (1992), pp. 151–72; Fraser (1992), pp. 60–162 (Iberia: 97–102).
20. Pym (2007), pp. 24–5.
21. Bernheimer (1952); Husband (1980); Mason (1990), pp. 71–94.
22. Bernheimer (1952), p. 69.
23. Bernheimer (1952), p. 11.
24. Bernheimer (1952), pp. 5–6, 9–10, 60–1, 115, 155.
25. O'Reilly (1998), pp. 105–6; McNally and Florescu (1974), pp. 31–126.
26. Bernheimer (1952), p. 134.
27. Bernheimer (1952), plate 29 and pp. 103–7.
28. Magasich-Airola and de Beer (2006).
29. Bartlett (2006), p. 139.
30. Gerald of Wales, i, cc. 2, 30; Bartlett (2006).

31. Gerald of Wales, ii, c. 52.
32. Gerald of Wales, ii, cc. 53–4, 56.
33. Gerald of Wales, iii, c. 93.
34. Gerald of Wales, iii, c. 93.
35. Gerald of Wales, iii, c. 93.
36. Gerald of Wales, iii, c. 94.
37. Gerald of Wales, iii, c. 98.
38. Gerald of Wales, iii, c. 103; Bartlett (2006), p. 134.
39. Friedman (1981); Flint (1992a) and (1992b), pp. 48–56.
40. Cf. Greenblatt (1991), pp. 26–51.
41. Mandeville, c. 22.
42. Mandeville, c. 21.
43. Abulafia, A.S. (1995), pp. 24, 88, 129, 133.
44. Cicero, *De legibus*, 1.7.22–3, pp. 320–1.
45. Abulafia, D. (1997), pp. 94–101.

Chapter 3: Images of Asia

1. Idrisi, cited by Yule in Marco Polo, ii, 256 (not identifiable in Idrisi, *Géographie*).
2. Flint (1992b), pp. 65–8.
3. E.g. Gonville and Caius College, Cambridge, MS 162/83.
4. Cf. Davidson (1997).
5. Mandeville, cc. 23–6.
6. Fuson (1995), pp. 118–19; Johnson, D. (1997), pp. 91–112.
7. Verlinden (1970), pp. 181–95; Focus Behaim-Globus (1992); also Fernández-Armesto (1991), p. xxi.
8. Keene (2003).
9. Von Verschuer (1988); Souyri (2001/2).
10. Marco Polo, ii, p. 253 cf. Pipino, f. 73v; Magasich-Airola and de Beer (2006), pp. 58–9.
11. Marco Polo, ii, pp. 254–5.
12. Marco Polo, ii, pp. 253–4; Pipino, f. 74v, adds cannibalistic Japanese, confusing Marco Polo ii, p. 264 (on India) with Japan.
13. Wood (1995).
14. Rumeu de Armas (1985), pp. 94–5.
15. Rumeu de Armas (1985), p. 96.
16. Marinescu (1994), pp. 13–28.
17. RC vi, DB c. 1.
18. RC vi, DB c. 36.
19. RC vi, DB c. 41.
20. RC vi, DB c. 51.
21. Vogt (1979), pp. 19–58; Hair (1994).
22. RC ii.
23. RC vi, DB c. 29.

Chapter 4: Innocence and Wildness in the Canary Islands

1. Cf. Thornton, I. (2007).
2. Cachey (1995), p. 18.
3. Martorell and Martí de Galba, *Tirant lo Blanc*, p. 8; Goodman (1998), pp. 131–3; Farrujia de la Rosa (2005), p. 11.
4. Idrisi, *Géographie*, i, pp. 101–5.
5. Merediz (2004), p. 22, n. 32.
6. Idrisi, *Géographie*, i, pp. 105–6.
7. Pifarré Torres (2002).
8. Abulafia, D. (1994), p. 208.
9. Moore (1972), pp. 387–400; also Mauny (1960).
10. Zurara, *Chronicle*, cc. 8–9, i. pp. 30–4.
11. There is fuller annotation in Abulafia, D. (2002).
12. *De Canaria*, p. 153.
13. *De Canaria*, p. 153.
14. Verlinden (1958c), pp. 1173–209.
15. *De Canaria*, p. 153.
16. *De Canaria*, p. 154.
17. *De Canaria*, pp. 153–4, 156.
18. *De Canaria*, p. 154.
19. *De Canaria*, pp. 154, 155.
20. *De Canaria*, p. 154; cf. Hyde (1993), p. 200.
21. *De Canaria*, p. 155.
22. *De Canaria*, p. 155.
23. *De Canaria*, p. 156.
24. *De Canaria*, p. 156.
25. Hyde (1993), p. 200.
26. *De Canaria*, p. 155.
27. *De Canaria*, pp. 145–6, p. 153; Hulme (1994), p. 181; Cachey (1995), pp. 115–16.
28. Cf. Hyde (1982), pp. 125–47; Hyde (1993), pp. 199–202; also Wallace (2004), pp. 203–38.
29. Pliny the Elder, 2.6.202.
30. Cachey (1995), pp. 89–93.
31. Cary and Warmington (1963), pp. 69, 125, 245; Manfredi (1996).
32. *De Canaria*, pp. 146–53; Hyde (1993), p. 202 (Domenico Silvestri and Domenico Bandini); Martínez (1996), pp. 155–204.
33. Hyde (1993), pp. 199–202; Cachey (1995), pp. 83–121.
34. Petrarca, *De vita solitaria*, pp. 125–6; Petrarch, *The life of solitude*, p. 267.
35. Hulme (1994), pp. 184, 182–3.
36. Petrarca, *De vita solitaria*, pp. 125–6.
37. Torriani, p. 159.
38. Hulme (1994), 182–3; cf. Scyllacius, pp. 48, 68, 91: *sine lege, nudo corpore*.

39. Hulme (1994), pp. 184–6, 163–4.
40. Espinosa, ii, c. 2.
41. Espinosa, ii, c. 3.
42. Espinosa, ii, c. 1.
43. Espinosa, ii, cc. 11–12.
44. I Samuel 5:10.
45. Espinosa, ii, c. 13, and preface.
46. Espinosa, ii, c. 4.
47. Espinosa, iv.
48. Espinosa, i, c. 10.
49. Espinosa, i, cc. 4, 10; cf. Merediz (2004), p. 34 (Bernáldez).
50. Espinosa, ii, c. 1.
51. Merediz (2004), pp. 45–53, 61–82.
52. Espinosa, preface; cf. Merediz (2004), p. 54 and n. 73.
53. Espinosa, i, c. 5.

Chapter 5: The Canary Islanders, 1341–1496

1. Verlinden (1958a); Fernández-Armesto (1986), pp. 12–34.
2. Espinosa, i, c. 9.
3. *African Myths of Origins*; Ryder (1969), pp. 4–11.
4. Merediz (2004), pp. 38–82.
5. Abreu Galindo, *Historia*, pp. 25–9.
6. Abreu Galindo, *Historia*, p. 41.
7. Aznar Vallejo (1994), pp. 140–1.
8. Espinosa, i, c. 9.
9. Jiménez González (1990), pp. 37–50.
10. Glas, *History* (2nd edn, 1767), vol. i, pp. i–viii, esp. p. v.
11. Glas, *History*, pp. 63–4; cf. Abreu Galindo, *Historia*, p. 147.
12. Scyllacius, pp. 48, 68, 92.
13. Espinosa, pp. xx–xxvi; Glas, *History*, pp. 174–80.
14. Farrujia de la Rosa (2005).
15. Aznar Vallejo (1994), pp. 136–7; cf. Concepción (1984).
16. Manfredi (1996); Cachey (1995).
17. Tejera Gaspar (1992).
18. Jiménez González (1992).
19. Martín Rodríguez (1992).
20. Cabrera Pérez (1992).
21. Navarro Mederos (1993).
22. De la Cruz Jiménez Gómez (1993).
23. Cabrera Pérez (1993).
24. As in Mercer (1980).
25. Bernáldez, *Memorias*, c. 64, pp. 138–9; c. 64, p. 139; c. 132, pp. 337–8; c. 134, pp. 339–41; also Merediz (2004), pp. 33–4.

26. Cod. 314, Secção de Reservados, Biblioteca Geral da Universidade de Coimbra.

27. Torriani, plate 28, f. 36v, c. 34, and pp. 81–2.

28. Torriani, plate 29, f. 81r, c. 59, and p. 158.

29. Zurara, *Chronicle*, cc. 79–83, vol. ii, pp. 237–44.

30. Zurara, *Chronicle*, c. 80, ii, pp. 241–2; Merediz (2004), p. 29.

31. Cà da Mosto, *Voyages*, c. 8, p. 14.

32. Jiménez González (1990), p. 183.

33. Jiménez González (1990), pp. 55–79.

34. Abreu Galindo, *Historia*, p. 160.

35. Hemmerlein, f. 105v.

36. Torriani, plate 27, f. 34r, c. 31, and p. 76.

37. www.piramidesdeguimar.net/ingles/pagina.htm.

38. Torriani, plate 25, f. 25r, c. 21, and p. 56.

39. Torriani, plate 26, f. 35r, c. 32, and p. 79.

40. Pérez Saavedra (1982).

41. Eddy (1989).

42. Torriani, plate 31, f. 37v, c. 35, and p. 83.

43. Espinosa, i, c. 9.

44. Espinosa, i, c. 9; cf. i, c. 10.

45. Espinosa, i, cc. 4, 10.

46. Cicero, *De legibus*, 1.8.24–5, pp. 324–5.

47. McGrade (1982), pp. 751–2; Luscombe (1982), pp. 760–1.

48. Abreu Galindo, *Historia*, p. 150; Glas, *History*, pp. 69–76; Tejera Gaspar (1987); Jiménez González (1990), pp. 235–54.

49. Zurara, *Chronicle*, c. 79, ii, p. 237.

50. Zurara, *Chronicle*, c. 82, ii, p. 243; cf. c. 80, ii, p. 242 (Gomera).

51. Abreu Galindo, *Historia*, p. 150; Glas, *History*, p. 69; Nuñez de la Pena, *Conquista*, p. 27: 'Harimaguadas'.

52. Cf. Merediz (2004), p. 34 (from Bernáldez).

53. Sannazaro, *Arcadia*, p. 44.

54. Nuñez de la Pena, *Conquista*, pp. 22–3, 27, expanding on Espinosa.

55. Espinosa, i, c. 8.

56. Espinosa, i, c. 8.

57. Abreu Galindo, *Historia*, p. 171; Glas, *History* p. 75.

58. Abreu Galindo, *Historia*, p. 149.

59. Glas, *History*, p. 71; Zurara, c. 79, ii, p. 241; Merediz (2004), p. 30.

60. Cf. Espinosa i, c. 7.

61. *Le Canarien*, pp. 145, 351; Torriani, p. 34.

62. Cà da Mosto, *Voyages*, c. 8, p. 13.

63. Zurara, *Chronicle*, c. 80, ii, p. 242.

64. Hemmerlein, f. 105r.

Chapter 6: Rights of Dominion, 1341–1496

1. Abreu Galindo, *Historia*, pp. 39–42.
2. Abulafia, D. (1994), pp. 16–17.
3. Telde, p. 40.
4. Telde, pp. 23–40 and docs 1–10; Fernández-Armesto (1987), pp. 159–66; Abulafia, D. (1994), pp. 208–14.
5. De la Roncière (1924), plate X; Catalan world map (1934), sheet 4.
6. Godinho (1956).
7. Hemmerlein, ff. 105r–106r; Telde, pp. 40–2, 92–6.
8. Hemmerlein, f. 105r.
9. Marinescu (1994), pp. 18, 199–200.
10. Hemmerlein, f. 105r, amending 'Adriatic' to 'Atlantic'.
11. Hemmerlein, f. 105v.
12. Hemmerlein, f. 105v.
13. Hemmerlein, f. 105v.
14. Hemmerlein, ff. 105v–106r.
15. Hemmerlein, f. 105v.
16. Hemmerlein, f. 106r.
17. Abulafia, D. (1997), pp. 94–101.
18. Abulafia, D. (1997), pp. 99–100.
19. Telde, pp. 183–4, doc. 18.
20. Rowell (1994); Mażeika (1994), pp. 63–76.
21. Muldoon (1979b), pp. 125–95; Muldoon (1998).
22. Abreu Galindo, *Historia*, p. 40; Weckmann (1992); Daumet (1913), pp. 38–67.
23. Muldoon (1979a), pp. 88–9, from Vatican Register 62.
24. Muldoon (1979a), p. 188.
25. Glas, *History*, p. 79; cf. Abreu Galindo, p. 42.
26. Glas, *History*, p. 80; cf. Abreu Galindo, p. 41.
27. Abreu Galindo, *Historia*, p. 41.
28. Abreu Galindo, *Historia*, p. 42; Glas, *History*, pp. 81–2.
29. Glas, *History*, pp. 81–2.

Chapter 7: Quarrelsome Conquerors, 1402–44

1. Goodman (1986), pp. 104–33; Keen (1986), pp. 121–34.
2. Fernández-Armesto (1987), p. 174.
3. Fernández-Armesto (1987), p. 176.
4. *Le Canarien*, pp. 72–5; Merediz (2004), p. 28.
5. Cf. Merediz (2004), p. 29.
6. Cf. Merediz (2004), p. 34 (from Bernáldez).
7. British Library, London, MS Egerton 2709, f. 22r.
8. MS Egerton 2709, f. 1v; *Le Canarien*, pp. 4–5, 148–9.
9. *Le Canarien*, pp. 8–9, 154–5.

10. MS Egerton 2709, f. 32r: *grant stature fors et hardis.*
11. Moniz de Bettencourt (1993).
12. Russell (2000), pp. 83, 270; cf. Russell (1984).
13. Also Johnson, H.B. (2004).
14. Russell (2000), p. 83.
15. Russell (2000), pp. 94, 98.
16. Verlinden (1970), pp. 98–112; Diffie (1960); Hanson (2001).
17. Barata (1998), pp. 134–7, 206–9, 398–408; Fonseca and Cadeddu (2001).
18. Ferreira Priegue (1988), pp. 733–44; Ferreira Priegue, *Fuentes.*
19. Marques (1998).
20. RC xiii, *FC* c. 5.
21. Blake, *Europeans*, i, doc. 1, pp. 64–7.
22. Zurara, *Chronicle*, c. 5, i, p. 18.
23. Zurara, *Chronicle*, c. 68, i, p. 207.
24. Zurara, *Chronicle*, cc. 68–9, i, pp. 208–13.
25. Muldoon (1979a), p. 121; cf. Hulme (1994), p. 187.
26. Muldoon (1979a), p. 121.
27. Muldoon (1979b), pp. 124–5; Williams (1990), pp. 71–2.
28. Muldoon (1979b), p. 125.
29. Merediz (2004), pp. 17–18.
30. Zurara, *Chronicle*, c. 68, i, p. 207–8.

Chapter 8: Gold and Slaves, 1444–96

1. Axelson (1973).
2. Saunders (1982), pp. 62–112; Blumenthal (2008); cf. Heers (1981); sugar: Abulafia, D. (2000), pp. 105–19.
3. Zurara, *Chronicle*, c. 26, i, p. 83; Saunders (1982), p. 35.
4. Zurara, *Chronicle*, c. 26, i, pp. 81, 84; cf. c. 25, pp. 80–3, and Wolf (1994).
5. Blumenthal (2007).
6. Oliver and Atmore (2001); cf. Davidson (1998).
7. Ryder (1969), pp. 24–41.
8. Ryder (1969), p. 30.
9. Cà da Mosto, *Voyages*, cc. 15–19, pp. 29–34; Saunders (1982); Thomas (1997); Thornton (1998).
10. Cà da Mosto, *Voyages*, c. 13, p. 20.
11. Cà da Mosto, *Voyages*, c. 31, p. 48.
12. Cà da Mosto, *Voyages*, c. 22, p. 38.
13. Cà da Mosto, *Voyages*, c. 25, p. 41; cf. Diogo Gomes in Cà da Mosto, p. 98.
14. Malfante in Cà da Mosto, *Voyages*, p. 89.
15. Diogo Gomes in Cà da Mosto, *Voyages*, p. 95.
16. Lowe in Lowe and Earle (2005), pp. 1–47; Blumenthal (2007).
17. Genesis 9:22–7; Blumenthal (2007); Schorsch (2004), pp. 17–49.
18. Glas, *History*, p. 142.

19. Belenguer Cebrià (1976); cf. Peláez (1981).
20. Abreu Galindo, *Historia*, p. 180; Glas, *History*, pp. 83–4.
21. Abreu Galindo, *Historia*, p. 211; Glas, *History*, pp. 104–7, esp. p. 106.
22. Espinosa, iii, c. 4.
23. Espinosa, iii, c. 3.
24. Espinosa, iii, c. 4; cf. c. 10.
25. Espinosa, iii, c. 4.
26. Espinosa, iii, c. 6.
27. Espinosa, iii, c. 11.
28. Espinosa, iii, c. 9.
29. Bernáldez, *Memorias*, c. 132, pp. 337–8; c. 134, p. 144; Merediz (2004), p. 34.
30. Espinosa, iii, c. 12; Fernández-Armesto (1982); Aznar Vallejo (1983).
31. Otte (1996).
32. Fernández-Armesto (1982), pp. 36–8; Blumenthal (2008).
33. Fernández-Armesto (1982), doc. 3, pp. 213–14.

Chapter 9: From the Old Canaries to the New Canaries, 1492

1. RC vi, DB c. 1.
2. RC vi, DB c. 4.
3. RC vi, DB c. 5.
4. RC vi, DB c. 22.
5. RC vi, DB c. 12.
6. RC vi, DB c. 26.
7. Zerubavel (1992), pp. 26–7.
8. Cf. Livingston (2004).
9. Cf. Henige (1991).
10. RC vi, DB c. 27.
11. *L. Am.*, pp. 58–9; also in *Spanish letter of Columbus* (Quaritch).
12. RC vi, DB c. 48.
13. RC vi, DB c. 29.
14. RC vi, DB c. 28.
15. RC vi, DB c. 28.
16. RC vi, DB c. 28.
17. RC vi, DB c. 29; but cf. *L. Am.*, pp. 52–3.
18. RC vi, DB c. 29.
19. RC vi, DB c. 29.
20. RC vi, DB c. 28.
21. RC vi, DB c. 28.
22. RC vi, DB c. 28.
23. RC vi, DB c. 30.
24. *L. Am*, pp. 28–9; Ife questionably translates *setas* as 'religious observance'.
25. RC vi, DB c. 30.

26. RC vi, DB c. 30.
27. RC vi, DB c. 29.

Chapter 10: Taínos and Caribs

1. Keegan (1992) for the Bahamas.
2. Keegan (1992), pp. 48–90.
3. Rouse (1992), pp. 26–70.
4. Rouse (1992), p. 27.
5. Tabío and Rey (1979); Dacal Moure and Rivero de la Calle (1996), pp. 14–20.
6. Cited by Sauer (1992), p. 184; cf. Keegan (1992), pp. 4–8.
7. Keegan (1992), p. 8.
8. Tabío and Rey (1979), pp. 18–95.
9. Dacal Moure and Rivero de la Calle (1996), colour plates 1–4, and illus. 1–11, pp. 71–5.
10. Granberry and Vescelius (2004).
11. Rouse (1992).
12. Rouse (1992), pp. 27, 37–42, and figs 11–12.
13. Rouse (1992), pp. 42–5.
14. Allaire (1997a), pp. 20–8; Wilson (2007), pp. 59–94.
15. Rouse (1992), pp. 71–137.
16. Rouse (1992), p. 7; Keegan (1992); Wilson (2007), pp. 4–8.
17. Rouse (1992), pp. 7–19; cf. Atkinson (2006), Siegel (2005).
18. Rouse (1992), p. 19.
19. Sauer (1992), pp. 53–4.
20. Sauer (1992), pp. 54–5.
21. Sauer (1992), p. 51.
22. Olsen (1974b), pp. 35–41; fig. 2, p. 36.
23. Iguana meat: RC v, *PM* 1.5.11.
24. Sauer (1992), p. 69.
25. Sauer (1992), pp. 65–6; Keegan (1992), pp. 159–60; Rosenblatt (1992), pp. 35–8.
26. Sale (1991); Walker (1991); Pieraccioli (1992); cf. Cassi (2007) and Wilson (2007), pp. 1, 10–11.
27. Sauer (1992), p. 61.
28. Sauer (1992), pp. 62–3.
29. Wilson, S. (1990), p. 57; Rouse (1992), fig. 4, p. 10, both reversing *bohío* and *caney*; cf. Sauer (1992), p. 63; Deagan and Cruxent (2002b), p. 34.
30. Plates in Kerchache (1994), pp. 32–57.
31. Plates in Kerchache (1994), pp. 158–221; cotton *zemís*: Kerchache (1994), pp. 158–65.
32. Rouse (1992), p. 117, fig. 29c.
33. Martinón-Torres (2007), pp. 194–204.

34. Olazagasti (1997), p. 132.
35. Rouse (1992), pp. 133–7; Dacal Moure and Rivero de la Calle (1996), pp. 47–50.
36. RC vi, DB c. 31.
37. Keegan (1992), pp. 49–51.
38. Cf. Olazagasti (1997), pp. 131–4.
39. Wilson, S. (1990), pp. 32–3 and *passim*.
40. Keegan (1992), pp. 106–11.
41. Sauer (1992), p. 50; Keegan (2007) for Caonabó.
42. Rouse (1992), p. 17.
43. Rouse (1992), pp. 112–15; Olazagasti (1997), pp. 137–9.
44. Rouse (1992), p. 114, fig. 28.
45. Keegan (1992), pp. 91–112.
46. *Four voyages*, i, pp. 30–1.
47. *Four voyages*, i, pp. 32–3.
48. *L. Am.*, pp. 40–1, amending to 'navigate' the inappropriate 'sail'.
49. Arens (1980); Barker, Hulme and Iversen (1998).
50. Keegan (1992), p. 9.
51. Lestringant (1994); cf. Hulme (1986); also Llewelyn Price (2003).
52. Hulme (1986), p. 81.
53. *Wild majesty*, p. 108; Cooper (1997).
54. Allaire (1997b), pp. 179–85.
55. Keegan (1992), pp. 8–10.
56. Rouse (1992), pp. 129–33; Allaire (1997b), p. 183.
57. Keegan (1992), p. 9; Allaire (1997b), p. 180.
58. *Wild majesty*, p. 105; see also Whitehead (1995).
59. *Wild majesty*, p. 112.
60. Cf. *Wild majesty*, p. 111.
61. *Wild majesty*, pp. 38–44, from 1580.
62. *Wild majesty*, p. 105.
63. *Wild majesty*, p. 109.
64. *Wild majesty*, p. 108.
65. *Wild majesty*, p. 109.
66. *Four voyages*, i, pp. 36–9.
67. *Four voyages*, i, pp. 38–9.
68. Rouse (1992), pp. 21–3; Cooper (1997), pp. 186–96.
69. *Four voyages*, i, pp. 40–1.

Chapter 11: Turtles, Shamans and Snorting Tubes

1. Pané, Introduction.
2. Stevens-Arroyo (2006).
3. See McDonald (2004).
4. Arrom in Pané, English ed., p. xiii.

5. Varela (2006), p. 35.
6. Las Casas in Pané, app. C, p. 72 (Spanish edn); p. 57 (English edn).
7. Abulafia, D. (1997), pp. 91–4.
8. Las Casas in Pané, app. C, p. 72 (Spanish edn); p. 56 (English edn).
9. Varela (2006), p. 203; also p. 103.
10. Columbus in Pané, app. A.
11. Varela (2006), pp. 100, 203.
12. Granberry and Vescelius (2004).
13. Las Casas in Pané, app. C, p. 72 (Spanish edn); p. 57 (English edn).
14. Varela (2006), p. 103.
15. Pané, cc. 25b–26.
16. Pané, app. A.
17. Pané, app. B and C.
18. Pané, Introduction.
19. Atkinson (2006); Siegel (2005); Curet (2005).
20. Las Casas in Pané, app. C, p. 72 (Spanish edn); p. 57 (English edn).
21. Las Casas in Pané, app. C, p. 72 (Spanish edn); p. 57 (English edn).
22. Pané, Introduction.
23. Pané, Introduction.
24. Pané, Introduction.
25. Las Casas in Pané, app. C, p. 76 (Spanish edn); p. 61 (English edn).
26. Las Casas in Pané, app. C, p. 74 (Spanish edn); p. 62 (English edn).
27. Pané, c. 1; cf. Stevens-Arroyo (2006).
28. Pané, c. 1.
29. Pané, cc. 3–4.
30. Pané, c. 5.
31. *Libro Copiador*, ii, 463.
32. Pané, c. 7.
33. Pané, c. 8 (amending Griswold); cf. Stevens-Arroyo (2006), pp. 171–2.
34. Pané, c. 9.
35. Pané, c. 10; cf. Stevens-Arroyo (2006), pp. 107–8.
36. Cf. Stevens-Arroyo (2006), pp. 100–1.
37. Pané, c. 11.
38. Peter Martyr in Pané, app. B, p. 63 (Spanish edn); p. 49 (English edn).
39. Pané, c. 11.
40. Cf. RC ix, *Oviedo*, 3.13.
41. Pané, c. 12.
42. Pané, c. 13.
43. Pané, c. 14.
44. Pané, c. 16.
45. Pané, c. 17.
46. Pané, cc. 18–18b.
47. Pané, c. 15.
48. Pané, cc. 15, 17.

49. Cf. Pané, c. 9.
50. Pané, c. 22.
51. Pané, c. 21.
52. Pané, c. 19; las Casas in Pané, app. C, p. 73 (Spanish edn); p. 57–8 (English edn).

Chapter 12: Cuba = Cipangu = Japan, 1492

1. RC vi, DB c. 31.
2. RC vi, DB c. 31.
3. RC vi, DB c. 31.
4. RC vi, DB c. 31.
5. Cf. Rouse (1992), p. 9.
6. RC vi, DB c. 31.
7. RC vi, DB c. 32.
8. RC vi, DB c. 32.
9. RC vi, DB c. 61.
10. Cf. Sale (1991), Whelan (1999).
11. RC vi, DB c. 34.
12. RC vi, DB c. 57.
13. RC vi, DB c. 38.
14. RC vi, DB c. 36.
15. RC vi, DB c. 41.
16. RC vi, DB c. 41.
17. RC vi, DB c. 42.
18. RC vi, DB c. 42.
19. RC vi, DB c. 42.
20. RC vi, DB c. 44.
21. RC vi, DB c. 45.
22. RC vi, DB c. 45.
23. Todorov (1984), pp. 30–1.
24. RC vi, DB c. 46.
25. RC vi, DB c. 53.
26. Martinón-Torres (2007), pp. 194–204.
27. RC vi, DB c. 51.
28. RC vi, DB c. 53.
29. RC xiii, FC, p. 50; cf. Sauer (1992), p. 60.
30. RC vi, DB c. 50.
31. RC vi, DB c. 51.
32. RC vi, DB c. 50.
33. RC vi, DB c. 50.
34. RC vi, DB c. 51.
35. RC vi, DB c. 51; cf. Granberry and Vescelius (2004).
36. RC vi, DB c. 58.

37. RC vi, DB c. 59; cf. RC vi, LC 59.
38. RC vi, DB c. 62.
39. Mandeville, c. 22.
40. RC vi, LC 59; cf. RC vi, DB cc. 70, 75.
41. RC vi, DB c. 62.
42. RC vi, DB c. 63.
43. RC vi, DB c. 63; cf. Greenblatt (1991) on wonder; also Cassi (2007).
44. RC vi, DB c. 64.
45. RC vi, DB c. 64.
46. RC vi, DB c. 65.
47. RC vi, DB c. 68.
48. RC vi, DB c. 68.

Chapter 13: La Navidad, 1492–3

1. RC vi, DB c. 79.
2. RC vi, DB c. 76.
3. RC vi, DB c. 76.
4. RC vi, DB c. 77.
5. RC vi, DB c. 77; cf. c. 80.
6. RC vi, DB c. 80.
7. RC vi, DB c. 81.
8. RC vi, DB c. 80.
9. RC vi, DB c. 82.
10. RC vi, DB c. 82.
11. RC vi, DB c. 84.
12. RC vi, DB c. 82.
13. RC vi, DB c. 82.
14. RC vi, DB c. 86.
15. RC vi, DB c. 85, 21 December 1492.
16. RC vi, DB c. 85.
17. RC vi, DB c. 85.
18. RC vi, DB c. 87.
19. RC vi, DB c. 88.
20. RC vi, DB c. 87.
21. RC vi, DB c. 89.
22. RC vi, DB c. 90.
23. RC vi, DB c. 91.
24. RC vi, DB c. 91.
25. RC vi, DB c. 91.
26. RC vi, DB c. 98.
27. RC vi, DB c. 94.
28. RC vi, DB c. 91.
29. RC vi, DB cc. 98, 102.

30. RC vi, DB c. 98.
31. RC vi, DB c. 99, note.
32. RC vi, DB c. 101.
33. RC vi, DB c. 103.
34. RC vi, DB c. 107.
35. *L. Am.*, pp. 40–1.
36. RC vi, DB c. 107.
37. *L. Am.*, pp. 40–1.
38. RC vi, DB c. 107.
39. *L. Am.*, pp. 40–1.
40. RC vi, DB c. 110; *L. Am.*, pp. 40–1; *Libro Copiador*, ii, 463; cf. Pané, c. 5.
41. RC vi, DB c. 109.
42. RC vi, DB c. 109.
43. RC vi, DB c. 109.

Chapter 14: First News of the New World

1. Catz (1993).
2. RC vi, DB c. 120.
3. *L. Am.*, pp. 35–9.
4. *Col. It.*, LX, giving 'cannibals are racked [*sic*]', but 'cannibal' is not in the text.
5. *L. Am.*, pp. 58–9.
6. *Col. It.*, XLV.
7. *Col. It.*, XLVII.
8. *Libretto*, ed. Wroth, pp. 4–6.
9. RC v, *PM* 1.1.3; *Libretto*, p. 3, f. 2r.
10. RC v, *PM* 1.1.3.
11. RC v, *PM* 1.1.11.
12. RC v, *PM* 1.1.11.
13. RC v, *PM* 1.1.6.
14. RC v, *PM* 1.1.6.
15. *Libretto*, p. 12, f. 6v.
16. RC v, *PM* 1.1.9.
17. RC v, *PM* 1.1.9.
18. *Libretto*, p. 4, f. 2v.
19. RC v, *PM* 1.1.8.
20. Cf. Gil and Varela, *Cartas*, p. 190 (Guillermo Coma).
21. RC v, *PM* 1.1.8.
22. RC v, *PM* 1.3.24.
23. *Col. It.*, XLV.
24. More, *Utopia*, pp. 18–20.
25. RC v, *PM* 1.2.13.
26. RC xii, 1.
27. RC xii, 2.

28. RC xii, 4.
29. RC x, *LD*, 1.
30. RC x, *LD*, 10.
31. Catz (1993).
32. RC vii, *LC* 3.3.17: *feliçes tierras, llenas de naciones infinitas.*
33. RC x, *LD*, 5–7.
34. RC x, *LD*, 5; RC vii, *LC* 3.3.18.
35. RC vii, *LC* 3.3.19.
36. RC x, *LD*, 6.
37. RC x, *LD*, 6.
38. RC x, *LD*, 6.
39. RC x, *LD*, 5, 6.
40. RC x, *LD*, 6.
41. RC x, *LD*, 7.
42. RC x, *LD*, 11.
43. See Abulafia, D. (1995).
44. Weckmann (1992).
45. RC x, *LD*, 7.

Chapter 15: Into the Caribbean, 1493–4

1. Gallinari (1999).
2. *Four voyages*, i, p. cxliv.
3. *Four voyages*, i, pp. 118–19: Bernáldez summarised the words of 'el doctor Anca ó Ochanca'.
4. *Four voyages*, i, pp. 24–5; RC xiii, *FC* 45; Scyllacius, pp. 50, 70, 97 (Dominica).
5. RC xiii, FC 46; cf. *Libro Copiador*, ii, 452.
6. *Four voyages*, i, pp. 26–7; Scyllacius, pp. 50, 70, 96.
7. Mandeville, c. 21.
8. Siegel (2005); Curet (2005).
9. RC xii, M. Cuneo, 7.2.1.5.
10. RC xii, M. Cuneo, 7.2.1.7.
11. *Four voyages*, i, pp. 28–9; RC xii, M. Cuneo, 7.2.1.7; the number of crew is given as seven or eleven.
12. *Four voyages*, i, pp. 30–1.
13. *Four voyages*, i, pp. 30–1.
14. *Four voyages*, i, pp. 30–1.
15. *Four voyages*, i, pp. 31–2.
16. *Four voyages*, i, pp. 32–3.
17. *Four voyages*, i, pp. 32–3.
18. *Four voyages*, i, pp. 32–3.
19. Scyllacius, pp. 52, 71, 101.
20. Cf. Montaigne, *Complete Works*, Essay 31.

21. *L. Am.*, pp. 40–1.
22. Cf. *Libro Copiador*, ii, 453 (S. Juan Baptista).
23. *Four voyages*, i, pp. 37–8, 44–5; RC xii, M. Cuneo, 7.2.1.7.
24. RC xii, M. Cuneo, 7.2.1.7.
25. RC xii, M. Cuneo, 7.2.1.7.
26. *Four voyages*, i, pp. 50–1.
27. *Four voyages*, i, pp. 45–5; also pp. 52–3.
28. *Four voyages*, i, pp. 53–5.
29. RC xii, M. Cuneo, 7.2.1.9.
30. *Four voyages*, i, pp. 53–5.
31. RC vii, *LC* 5.2.15.
32. *Libro Copiador*, ii, 459.
33. RC vii, *LC* 5.2.4.
34. RC vii, *LC* 5.2.5.
35. *Four voyages*, i, pp. 58–9.
36. RC vii, *LC* 5.2.6.
37. *Four voyages*, i, pp. 65–6.
38. *Four voyages*, i, pp. 66–7.
39. *Four voyages*, i, pp. 66–7.
40. Deagan and Cruxent (2002a and 2002b).
41. Cf. DeCorse (2001).
42. Deagan and Cruxent (2002b), pp. 53, 57, 96–7, 180–1.
43. *Four voyages*, i, pp. 64–5.
44. Deagan and Cruxent (2002b), pp. 198–200.
45. Deagan and Cruxent (2002b), pp. 146, 191–2.
46. Deagan and Cruxent (2002b), p. 198.
47. Deagan and Cruxent (2002b), pp. 194–8.

Chapter 16: Misrule in Hispaniola, 1494–6

1. *Four voyages*, i, pp. 116–17.
2. RC xiii, *FC* 55, p. 122.
3. *Four voyages*, i, pp. 126–7.
4. *Four voyages*, i, pp. 126–7.
5. *Four voyages*, i, pp. 130–1, 134–5, 136–7, 138–9.
6. *Four voyages*, i, pp. 138–9; also Bernáldez in *Four voyages*, i, pp. 142–3, 146–7.
7. *Four voyages*, i, pp. 142–3; RC xiii, *FC* 56, p. 123.
8. *Four voyages*, i, pp. 91–3.
9. RC vii, 5.4.41.
10. Keegan (2007).
11. RC xiii, *FC* 60, p. 130.
12. RC vii, 5.4.5.
13. RC vii, 5.4.5.
14. RC vii, 5.4.5.

15. RC vii, 5.4.6.
16. RC vii, 5.4.9.
17. Varela (2006), p. 98.
18. Varela (2006), pp. 99–100.
19. LC, *DI*, p. 41.
20. RC vii, 5.4.11–12.
21. RC vii, 5.4.11.
22. RC vii, 5.4.11.
23. RC vii, 5.4.22.
24. RC vii, 5.4.51.
25. Martinón-Torres (2007), pp. 194–204.
26. RC vii, 5.4.25–6.
27. RC vii, 5.4.30.
28. RC xiii, FC 61, p. 133; cf. Keegan (2007).
29. RC vii, 5.4.30; cf. 5.4.61.
30. LC, *DI*, p. 37.
31. RC vii, 5.4.46.
32. RC vii, 5.4.44.
33. RC vii, 5.4.47.
34. RC vii, 5.4.48.
35. Cook (1998).
36. RC vii, 5.4.51.
37. RC xiii, *FC* 60, p. 131; cf. RC vii, 5.4.48.
38. RC vii, 5.4.70.
39. RC vii, 5.4.49.
40. RC vii, 5.4.70.
41. LC, *DI*, p. 36.
42. LC, *DI*, p. 38.
43. RC vii, 5.4.50.
44. RC vii, 5.5.2.
45. LC, *DI*, p. 40.
46. Cf. Varela (2006).
47. Cf. Curet (2005).

Chapter 17: The Project Unravels, 1497–8

1. Symcox and Sullivan, *Christopher Columbus*, doc. 26, p. 151.
2. RC xiii, *FC* 64, p. 153.
3. Varela (1991).
4. RC xiii, *FC* 65, p. 155.
5. *Four voyages*, ii, pp. 14–15.
6. *Four voyages*, ii, pp. 14–15; cf. pp. 22–3; also Greenblatt (1991), pp. 86, 90–1, 93.

7. RC xiii, *FC* 68, pp. 159–60; cf. *Four voyages*, ii, pp. 14–17.
8. RC xiii, *FC* 68, p. 160.
9. RC xiii, *FC* 70, p. 162.
10. *Four voyages*, ii, pp. 24–5; RC xiii, *FC* 70, p. 162.
11. *Four voyages*, ii, pp. 23–5.
12. *Four voyages*, ii, pp. 24–5.
13. Flint (1992b), p. 51.
14. RC xiii, *FC* 71, p. 163.
15. *Four voyages*, ii, pp. 30–1.
16. Genesis 3:24.
17. *Cabot voyages*, no. 13, pp. 199–200.
18. *Cabot voyages*, no. 16, pp. 202–3.
19. *Cabot voyages*, no. 12, pp. 196–9; Ballesteros (1997), pp. 133–50.
20. *Cabot voyages*, nos 6–7, pp. 187–9; Quinn (1961); cf. Wilson, I. (1991).
21. Seaver (1996).
22. Fagan (2006).
23. *Cabot voyages*, no. 24, p. 210.
24. *Cabot voyages*, no. 18, pp. 204–5.
25. *Cabot voyages*, nos 19–20, p. 206.
26. Pope (1997).
27. *Cabot voyages*, no. 23, pp. 208–9.
28. *Cabot voyages*, no. 25, p. 213; Gil and Varela, *Cartas*, pp. 267–9.
29. *Cabot voyages*, no. 25, p. 212.
30. *Cabot voyages*, no. 21, p. 207.
31. *Cabot voyages*, no. 25, p. 212.
32. *Cabot voyages*, no. 31, i, p. 220.
33. RC x, no. 26.
34. *Cabot voyages*, no. 21, p. 207.
35. Subrahmanyam (1997); Fonseca (1998); Ames (2004).
36. Da Gama, pp. 6–7.
37. Da Gama, pp. 11, 13.
38. Da Gama, pp. 17–18.
39. Da Gama, p. 20.
40. Da Gama, p. 23.
41. Da Gama, p. 23.
42. Da Gama, p. 36.
43. Da Gama, p. 48.
44. Da Gama, p. 53.
45. Da Gama, p. 54.
46. Da Gama, p. 55.
47. Da Gama, p. 52, note 3; p. 53, illustration; pp. 53–4, note 2; p. 54, note 2, and pp. 114–5.
48. Da Gama, p. 36, note 1.

Chapter 18: Columbus Eclipsed, 1498–1506

1. RC xiii, *FC* 73.
2. RC xiii, *FC* 73.
3. RC xiii, *FC* 73, note 342; cf. Floyd (1973), pp. 39–40.
4. RC xiii, *FC* 74.
5. RC xiii, *FC* 74.
6. RC xiii, *FC* 75.
7. RC xiii, *FC* 75, and note 347.
8. RC xiii, *FC* 75.
9. RC xiii, *FC* 75.
10. RC xiii, *FC* 76–77.
11. RC xiii, *FC* 79.
12. RC xiii, *FC* 84.
13. RC xiii, *FC* 83.
14. RC xiii, *FC* 84.
15. RC xiii, *FC* 84.
16. RC xiii, *FC* 85.
17. RC xiii, *FC* 86.
18. Cf. Greenblatt (1991), p. 66.
19. Psalms 22:28; *Book of prophecies*, p. 115 (as Psalm 21); cf. RC ix, *Oviedo*, 3.8.5.
20. *Book of prophecies*, pp. 134–41.
21. *Book of prophecies*, pp. 238–9.
22. *Book of prophecies*, pp. 226–7.
23. *Book of prophecies*, pp. 248–55; quotation from Isaiah 42:4 on pp. 250–1; also pp. 140–1, 154–5.
24. RC xiii, *FC* 87.
25. Floyd (1973), pp. 51–5.
26. RC vii, *LC* 9.1.1.
27. RC xiii, *FC* 88 (eyewitness account); RC vii, *LC* 9.1.8–10.
28. RC xiii, *FC* 88.
29. RC vii, *LC* 9.1.10.
30. RC vii, *LC* 9.1.9.
31. RC xiii, *FC* 89; Incer Barquero (2002).
32. RC xiii, *FC* 89.
33. RC vii, *LC* 9.2.7, though las Casas claims that he did provide gifts in return.
34. RC xiii, *FC* 9.
35. RC xiii, *FC* 89.
36. RC xiii, *FC* 90.
37. *Four voyages*, ii, pp. 82–5.
38. RC xiii, *FC* 90.
39. RC xiii, *FC* 91 speaking paper: p. 282 *supra*.
40. RC xiii, *FC* 91.
41. RC xiii, *FC* 91; RC vii, *LC* 9.1.20.

42. RC vii, *LC* 9.1.23; cf. RC xiii, *FC* 92.
43. RC vii, *LC* 9.1.23.
44. RC xiii, *FC* 92.
45. *Four voyages*, ii, pp. 80–3.
46. *Four voyages*, ii, pp. 82–3; cf. RC xiii, *FC* 96.
47. RC vii, *LC* 9.1.42.
48. RC vii, *LC* 9.1.36–8.
49. RC xiii, *FC* 96.
50. RC vii, *LC* 9.1.42.
51. RC xiii, *FC* 95–6.
52. *Four voyages*, ii, pp. 90–1, RC xiii, *FC* 97.
53. RC vii, *LC* 9.1.59; also RC vii, *LC* 9.1.74.
54. *Four voyages*, ii, pp. 90–1.
55. *Four voyages*, ii, pp. 90–3.
56. RC xiii, *FC* 97–100.
57. *Four voyages*, ii, pp. 94–5.
58. Cf. Atkinson (2006).
59. RC xiii, *FC* 101.
60. *Four voyages*, ii, pp. 72–111; cf. pp. 112–43 (Diego Méndez).
61. *Four voyages*, ii, pp. 113–42; cf. RC xiii, *FC* 105.
62. RC xiii, *FC* 102.
63. RC xiii, *FC* 103.
64. RC xiii, *FC* 103.
65. Joel 2:31; *Book of prophecies*, pp. 196–7.
66. *Book of prophecies*, pp. 226–7.
67. RC xiii, *FC* 104.
68. RC xiii, *FC* 108.
69. Floyd (1973), pp. 92–3.
70. Cf. RC viii.
71. Chamberlain (1939/70).

Chapter 19: Vespucci's Tabloid Journalism, 1497–1504

1. Fernández-Armesto (2006).
2. Johnson, C. (2006), p. 9.
3. More, *Utopia*, p. 10.
4. Vespucci, app. E, pp. 126–7.
5. Vespucci, app. E, p. 141.
6. Formisano in Vespucci, p. xxiii.
7. Formisano in Vespucci, p. xxi.
8. Vespucci, ep. V, pp. 45–56; *Mundus Novus*, ff. 1r–4v.
9. *Cosmographiae Introductio*.
10. Varela (1991).
11. See RC x.

12. Vespucci, ep. VI, p. 59; *Lettera*, ff. 1v–2r.
13. Cf. Fernández-Armesto (2006).
14. Vespucci, app. E, p. 128.
15. Vespucci, app. E, p. 129.
16. Fernández-Armesto (2006).
17. Vespucci, app. E, p. 151.
18. Vespucci, ep. VI, p. 60; *Lettera*, f. 2v.
19. Vespucci, app. E, p. 131.
20. Cf. RC x and RC xii.
21. Vespucci, ep. VI, p. 61; *Lettera*, f. 3r.
22. RC x, p. 43, no. 13; cf. Vespucci, ep. IV, p. 39.
23. Vespucci, ep. VI, p. 64; *Lettera*, f. 4r.
24. Cf. Vespucci, ep. V, p. 50; *Mundus Novus*, f. 2v.
25. Vespucci, ep. VI, pp. 61–2; *Lettera*, f. 3r.
26. Vespucci, ep. VI, p. 64; *Lettera*, f. 4r.
27. Vespucci, ep. VI, p. 62; *Lettera*, f. 3v.
28. Cf. Vespucci, ep. III, p. 31; Vespucci, ep. V, p. 49 and *Mundus Novus*, f. 2v.
29. Vespucci, ep. VI, p. 63; *Lettera*, f. 3v.
30. Vespucci, ep. VI, p. 64; *Lettera*, f. 4r.
31. Vespucci, ep. V, pp. 49–50 and *Mundus Novus*, f. 2v; cf. ep. IV, p. 42.
32. Vespucci, ep. VI, p. 66; *Lettera*, f. 4v.
33. Vespucci, ep. VI, pp. 63–4 and *Lettera*, f. 4r; cf. Vespucci, ep. III, p. 32.
34. Vespucci, ep. VI, p. 64; *Lettera*, f. 4r.
35. Vespucci, ep. V, pp. 49–50; *Mundus Novus*, ff. 2v–3r.
36. Vespucci, ep. VI, p. 65 and *Lettera*, f. 4v; cf. Zurara, *Chronicle*, c. 80, ii, p. 242.
37. Vespucci, ep. III, p. 32.
38. Cf. Vespucci, ep. III, pp. 31–2 (third voyage).
39. Vespucci, ep. VI, p. 65; *Lettera*, f. 4r.
40. Vespucci, ep. VI, p. 67; *Lettera*, f. 5v.
41. Vespucci, ep. VI, p. 68; *Lettera*, f. 5v.
42. Vespucci, ep. VI, p. 69; *Lettera*, f. 6r.
43. Vespucci, ep. VI, p. 69; *Lettera*, f. 6r.
44. Vespucci, ep. VI, p. 71; *Lettera*, f. 7r.
45. Vespucci, ep. VI, p. 72; *Lettera*, f. 7r.
46. Cf. Vespucci, ep. V, p. 48; *Mundus Novus*, f. 2r.
47. Cf. Vespucci, ep. I, p. 11.
48. Vespucci, ep. VI, p. 73; *Lettera*, f. 7v.
49. Vespucci, ep. VI, p. 74; *Lettera*, ff. 7v–8r.
50. Vespucci, ep. VI, pp. 75; *Lettera*, f. 8r; cf. Vespucci, Notes, p. 191.
51. Vespucci, ep. VI, p. 76; *Lettera*, f. 8v.
52. Vespucci, app. E, p. 151.
53. Vespucci, ep. I, p. 11.
54. Vespucci, ep. VI, p. 79 and *Lettera*, f. 10r; cf. Vespucci, ep. III, p. 32 (third voyage) and RC x, p. 43, no. 13.

55. Vespucci, ep. I, p. 9.
56. Vespucci, ep. I, p. 10.
57. Vespucci, ep. VI, p. 81; *Lettera*, f. 10v.
58. Vespucci, ep. VI, pp. 81–2; *Lettera*, f. 11r.
59. Vespucci, ep. II, pp. 20–6.
60. Vespucci, ep. II, pp. 21.
61. Vespucci, ep. III, pp. 19–20.
62. Vespucci, ep. II, p. 19 (13 May); Vespucci, ep. V, p. 45 (14 May) and *Mundus Novus*, f. 1r; Vespucci, ep. VI, p. 86 (10 May) and *Lettera*, f. 13r.
63. Vespucci, ep. III, p. 32.
64. Vespucci, ep. III, p. 32.
65. Vespucci, ep. V, p. 49; *Mundus Novus*, f. 2v.
66. Vespucci, ep. V, p. 48; *Mundus Novus*, f. 2v.
67. Vespucci, ep. V, p. 49; *Mundus Novus*, f. 2v.
68. Vespucci, ep. III, p. 32; cf. Vespucci, ep. V, p. 49 and *Mundus Novus*, f. 2r.
69. Vespucci, ep. III, p. 31.
70. Vespucci, ep. III, p. 31.
71. Vespucci, ep. III, p. 33.
72. Vespucci, ep. III, p. 34.
73. Vespucci, ep. III, p. 34.
74. Cf. Vespucci, ep. V, p. 49; *Mundus Novus*, f. 2r.
75. Vespucci, ep. VI, p. 62; *Lettera*, f. 3v.
76. Vespucci, ep. IV, p. 43.
77. Pigafetta, *Magellan's Voyage*, vii, pp. 43–4.
78. Vespucci, ep. III, p. 33.
79. Vespucci, ep. III, p. 34; cf. Vespucci, ep. V, p. 50 and *Mundus Novus*, f. 2v.
80. Vespucci, ep. III, p. 32.
81. Vespucci, ep. VI, pp. 88–9; *Lettera*, f. 13v.
82. Vespucci, ep. III, p. 32.
83. Vespucci, ep. III, p. 33.
84. Vespucci, plate I.
85. Vespucci, ep. VI, pp. 92–6.
86. RC viii.
87. RC v, *PM* 1.9.8.
88. Cf. RC viii, 13.4; Verlinden (1961), pp. 399–400.
89. Blumenthal (2008).
90. Vigneras (1976), p. 92.
91. Vigneras (1976), p. 124.
92. Vigneras (1976), pp. 103–4.
93. Vespucci, ep. III, pp. 30–1; but cf. Vespucci, ep. V, p. 52.
94. Vespucci, ep. V, p. 47.
95. Vespucci, app. A, p. 101.
96. Vespucci, ep. V, p. 45.
97. Vespucci, ep. V, p. 47.

98. *Cosmographiae Introductio*, f. 13r.
99. Vespucci, app. D, pp. 116–17; Johnson, C. (2006), pp. 3–43.

Chapter 20: The Land of the Holy Cross, 1500

1. Cf. Amado and Figueiredo, *Brasil 1500*; Magalhães and Miranda, *Os primeiros 14 documentos*.
2. McEwen, Barreto and Neves (2001); Hemming (1978a), pp. 52–3.
3. Hemming (1978a), p. 57.
4. Hemming (1978a), pp. 46–7, 57; cf. RC ix, *Oviedo*, 3.8.5.
5. Hemming (1978a), p. 48.
6. Gandavo, *A primeiro história*, p. 100; Hemming (1978a), p. 67.
7. *Cabral's voyage*, plate opposite p. 8.
8. Hemming (1978a), pp. 66–8.
9. Vespucci, ep. V, p 49.
10. Hemming (1978a), p. 28.
11. Hemming (1978a), p. 31.
12. Léry, *History*, pp. 122–34; Staden *True History*, part i, chs 18–51, pp. 62–120.
13. Montaigne, *Complete Works*, Essay 31, pp. 191–2.
14. Cf. Scyllacius, pp. 52, 71, 101.
15. Hemming (1978a), pp. 33–4.
16. Montaigne, *Complete Works*, Essay 31, p. 182; Greenblatt (1991), pp. 146–50; cf. Hemming (1978a), pp. 12–13.
17. Montaigne, *Complete Works*, Essay 31, pp. 185–9.
18. Matthew 26:26; Hulme (1986), p. 85; Llewelyn Price (2003), pp. 25–41.
19. Léry, *History*, p. 41; cf. pp. 29, 236; cf. Bynum (2007) on blood.
20. Tierney (1997), pp. 256–72.
21. Vitoria, *Political Writings*, pp. 208–12.
22. Vitoria, *Political Writings*, p. 225.
23. *Cabral's voyage*, p. 5.
24. *Cabral's voyage*, pp. 53–94; cf. RC x, no. 24 (M. Cretico).
25. Fonseca (1999b).
26. *Cabral's voyage*, p. 33.
27. *Cabral's voyage*, p. 8.
28. *Cabral's voyage*, p. 10.
29. *Cabral's voyage*, p. 15.
30. *Cabral's voyage*, p. 24.
31. *Cabral's voyage*, p. 11; cf. p. 58.
32. *Cabral's voyage*, p. 15; cf. p. 59.
33. *Cabral's voyage*, p. 16.
34. *Cabral's voyage*, p. 21.
35. *Cabral's voyage*, p. 23.
36. *Cabral's voyage*, p. 15.
37. *Cabral's voyage*, p. 21; cf. p. 59.

38. *Cabral's voyage*, p. 11.
39. *Cabral's voyage*, p. 12.
40. *Cabral's voyage*, p. 29.
41. Cf. *Cabral's voyage*, p. 16.
42. *Cabral's voyage*, p. 13.
43. *Cabral's voyage*, pp. 14, 16.
44. *Cabral's voyage*, pp. 14–15.
45. *Cabral's voyage*, p. 24; cf. p. 59.
46. *Cabral's voyage*, p. 16.
47. *Cabral's voyage*, p. 19.
48. *Cabral's voyage*, p. 19.
49. *Cabral's voyage*, p. 20.
50. *Cabral's voyage*, p. 25; cf. p. 59.
51. *Cabral's voyage*, p. 26.
52. *Cabral's voyage*, pp. 26–7.
53. *Cabral's voyage*, p. 29.
54. *Cabral's voyage*, p. 29.
55. *Cabral's voyage*, p. 30.
56. *Cabral's voyage*, p. 32.
57. *Cabral's voyage*, p. 31.
58. *Cabral's voyage*, p. 31.
59. *Cabral's voyage*, p. 32.
60. *Cabral's voyage*, p. 33; cf. Master John's letter, *Cabral's voyage*, pp. 36–40.
61. *Cabral's voyage*, p. 43; cf. p. 44.
62. *Cabral's voyage*, pp. 58–9.
63. *Cabral's voyage*, pp. 114–50.

Chapter 21: The Realm of King Arosca, 1505

1. Dos Santos, *Découverte de Brésil*, pp. 143–59.
2. Gonneville, p. 88.
3. Gonneville, pp. 88–91.
4. Verlinden (1958b).
5. Gonneville, p. 93.
6. Gonneville, p. 95.
7. Léry, *History*, p. 29.
8. Gonneville, p. 96; cf. p. 100.
9. Gonneville, p. 97.
10. Gonneville, p. 96.
11. Gonneville, p. 99.
12. Gonneville, p. 97.
13. Gonneville, p. 98.
14. Gonneville, pp. 98–9.
15. Gonneville, p. 99.

16. Gonneville, p. 102.
17. Gonneville, pp. 100–1.
18. Gonneville, p. 102.
19. Gonneville, p. 103.
20. Gonneville, p. 105.
21. Gonneville, p. 105.
22. Gonneville, p. 106.
23. Gonneville, p. 106.
24. Gonneville, p. 109.
25. Gonneville, p. 110.
26. Gonneville, p. 6.

Chapter 22: A Compulsory Voluntary 'Requirement', 1511–20

1. Floyd (1973), pp. 83–8.
2. RC ix, RC ix, *Oviedo*, 3.30.1; also 3.3.1, 3.8.5.
3. RC ix, RC ix, *Oviedo*, 3.4.2.
4. RC ix, RC ix, *Oviedo*, 3.25, 3.25.1.
5. Genesis 1:28.
6. Pagden (1986), p. 17; Aristotle, *Politics*, 1252a1; cf. 1253a5–10.
7. Aristotle, *Nic. Eth.*, 1145a31.
8. Pagden (1986), p. 18; Aristotle, *Nic. Eth.*, 1148b17–19, and *Politics*, 1338b19.
9. Aristotle, *Politics*, 1260a7–14; Garnsey (1996), pp. 114–15.
10. McGrade (1982), pp. 751–3; Luscombe (1982), pp. 760–1.
11. Aristotle, *Politics*, 1280a31–35.
12. Cited from MS in Pagden (1986), p. 48.
13. Garnsey (1996), pp. 107–27; Aristotle, *Politics*, 1254a20–24.
14. Aristotle, *Politics*, 1255a5.
15. Pagden (1986), pp. 42, 45, 47; also Garnsey (1996).
16. Aristotle, *Nic. Eth.*, 1161a30–b6; Garnsey (1996), p. 119.
17. Pagden (1986), p. 49.
18. Pagden (1986), pp. 28–31.
19. Palacios Rubios, pp. xiv–xvii, Bibl. Noc. Madrid, MS 17641.
20. Palacios Rubios, p. 32, f. 13r, also ff. 11v, 13v, 16v.
21. Palacios Rubios, pp. 108, 112, etc.; ff. 50r, 5lv, 52v, 53r, etc.
22. Palacios Rubios, p. 9, f. 4r.
23. Palacios Rubios, p. 39, f. 16r–v.
24. Palacios Rubios, pp. 9–10, f. 4r–v.
25. Palacios Rubios, p. 11, ff. 4v–5r.
26. Palacios Rubios, p. 13, f. 6r.
27. Aristotle, *Politics*, 1254a24; Palacios Rubios, p. 25 and n. 2, f. 11r; cf. Vitoria, *Political Writings*, p. 239, and Pagden (1986), pp. 67–78.

28. Palacios Rubios, pp. 26, 39–55, 58, 60–1, ff. 11v, 16r–24r, f. 25v, 26r–27r; cf. Vitoria, *Political Writings*, pp. 244, 246–7.
29. Palacios Rubios, p. 149, f. 65v.
30. Palacios Rubios, pp. 163–5, f. 70r–v.
31. Laws of Burgos, xx.
32. Laws of Burgos, prologue, p. 11.
33. Laws of Burgos, xx, xxii, pp. 28–31.
34. Laws of Burgos, xxxv, p. 38.
35. Laws of Burgos, xviii, p. 34.
36. Laws of Burgos, xxiv, p. 32.
37. Laws of Burgos, prologue, pp. 11–12.
38. Laws of Burgos, xiii, p. 24.
39. Preserved in Seville, Archivo General de Indias, Audiencia de Panamá, Leg. 233, lib. 1, ff. 49–50v; www.dickinson.edu/~borges/Resources-Requerimiento. htm; Fuson (2000), pp. 132–6.
40. Cf. Verlinden (1961), pp. 400–3.
41. Seed (1995), p. 71.
42. Matías de Paz, p. 239; cf. pp. 228, 234.
43. Matías de Paz, pp. xxviii–xxix.
44. Seed (1995), pp. 69–99.
45. The Koran, 2:256; Seed (1995), p. 77.
46. Seed (1995), pp. 78–83.
47. Abulafia, D. (1997), pp. 40, 43.
48. Deuteronomy 20:15; Seed (1995), pp. 89–92.
49. Deuteronomy 20:10–13.
50. Palacios Rubios, pp. 36–7, f. 15r–v.
51. Matthew 10:11–13; cf. Mark 6:10–11, Luke 9:5, 10–11.
52. Palacios Rubios, p. 37, f. 15r–v.
53. Thomas (2003), pp. 274–85; Jamaica: Morales Padrón (2003), Atkinson (2006).
54. Thomas (2003), pp. 276, 283.
55. LC, *DI*, p. 43; cf. Morales Padrón (2003); also Siegel (2005); Curet (2005); Atkinson (2006).
56. LC, *DI*, p. 44.
57. Martinón-Torres (2007), pp. 194–204.
58. Thomas (2003), p. 277.
59. LC, *DI*, p. 45.
60. LC, *DI*, p. 46.
61. Thomas (2003), p. 278.
62. LC, *DI*, pp. 46–7.
63. LC, *DI*, p. 47; Thomas (2003), p. 282.
64. LC, *DI*, p. 47.
65. Thomas (2003), p. 282.

66. Thomas (2003), p. 283; Fernández-Armesto (1982), pp. 21–32; Schwartz (2004).
67. Mira Caballos (2000); Ladero Quesada (2002); also Floyd (1973), pp. 50, 72.
68. Thomas (2003), pp. 277, 283.
69. Thomas (1993); Prescott (1994), and earlier editions; also Todorov (1984), pp. 53–123.
70. Cortes, Letters from Mexico, pp. lxi–lxiii.
71. Díaz del Castillo, *Historia*, ii, c. 88; Bernal (1975), pp. 1–3.
72. Díaz del Castillo, *Historia*, ii, c. 92.
73. Cortes, Letters from Mexico, pp. 103–4; Díaz del Castillo, *Historia*, ii, c. 92.
74. Cortes, Letters from Mexico, p. 104.
75. Cortes, Letters from Mexico, p. 110.
76. Cortes, Letters from Mexico, p. lxii.
77. Cortes, Letters from Mexico, p. 102; cf. Todorov (1984), pp. 128–9.
78. Cortes, Letters from Mexico, p. 108.

Conclusion: The Renaissance Discovery of Man

1. Cf. Michelet in 1855: Elliot (1989), p. 42.
2. Burckhardt (1990), pp. 187, 195–7; cf. Flint (1992b), pp. 56–61.
3. Burckhardt (1990), p. 186.
4. Abulafia, A.S. (1995).
5. O'Gorman (1961); Zerubavel (1992).
6. Hemming (1978b).
7. Milanich (1994, 1995, 1996, 1998); Fuson (2000); cf. Devereux (1993).
8. Pigafetta, *Magellan's Voyage*, viii, pp. 45–50.
9. Pigafetta, *Magellan's Voyage*, xviii, pp. 68–9; xxvi, p. 85, etc.
10. Lazcano Sahagún (2000); Montané Martí and Lazcano Sahagún (2001); Miller (1988).
11. Cabeza de Vaca, *Castaways*.
12. Bucher (1981); also www.csulb.edu/~aisstudy/woodcuts/.
13. Sloane (2007).
14. Elliott (1989), pp. 63–4.
15. Malachi 2:10.

BIBLIOGRAPHY

Primary Sources – Manuscripts

ENGLAND

Cambridge: Gonville and Caius College, MS 162/83 (Pipino).
London: British Library: MS Egerton 2709 (*Le Canarien*).

GERMANY

Nuremberg: Germanisches National-Museum, Martin Behaim globe.

PORTUGAL

Coimbra: Biblioteca Geral da Universidade de Coimbra, Portugal, Secção de Reservados: Cod. 314 (Torriani).

SPAIN

Madrid: Biblioteca Nacional: MS 17641 (Palacios Rubios).

Primary Sources – Printed

Abreu Galindo, J. de, *Historia de la conquista de las siete isles de Canaria*, ed. A. Cioranescu, Santa Cruz de Tenerife, 1977 (*see also* Glas, Captain G.).
African Myths of Origins, ed. S. Belcher, Harmondsworth, 2005.
Airaldi, G., ed., *La terra di Brasile nelle relazioni di Amerigo Vespucci, Pero Vaz de Caminha, Paulmier de Gonneville, Jean de Léry*, Verona, 1991.
Amado, J., and Figueiredo, L.C., *Brasil 1500: quarenta documentos*, Brasilia and São Paulo, 2001.
Aristotle, *Politics*, ed. and trans. H. Rackham, Cambridge MA, 1932.
Aristotle, *Nicomachean Ethics*, ed. and trans. H. Rackham, 2nd edn, Cambridge MA, 1934.
Augustine of Hippo, St, *The City of God against the pagans*, ed. and trans. R.W. Dyson, Cambridge, 1998.

Axelson, E., ed., *Vasco da Gama. The diary of his travels through African waters, 1497–1499*, Somerset West (S. Africa), 1998.

Bernáldez, Andrés, *Memorias del reinado de los Reyes Católicos*, ed. M. Gómez Moreno and J. de Mata Carriazo, Madrid, 1962.

Blake, J.W., ed., *Europeans in West Africa (1450–1560). Documents to illustrate the nature and scope of Portuguese enterprise in West Africa*, 2 vols, Hakluyt Society, London, 1942.

Cà da Mosto, Alvise da (Cadamosto, da Mosto), *The voyages of Cadamosto and other documents on western Africa in the second half of the fifteenth century*, ed. G.R. Crone, Hakluyt Society, London, 1937.

Cà da Mosto, Alvise, *Voyages en Afrique Noire d'Alvise Cà da Mosto (1455 et 1456)*, ed. F. Verrier, Collection Magellane, Paris, 1994.

Cà da Mosto, Alvise da (Cadamosto, da Mosto), *Questa e una opera necessaria a tutti li naviga[n]ti (1490)*, ed. F. Fernández-Armesto, Delmar, NY 1992 (*see also* Martyr, Peter).

Cabeza de Vaca, Alvar Nuñez, *Castaways: the narrative of Alvar Nuñez Cabeza de Vaca*, ed. E. Pupo-Walker, trans. F.M. López-Morillas, Berkeley CA, 1993: also *Chronicle of the Narváez expedition*, ed. I. Stevens et al., Harmondsworth, 2002.

Caminha, Pero Vaz de, *A Carta de Pero Vaz de Caminha*, ed. M. Mendonça, M. Garcoz Ventura and J. Veríssimo Serrão, Ericeira, 2000.

Caminha, Pero Vaz de, *A Carta de Pero Vaz de Caminha: o descobrimento do Brasil*, ed. S. Castro, Porto Alegre and São Paulo, 2000.

Caminha, Pero Vaz de, *Carta a el-Rei D. Manuel sobre o achamento do Brasil*, ed. M.P. Caetano and N. Aguas, Mem Martins, 2000.

Caminha, Pero Vaz de, *De ontdekking van Brazilië*, ed. and trans. A. Willemsen, privately printed, Amsterdam, 1999.

Caminha, Pero Vaz de, 'Letter to King Manuel of Portugal', in: Greenlee, W.B., ed., *Cabral's voyage to Brazil and India*, Hakluyt Society, London, 1938, pp. 3–33; repr. in: Ley, C.D., ed., *Portuguese Voyages, 1498–1663*, 3rd edn, London, 2000, pp. 41–53.

Camões, Luis de, *The Lusiads*, trans. L. White, Oxford, 1997.

Canarian, The, trans. R.H. Major, Hakluyt Society, London, 1872.

Canarien, Le, ed. A. Cioranescu and E. Serra Ràfols, 3 vols, La Laguna, 1959.

Canarien, Le: manuscritos, transcripción y traducción, ed. B. Pico, E. Aznar and D. Corbella, Fontes Rerum Canariarum, vol. 12, La Laguna, Tenerife, 2003.

Caraci Luzzana, B., Symcox, G., and Sullivan, B., eds, *The history of the life and deeds of the Admiral Don Christopher Columbus attributed to his son Fernando Colón*, Repertorium Columbianum, vol. 13, Turnhout, 2004.

Carrillo, J., *Oviedo on Columbus*, Repertorium Columbianum, vol. 9, Turnhout, 2000.

Catalan world-map of the R. Biblioteca Estense at Modena, The Royal Geographical Society, London, 1934.

Cicero, Marcus Tullius, *De Legibus*, ed. C.W. Keyes, London, 1977.

Columbus, Ferdinand (Fernando Colón): *see* Caraci Luzzana, B., Symcox, G., and Sullivan, B., *and* Keen, B., *and* Taviani, P.E.

Cortés, Hernán, *Letters from Mexico*, ed. and trans. A. Pagden, 2nd edn, New Haven, CT and London, 1986.

Cosmographiae Introductio cum quibusdam Geometriae ac Astronomiae principiis ad eam rem necessariis insuper quattuor Americi Vespucij nauigationes, Saint-Dié, 1507.

Cummins, J., ed., *The voyage of Christopher Columbus*, London, 1992.

Davies, M., ed., *Columbus in Italy: an Italian versification of the Letter on the Discovery of the New World*, London, 1991.

Díaz del Castillo, Bernal, *Historia verdadera de la conquista de la Nueva España*, ed. M. León-Portilla, 2 vols, Madrid, 1984.

Dos Santos, I. Mendes, eds, *La découverte du Brésil: les premiers témoignages (1500–1549)*, Paris, 2000.

Dotson, J., and Agosto, A., eds, *Christopher Columbus and his family*, Repertorium Columbianum, vol. 4, Turnhout, 1998.

Eatough, G., ed., *Selections from Peter Martyr*, Repertorium Columbianum, vol. 5, Turnhout, 1998.

Espinosa, Alonso de, *The Guanches of Tenerife* ed. and trans. C. Markham, Hakluyt Society, London, 1907.

Eustache de la Fosse, *Voyage d'Eustache Delafosse*, Collection Magellane, Paris, 1992.

Fernández-Armesto, F., ed., *Columbus on himself*, London, 1992.

Ferreira Priegue, M.E., *Fuentes para la exportación gallega de la segunda mitad del siglo XV*, Santiago de Compostela, 1984.

Formisano, L., *Italian Reports on America 1493–1522: accounts by contemporary observers*, Repertorium Columbianum, vol. 12, Turnhout, 2002.

Formisano, L., ed., *Letters from a New World: Amerigo Vespucci's discovery of America*, 1992.

Gandavo, Pero Magalhães de, *A primeira história do Brasil: História da província Santa Cruz a que vulgarmente chamamos Brasil*, Lisbon, 2004 (first. edn 1576).

Gerald of Wales, *The history and topography of Ireland*, trans. J.J. O'Meara, Harmondsworth, 1982.

Gil, J., and Varela, C., *Cartas de particulares a Colón y relaciones coetáneas*, Madrid, 1984.

Glas, Captain G., *The history of the discovery and conquest of the Canary Islands translated from a Spanish manuscript, lately found in the island of Palma, with an enquiry into the origin of the ancient inhabitants*, London, 1764 (also 2nd edn, 2 vols, Dublin, 1767).

Gonneville, Paulmier de, *Relation authentique du voyage du Capitaine de Gonneville ès nouvelles terres des Indes*, ed. M. d'Avézac, Paris, 1869.

Gonneville, Paulmier de, *Vinte Luas: viagem de Paulmier de Gonneville ao Brasil: 1503–1505*, ed. L. Perrone-Moyses, São Paulo, 1992; French edn: *Le voyage de*

Gonneville (1501–1505) et la découverte de la Normandie par les indiens du Brésil, Collection Magellane, Paris, 1995.

Gonneville, Paulmier de, 'Voyage au Brésil', ed. C.A. Sulier, in: Tomlinson, R.J., *The Struggle for Brazil*, 1970.

Greenlee, W.B., ed., *Cabral's voyage to Brazil and India*, Hakluyt Society, London, 1938.

Griffin, N., ed., *Las Casas on Columbus: background and the second and fourth voyages*, Repertorium Columbianum, vol. 7, Turnhout, 1999.

Hemmerlein, F., *Felicis Malleoli vulgo Hemmerlein Decretorum Doctoris Iureconsultissimi, De nobilitate et rusticitate Dialogus*, 1497.

Hulme, P., and Whitehead, N., *Wild Majesty: Encounters with Caribs from Columbus to the present day*, Oxford, 1992.

Idrisi, Muhammad al-, *Géographie d'Edrisi*, ed. and trans. A. Jaubert, 2 vols, Paris, 1836–40.

Ife, B.W., *Letters from America: Columbus's first accounts of the 1492 voyages*, King's College London School of Humanities, London, 1992.

Jane., C., ed., *The Four Voyages of Columbus*, 2 vols, Hakluyt Society (and later one-vol. edition; English translation on even pages), London, 1929–32.

Keen, B., ed., *The Life of the Admiral Christopher Columbus by his son Ferdinand*, 2nd edn, Brunswick NJ, 1992 (see newer edition of Caraci Luzzana, Symcox and Sullivan).

Lardicci, F., ed., *A synoptic edition of the log of Columbus' first voyage*, Repertorium Columbianum, vol. 6, 1999.

Las Casas, Bartolomé de: *see* Griffin, N., *and* Symcox, G., and Carrillo, J.

Las Casas, Bartolomé de, *A short account of the destruction of the Indies*, ed. A. Pagden and N. Griffin, Harmondsworth, 1992; Briffault, H., trans., *The devastation of the Indies: a brief account*, Baltimore MD, 1992.

Las Casas, Bartolomé de, *In defense of the Indians*, ed. S. Poole and M.E. Marty, DeKalb IL, 1992.

Léry, Jean de, *History of a voyage to the land of Brazil*, ed. and trans. J. Whatley, Berkeley CA, 1990.

Lettera di Amerigo Vespucci delle isole nouamente trouate in quattro suoi viaggi, Florence, 1505.

Libro Copiador de Cristóbal Colón, ed. A. Rumeu de Armas, 2 vols, Madrid, 1989.

Lunardi, E., Magioncalda, E., and Mazzacane, R., *The discovery of the New World in the writings of Peter Martyr of Anghiera*, Nuova Raccolta Colombiana, English edition, vol. 2, Rome, 1992.

Magalhães, J. Romero, and Miranda, S. Münch, eds, *Os primeiros 14 documentos relativos à Armada de Pedro Álvares Cabral*, Lisbon, 1999.

Major, R.H., ed., *The Canarian*, Hakluyt Society, London, 1872 (including the translation of the letter by Giovanni Boccaccio, *De Canaria*).

Mandeville, John, *The Travels of John Mandeville*, trans. C.W.R.D. Moseley, Harmondsworth, 1983.

Marco Polo, *The book of Ser Marco Polo*, ed. H. Yule, 3rd edn, 2 vols, London, 1903.

Marques, A.H. de Oliveira, ed., 1996, *A expansío quatro centista*, Nova história da expansío portuguesa, vol. 2, Lisbon.

Martorell, J., and Martí de Galba, J., *Tirant lo Blanc*, trans. D.H. Rosenthal, London, 1984.

Martyr, Peter: *see* Eatough, G., *and* Lunardi, E.

Martyr, Peter, *Libretto de tutta la nauigatione de re de Spagna de le isole et terreni nouamente trouati, Venice, 1504: a facsimile from the only known perfect copy, now in the John Carter Brown Library, of the famous little book of the King of Spain's voyages*, ed. L.C. Wroth, Paris, 1929.

Martyr, Peter, *Libretto de tutta la nauigatione de re de Spagna de le isole et terreni nouamente trouati*, in: Alvise Cà da Mosto ('Luigi Cadamosto'), *Questa e una opera necessaria a tutti li naviga[n]ti (1490)*, ed. F. Fernández-Armesto, Delmar NY, 1992.

Martyr, Peter, 'The eight decades': in Dahlberg, E., ed., *The Gold of Ophir*, New York, 1972, pp. 31–113.

Montaigne, Michel de, *The Complete Works*, trans. D.M. Frame, London, 2003.

Monumenta Henricina, Coimbra, 1960, vol. 1, pp. 202–6 (Boccaccio, *De Canaria*).

More, Thomas, *Utopia*, ed. G.M. Logan and R.M. Adams, Cambridge, 1989.

Mundus Novus. Albericus Vesputius Laurentio Petri de Medicis salutem plurimam dixit, Rome, circa 1502.

Nader, H., and Formisano, L., eds, *The Book of Privileges issued to Christopher Columbus by King Fernando and Queen Isabel*, Repertorium Columbianum, vol. 2, Berkeley CA, 1996.

Nuñez de la Pena, J., *Conquista y antiguedades de las Islas de la Gran Canaria y su descripción*, Madrid, 1676; facsimile, ed. A. de Béthencourt Massieu, Las Palmas de Gran Canaria, 1994.

Oviedo: *see* Carrillo, J.

Pané, Ramón, *Relación acerca de las antigüedades de los Indios*, ed. J.J. Arrom, 8th edn, Mexico and Buenos Aires, 1988; English edition: *An account of the antiquities of the Indians*, ed. J.J. Arrom, trans. S.C. Griswold, Durham NC, 1999.

Pastore Stocchi, M., 'Il *De Canaria* boccaccesco e un "locus deperditus" nel *De Insulis* di Domenico Silvestri', *Rinascimento*, 10 (1959), pp. 153–6.

Petrarca, F., *De Vita Solitaria*, ed. A. Altamura, Naples, 1963.

Petrarch, *The Life of Solitude*, trans. J. Zeitlin, Chicago, 1924.

Phillips, W.D., ed., *Testimonies from the Columbian lawsuits*, Repertorium Columbianum, vol. 8, Turnhout, 2000.

Pigafetta, Antonio, *Magellan's voyage*, ed. and trans. R.A. Skelton, New Haven CT, 1969.

Pliny the Elder, *Natural history*, ed. and trans. H. Rackham et al., 10 vols, Loeb Classical Library, London, 1938–80.

Ravenstein, E.G., ed., *Journal of the first voyage of Vasco da Gama, 1497–1499*, Hakluyt Society, London, 1898.

Rudulet, C., *Terra Brasil 1500: a viagem de Pedro Álvares Cabral, testimonhos e comentários*, Lisbon, 1999.

Sannazaro, J., *Arcadia and piscatorial eclogues*, trans. R. Nash, Detroit MI, 1969.

Schmitt, E., and Verlinden, C., eds, *Die mittelalterlichen Ursprünge des europäischen Expansion*, Munich, 1986.

Scillacio [Scyllacius], Nicola, *Delle isole del mare meridiano e indiano recentemente scoperte*, ed. O. Baldacci, Florence, 1992.

Scillacio [Scyllacius], Nicolò, *Sulle isole meridionali e del mare indico nuovamente trovate*, ed. and trans. M.G. Scelfo Micci, Rome, 1990.

Simpson, J.B., ed. and trans., *The Laws of Burgos of 1512–1513: royal ordinances for the good government and treatment of the Indians*, San Francisco, 1960.

Spanish letter of Columbus to Luis de Sant'Angel Escribano de Racion of the Kingdom of Aragon dated 15 February 1493, facsimile of Bernard Quaritch's original 1891 edition with essays by F. Fernández-Armesto et al., London, 2006.

Staden, Hans, *The True History of his Captivity 1557*, ed. and trans. M. Letts, London, 1928.

Symcox, G., ed., *Italian Reports on America 1493–1522: letters, dispatches, and papal bulls*, Repertorium Columbianum, vol. 10, 2001.

Symcox, G., and Carrillo, J., eds, *Las Casas on Columbus: the third voyage*, Repertorium Columbianum, vol. 11, Turnhout, 2001.

Symcox, G., and Sullivan, B., eds, *Christopher Columbus and the enterprise of the Indies*, Boston and New York, 2005 (selected texts mainly from Repertorium Colombianum, vols 2–12).

Taviani, P.E., *Accounts and letters of the second, third and fourth voyages*, Nuova Raccolta Colombiana, English edition, vol. 6, Rome, 1994.

Taviani, P.E., and Luzzana Caraci, I., *Historie concerning the life and deeds of the admiral don C. Columbus* [by his son Ferdinand], Nuova Raccolta Colombiana, English edition, vol. 4, Rome, 2001.

Taviani, P.E., and Varela, C., *The journal: account of the first voyage and discovery of the Indies*, Nuova Raccolta Colombiana, English edition, vol. 1, Rome, 1992.

Thevet, André, *Le Brésil d'André Thevet*, ed. F. Lestringant, Collection Magellane, Paris, 1997.

Torriani, L. *Descrição e história do Reino das Ilhas Canarias antes ditas Afortunadas, com o paracer das suas fortificações*, ed. J.M. Azevedo e Silva, Lisbon, 1999.

Tyler, S.L., ed., *Two worlds: the Indian encounter with the European, 1492–1509* 1988 (selection of sources concerning Columbus).

Unali, A., *Christopher Columbus' discoveries in the testimonials of Diego Álvarez Chanca and Andrés Bernáldez*, Nuova Raccolta Colombiana, English edition, vol. 5, Rome, 1992.

Varela, C., ed., *Textos y documentos completos: relaciones de viajes, cartas y memorias*, Madrid, 1982.

Vitoria, F., *Political Writings*, ed. A. Pagden and J. Lawrance, Cambridge, 1991.
Waldseemüller World Map, Seattle, 2003.
West, D.C., and Kling, A., *The* libro de las profecías *of Christopher Columbus*, Gainesville FL, 1991.
Williamson, J.A., *The Cabot voyages and Bristol discovery under Henry VIII*, Hakluyt Society, London, 1962.
Woolf, L., ed., *Jews in the Canary Islands*, London, 1926; New York, 2001.
Zavala, S., and Millares Carlo, A., eds and trans, Juan López de Palacios Rubios, *De las isles del mar Océano*, Fray Matías de Paz, *Del dominio de los Reyes de España sobre los indios*, Mexico City and Buenos Aires, 1954 (in one volume).
Zurara, Gomes Eanes de, *Chronique de Guinée (1453)*, ed. L. Bourdon, Collection Magellane, Paris, 1994.
Zurara, Gomes Eanes de, *The chronicle of the discovery and conquest of Guinea written by Gomes Eannes de Azurara*, ed. C.R. Beazley and E. Prestage, Hakluyt Society, 2 vols, London, 1896–9.

Secondary Literature

Abreu, J. Capistrano de, 1999, *O descobrimento do Brasil*, São Paulo.
Abulafia, A. Sapir, 1995, *Christians and Jews in the twelfth-century Renaissance*, London.
Abulafia, D., 1992, *Spain and 1492. Unity and uniformity under Ferdinand and Isabella*, Bangor.
Abulafia, D., 1994, *A Mediterranean emporium: the Catalan kingdom of Majorca*, Cambridge.
Abulafia, D., ed., 1995, *The French descent into Renaissance Italy, 1494–95: antecedents and effects*, Aldershot.
Abulafia, D., 1997, *The western Mediterranean kingdoms: the struggle for dominion, 1200–1500*, London.
Abulafia, D., 2000, 'La produzione dello zucchero nei domini della Corona d'Aragona', in Rossetti, G., and Vitolo, G., eds, *Medioevo Mezzogiorno Mediterraneo: studi in onore di Mario del Treppo*, 2 vols, Naples, vol. 2, pp. 105–19.
Abulafia, D., 2002, 'Neolithic meets medieval: first encounters in the Canary Islands', in Abulafia, D., and Berend, N., eds, *Medieval frontiers: concepts and practices*, Aldershot, pp. 255–78.
Abulafia, D., 2004, '*Nam iudei servi regis sunt*: the Jews in the municipal fuero of Teruel (1176–7)', in *Jews, Muslims and Christians in and around the Crown of Aragon: essays in honour of Professor Elena Lourie*, ed. H. Hames, Leiden, pp. 97–123.
Abulafia, D., 2006, 'Ferdinand the Catholic and the Kingdom of Naples', in Shaw, C., ed., *Italy and the European powers: the impact of war 1500–1530*, Leiden, pp. 129–58.
Albuquerque, L. de, 1989, *Introdução à história dos descobrimentos portugueses*, 4th ed., Mem Martins.

Allaire, L., 1997a, 'The Lesser Antilles before Columbus', in *The indigenous people of the Caribbean*, ed. S. Wilson, Gainesville FL, pp. 20–8.

Allaire, L., 1997b, 'The Caribs of the Lesser Antilles', in *The indigenous people of the Caribbean*, ed. S. Wilson, Gainesville FL, pp. 179–85.

Alvarez, M., 1999, *Arqueologia linguistica: estudios modernos dirigidos al rescate y reconstrucción del arahuaco taino*, San Juan de Puerto Rico.

Amazon to Caribbean: early peoples of the rainforest, 2005, Horniman Museum, London.

Ames, G.J., 2004, *Vasco da Gama: Renaissance crusader*, New York.

Angra, a Terceira e os Açores nas rotas da Índia e das Américas, 1999, Angra do Heroismo.

Aram, B., 2005, *Juana the Mad: sovereignty and dynasty in Renaissance Europe*, Baltimore MD.

Arciniegas, G., 1955, *Amerigo and the New World: the life and times of Amerigo Vespucci*, New York NY.

Arens, W., 1980, *The man-eating myth*, New York NY.

Arranz Márquez, L., 2006, *Cristóbal Colón: misterio y grandeza*, Madrid.

Arrom, J.J., and García Arévalo, M.A., 1986, *Cimarrón*, Santo Domingo.

Atkinson, L.-G., ed., 2006, *The earliest inhabitants: the dynamics of the Jamaican Taíno*, Kingston, Jamaica.

Axelson, E., 1973, *Congo to Cape: early Portuguese explorers*, London.

Aznar Vallejo, E., 1979, *La organización económica de la Islas Canarias después de la Conquista (1478–1527)*, Coll. Guagua, Las Palmas de Gran Canaria.

Aznar Vallejo, E., 1983, *La integración de las Islas Canarias en la Corona de Castilla (1478–1526)*, La Laguna and Seville.

Aznar Vallejo, E., 1994, 'The conquests of the Canary Islands', in Schwartz, S., ed., *Implicit understandings: observing, reporting and reflecting on the encounters between Europeans and other peoples in the early modern era*, Cambridge, pp. 134–56.

Bailyn, B., 2005, *Atlantic history: concept and contours*, Cambridge MA.

Baldacci, O., 1997, *Columbian atlas of the great discovery*, Nuova Raccolta Colombiana, English edition, vol. 9, Rome.

Ballesteros Gaibrois, M., 1997, *Juan Caboto*, Cuadernos Colombinos, vol. 21, Valladolid.

Barata, F. Themudo, 1998, *Navegação, comércio e relações políticas: os portugueses no Mediterrâneo Ocidental (1385–1466)*, Lisbon.

Barker, F., Hulme, P., and Iversen, M., eds, 1998, *Cannibalism and the colonial world*, Cambridge.

Bartlett, R., 1993, *The making of Europe: conquest, colonization and cultural change, 950–1350*, London.

Bartlett, R., 2006, *Gerald of Wales: a voice of the Middle Ages*, 2nd edn, Stroud.

Bedini, S., ed., 1991, *Christopher Columbus encyclopædia*, 2 vols, Basingstoke (repr. in one-vol. paperback edn as: Bedini, S., *Christopher Columbus and the age of exploration*, New York, 1998).

Belenguer Cebrià, E., 1976, *València en la crisi del segle XV*, Barcelona.

Belenguer Cebrià, E., 2001, *Fernando el Católico: un monarca decisivo en las encrucijadas de su época*, 3rd edn, Barcelona.

Bernal, I., 1975, *Mexico before Cortez: art, history, legend*, 2nd edn, Garden City NY.

Bernárdez Vilar, X., 2001, *Antes da invención de América: as descubertas precolombinas dos século XV*, Vigo.

Bernheimer, R., 1952, *Wild men in the Middle Ages*, Cambridge MA.

Birmingham, D., 2000, *Trade and empire in the Atlantic, 1400–1600*, London.

Bitterli, U., 1989, *Cultures in conflict: encounters between European and non-European cultures, 1492–1800*, Cambridge.

Blake, J.W., 1977, *West Africa: quest for God and gold, 1454–1578*, London (previous edn: *European beginnings in West Africa*, London, 1937).

Blumenthal, D., 2008, *Enemies and familiars: Muslim, eastern, and black African slaves in late medieval Valencia*, Philadelphia.

Boas, G., 1948, *Essays on primitivism and related ideas in the Middle Ages* (reprinted in 1999 as: *Primitivism and related ideas in the Middle Ages*), Baltimore MD.

Boruchoff, D.A., ed., 2003, *Isabel la Católica*, Basingstoke.

Boucher, P., 1993, *Cannibal encounters: Europeans and Island Caribs, 1492–1763*, Baltimore MD.

Boxer, C.R., 1969, *The Portuguese seaborne empire 1415–1825*, London.

Bray, W., ed., 1993, *The meeting of two worlds: Europe and the Americas 1492–1650*, also published as *Proceedings of the British Academy*, vol. 81, London.

Brett, M., and Fentress, E., 1996, *The Berbers*, Oxford.

Brotton, J., 1997, *Trading territories: mapping the early modern world*, London.

Bucher, B., 1981, *Icon and conquest: a structural analysis of the illustrations of de Bry's Great Voyages*, Chicago.

Bueno, E., 1998, *A viagem do descobrimento: a verdadeira história da expedição de Cabral*, Rio de Janeiro.

Burckhardt, J., 1990, *The civilization of the Renaissance in Italy*, trans. S.G.C. Middlemore, ed. P. Burke, Harmondsworth.

Bynum, C.W., 2007, *Wonderful Blood: theology and practice in late medieval northern Germany and beyond*, Philadelphia.

Cabrera Pérez, J.C., 1992, *Lanzarote y los Majos*, La Prehistoria de Canarias, vol. 4, Santa Cruz de Tenerife.

Cabrera Pérez, J.C., 1993, *Fuerteventura y los Majoreros*, La Prehistoria de Canarias, vol. 7, Santa Cruz de Tenerife.

Cachey, T., 1995, *Le Isole Fortunate: appunti di storia letteraria italiana*, Rome.

Campbell, M.R., 1988, *The witness and the other world: exotic European travel writing, 400–1600*, Ithaca NY.

Carita, R., 1989, *Historia da Madeira (1420–1566): povoamento e produção açucareira*, Funchal.

Carus-Wilson, E., 1954, *Medieval merchant venturers*, London.

Cary, M., and Warmington, E.H., 1963, *The ancient explorers*, 2nd edn, Harmondsworth.

Cassi, A.A., 2007, *Ultramar: l'invenzione europea del Nuovo Mondo*, Bari and Rome.

Catz, R., 1993, *Christopher Columbus and the Portuguese, 1476–1498*, Westport CT.

Chamberlain, R.S., 1939/1970, 'Castilian backgrounds of the *Repartimiento-Encomienda*', Carnegie Institution of Washington, *Contributions to American Anthropology and History*, vol. 5, 1939, pp. 33–52; partly repr. as 'The roots of lordship; the *Encomienda* in medieval Castile', in Johnson, H.B., *From reconquest to Empire*, New York NY, 1970, pp. 124–47.

Chaunu, P., 1977, *Séville et l'Amérique, XVIe–XVII siècle*, Paris.

Chaunu, P., 1979, *European expansion in the later Middle Ages*, Amsterdam.

Concepción, J.L., 1984, *The Guanches: survivors and their descendants*, Santa Cruz de Tenerife.

Cook, N.D., 1998, *Born to die: disease and New World conquest, 1492–1650*, Cambridge.

Cooper, V.O., 1997, 'Language and gender among the Kalinago of fifteenth-century St Croix', in Wilson, S., ed., *The indigenous people of the Caribbean*, Gainesville FL, pp. 186–96.

Corrêa, Marquez de Jacome, 1926, *Historia da descoberta das ilhas*, Coimbra.

Cortesão, J., *A expedição de Pedro Álvares Cabral e o descobrimento do Brasil*, Casa da Moeda, 1994.

Couto, J., 1997, *A Construção do Brasil: Ameríndios, Portugueses a Africanos, do início do povoamento a finais de Quinhentos*, 2nd edn, Lisbon.

Crosby, A., 1986, *Ecological imperialism: the biological expansion of Europe, 900–1900*, Cambridge.

Curet, L.A., 2005, *Caribbean paleodemography: population, culture history, and sociological processes in ancient Puerto Rico*, Tuscaloosa AL.

Curet, L.A., Dawdy, S.L., and La Rosa Corzo, G., eds, 2005, *Dialogues in Cuban archaeology*, Tuscaloosa AL.

Curtin, P.D., 1990, *The rise and fall of the plantation complex*, Cambridge.

Dacal Moure, R., and Rivero De La Calle, M., 1996, *Art and archaeology of pre-Columbian Cuba*, Pittsburgh PA.

Das Neves, João Alves, 1991, *Pedro Álvares Cabral, o descobridor do Brasil*, 2nd edn, Oporto.

Daumet, G., 1913, 'Luis de la Cerda ou d'Espagne', *Bulletin hispanique*, vol. 15, pp. 38–67.

Davidson, B., 1998, *West Africa before the colonial era*, London.

Davidson, M., 1997, *Columbus then and now*, Norman OK.

Davies, P., 1995, *Are we alone? Implications of the discovery of extra-terrestrial life*, Harmondsworth.

Deagan, K., and Cruxent, J.M., 2002a, *Archaeology at La Isabela: America's first European town*, New Haven CT and London.

Deagan, K., and Cruxent, J.M., 2002b, *Columbus's outpost among the Taínos: Spain and America at La Isabela, 1493–1498*, New Haven CT and London.

De Boer, D.E.H., 1998, *Kennis op Kamelen: Europa en de buiten-Europese wereld (1150–1350)*, Amsterdam.

DeCorse, C.R., 2001, *An archaeology of Elmina: Africans and Europeans on the Gold Coast, 1400–1900*, Washington DC.

De la Cruz Jiménez Gómez, M., 1993, *El Hierro y los Bimbachos*, La Prehistoria de Canarias, vol. 6, Santa Cruz de Tenerife.

De la Roncière, C., 1924, *La découverte de l'Afrique au moyen âge*, Mémoires de la Société Royale de Géographie d'Égypte, vol. 5, Cairo.

Denevan, W.M., ed., 1992, *The native population of the Americas in 1492*, 2nd edn, Madison WI.

Devereux, A.Q., 1993, *Juan Ponce de León, King Ferdinand and the Fountain of Youth*, Spartanburg SC.

Diffie, B.W., 1960, *Prelude to empire: Portugal overseas before Henry the Navigator*, Lincoln NE.

Disney, A., and Booth, E., eds, 2000, *Vasco de Gama and the linking of Europe and Asia*, Oxford and New Delhi.

Doussinague, J.M., 1944, *La política internacional de Fernando el Católico*, Madrid.

Drewett, P., et al., 1991, *Prehistoric Barbados*, Barbados and London.

Dreyer, E.L., 2007, *Zheng He: China and the oceans in the early Ming Dynasty, 1403–1433*, New York.

Dugard, M., 2005, *The last voyage of Columbus*, New York and Boston.

Earle, T.F., and Lowe, K.J.P., eds, 2005, *Black Africans in Renaissance Europe*, Cambridge.

Eddy, M., 1989, *Crafts and traditions of the Canary Islands*, Aylesbury.

Edwards, J., 2000, *The Spain of the Catholic Monarchs, 1474–1520*, Oxford.

Edwards, J., 2005, *Ferdinand and Isabella*, Harlow, 2005.

Elliott, J.H., 1963, *Imperial Spain, 1469–1716*, London.

Elliott, J.H., 1970, *The Old World and the New, 1492–1650*, Cambridge.

Elliott, J. H., 1989, *Spain and its World 1500–1700*, New Haven CT and London.

Emmer, P.C., ed., 1999, *New societies: the Caribbean in the long sixteenth century*, UNESCO General History of the Caribbean, vol. 2, London.

Enterline, J.R., 2002, *Erikson, Eskimos and Columbus: medieval European knowledge of America*, Baltimore MD.

Ewen, C.R., 1991, *From Spaniard to Creole: the archaeology of cultural formation at Puerto Real Haiti*, Tuscaloosa AL.

Fagan, B., 2006, *Fish on Friday: feasting, fasting and the discovery of the New World*, Boston and New York.

Farnsworth, P., ed., 2001, *Island lives: historical archaeologies of the Caribbean*, Tuscaloosa AL.

Farrujia de la Rosa, A.J., 2005, *Imperialist archaeology in the Canary Islands*, British Archaeological Reports, no. S1333, Oxford.

Fernández-Armesto, F., 1982, *The Canary Islands after the conquest*, Oxford.

Fernández-Armesto, F., 1986, 'Atlantic exploration before Columbus: the evidence of maps', *Renaissance and Modern Studies*, 30, 1986, pp. 12–34, repr. in F. Fernández-Armesto, ed., *The European Opportunity*, vol. 2, *An Expanding World*, Aldershot, 1995, pp. 278–300.

Fernández-Armesto, F., 1987, *Before Columbus. Exploration and colonisation from the Mediterranean to the Atlantic, 1229–1492*, London.

Fernández-Armesto, F., 1991, *Columbus*, Oxford, 1991.

Fernández-Armesto, F., 2000, *Columbus and the conquest of the impossible*, 2nd edn, London.

Fernández-Armesto, F., 2004, *So you think you're human?*, Oxford, 2004.

Fernández-Armesto, F., 2006, *Amerigo: the man who gave his name to America*, London.

Ferreira Priegue, M.E., 1988, *Galicia en el comercio maritimo medieval*, A Coruna.

Ferro, G., 1992, *Liguria and Genoa at the time of Columbus*, Nuova Raccolta Colombiana, English edition, vol. 3, 2 vols, Rome.

Ferro, G., 1996, *The Genoese cartographic tradition and Christopher Columbus*, Nuova Raccolta Colombiana, English edition, vol. 12, Rome.

Ferro, G., Faldini, F., and Milanesi, M., 1992, *Columbian iconography*, Nuova Raccolta Colombiana, English edition, vol. 11, Rome.

Flint, V., 1992a, 'Christopher Columbus and the friars', in L. Smith and B. Ward, eds, *Intellectual life in the Middle Ages: essays presented to Margaret Gibson*, London, pp. 295–310.

Flint, V., 1992b, *The imaginative landscape of Christopher Columbus*, Princeton NJ.

Floyd, T.S., 1973, *The Columbus dynasty in the Caribbean 1492–1526*, Albuquerque NM.

Focus Behaim-Globus, 1992, catalogue of an exhibition at the Germanisches National-Museum, Nuremberg, 2 vols, Nuremberg.

Fonseca, L. Adão de, 1998, *Vasco da Gama: o homem, a viagem, a época*, Lisbon.

Fonseca, L. Adão de, 1999a, *Os descobrimentos e a formação do oceano Atlântico*, Lisbon.

Fonseca, L. Adão de, 1999b, *Pedro Álvares Cabral: uma viagem*, Lisbon.

Fonseca, L. Adão de, and Cadeddu, M.E., 2001, *Portogallo mediterraneo*, Cagliari.

Forbes, J.D., 2007, *The American discovery of Europe*, Urbana IL.

Fraser, A., 1992, *The Gypsies*, Oxford.

Friedman, J.B., 1981, *The monstrous races in medieval art and thought*, Cambridge MA.

Fuson, R.H., 2000, *Juan Ponce de León and the Spanish discovery of Puerto Rico and Florida*, Blacksburg VA.

Fuson, R.H., 1995, *Legendary islands of the Ocean Sea*, Sarasota FL.

Gallinari, L. 1992, *Diego Alvarez Chanca, medico di Cristoforo Colombo*, Cagliari.

Garnsey, P., 1996, *Ideas of slavery from Aristotle to Augustine*, Cambridge.

Gay, F., 1997, *The ships of Christopher Columbus*, Nuova Raccolta Colombiana, English edition, vol. 7, Rome.

Gerbi, A., 1985, *Nature in the New World*, Pittsburgh PA.

Geremek, B., 1992, *Uomini senza padrone: poveri e marginali tra medioevo e età moderna*, Turin.

Gil, J., 1989, *Mitos y utopías del descubrimiento*, vol. 1, *Colón y su tiempo*, Madrid.

Godinho, V. Magalhães, 1956, *O 'Mediterrâneo' Saariano e as Caravanas do Ouro: Geografia econômica e social do Sáara Ocidental e Central do XI ao XV século*, São Paulo.

González Antón, R., and Antón Tejera, A., 1990, *Los Aborígines Canarios: Gran Canaria y Tenerife*, 2nd edn, Madrid.

Goodman, J., 1986, *Chivalry and exploration 1298–1630*, Woodbridge.

Grafton, A., with Shelford, A., and Siraisi, N., 1992, *New worlds, ancient texts: the power of tradition and the shock of discovery*, Cambridge MA.

Granberry, J., and Vescelius, G., 2004, *The languages of the pre-Columbian Antilles*, Tuscaloosa AL.

Greenblatt, S., 1991, *Marvelous possessions: the wonder of the New World*, Oxford.

Gregório, Rute Dias, 2001, *Pero Anes do Canto: um homem e um património (1473–1556)*, Ponta Delgada.

Guerreiro, M. Viegas, 1992, *A carta de Pero Vaz de Caminha lida por um etnógrafo*, Lisbon.

Hair, P.E.H., 1994, *The founding of the Castelo de São Jorge de Mina* (University of Wisconsin African Studies Program), Madison WI.

Hanke, L., 1959, *Aristotle and the American Indians: a study in race prejudice in the modern world*, London.

Hanke, L., 2002, *The Spanish struggle for justice in the conquest of America*, 2nd edn, Dallas TX.

Hanson, C., 2001, *Atlantic emporium: Portugal and the wider world 1147–1497*, New Orleans LA.

Hart, J., 2001, *Representing the New World*, Basingstoke.

Hart, J., 2003a, *Columbus, Shakespeare and the interpretation of the New World*, Basingstoke.

Hart, J., 2003b, *Comparing empires*, Basingstoke.

Hart, J., 2005, *Contesting empires*, Basingstoke.

Hattendorf, J.B., and King, E.J., 1996, *Maritime History*, vol. 1, *The Age of Discovery*, Malabar FL.

Heers, J., 1981, *Esclaves et domestiques au moyen âge dans le monde méditerranéen*, Paris.

Hemming, J., 1978a, *Red gold: the conquest of the Brazilian Indians*, London.

Hemming, J., 1978b, *The search for El Dorado*, London.

Henige, D., 1991, *In search of Columbus: the sources for the first voyage*, Tucson AR.

Hernando Sánchez, C.J., 1996, *Las Indias en la Monarquía Católica: imagines e ideas políticas*, Valladolid.

Highfield, A.R., 1997, 'Some observations on the Taino language', in Wilson, S., ed., *The indigenous people of the Caribbean*, Gainesville FL, pp. 154–68.

Highfield, R., ed., 1972, *Spain in the fifteenth century 1369–1516*, London.

Hillgarth, J., 1978, *The Spanish kingdoms*, vol. 2, *Castilian hegemony, 1410–1516*, Oxford.

Hodgen, M.T., 1964, *Early anthropology in the sixteenth and seventeenth centuries*, Philadelphia PA.

Hulme, P., 1986, *Colonial encounters: Europe and the native Caribbean, 1492–1797*, London.

Hulme, P., 1994, 'Tales of distinction: European ethnography and the Caribbean', in Schwartz, S., ed., *Implicit understandings: observing, reporting and reflecting on the encounters between Europeans and other peoples in the early modern era*, Cambridge, pp. 157–97.

Husband, T., with Gilmore-House, G., 1980, *The wild man: symbolism and thought*, New York.

Hyde, J.K., 1982, 'Real and imaginary journeys in the later Middle Ages', *Bulletin of the John Rylands University Library*, vol. 65, pp. 125–47.

Hyde, J.K., 1993, *Literacy and its uses: studies on late medieval Italy*, ed. D. Waley, Manchester.

Incer Barquero, J., ed., 2002, *Colón y la Costa Caribe de Centroamérica*, Managua.

Janiga-Perkins, C.G., 2001, *Immaterial transcendences: colonial subjectivity as process in Brazil's Letter of Discovery (1500)*, New York.

Janssen Perio, E.M., 1994, *Een nieuwe wereld: Europese ontdekkingsreizen en renaissance rond 1500*, Baarn.

Jiménez González, J.J, 1990, *Los Canarios*, Santa Cruz de Tenerife.

Jiménez González, J.J., 1992, *Gran Canaria y los Canarios*, La Prehistoria de Canarias, vol. 2, Santa Cruz de Tenerife.

Johnson, C., 2006, 'Renaissance German cosmographers and the naming of America', *Past and present*, no. 191.

Johnson, D., 1997, *Phantom islands of the Atlantic: the legends of seven islands that never were*, London.

Johnson, H.B., ed., 1970, *From reconquest to empire: the Iberian background to Latin American history*, New York.

Johnson, H.B., 1997, *Camponeses e colonizadores: estudios de história luso-brasileira*, Lisbon.

Johnson, H.B., 2004, *Dos estudos polemicos*, Tucson AR.

Kadir, D., 1992, *Columbus and the ends of the Earth: Europe's prophetic rhetoric as conquering ideology*, Berkeley CA.

Kamen, H., 2002, *Spain's road to Empire*, London, 2002 (American edition: *Empire*, New York).

Kayserling, M., 2002, *Christopher Columbus and the participation of the Jews in the Spanish and Portuguese discoveries*, Albuquerque NM, repr. from 1st edn, 1894.

Kedar, B.Z., 1984, *Crusade and mission: European approaches toward the Muslims*, Princeton, NJ.

Keegan, W., 1992, *The people who discovered Columbus*, Gainesville FL.

Keegan, W., 2007, *Taino Indian myth and practice: the arrival of the stranger king*, Gainesville FL.

Keen, M., 1986, 'Gadifer de la Salle: a late medieval knight errant', in C. Harper-Bill and R. Harvey, eds, *The ideals and practice of medieval knighthood: papers from the first and second Strawberry Hill conferences*, Woodbridge, 1986, pp. 121–34.

Keene, D., 2003, *Yoshimasa and the silver pavilion: the creation of the soul of Japan*, New York NY.

Kerchache, J., 1994, *L'art taíno*, Musée du Petit Palais, Paris.

Kikkert, O., 1992, *Taíno: Columbus' verstoorde Paradijs*, Kampen.

Kretzmann, N., Kenny, A., and Pinborg, J., eds, 1982, *The Cambridge history of later medieval philosophy*, Cambridge.

Ladero Quesada, M.A., 1979, *Los primeros Europeos en Canarias (siglos XIV y XV)*, Coll. Guagua, Las Palmas de Gran Canaria.

Ladero Quesada, M.A., 2002, *El primer oro de América: los comienzos de la Casa de la Contratación de las Yndias (1503–1511)*, Madrid.

Larsen, S., 1983, *Danimarca e Portugal o século XV*, Lisbon.

Lazcana Sahagún, C., 2000, *Pa-Tai: la historia olvidada de Ensenada*, Ensenada.

Lestringant, F., 1994, *Cannibals*, Cambridge.

Lewis, B., 1995, *Cultures in conflict: Christians, Muslims and Jews in the age of discovery*, New York.

Liss, P., 2005, *Isabel the queen*, 2nd edn, New York and Oxford.

Livingston, M., 2004, 'More Vinland maps and texts: discovering the New World in Higden's *Polychronicon*', *Journal of medieval history*, vol. 30, pp. 25–44.

Llewelyn Price, M., 2003, *Consuming passions: the uses of cannibalism in late medieval and early modern Europe*, New York and London.

Lowe, K.J.P., ed., 2000, *Cultural links between Portugal and Italy in the Renaissance*, Oxford.

Lowe, K.J.P., and Earle, T.F., eds, 2005, *Black Africans in Renaissance Europe*, Cambridge.

Luscombe, D., 1982, 'The state of nature and the origins of the state', in Kretzmann, N., Kenny, A., and Pinborg, J., eds, *The Cambridge history of later medieval philosophy*, Cambridge, pp. 757–70.

McCrank, L., ed., 1993, *Discovery in the archives of Spain and Portugal: quincentenary essays*, New York.

McDonald, M., 2004, *The print collection of Ferdinand Columbus, 1488–1539*, 2 vols, London.

MacDonald, N.P., 1996, *The making of Brazil: Portuguese roots 1500–1822*, Lewes.

McEwen, C., Barreto, C., and Neves, E., eds, 2001, *Unknown Amazon: culture in nature in ancient Brazil*, London.

McGrade, A.S., 1982, 'Rights, natural rights, and the philosophy of law', in Kretzmann, N., Kenny, A., and Pinborg, J., eds, *The Cambridge history of later medieval philosophy*, Cambridge, pp. 738–56.

McNally, R.T., and Florescu, R., 1974, *In search of Dracula*, London.

Magasich-Airola, J., and de Beer, J.-M., 2006, *America magica: when Renaissance Europe thought it had conquered Paradise*, London.

Manfredi, V., 1996, *Le Isole Fortunate*, Rome.

Marchant, A., 1942, *From barter to slavery. The economic relations of Portuguese and Indians in the settlement of Brazil, 1500–1580*, published as monograph in Johns Hopkins University Studies in Historical and Political Science, series lx, no. 1, 1942, Baltimore MD; and separately, 1966, Gloucester MA.

Marcus, G.J., 1980, *The conquest of the North Atlantic*, Ipswich.

Marinescu, C., 1994, *La politique orientale d'Alfonse V d'Aragon, roi de Naples (1416–1458)*, Institut d'Estudis Catalans, Memòries de la Secció historico-arqueológico, vol. 46, Barcelona.

Marques, A.H. de Oliveira, ed., 1996, *A expansão quatrocentista*, Nova história da expansão portuguesa, vol. 2, Lisbon.

Martínez, M., 1996, *Las isles Canarias de la antigüedad al Renacimiento: nuevos aspectos*, Santa Cruz de Tenerife.

Martínez, M., 2002, *Las Canarias en la antigüedad clásica: mito, historia e imaginario*, Las Palmas de Gran Canaria and Santa Cruz de Tenerife.

Martínez Arango, F., 1997, *Los Aborígines de la Cuenca de Santiago de Cuba*, Miami FL.

Martinho, T., 2001, *Pedro Álvares Cabral: o homem, o feito e a memória*, V.N. de Gaia.

Martinón-Torres, M., Valcárcel Rojas, R., Cooper, J., and Rehren, T., 2007, 'Metals, microanalysis and meaning: a study of metal objects excavated from the indigenous cemetery of El Chorro de Maíta, Cuba', *Journal of archaeological science*, vol. 34, pp. 194–204.

Martín Rodríguez, E., 1992, *La Palma y los Auaritas*, La Prehistoria de Canarias, vol. 3, Santa Cruz de Tenerife.

Mason, P., 1990, *Deconstructing America: representations of the Other*, London.

Mauny, R., 1960, *Les navigations médiévales sur les côtes sahariennes*, Lisbon.

Mazeika, R., 1994, 'Of cabbages and knights: trade and trade treaties with the infidel on the northern frontier, 1200–1340', *Journal of medieval history*, vol. 20, pp. 63–76.

Menocal, M.R., 2002, *The ornament of the world: how Muslims, Jews, and Christians created a culture of tolerance in medieval Spain*, Boston.

Mercer, J., 1973, *Canary Islands: Fuerteventura*, Newton Abbot.

Mercer, J., 1980, *The Canary islanders*, London.

Merediz, E., 2004, *Refracted images. The Canary Islands through a New World lens*, Phoenix AR.

Metcalf, A.C., 2005, *Go-betweens and the colonization of Brazil 1500–1600*, Austin TX.

Mignolo, W.D., 1995, *The darker side of the Renaissance*, Ann Arbor MI.

Milanich, J.T., 1994, *Archaeology of pre-Columbian Florida*, Gainesville FL.

Milanich, J.T., 1995, *Florida Indians and the invasion from Europe*, Gainesville FL.

Milanich, J.T., 1996, *The Timucua*, Oxford.

Milanich, J.T., 1998, *Florida's Indians from ancient times to the present*, Gainesville FL.

Milanich, J.T., and Milbrath, S., eds, 1989, *First encounters: Spanish exploration in the Caribbean and the United States, 1492–1570*, Gainesville FL.

Millares Torres A., 1997, *Historia de la Gran Canaria*, vol. 1, new ed., Las Palmas de Gran Canaria.

Miller, B.W., 1988, *Chumash: a picture of their world*, Los Osos CA.

Miner Solá, E., 2002, *Diccionario Taíno ilustrado*, San Juan de Puerto Rico.

Mira Caballos, E., 2000, *Las Antillas Mayores 1492–1550: ensayos y documentos*, Madrid.

Moffitt, J.F., and Sebastian, S., 1996, *O brave new people: the European invention of the American Indian*, Albuquerque NM.

Moniz de Bettencourt, J., 1993, *Os Bettencourt, da origines normandas a expansão atlántica*, Lisbon.

Montané Martí, J.C., and Lazcano Sahagún, C., 2001, *El descubrimiento de California: las expediciones de Becerra y Grijala a la Mar del Sur 1533–1534*, Ensenada.

Montbrun, C., 1984, *Les Petites Antilles avant Christophe Colomb*, Paris.

Montell, J., 2003, *La caída de Mexico-Tenochtitlán*, Mexico City.

Moore, G., 1972, 'La spedizione dei fratelli Vivaldi e nuovi documenti d'archivio', *Atti della Società Ligure di Storia Patria*, nuova serie, vol. 12, pp. 387–400.

Morales Padrón, F., 2003, *Spanish Jamaica*, Kingston, Jamaica.

Moreau, J.-P., 1992, *Les Petites Antilles de Christophe Colomb à Richelieu*, Paris.

Morison, S.E., 1940, *Portuguese voyages to America in the fifteenth century*, Cambridge MA.

Morison, S.E., 1992, *Admiral of the Ocean Sea*, new edn, New York.

Muldoon, J., 1978, 'Papal responsibility for the infidel: another look at Alexander VI's *Inter Caetera*', *Catholic historical review*, vol. 64, pp. 168–84.

Muldoon, J., 1979a, *Popes, lawyers and infidels: the Church and the non-Christian world, 1250–1500*, Liverpool.

Muldoon, J., 1979b, 'The Avignon papacy and the frontiers of Christendom: the evidence of Vatican Register 62', *Archivum historiae pontificiae*, vol. 17, pp. 125–95, repr. in. Muldoon (1998).

Muldoon, J., 1998, *Canon law, the expansion of Europe, and world order*, Aldershot.

Nakamura, H., 1962, *East Asia in old maps*, Centre for East Asian Cultural Studies, Tokyo.

Navarro Mederos, J.F., 1993, *La Gomera y los Gomeros*, La Prehistoria de Canarias, vol. 5, Santa Cruz de Tenerife.

Newitt, M., 2005, *A History of Portuguese overseas expansion 1400–1668*, Abingdon.

Nicholson, D.V., 1983, *The story of the Arawaks in Antigua and Barbuda*, Antigua.

O'Gorman, E., 1961, *The invention of America: an enquiry into the historical nature of the New World and the meaning of its history*, Bloomington IN.

Olazagasti, I., 1997, 'The material culture of the Taino Indians', in Wilson, S., ed., *The indigenous people of the Caribbean*, Gainesville FL, pp. 131–9.

Oliver, J.R., 1997, 'The Taino Cosmos', in Wilson, S., ed., *The indigenous people of the Caribbean*, Gainesville FL, pp. 140–53.

Oliver, R., and Atmore, A., 2001, *Medieval Africa 1250–1800*, Cambridge.

Olsen, F., 1974a, *Indian Creek: Arawak site on Antigua, West Indies*, Norman OK.

Olsen, F., 1974b, *On the trail of the Arawaks*, Norman OK.

O'Reilly, W., 1998, 'Conceptualizing America in early modern central Europe', *Explorations in early American culture*, special issue of *Pennsylvania history, a journal of mid-Atlantic studies*, vol. 65, pp. 101–21.

Otte, E., 1996, *Sevilla y sus mercaderes a fines de la Edad Media*, Seville.

Padoan, G., 1964, 'Petrarca, Boccaccio e la scoperta della Canarie', *Italia medioevale e umanistica*, vol. 7, pp. 263–77, repr. with additional material in Padoan, G., *Il Boccaccio, le Muse, il Parnasso e l'Arno*, Florence, 1978, pp. 277–91.

Padrón, R., 2004, *The spacious word: cartography, literature, and empire in early modern Spain*, Chicago.

Pagden, A., 1986, *The fall of natural man. The American Indian and the origins of comparative ethnography*, 2nd edn, Cambridge.

Pagden, A., 1993, *European encounters with the New World*, New Haven CT and London.

Paiewonsky, M., 1991, *Conquest of Eden, 1493–1515: other voyages of Columbus, Guadeloupe, Puerto Rico, Hispaniola, Virgin Islands*, Rome.

Palmer, S.H., and Reinhartz, D., 1988, *Essays on the history of North American discovery and exploration*, Arlington TX.

Parry, J.H., 1963, *The Age of Reconnaissance: discovery, exploration and settlement 1450–1650*, London.

Parry, J.H., 1979, *The discovery of South America*, London.

Peck, D.T., 1995, *Ponce de León and the discovery of Florida: the man, the myth and the truth*, Florida.

Peláez, M.J., 1981, *Catalunya després de la guerra civil del segle XV: institucions, formes de govern i relacions socials i econòmiques (1472–1479)*, Barcelona.

Pérez Saavedra, F., 1982, *La mujer en la sociedad indigena de Canarias*, Las Palmas de Gran Canaria.

Phillips, J.R.S., 1998, *The medieval expansion of Europe*, 2nd edn, Oxford.

Phillips, W.D., 1992a, *Before 1492: Christopher Columbus' formative years*, American Historical Association, Essays on the Columbian Encounter, Washington DC.

Phillips, W.D. and C.R., 1992b, *The worlds of Christopher Columbus*, Cambridge.

Picard, C., 1997, *L'océan atlantique musulman de la conquête arabe à l'époque almohade: navigation et mise en valeur des côtes d'al-Andalus et du Maghreb occidental (Portugal-Espagne-Maroc)*, Paris.

Pieper, R., 2000, *Die Vermittlung einer neuen Welt: Amerika im nachrichtennetz des Habsburgischen Imperiums 1493–1598*, Mainz.

Pieraccioli, R., 1992, *Hispaniola 1492: cronaca di un etnocidio*, San Domenico di Fiesole.

Pifarré Torres, D., 2002, *El comerç internacional de Barcelona i el Mar del Nord (Bruges) al final del segle XIV*, Montserrat.

Pike, R., 1966, *Enterprise and adventure: the Genoese in Seville and the opening of the New World*, Ithaca NY.

Pleij, H., 2001, *Dreaming of Cockaigne: medieval fantasies of the perfect life*, New York.

Pope, P., 1997, *The many landfalls of John Cabot*, Toronto.

Prescott, W.H., 1994, *History of the conquest of Mexico*, ed. F. Fernández-Armesto, London.

Pym, R., 2007, *The Gypsies of early modern Spain, 1425–1783*, Basingstoke.

Quinn, D.B., 1961, 'The argument for the English discovery of America between 1480 and 1494', *The geographical journal*, vol. 127, pp. 277–85.

Ramsey, J.F., 1973, *Spain: the rise of the first world power*, University AL.

Rau, V., 1970, 'The Madeiran sugar cane plantations', in Johnson, H.B., ed., *From reconquest to empire: the Iberian background to Latin American history*, New York, pp. 71–84.

Restall, M., 2003, *Seven myths of the Spanish conquest*, Oxford and New York.

Reston, J., 2005/6, *Dogs of God: Columbus, the Inquisition and the defeat of the Moors*, New York and London.

Ríos Lloret, R., 2003, *Germana de Foix, una mujer, una reina, una corte*, Valencia.

Rosenblatt, Á., 'The Caribbean, central America and Yucatán', in Denevan, W.M, ed., 1992, *The native population of the Americas in 1492*, 2nd edn, Madison WI, pp. 35–41.

Rouse, I., 1992, *The Tainos: rise and decline of the people who greeted Columbus*, New Haven CT.

Rowell, S., 1994, *Lithuania ascending: a pagan empire within east-central Europe, 1295–1345*, Cambridge.

Rubiés, J.-P., 2000, *Travel and ethnology in the Renaissance*, Cambridge.

Rubiés, J.-P., 2006, 'Travel writing and humanistic culture: a blunted impact?', *Journal of modern history*, vol. 10, pp. 131–68.

Ruiz, T., 2007, *Spain's Centuries of Crisis 1300–1474*, Oxford.

Rumeu de Armas, A., 1985, *Nueva luz sobre las capitulaciones de Santa Fé*, Madrid.

Rumeu de Armas, A., 1986, *El Obispado de Telde: misioneros mallorquines y catalanes en el Atlántico*, 2nd edn, Madrid and Telde.

Russell, P.E., 1979, *O infante D. Henrique e as Ilhas Canárias: una dimensão mal compreendida da biografia henriquina*, Academia das Ciências de Lisboa, Instituto de Altos Estudios, n.s., fasc. 5, Lisbon, 1979.

Russell, P.E., 1984, *Prince Henry the Navigator. The rise and fall of a culture hero*, Oxford, reprinted in Russell (1995).

Russell, P.E., 1995, *Portugal, Spain and the African Atlantic, 1343–1490*, Aldershot.

Russell, P.E., 2000, *Prince Henry 'the Navigator': a life*, New Haven CT and London.

Russell-Wood, A.J.R., 1992, *The Portuguese Empire, 1415–1808: a world on the move*, Baltimore MD.

Ryder, A., 1969, *Benin and the Europeans, 1485–1897*, London.

Sale, K., 1991, *Conquest of Paradise: Christopher Columbus and the Columbian legacy*, London.

Salomon, F., and Schwartz, S.B., eds, 1999–2000, *The Cambridge history of the native peoples of America*, vol. 3, *South America*, parts 1 and 2, Cambridge.

Sauer, C.W., 1992, *The early Spanish Main*, 4th edn, with intro. by A. Pagden, Berkeley CA.

Saunders, A. de C.M., 1982, *Black slaves and freedmen in Portugal, 1441–1555*, Cambridge.

Scammell, G., 1981, *The world encompassed*, London.

Schorsch, J., 2004, *Jews and blacks in the early modern world*, Cambridge.

Schwartz, S.B., 1986, *The Iberian Mediterranean and Atlantic traditions in the formation of Columbus as a colonizer*, Minneapolis.

Schwartz, S.B., ed., 1994, *Implicit understandings: observing, reporting and reflecting on the encounters between Europeans and other peoples in the early modern period*, Cambridge.

Schwartz, S.B., ed., 2004, *Tropical Babylons: sugar and the making of the Atlantic world 1450–1680*, Durham NC.

Seaver, K., 1996, *The frozen echo: Greenland and the exploration of North America, ca. AD 1000–1500*, Stanford CA.

Seaver, K., 2004, *Maps, myths and men: the story of the Vinland Map*, Stanford CA.

Seed, P., 1995, *Ceremonies of possession in Europe's conquest of the New World, 1492–1640*, Cambridge.

Shepherd, V., and Beckles, H. McD., eds, 2000, *Caribbean slavery in the Atlantic world*, Oxford and Kingston, Jamaica.

Siegel, P.E., ed., 2005, *Ancient Borinquen: archaeology and ethnography of native Puerto Rico*, Tuscaloosa AL.

Skelton, R.A., Marston, T.E., and Painter, G., 1995, *The Vinland Map and the Tartar Relation*, 2nd edn, New Haven CT and London.

Sloane, K., 2007, *A New World: England's first view of America*, London.

Smith, R., 1993, *Vanguard of empire: ships of exploration in the age of Columbus*, New York and Oxford.

Souyri, P., 2001/2, *The world turned upside down: medieval Japanese society*, New York and London.

Stevens-Arroyo, A.M., 1993, 'The inter-island paradigm: the failure of Spanish medieval colonization of the Canary and Caribbean islands', *Comparative studies in society and history*, vol. 35, pp. 515–43; repr. in Black, J., ed., *The Atlantic slave trade*, vol. 1, *Origins-1600*, Aldershot, 2006.

Stevens-Arroyo, A.M., 2006, *The Cave of the Jagua: the mythological world of the Taínos*, 2nd edn, Scranton PA.

Suárez Acosta, J.J., Rodríguez Lorenzo, F., and Quintero Padrón, C.L., 1988, *Conquista y colonización*, Las Palmas de Gran Canaria, 1988.

Subrahmanyam, S., 1997, *The career and legend of Vasco da Gama*, Cambridge.

Sued-Badillo, J., ed., 2003, *Autochthonous societies*, UNESCO General History of the Caribbean, vol. 1, London.

Tabío, E., and Rey, E., 1979, *Prehistoria de Cuba*, Havana.

Taíno: pre-Columbian art and culture from the Caribbean, 1997, Museo del Barrio, New York.

Taviani, E., 1985, *Christopher Columbus*, London.

Tejera Gaspar, A., 1987, *La religión de los Guanches (ritos, mitos y leyendas)*, La Laguna.

Tejera Gaspar, A., 1992, *Tenerife y los Guanches*, La Prehistoria de Canarias, vol. 1, Santa Cruz de Tenerife.

Thomas, D.H., ed., 1990, *Columbian consequences*, vol. 2, *Archaeological and historical perspectives on the Spanish borderlands east*, Washington DC.

Thomas, H., 1993, *The conquest of Mexico*, London.

Thomas, H., 1997, *The slave trade: the history of the Atlantic slave trade, 1440–1870*, London.

Thomas, H., 2003, *Rivers of gold: the rise of the Spanish Empire*, London.

Thomaz, L.F.F.R., 1994, *De Ceuta a Timor*, 2nd edn, Lisbon.

Thornton, I., 2007, *Island colonization: the origin and development of island communities*, ed. T. New, Cambridge.

Thornton, J., 1998, *Africa and Africans in the making of the Atlantic world 1400–1680*, Cambridge.

Tierney, B., 1997, *The idea of natural rights: studies on natural rights, natural law, and Church law, 1150–1625*, Atlanta GA.

Todorov, Tz., 1984, *The conquest of America: the question of the Other*, New York.

Tomlinson, R.S., 1970, *The struggle for Brazil: Portugal and 'the French interlopers' (1500–1550)*, New York.

Trinkaus, E., and Shipman, P., 1993, *The Neandertals: changing the image of mankind*, London.

Unali, A., 2000, *Ceuta 1415: alle origini dell'espansione europea in Africa*, Rome.

Varela, C., 1991, *Colombo e i fiorentini*, Florence.

Varela, C., 2006, *La caída de Colón: el juicio de Bobadilla*, Madrid.

Verlinden, C., 1958a, 'De Ontdekking der Kanarische Eilanden in de XIVe eeuw volgens de geschreven Bronnen en de Kartographie', *Mededelingen van de Koninklijke Vlaamse Academie voor Wetenschappen, Letteren en Schone Kunsten van België*, Klasse der Wetenschappen, vol. 20, fasc. 6.

Verlinden, C., 1958b, 'Paulmier de Gonneville en de Braziliaanse Inboorlingen in 1504', *Mededelingen van de Koninklijke Vlaamse Academie voor Wetenschappen, Letteren en Schone Kunsten van België*, Klasse der Wetenschappen, vol. 20, fasc. 6.

Verlinden, C., 1958c, 'Lanzarotto Malocello et la découverte portugaise des Canaries', *Revue belge de philologie et d'histoire*, vol. 36, pp. 1173–1209.

Verlinden, C., 1961, 'Le "Requerimiento" et la "Paix coloniale" dans l'Empire espagnol d'Amérique', *Recueil de la Société Jean Bodin*, vol. 15, *La paix*, Brussels.

Verlinden, C., 1970, *The beginnings of modern colonization*, Ithaca NY.

Verlinden, C., and Pérez-Embid, F., 2006, *Cristóbal Colón y el descubrimiento de América*, 2nd edn, Madrid.

Vieira, A., 1987, *O Comercio inter-insular nos séculos XV e XVI: Madeira, Açores e Canarias*, Funchal.

Vigneras, L.A., 1976, *The discovery of South America and the Andalusian voyages*, Chicago.

Vogt, J., 1979, *Portuguese rule on the Gold Coast 1469–1692*, Athens GA.

Von Verschuer, C., 1988, *Commerce extérieur du Japon: des origines au XVIe siècle*, Paris.

Walker, D., 1991, *Columbus and the golden world of the island Arawaks: the story of the first Americans and their Caribbean environment*, Lewes.

Wallace, D., 2004, *Pre-modern places: Calais to Surinam, Chaucer to Aphra Behn*, Oxford.

Weckmann, L., 1992, *Constantino el Grande y Cristobal Colón: estudio de la supermacía papal sobre islas, 1091–1493*, Mexico City (new edn of *Las bulas alejandrinas de 1493*, 1949).

Whelan, R., 1999, *Wild in woods. The myth of the noble eco-savage*, IEA Studies on the Environment, London.

Whitehead, N., ed., 1995, *Wolves from the sea: readings in the anthropology of the native Caribbean*, Leiden.

Williams, R., 1990, *The American Indian in Western Legal Thought: the discourses of conquest*, Oxford and New York.

Wilson, I., 1991, *The Columbus myth: did men of Bristol reach America before Columbus?*, London.

Wilson, S., 1990, *Hispaniola: Caribbean chiefdoms in the age of Columbus*, Tuscaloosa AL.

Wilson, S., ed., 1997, *The indigenous people of the Caribbean*, Gainesville FL.

Wilson, S., 2007, *The Archaeology of the Caribbean*, Cambridge.

Wolf, K.B., 1994, 'The "Moors" of West Africa and the Beginnings of the Portuguese Slave Trade', *Journal of Medieval and Renaissance Studies*, vol. 24, pp. 449–69.

Wood, F., 1995, *Did Marco Polo go to China?*, London.

Yacou, A., and Adelaïde-Merlande, J., 1993, *La découverte et la conquête de Guadeloupe*, Paris.

Zerubavel, E., 1992, *Terra cognita: the mental discovery of America*, New Brunswick NJ.

Zheng Kan Zhu, 2005, *Zheng He vs. Ge Lun Bu*, Hong Kong.

INDEX